DISCOVERY HOUSE

BIBLE ATLAS

Dr. John A. Beck

Discovery House
from Our Daily Bread Ministries

For Marmy, my bride, backpacking partner, and co-adventurer.

For Isaiah and Eliza, our grandchildren, who joined our family
and God's kingdom during the writing of this atlas.

Discovery House Bible Atlas
© 2015 by John A. Beck
All rights reserved.

Discovery House is affiliated with Our Daily Bread Ministries, Grand Rapids, Michigan.

Requests for permission to quote from this book should be directed to: Permissions Department,
Discovery House Publishers, P.O. Box 3566, Grand Rapids, MI 49501, or contact us by e-mail at
permissionsdept@dhp.org

Interior design by Sherri L. Hoffman

Library of Congress Cataloging-in-Publication Data

Beck, John A., 1956-
 Discovery House Bible atlas / Dr. John A. Beck.
       pages   cm
 Includes bibliographical references and index.
 ISBN 978-1-57293-801-4
 1. Bible—Geography. 2. Bible—Geography—Maps. I. Title.
 BS630.B43 2015
 220.9'1—dc23   2014034096

Printed in Italy

First printing in 2015

CONTENTS

MAPS

‹ **Opposite page**
Top: *Worshipers at Jerusalem's Western Wall;* **Bottom left:** *Jerusalem's Old City market;* **Bottom center:** *Colorful Jerusalem;*
Bottom right: *Music greets the visitor at a Jerusalem city gate*

Sea of Galilee

Introduction

GEOGRAPHY AND THE HUMAN SPIRIT

We are bound to the natural world by divine design. This dependence is not due to our sinfulness. It is how God made us. The first pages of the Bible highlight this connection. Before the Lord created Adam and Eve, the first humans, he meticulously shaped the world where they would live and on which they would depend.

What the Bible says about our connection to the natural world is confirmed in our everyday experiences. The earth's gravity keeps us from drifting into the perilous vacuum of space. Precipitation falls to the earth and is ultimately drawn from the earth to hydrate our bodies. The rich soil that covers the earth nurtures crops and pastures, which in turn provide us with food—vegetables, fruit, grain, meat, milk. And the many plants and trees provide medicines that

∧ *Wheat ripening in Judah's Shephelah*

∧ Snow-covered heights of Mount Hermon

address a variety of our ills. As mortals, we are bound to the natural world.

Despite the vital relationship we have with our living space, we are prone to think about it less and less. Insulated from the natural world by the buildings where we work and the homes where we live, we can spend days away from the sights, sounds, and smells of nature. Future generations are increasingly likely to experience the natural world by watching nature programs on electronic devices—a virtual experience substituting for a real one. Our sheltered indoor living makes us less attentive to the signs in the atmosphere that signal a change in weather. Traveling in our vehicles instead of walking, we are less sensitive to changes in the elevation along our route. And when we see wildlife, it's merely a glimpse through a window rather than while walking in the wild.

This disconnection from the natural world comes with a price. We are deprived of the lessons the natural world can teach us. Immersed as we are in the paraphernalia of modern living, we experience what lies outside our bubble only in virtual ways. But when we feel the pulsating power unleashed in a thunderstorm or stand at the base of a mountain looking up,

∧ Nubian ibex in the Judean Wilderness

we gain a broader, more accurate perspective of our world. The complexity of the ecosystem and the real limitations imposed on us by the natural world direct us to the ultimate architect and power broker of this world. If this sounds like just so much nature talk, realize that Scripture itself celebrates what nature can do. God left evidence of his power and wisdom in the natural world so that every mortal might search for a fuller understanding of him (Romans 1:20).[1]

The natural world is also a place that can restore a greater sense of well-being. John Muir, a Christian with a powerful love of nature, plunged himself wholeheartedly into the wilderness and found a peace that no urban setting could offer. His frequent trips into the wilderness led him to offer this unqualified encouragement: "Climb the mountains and get their good tidings. Nature's peace will flow into you as sunshine flows into trees. The winds will blow their own freshness into you, and the storms their energy, while cares will drop away from you like the leaves of Autumn."[2] That is why it is so healthy for us to spend time in natural settings listening to the wild sounds, smelling the freshness, and immersing ourselves in the restoration nature dispenses. Nature can reinvigorate tired beings in ways that other settings cannot. Those who have known the experience join with Muir when he says, "In every walk with Nature one receives far more than he seeks. . . . Everyone needs beauty as well as bread, places to play and pray, where nature heals and gives strength to body and soul alike."[3]

Map I.1—Ancient Near East

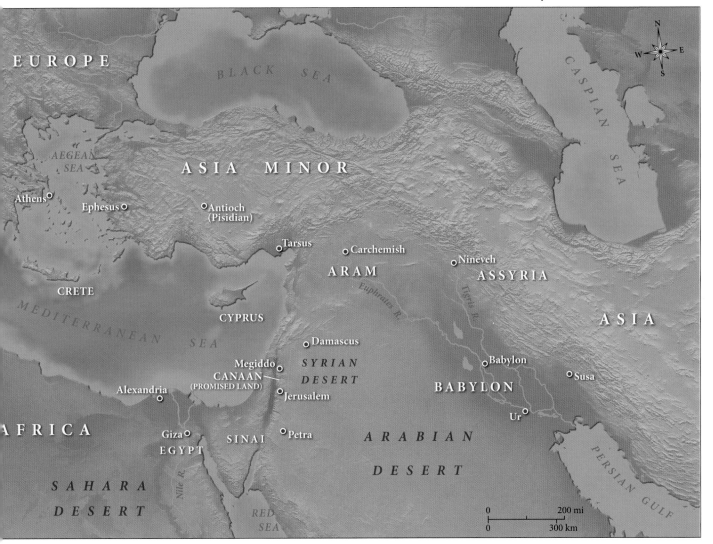

Geography and the Bible

When we stop paying attention to the geography of the natural world around us, we disable our sensitivity to the geographical world presented to us in the Bible. The Bible is unique among the sacred writings of the world in that it makes frequent mention of geography.[4] When we pay attention to these geographic details, we become aware of the important role geography played in shaping events during Bible times. Even more importantly, we will consider the role that the geography plays in shaping those who read the Bible. Our study of geography and the Bible in this atlas is formed by two types of investigation:

- Historical geography, a study of how geography shaped events.
- Literary geography, a study of how the geography mentioned in the Bible shapes readers.

Historical Geography

The geography of a region shapes the events, cultures, and worldview of that region. The study of geography along with the history of Bible times reveals the influence geography had on how the people lived. Geopolitical borders often coincided with natural boundaries imposed by water courses or rising terrain. People established cities where they could best take advantage of natural resources, natural defenses, and natural trade corridors. The principle diet of a region and the raw materials residents used to make their clothing and homes and tools were influenced by what was available locally. Worship of a solar deity or a rain deity was strongly influenced by the way the people obtained their water.

The Bible tells the stories of people and events, but it also is a book about place. Many events have a geographic backstory. For example, Israel's insidious attraction to the worship of the rain deity Baal is a product of the uncertain rainfall in parts of the Promised Land. King David's selection of Jerusalem as his capital city was influenced by the site's natural defenses. Jesus' decision to create a ministry base at

Elah Valley, setting of the fight between David and Goliath

Capernaum is better understood when we see this city sitting near a major international transportation route.

Thoughtful Bible readers and interpreters have made a point of honoring and studying this link between place and Bible event. Among the earliest was the church father Jerome, who moved to Bethlehem while translating the Old Testament into Latin. He believed that a better understanding of the Promised Land and its culture would help the cause of Bible translation and interpretation. In the introduction to his commentary on Chronicles, he wrote, "Just as those who have seen Athens understand Greek history better, and just as those who have seen Troy understand the words of the poet Virgil, thus one will comprehend the Holy Scriptures with a clearer understanding

Jerome, Church of St. Catherine, Bethlehem

who has seen the land of Judah with his own eyes."[5]

Literary Geography

Geography was not just a shaper of Bible events. Biblical authors used geographic details to influence and shape the thoughts and beliefs of readers. For example, the poet of Psalm 125 refers to specific topography to increase the reader's confidence in the Lord: "Those who trust in the LORD are like Mount Zion, which cannot be shaken but endures forever. As the mountains surround Jerusalem, so the LORD surrounds his people both now and forevermore" (Psalm 125:1–2).

The people of Bible times obviously did not have Bibles to carry with them as we do today. But they had the stories and the promises of God passed on from one generation to the next. As they walked the land of the Bible, they passed the places that had been the setting for Bible events. Some of these places were even given names that helped to recall those events, like "The LORD Will Provide," "Ebenezer," and "Perez Uzzah" (Genesis 22:14; 1 Samuel 7:12; 2 Samuel 6:8). Their walks became opportunities for spiritual reflection; the places they passed gave them an opportunity to teach their children the Bible stories that defined them as God's people. "These commandments that I give you today are to be on your hearts. Impress them on your children. Talk about them when you sit at home and when you *walk along the road*, when you lie down and when you get up" (Deuteronomy 6:6–7, emphasis added). To walk the land was to "read" their Bible.

This teaching via landscape is interwoven into the fabric of the Bible's communication. The Bible is not a geography book, but it is a book that employs geography. As the biblical authors received the thoughts of God and recorded them in the language of mortals, the Holy Spirit led them to include geographic details.

While some Bible passages are geography free, others, like Psalm 104 and Obadiah 1, are filled with descriptions of the natural world. Entire books, like the book of Acts, employ geography as their organizing principle.

The risk for us is that we will skip those passages with geography and won't consider the way the geography contributes to the message. For example, even the most inexperienced Bible readers are likely to know the main details of the story about David and Goliath. But how many have weighed the role geography played in this event? This familiar story begins with some unfamiliar geography. "Now the Philistines gathered their forces for war and assembled at Sokoh in Judah. They pitched camp at Ephes Dammim, between Sokoh and Azekah. Saul and the Israelites assembled and camped in the Valley of Elah" (1 Samuel 17:1–2). If we skip this geography, we miss the grave national crisis the Israelites were facing. The land on which the Philistines camped was the very land the Israelites had to hold in order to protect access routes that led into their heartland. In this

∨ *Iron Age fortress at Arad, strategically located in the Negev*

story, we consider who is the best leader for Israel, David or Saul. That evaluation takes place during a national crisis that is, in part, defined by the geography at the start of this story.

Geography is not just incidental in the stories of the Bible. It's an integral part of the Bible's communication with us, and we need to recognize its role in shaping the meaning and message of a text. That is where literary geography comes in. This idea is likely new to you. Here are three steps that help Bible readers evaluate the role of geography in a given passage of Scripture.

- Notice the Bible's mention of geography or natural history.
- Learn about that geography—the topography of a place, its geology, the forces that work on the land, like the wind and the rain. Understand how the people use that place to build their homes, grow their food, and develop roadways. Take into account the appearance and behavior of birds, animals, and plants.
- Ask this question: How does this geographic detail help to deliver the message of this passage of Scripture?

How This Atlas Builds Better Bible Readers

Over the last two decades, I have been speaking, teaching, and writing about the important relationship between geography and Bible reading. This includes my many trips to the Holy Land where I have seen the effect that studying the Bible while surrounded by its geography has had on people. This atlas taps into that Holy Land experience for you, the reader. As you read, you become a "visitor" to the Holy Land and can improve your sense of orientation in the region, learn the connotations attached to places, and see the vital role geography plays in the Bible's communication with us.

Map I.2—Modern Middle East

Map I.3—Major Cities of Biblical Israel

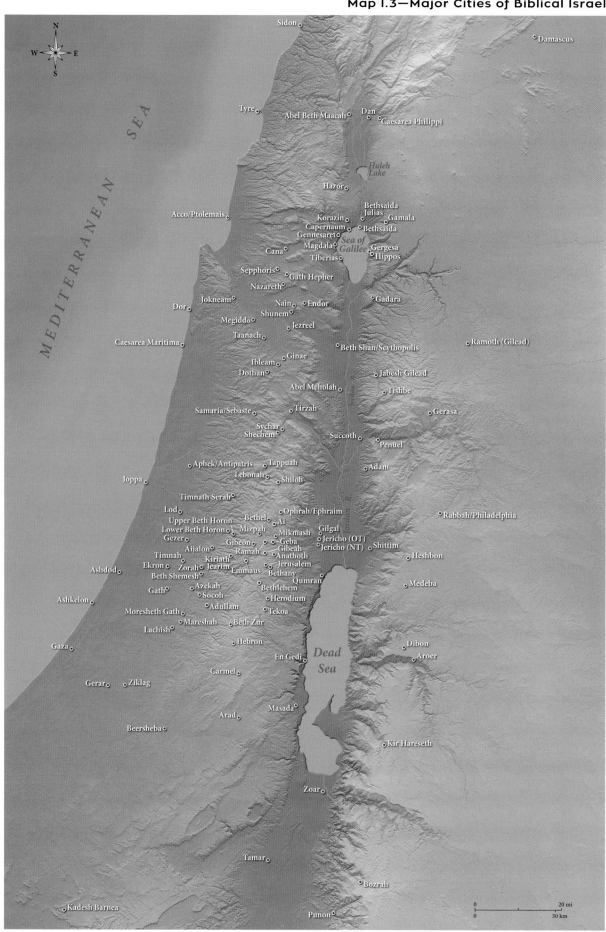

The people of Bible times carried a mental map that allowed them to quickly orient themselves to the geography mentioned in Scripture. This mental map is similar to the one we have that allows us to run errands, find our way to school or to work, and walk about in our neighborhood, all without consulting a physical map of any kind. Back in Bible times, the people knew where Bethlehem was in comparison to Capernaum. They knew which direction to point when someone asked the way to the Dead Sea or to Galilee. The intent of this atlas is to help Bible readers develop a similar familiarity with the important places mentioned in the Bible.

Both the maps and the photographs in this atlas are designed to help with that orientation. Some of the maps show a particular period of Bible history while others focus on a specific event or series of events. The photographs capture a modern-day view of some of the historic places the Bible authors would want you to see.

It is important not just to know where a place is but to know what people thought about it. That perception is formed by the events that occurred there and by the nature of the place. Consider the differing impressions and feelings communicated by mention of places like Hollywood, Pearl Harbor, the Alamo, the World Trade Center in New York, the Korean Demilitarized Zone (DMZ), or the Great Wall of China. Prior events shape our response. The nature of a place can also give it a distinctive connotation. Think of the different impressions you have of Death Valley, the Everglades, and the Rock of Gibraltar.

The same is true for Bible places. They have distinctive connotations formed by the nature of the place and its history. The articles that accompany the maps and photographs in this atlas explore how the biblical authors use these in their writing. For example, we will see how the city of Dan became associated with infamy and how Bethlehem became a place associated with solutions.

The articles in this atlas call attention to the often forgotten connections in what God has to say to us

∧ *Black basalt foundation of the first-century synagogue at Capernaum*

through the use of geography in the Bible. My prayer is that readers, after exploring these connections, might say the same thing I hear from students in the Holy Land: "This experience has completely changed the way I read my Bible."

Our connection to the natural world has a profound impact on how we think and how we communicate. So it should come as no surprise that the biblical authors also were influenced by where they lived and that this influence becomes a part of how God communicates with us in his Word. This atlas gives special attention to that connection between the words of God and our physical world. It does not address every passage in Holy Scripture or even every passage that involves geography. But it will open a new way to read the Bible as it discusses key passages, illustrating how geography helps to communicate what our God wants us to know.

Map I.4—Old Testament Regions

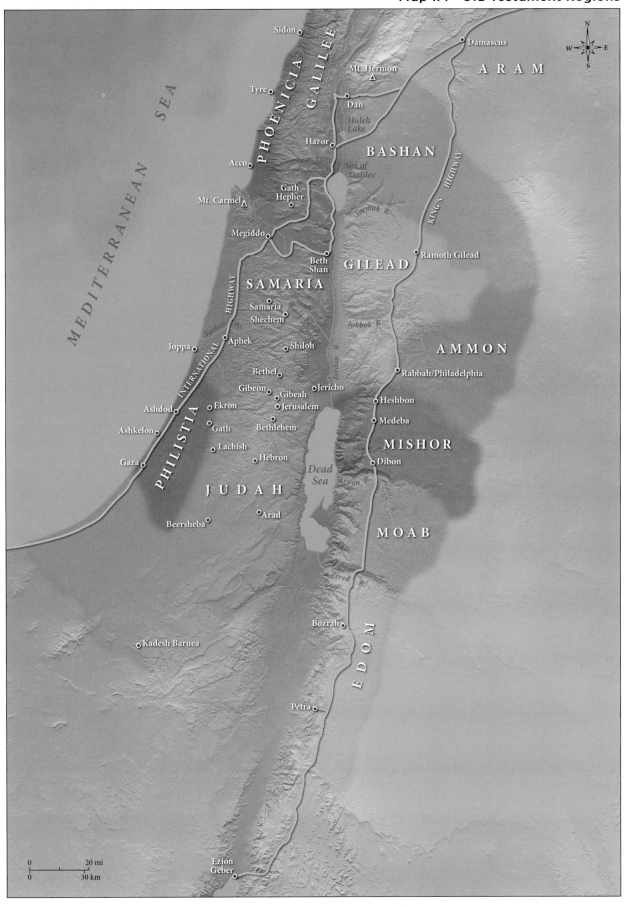

Map I.5—New Testament Regions

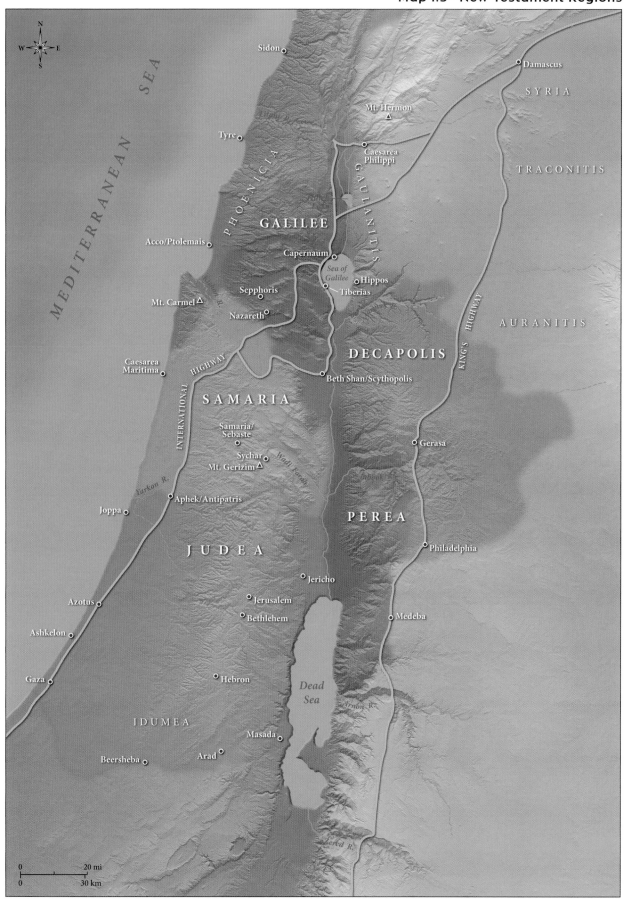

∧ *Arnon Gorge in the Transjordan*

Chapter 1

GENERAL GEOGRAPHY OF THE PROMISED LAND

Over the centuries, first-time travelers to the Promised Land have imagined how this holy land would appear. Almost always, they have gotten it wrong. Some have expected a barren sandy desert, while others have envisioned an oasis laden with palm trees. Still others expected fertile farmland and green pastures with sheep and goats grazing. While each of these descriptions aptly portrays a portion of the Promised Land, none characterizes the land as a whole. No single picture of the Promised Land can do it justice; it would take an entire album of photographs to capture the diversity of this landscape. It is a land that includes cold, windswept tundra and barren desert, pine trees and palm trees, snowcapped mountains and rich valleys, inland lakes of saltwater or freshwater, rivers, and a Mediterranean shoreline. And all of this diversity is captured within a remarkably small space, an area roughly equivalent in size to Lake Erie, the state of Massachusetts, or the country of Belize.[1]

The land has four geographic zones. From west to east, the land is made up of the coastal plain, the central mountain range, the Jordan Valley, and the Transjordan Plateau.[2]

GENERAL GEOGRAPHY OF THE PROMISED LAND | 19

The Coastal Plain

The coastal plain extends eastward from the Mediterranean Sea (see map 1.1). As the name implies, this zone is primarily level. The scattered hills that break the monotony of the plain are modest in elevation, rising to little more than 150 feet (45.7 m) above sea level. This zone is rich in natural resources to sustain life. It is the first to benefit from the eastward marching rain showers of the rainy season, receiving between 16 and 25 inches (40 and 63.5 cm) of precipitation. Even more moisture is realized from the rain that falls on the west side of the central mountains, the mountain runoff depositing nutrient-rich soil as it makes its way to the Mediterranean Sea. And when rainfall takes its yearly hiatus, this zone's proximity to the Mediterranean guarantees life-giving dewfall for the maturing summer fruit crops.

Those who lived on or traveled through the coastal plain found both advantages and disadvantages. The southern portion of the coastal plain, dubbed the Philistine Plain after its Old Testament residents, was prime grain-growing country. The gently rolling plain was easy to travel, devoid of energy-sapping elevation changes. It was an ideal route for traders on their north-south journey en route to Mesopotamia or Africa. They used this natural land bridge in their bid to link international markets. But this merchant-rich environment also drew world powers that invaded and took control of this land bridge to tax the trade goods and collect fees from the traveling merchants. The empires used this land bridge as a defensive buffer zone to prevent aggressors from crossing into their own homelands.

A quick look at the map could lead you to the conclusion that the coastal plain and its miles of shoreline

⋁ *Mediterranean coastline at Caesarea Maritima*

Map 1.1—The Four Geographical Zones

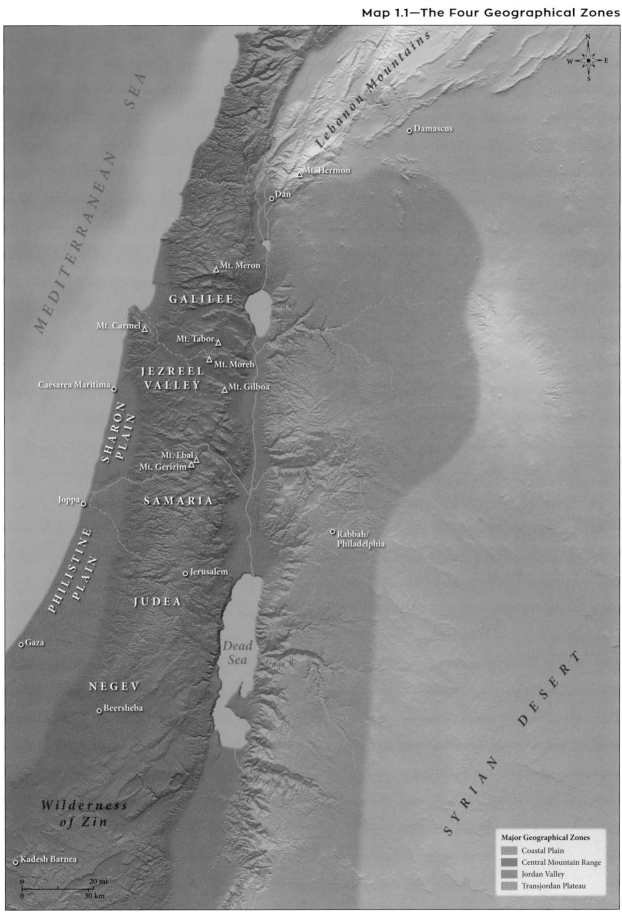

MEDITERRANEAN SEA

Lebanon Mountains

Damascus

△ Mt. Hermon

Dan

△ Mt. Meron

GALILEE

Sea of Galilee

Mt. Carmel △

Mt. Tabor △

△ Mt. Moreh

JEZREEL VALLEY

Caesarea Maritima

△ Mt. Gilboa

SHARON PLAIN

Mt. Ebal △
Mt. Gerizim △

Jabbok R.

Joppa

SAMARIA

Rabbah/ Philadelphia

PHILISTINE PLAIN

Jerusalem

JUDEA

Dead Sea

Arnon R.

Gaza

SYRIAN DESERT

NEGEV

Beersheba

Wilderness of Zin

Zered R.

Kadesh Barnea

| 0 | | 20 mi |
| 0 | | 30 km |

Major Geographical Zones
Coastal Plain
Central Mountain Range
Jordan Valley
Transjordan Plateau

are ideal for harbors and a thriving maritime culture. But that is not the case. The shallow waters along the shoreline make it inhospitable for shipping. So while there were coastal cities that had harbors—like Joppa, Dor, and Caesarea Maritima—they could not compare to the natural deepwater harbors enjoyed by the Phoenicians to the north, who had a strong culture of shipbuilding and maritime commerce.

The Central Mountain Range

The central mountain range runs north and south through the heart of the Promised Land, from Galilee in the north to the Negev highlands. Once east of the lower foothills along the western edge of this zone, these limestone mountains rise abruptly, to elevations of 1,500 to 3,000 feet (457 to 914 m), with some segments reaching to 3,330 feet (1,006 m). The character of these mountains and their valleys changes as we move from south to north. For example, Judah's hill country has bare steep-sided slopes that plunge into narrow V-shaped valleys. As we travel north into Samaria, the mountain elevations decrease and the valleys become wider. Still farther north, the ridges of Lower Galilee are lower and the valleys are even broader and take on an east-west orientation. This trend changes when we get to Upper Galilee, with its block of mountains twice the elevation of those in Lower Galilee. These

∨ *Lower Galilee, north of Sepphoris*

mountains make access difficult and discourage formation of large urban centers.

Variations in soil quality and annual precipitation also affect how the land in this central mountain zone is used. Generally the southern sections of the central mountain range receive less precipitation than the mountains on the north end, and the western slopes receive considerably more precipitation than the eastern slopes. This east-west difference in rainfall joins with changes in soil quality to make the area of the Shephelah west of Judah's hill country and the Judean Wilderness east of the hill country of Judah strikingly different. In the Shephelah, we find rain-soaked grain fields and sycamore trees, while the Judean Wilderness only 18 miles (29 km) to the east is arid, with few trees and no agriculture.

Among the most enduring of the natural resources in the central mountain zone is the hard building stone harvested from these mountains. This hard limestone erodes at a rate of just .4 inches (1 cm) in a thousand years.[3] Foundations of buildings, walls, and gates built thousands of years ago from this durable stone can still be seen today in Jerusalem. They date as far back as the time of King Hezekiah and his efforts to prepare the city for invasion by the Assyrians (c. 705 BC).

These mountains have not changed appreciably since Bible times. Their presence had a major impact on travel. Because of their north-south orientation, it was extremely difficult to move from east to west through the core of the mountain zone without many hours of thigh-burning climbs and descents. Consequently the international travelers and armies tended to avoid this region. Even local travelers moving north or south favored the ridges to minimize elevation change as they walked. The exception is in Lower Galilee, where the usual north-south orientation to ridges and valleys changes to east-west.

The differences found in the central mountain range produce a variety of cultural realities. Agriculture is most dominant in the rain-rich north due

Left: Judah's hill country, west of Jerusalem, from Mount Eitan; ***Right:*** *Mountains of Samaria north of Shiloh*

to the wider valley floors for farming. While grapes, olives, and wheat are grown throughout this mountainous region, Judah tends to produce better grapes, Samaria better olives, and Galilee in the north better wheat. The diminishing rainfall in the south causes a transition to pastoral pursuits, to the herding of sheep and goats. The more rugged landscapes in the south were the easiest lands to defend against foreign invasion. In the north, the ease of travel opened the way for merchants to bring foreign goods into this region. That open door to the outside also meant that foreign armies and pagan ideology could more easily invade the area and the lives of the people who lived there.

The Jordan Valley

The Jordan Valley extends from Huleh Basin in the north through the Dead Sea. It lies between the high mountains of the central mountain range and the even higher mountains of the Transjordan Plateau. This valley is just one segment of a much larger intrusion in the surface of the earth called the Afro-Arabian Rift Valley, which extends for more than 4,000 miles (6,437 km) from Turkey into East Africa (see figure 1.1). Within the Promised Land, the Jordan Valley is a sunken block between two fault lines,[4] land that in almost all locations is below sea level. For example, the Sea of Galilee sits at approximately 700 feet (213 m) below sea level, and the Dead Sea is 1,300 feet (396 m) below sea level. As in the mountains to the west of this zone, the annual rainfall is greatest in the north. The city of Dan at the northern end gets 24 inches (61 cm) of precipitation, and the southern end of the Dead Sea is limited to just 2 inches (5 cm) of rainfall (see map 1.2). A map of this region can make it seem as if freshwater is plentiful, but the reality is quite different. The low elevation of the lakes and rivers, their distance from the best agricultural lands in other

Figure 1.1—Geographical Cross Section of Afro-Arabian Rift Valley

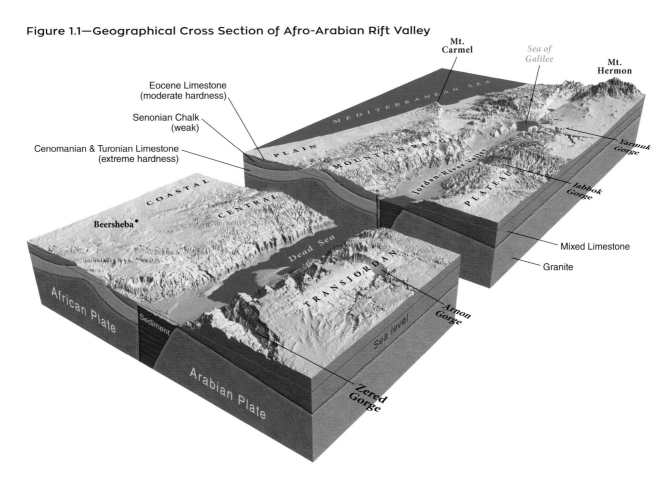

zones, and the increasing salinity of the water as it moves down the Jordan River to the Dead Sea mean this area has little freshwater to offer those living in the Promised Land.

The Sea of Galilee basin offers the most advantages in rainfall, agriculture, and fishing. The northwestern and northeastern plains of this inland lake are both fertile and rain rich. Early volcanic activity in the Galilee area provided not only the rich dark soils that favored agriculture but also the black basalt boulders that were ideal for fashioning ancient grinding mills. The Sea of Galilee with its array of fish hosted a thriving fishing industry. The agricultural and fishing images that Jesus used in teaching about the kingdom of God were drawn from these plains.

The Dead Sea in the south also offered business opportunities. The salt so prevalent in this region was mined and transported around the country, where it was used not only to season food but also to preserve meat and fish in an era without refrigeration. Bitumen, also referred to as "tar," was harvested from natural deposits found near the Dead Sea or floating on the water. It was sold to those who used it to waterproof the seams of their wooden boats and to Egyptians for their embalming process.

Because of the difficulty of moving through the central mountain range, we might expect that a continuous north-south valley like the Jordan Valley would host a primary road system. But the extremely warm temperatures of summer, the rigors of descending into and climbing out of the low valley, and the presence of large predators like lions, bears, wolves, and hyenas in the northern end of the valley discouraged travel. Most of the travel in the Jordan Valley was east-west, using natural fords of the Jordan River that linked the international traffic moving on the coastal plain with the international traffic moving on the heights of the Transjordan Plateau.[5]

The Jordan River flows from the Sea of Galilee to the Dead Sea. This river channel runs within two larger valley structures. The broader valley system, which stretches between rising terrain on the east and

∨ *Looking east toward the Jordan River Valley over the ruins of an Iron Age Israelite fortress at Beth Shan*

∧ *Sea of Galilee, looking southwest toward modern Tiberias*

west, is called the Ghor. Within the Ghor valley is the smaller cut of the *qattara*, looking like a miniature badlands, infertile and void of vegetation most of the year. The Jordan River proper is in the bottom of this *qattara*, requiring one to descend as many as 150 feet (46 m) to reach the river channel. In Bible times, the Jordan River was an average of 100 feet (30.5 m) wide and was as deep as 10 feet (3 m), but it was not generally used for transporting people or goods, mainly because of the violent flow of its current. In 1848 United States explorer W. F. Lynch set out to travel this river in small boats from the Sea of Galilee to the Dead Sea. His group encountered 27 significant whitewater rapids. Some were so threatening they were unrunable, forcing his expedition to portage again and again.[6]

The Transjordan Plateau

East from the Jordan Valley is the dramatic façade of the Transjordan mountains. The elevation of this terrain significantly exceeds the highest mountains west of the Jordan Valley, rising to well over 5,000 feet (1,524 m) in places. However, once we move past this dramatic wall of stone, we find ourselves on a plateau, the Transjordan Plateau, that tilts in the direction of the Arabian Desert. This plateau is most evident in the regions of Bashan and the Mishor, but it does not continue without interruption. The plateau is broken into segments by mountain groups, as in the regions of Gilead, Moab, and Edom. The plentiful rainfall of the north diminishes quickly as we move south. Mount Hermon receives 60 inches (152 cm) of precipitation annually. The southernmost reaches of Edom receive as little as 1 inch (2.5 cm) per year. Because the Transjordan mountains are higher than the mountains west of the Jordan River, the western edges of this region receive more rainfall and totals diminish quickly to the east.

Changes in the natural resources prompted changes in how the people lived throughout this region. In the Bashan region, rich volcanic soils and plentiful rainfall make this a desirable spot for raising cattle and sheep and for wheat farming. The mountains of Gilead receive ample precipitation, where the favored produce shifts to olives and grapes. The Medeba (Mishor) Plateau has less rain but still receives sufficient precipitation for wheat farming. South of the Arnon River, we enter the land the Lord gave to Moab

∧ *Moab's geography favored the raising of sheep and goats*

(Deuteronomy 2:9). Agriculture becomes increasingly difficult here due to infrequent rainfall, so the focus turns to the raising of sheep and goats.

Throughout this zone, we can trace the ancient north-south international trade road called the King's Highway, which generally follows the watershed. But by contrast to the level road system on the coastal plain, travelers in the Transjordan Plateau had to negotiate a number of deep canyons, including those of the Arnon and Zered Rivers. When we cross the Zered River canyon heading south, we enter the land of the Edomites. The high mountains and difficult access from the west gave them a high degree of security. Their overconfidence becomes a target of Jeremiah's criticism. "'The terror you inspire and the pride of your heart have deceived you, you who live in the clefts of the rocks, who occupy the heights of the hill. Though you build your nest as high as the eagle's, from there I will bring you down,' declares the LORD" (Jeremiah 49:16). The diminishing rainfall of Edom takes its toll on farm fields and pastures. Thus we find the Edomites and others within this region oriented more toward trade than the agricultural and pastoral pursuits that define the northern part of the Transjordan Plateau.

Hydrology and Climate

Water and weather exert a powerful influence on the residents of each of these geographic zones. Access to potable water defines where people live and travel. The weather within a region and its seasonal changes influence what forms of agriculture are favored, the time of the year when countries make war, and even the time of year when religious festivals are held. This striking influence of water and weather becomes part of the communication used by the biblical authors, who also made use of weather-related metaphors in telling stories. The weather patterns with their seasonal variations are either mentioned or alluded to by the Bible's authors when writing about agriculture or travel.[7]

Hydrology

Any study of the Promised Land has to include an understanding of the primary source of water, its unequal distribution throughout the land, the meager amount of freshwater available, and the mechanisms used to secure a supply of water for local residents and their animals and crops. The Israelites faced many challenges after they left Egypt during the 40 years they lived in the wilderness. When they were about to enter the Promised Land to make permanent homes, one of their biggest concerns had to do with securing an adequate supply of freshwater.

Moses, in his final words to the Israelites when they stood poised to enter the land of Canaan, made special mention of the source of water. "The land you are entering to take over is not like the land of Egypt, from which you have come, where you planted your seed and irrigated it by foot as in a vegetable garden. But the land you are crossing the Jordan to take possession of is a land of mountains and valleys that drinks rain from heaven" (Deuteronomy 11:10–11).

In Egypt, the water the people and their animals drank as well as the water they used to irrigate their farm fields was drawn from the Nile River. This is the river-based hydrology that God's people had known for centuries. But the Promised Land had a rain-based hydrology.[8] No major river provided water for them. The water people drank when they were thirsty and the water for their animals and wheat fields and pastures was rainwater. The Sea of Galilee and the northern segment of the Lower Jordan River had good water, but the people had no system to raise that water 700 feet (213 m) from the river or the lake to irrigate their agricultural fields on higher ground.

The rainfall the people of this land depended on is unevenly distributed during the year and throughout the land. The majority of rain falls during the months of November through February. The region receives almost no rain from May through August (see figure 1.2). When there is rain, 75 percent of it falls on 25 percent of the land. The rainfall on map 1.2 illustrates that the northern portions of the land receive much more precipitation than the southern regions, and the west side of rising terrain receives much more precipitation than the east side.[9]

Even under the best of conditions, the amount of freshwater available in the Promised Land during Bible times was a fraction of the freshwater available in most modern countries. When we compare the amount of water per capita enjoyed by residents of the US, for example, with the amount available to those living in the Promised Land during Bible times, the difference is stunning. Think of reducing your water supply by 98 percent. Only a handful of countries have less freshwater per capita than Israel.[10] Given the challenges of providing water for their families, fields, and herds, the people of Bible times spent a considerable portion of their month identifying, securing, storing, and defending their supply of water. It is no wonder that water

∨ *Judah's Wilderness formed in a rainfall shadow*

Map 1.2—Rainfall Distribution

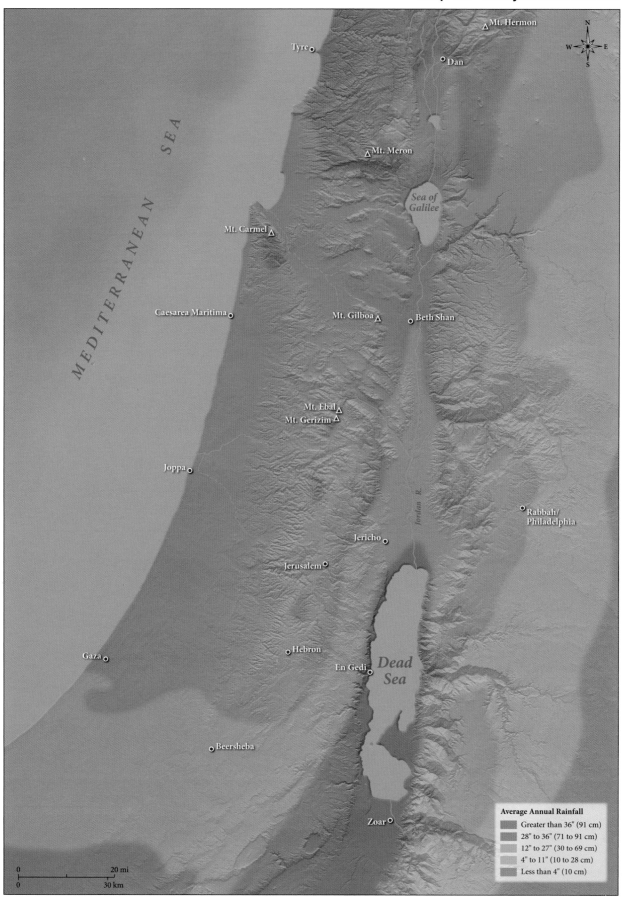

MEDITERRANEAN SEA

△ Mt. Hermon

Tyre ○

○ Dan

△ Mt. Meron

Sea of Galilee

Mt. Carmel △

Caesarea Maritima ○

Mt. Gilboa △   ○ Beth Shan

Mt. Ebal △
Mt. Gerizim △

Joppa ○

Jordan R.

○ Rabbah/ Philadelphia

Jericho ○

Jerusalem ○

Hebron ○

Gaza ○

En Gedi ○

Dead Sea

Beersheba ○

Zoar ○

Average Annual Rainfall
Greater than 36" (91 cm)
28" to 36" (71 to 91 cm)
12" to 27" (30 to 69 cm)
4" to 11" (10 to 28 cm)
Less than 4" (10 cm)

0   20 mi
0   30 km

∧ Roman aqueduct that carried water to first-century Caesarea Maritima

was linked to the gospel message and to fellowship with the living God (Psalm 42:1–2; John 4:13–14).

Sources of freshwater depended on where one lived and the resources available to transport water to another location. In most cases, the people were getting rainwater for drinking in one of three ways: springs, wells, and cisterns. A spring, where water from the underground water table intersects with the earth's crust and bubbles to the surface, provided naturally filtered drinking water with a minimum of labor. However, natural springs were modest in size and not evenly distributed in the land. So where there were no springs, people had to rely on man-made wells and cisterns for much of their water. A well was a shaft of up to 6 feet (1.8 m) in diameter dug down to the water table. The sides of the well were lined with fieldstone to prevent them from collapsing. A well cap was put in place to prevent contamination. A cistern was a water storage chamber dug in the ground to collect surface water that otherwise would run off and be lost. This storage chamber also required a cap to prevent evaporation and contamination. The cistern walls were sealed with plaster and maintained to prevent the water from seeping out of the chamber.

These were the systems that provided water for most households. But when a strong central government was in place, water often was transported over long distances via channels and aqueducts to reservoirs where people could go to collect the water they needed. Archaeological evidence of subterranean

∨ Limestone well cap with a stone cover

tunnels, aboveground aqueducts, and reservoirs survives from Bible times.[11]

Climate

The weather of the Promised Land has two main seasons—summer and winter (see figure 1.2). Summer in Israel extends from mid-June to mid-September, when the region is dominated by high pressure that brings generally sunny skies, high humidity, and warmer temperatures. Within the mountainous interior, the average summer temperature reaches 77°F (25°C) and cools to the mid-50s (10°C) in the evening. The most defining feature of this time of year is the near absence of any rainfall.

This is when fruit crops are ripening, readying for harvest at the end of summer. The olives, dates, grapes, pomegranates, melons, and figs must rely on water in the soil as well as on the dewfall of summer. This vital dewfall can occur on as many as 250 nights during the year,[12] saturating the soil with moisture and giving evidence of the Lord's blessing (Deuteronomy 33:28; Zechariah 8:12). During the summer months, the sun's rays evaporate that dewfall by the close of the morning. Residents of this land during Bible times scurried for any shade they could find, whether offered by bush, residence, or rock (Isaiah 32:2). Pastures for sheep and goats become more difficult to find in the summer, so shepherds turn to the harvested grain fields where they are welcomed by the farmers who benefit from the manure that enriches the soil in advance of fall planting. Roads dry out and temperatures warm. Those unburdened by the demands of the grain-producing season find this the best time to travel. For the same reasons, kings pick the beginning of summer as the season for going off to war (2 Samuel 11:1).

October through mid-June marks a change in the atmosphere and brings new climatic conditions to the Promised Land. High pressure yields to a series of low-pressure areas that spill off the Mediterranean Sea brimming with moisture. These migrating lows are built to make rain, lifting and cooling the moist air within them past the dew point. Cooler temperatures accompany the rain. The daily high and low in the central mountain ranges is from an average of 48°F (9°C) to a chilly evening average of 30°F (-1°C). This is the season when clouds hang in the air more frequently and the blessing of life-giving rain begins. It does not rain every day during these months, and the rainfall patterns vary in the winter season. But this is the time of year when steady rainfall can last for a

Figure 1.2—Agricultural Calendar of the Promised Land

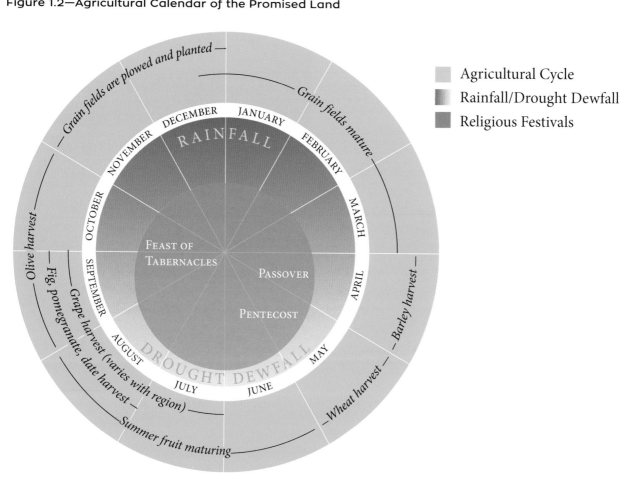

Agricultural Cycle
Rainfall/Drought Dewfall
Religious Festivals

∧ Winter rains green wilderness pastures

full day and be bracketed by days of showery precipitation. These days of rain are often followed by a full week or more of sunshine before the cycle begins again. In the higher elevations, snow is possible. Jerusalem receives snow on average two days a year.[13]

When the rains begin, people turn from traveling and making war to planting grain. The light early rains soften the soil baked hard by the summer sun. As soon as the scratch plow can penetrate the surface, families are plowing and planting their fields in anticipation of the middle and late rains of the winter season. This is the rainfall that ripens the grain and greens the land, including the wilderness areas. No longer welcome in the farm fields, the shepherds move their animals to the greening hillsides of the wilderness. This rainfall also recharges the groundwater supply, increasing the productivity of springs and wells, and fills cisterns for the coming year.[14]

Common to both the summer and winter seasons is wind, but not all forms of wind have the same force, source, and connotations. The winds most often associated with the winter season and rain are the frontal winds that seek to equalize high- and low-pressure areas. These are the winter storm winds that threaten shipping on the Mediterranean Sea (Acts 27:9). In the

summer, the onshore Mediterranean Sea breeze is steady and predictable. It is the cooling breeze that provides relief from the summer heat and is used to winnow grain to get rid of the chaff. This breeze is felt first along the Mediterranean coast about eight in the morning. Because the air over land warms more quickly than that over the sea, the warmer air rises and the cooler sea breeze fills the void, creating an onshore breeze that reaches Jerusalem by about noon.

In stark contrast to the pleasant sea breeze are the hot, dry winds from the south and east that flow out of the desert in the weeks at the end of summer. They are known as the Hamsin, or sirocco, winds. There is nothing redeeming about these hot winds that fill the

∨ Ripe pomegranates signal the end of summer drought

∧ *Ripe grain fields signal the start of the dry summer season*

air with gritty dust, send the relative humidity plummeting, and sharply increase the temperature. People view these winds negatively (Isaiah 27:8; Jeremiah 18:17; Hosea 12:1).

There is one local wind that begs for inclusion in our list. That is the *sharquia* wind of the Sea of Galilee basin. This unpredictable wind occurs when the cool air on the ridges above the lake descends violently into the lake basin. This cold air can plummet at more than 60 miles (96.5 km) per hour into the lake basin, whipping up waves and threatening any vessels caught on the lake when they strike (Matthew 14:22–36; Mark 4:35–41; Luke 8:22–25).[15]

Transportation

The people of Bible times were travelers who moved about for many reasons—family visits, business, diplomacy, war, to worship at a distant sanctuary, and in ministry (Genesis 37:25; 1 Samuel 7:15–17; 2 Kings 20:12–13; 23:29–30; Luke 1:39–40; 2:1–3, 42; Acts 2:5–11; 14). Their footsteps wore paths that became the primary road systems of the Promised Land.

Although donkeys, camels, and chariots were available, there is little doubt that when most people moved from place to place, they walked. Many walked great distances, often over difficult terrain. Ancient documentation of a day's walk indicates that those traveling would average upwards of 20 miles (32 km) per day.[16]

Route Selection

The routes used on these trips mark the beginning of the road systems. The shortest and most direct route between two locations was always the favored route. But geography tends to eliminate a direct route in all but a few instances. Four factors caused people to take a longer route. One was elevation change. The

Map 1.3—Road Systems of the Fertile Crescent

^ *The gentle slope of the Harod Valley creates a desirable travel route*

Promised Land is filled with sharply rising terrain, so those who walked this land would look for ways to avoid or minimize steep climbs even at the expense of adding distance to the route. If they could not follow a broad valley floor, they would look for natural ramps, plateaus, and mountain passes. And when mountain travel was required, the people would follow the twists and turns of the watershed ridge to minimize the amount of climbing and descending required.

A second factor was natural obstacles other than mountains that hampered travelers. Vegetation-clogged slopes, lakes, malaria-stricken swamps, forbidding canyons, and the unrelenting heat of a desert were all cause for a detour. Because most of those living in Bible times did not know how to swim, river crossings were avoided. Travelers would go out of their way to use natural fords with shallow water they could walk across to lessen the risks of a river crossing.

The third factor for taking a longer route was to have water and food along the way. Most travelers couldn't carry enough water and food for a long trip, so careful planning was needed to bring them to known water sources as well as population centers where food could be purchased. Crossing the Judean Wilderness was especially difficult. Merchants and soldiers would begin their trip across the wilderness at a known water source, like En Gedi or Jericho, and then carry enough water to last for the rest of the trip.

The fourth factor was exposure to thieves and large predators, such as lions, bears, and wolves, that prowled unpopulated areas in search of prey, including vulnerable travelers. Jacob, when he saw the bloody coat of his son Joseph, concluded that he had been killed by a large predator (Genesis 37:33). Thieves were a risk when traveling far from cities and villages. Jesus tells the story of a man traveling from Jerusalem to Jericho who fell into the hands of thieves (Luke 10:30–37). For these reasons, travelers would walk far out of their way to spend the night in a village that provided safety from these travel dangers.

Major Routes

These routes walked by the earliest travelers are still being used thousands of years later.[17] Given the needs of engineers to respond to the same geographic realities, many modern roads were built on or near these well-traveled paths of the past.

The four major road systems of Bible times were the International Highway, the Ridge Route, the Jericho-Gezer Road, and the King's Highway (see map 1.4). Each had a unique role. But don't be misled by the word *road*. These were nothing but paths, modestly improved by clearing away brush and larger rocks. This remained the case with roads in the open country of the Promised Land until well into the Roman period.[18] This means that all the roads, even those with the heavy traffic of international commerce, were little more than hiking trails, hardly varying in appearance from the local roads that branched off the "highways" into the interior.

The International Highway was the prime road system. It passed through the geographic bottleneck of the Promised Land to connect the far-flung population centers of the ancient Near East. It extended from Babylonia at the head of the Persian Gulf, through the Tigris and Euphrates River basins of Mesopotamia, and then south through Israel en route to Egypt (see map 1.3). When painted on a map, this route forms an arch some 1,800 miles (2,897 km) long. It transits the region dubbed the Fertile Crescent, the area with sufficient rainfall and irrigation potential to grow the grain vital for sustaining life. This road became the travel corridor that linked Ur in Mesopotamia with Egypt in Africa. Its dusty surface knew the footsteps of mighty armies as well as the seasoned steps of merchants.

This international route included the user-friendly passage through the Promised Land. From Gaza, a traveler on the International Highway moves north along the coastal plain and dodges eastward to avoid the ancient swamps of the Sharon Plain. The road

∨ *The International Highway crosses the Jezreel Valley toward dome-shaped Mount Tabor (right)*

Map 1.4—Roads Within the Promised Land

MEDITERRANEAN SEA

Damascus

Mt. Hermon △

Dan
Caesarea
Philippi

Hazor

Capernaum

Sea of
Galilee

Mt. Carmel △

Megiddo
Jezreel

Beth Shan/Scythopolis
Ramoth Gilead

Dothan

Tirzah
Gerasa

Samaria/
Sebaste
Shechem
Sychar
Succoth

Aphek/
Antipatris
Adam

Shiloh

Bethel
Mikmash
Lower
Beth Horon
Rabbah/
Philadelphia

Gezer
Gibeon
Gibeah
Jericho

Ashdod
Heshbon

Jerusalem

Ashkelon
Bethlehem

Gaza
Hebron
Dead
Sea
Dibon

Gerar

Arad
Beersheba

Tamar

Bozrah

	International Highway
	King's Highway
	Ridge Route
	Secondary roads

0 ___ 20 mi
0 ___ 30 km

continues north, transiting the extended ridge of Mount Carmel through one of the soft limestone valleys that bisect this rising terrain, and then travels through the Jezreel Valley, the easiest location in the country to move from east to west. It is here where the various empires and the Israelites could most successfully tax trade goods and manage the movement of international armies.[19] From the Jezreel Valley, this critical artery moves north into Galilee, runs near the western shoreline of the Sea of Galilee, and continues north through Huleh Basin en route to Damascus and beyond.

The second most important road system for international travel is the King's Highway (Numbers 20:17; 21:22). This road connected the Gulf of Aqaba and the Red Sea with Damascus and ran along the central ridge of the Transjordan Plateau.[20] The exotic perfumes and spices of southern Arabia were transported to their eastern markets via this road system.[21] This road connected the important cities of the Transjordan, such as Bozrah, Dibon, Medeba, Heshbon, Rabbath-Ammon, Gerasa, and Ramoth-Gilead. While it shortened the travel distance between the town of Ezion Geber on the Gulf of Aqaba and Damascus in the north, this road had one major liability. It required travelers to work their way through deep river canyons like the Arnon.

While the International Highway and King's Highway primarily served an international clientele, the Ridge Route was the local north-south road that connected residents of the Promised Land with key locations in the interior of this mountainous terrain. This path was formed by the feet of thousands who had the same goal: to find a route with the least change of elevation. This route joins the Beersheba and Arad areas with Hebron, Bethlehem, Jerusalem, Gibeah, Bethel, Shiloh, Shechem, and Samaria en route to the Jezreel Valley. When we hear of Abraham and Sarah traveling great distances with their sheep and goats, or Mary

∨ *The Ridge Route travels through this pass at Shechem*

and Joseph traveling to be counted in a tax census, this is the road they would have been on. It is the local road most often used by the people mentioned in the Bible as they moved about the Promised Land.

Moving east and west through the Promised Land was never easy, except for those traveling the east-west route in the Jezreel Valley. Local travelers used another crossing point. This was on the Benjamin plateau just north of Jerusalem. We call this route the Jericho-Gezer Road after the two cities connected by this east-west path. The Jericho-Gezer Road begins in the east with a difficult and dramatic climb from Jericho, runs through the Judean Wilderness, and goes into the central mountain range. Taking a heading toward Gibeon, the traveler would find the changes in elevation becoming more modest as they came to the east-west plateau in western Benjamin. Once across the plateau, it is down the Beth Horon Ridge and into the Aijalon Valley toward Gezer. This route was generally used by locals, but saw action when invaders had their hearts set on capturing the internal crossroads of the country located near Gibeon. When

∨ *The Jericho-Gezer Road crosses the central mountains via this plateau in Benjamin*

we place the attack route of Joshua on the map, we find that he followed this route from Jericho into the interior, both to divide the opposition and to capture a critical transportation hub. Later in Israel's history and on more than one occasion, foreign invaders would use this route, entering at Gezer and marching toward Gibeon, where they would turn south to attack the city of Jerusalem on its most vulnerable side.

This introduction to the geographical zones of the Promised Land, its water realities, climate, and transportation routes has highlighted the uniqueness of the land that influenced the people and events we read about in the Bible. As the inspired authors of the Bible wrote the words we cherish, they often mentioned geographical details like these. In the chapters that follow, we will explore the ways in which that geography shapes God's message for us.

∧ *Roman mile markers identify the location of roads whose worn paths have vanished*

∧ Pomegranate blossoms

Chapter 2

CREATION AND ABRAHAM'S FAMILY

The Garden of Eden

While many places mentioned in the Bible can be placed on a map with reasonable certainty, the Garden of Eden is not among them—despite the fact that all sorts of geographic assistance on its location appears to be in place. Genesis 2:8–14 says a river that waters this garden exits it and divides into four rivers: the Pishon associated with Havilah, the Gihon associated with Cush, the Tigris that ran along the east side of Ashur, and the Euphrates. The difficulty is in understanding this language to determine the most likely location of the garden.

To understand the place names associated with the Garden of Eden, we ask if these are the names of rivers and regions prior to the Flood, or the names used at the time of Moses for these rivers, or both. The inability to answer these questions with certainty has led to wildly divergent theories on where the Garden of Eden might have been located.[1]

Map 2.1—Possible Locations of the Garden of Eden

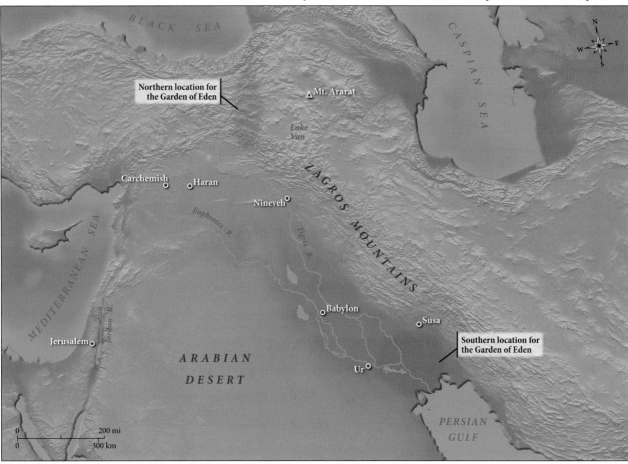

While there is no consensus, most scholars place the Garden of Eden in Mesopotamia. Their reasoning connects the word *Eden* with the Akkadian/Sumerian word *edinu* used to refer to the plain of Mesopotamia watered by the Tigris and Euphrates Rivers.[2] Genesis

∧ *Persian cyclamen*

says that a single river left the garden and then formed four streams. In an effort to find this description in the modern landscape, some scholars place this garden in northern Mesopotamia near the current headwaters of the Tigris and Euphrates Rivers (see map 2.1). This location in eastern Turkey is where we find the Choruk and Araxes Rivers that may be linked to the Pishon and Gihon of the Bible (Genesis 2:10–14). The headwaters of the Choruk and Araxes are in this same general area as the headwaters of the Tigris and Euphrates. Others place the Garden of Eden in the southern part of modern Iraq where the Tigris and Euphrates Rivers empty into the Persian Gulf. The Pishon and Gihon in this region could be two of the tributaries of these larger rivers.[3] Nothing more certain can be said about the location of the Garden of Eden.

But there is much more to be said about the enduring message the geography helps to deliver. The place names linked to the Garden of Eden and the other information about this garden give it a ring of familiarity. The Garden of Eden was not an otherworldly place. It was a place with soil, water, plants, trees, birds, and animals. It had fruit and the sweet smell of flower blossoms. It was in an area of named regions and rivers, some of which still appear on maps today. In striking contrast to other ancient Near Eastern accounts that describe the origins of the world, Genesis describes a real world that looks much like the one we enjoy now.

Because Adam and Eve lived in this physical world surrounded by plants, animals, rivers, and mountains prior to their fall into sin, we can be assured that our life in the natural world is not a product of our

∨ **Top:** *The Dan Stream at the base of Mount Hermon;* **Bottom Left:** *Crown anemone;* **Bottom Right:** *Fruit stand in Nazareth*

sinfulness, but reflects the intensions of our Creator. In the book of Revelation, as the Bible comes to a close, we find language reflective of the Garden of Eden with its river and fruit trees (Revelation 22:1–2). Given what we know of the Garden of Eden, the eternal home will be a place to feel the softness of the spring grass, to hear birds sing, to enjoy bright flowers, to indulge in time with animals, to walk the high ridgelines of lofty mountain ranges.

The Bible's description of the Garden of Eden is not intended to draw a treasure map we can use to find the location of this garden. It is there to show the Garden of Eden as a real place in the past that helps us to anticipate what our future home will be like.

The Table of Nations

Even the most dedicated Bible readers are tempted to turn past the pages of Genesis 10 that contain the Table of Nations. This portion of God's Word is anything but an easy read. Those who brave its verses will quickly find themselves drowning in a sea of names and geographic details that resist interpretation. Yet this chapter can be seen as a literary bridge between Eden and Abram.

So just what is this Table of Nations? That question is difficult to answer. There is no other document like it in the surviving literature from the ancient Near Eastern world and nothing exactly like it in the rest of the Bible.[4] What we have in this chapter is part genealogy and part geography, or what we will call a geographically informed genealogy. It lists the names of the descendants of Noah via his three sons, Japheth, Ham, and Shem. It also identifies generally the regions where the various clans settled (see map 2.2).

∨ *Canaanite wall on the eastern slope of the City of David*

∧ **A**bove: *Dome of the Rock in Jerusalem;* **Below:** *Canaanite wall bracket for burning incense or providing light*

The organization of the names in the list can be viewed both from the perspective of biological relationship and geography. The biblical author begins by tracing the descendants of Japheth (Genesis 10:2–5), continues with the descendants of Ham (10:6–20), and ends with the descendants of Shem (10:21–31). What is not apparent is the role geography plays in the organization of the list.[5] The word map of Genesis 10 is drawn from the perspective of Canaan (the yet-to-be-named Promised Land). Mentioned first in the Table of Nations are the descendants of Japheth, who settled farthest away, residing north and northwest of Canaan. In the Bible's presentation of Israel's history, these regions will have the least sustained interaction with the Promised Land. The descendants of Shem are linked to lands that are east and southeast of Canaan. They also are listed in order from most distant to least distant from Canaan. The names of the descendants of Ham follow the same pattern on distance, but some actually settled in the

Promised Land and will fight against the Israelites for ownership of this land.

If we remove this list from its literary context and attempt to make it do things that it was not designed to do, then frustration is likely to follow. Genesis 10 was not designed to be and does not provide a complete map of the ancient Near Eastern world. Nor does it give a full genealogical record of the descendants of Noah or a map of the languages of the ancient world.

Instead it creates a literary bridge between Eden and Abram. It shows that Abram was a direct descendant of Adam and Eve. Theologically this is a vital connection. The Redeemer who was promised in the Garden of Eden had to be a biological descendant of Adam and Eve (Genesis 3:15). Genesis 5:3–32 links Adam to Noah, Genesis 10:1, 21 link Noah with Eber, and Genesis 11:16–31 links Eber to Abram. Thus the link between the Messiah and Adam and Eve comes through Abram.

Genesis 10 also creates a bridge by shifting our geographic focus from Eden to Canaan. In Genesis 1–2, the reader's attention is on the Garden of Eden. By the close of Genesis 3, Adam and Eve have been driven from the Garden of Eden and barred from ever entering it again. We remain uncertain just where to look next until Genesis 12:1–7, when the land of Canaan, henceforth the Promised Land, becomes our geographic focus. Genesis 10 creates the transition. Both by the sheer number of peoples associated with Canaan (10:15–19) and by the fact that this geographically informed genealogy is organized from the perspective of Canaan, our focus of interest moves from the Garden of Eden to the land of Canaan.

Also, Genesis 10 helps us understand the map of the "earth" the author of Genesis had in mind when recording this promise the Lord made to Abram: "All peoples on earth will be blessed through you" (Genesis 12:3). The details include not only the names of places but also the number of nations in this Table of Nations—70. Since genealogies in the Bible can be organized to have numerical significance (Matthew 1:17), and given that 70 is a multiplication of two numbers, 7 and 10, that independently may be used to communicate the idea of completeness, the number of nations in the list indicates "all people of earth."[6] The story of Abram's family is, for the most part, a local story. But what happens in Canaan will change the world defined by Genesis 10.

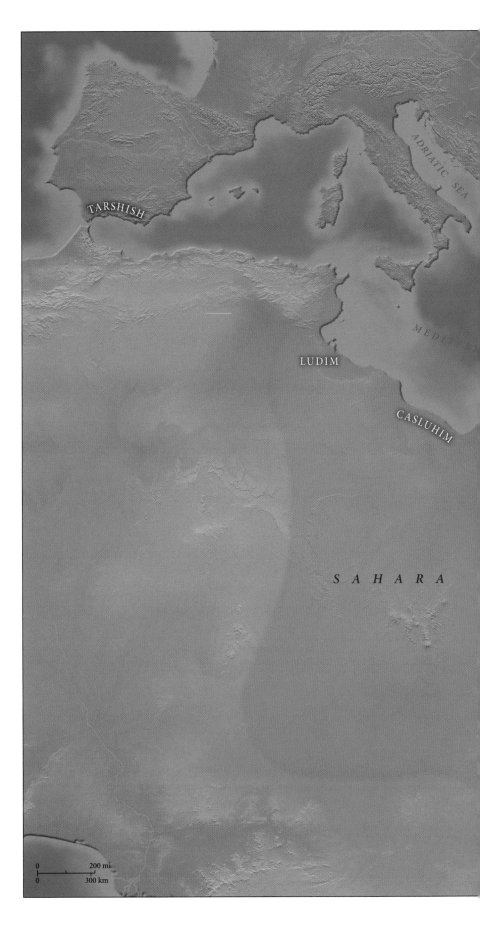

Map 2.2—Table of Nations

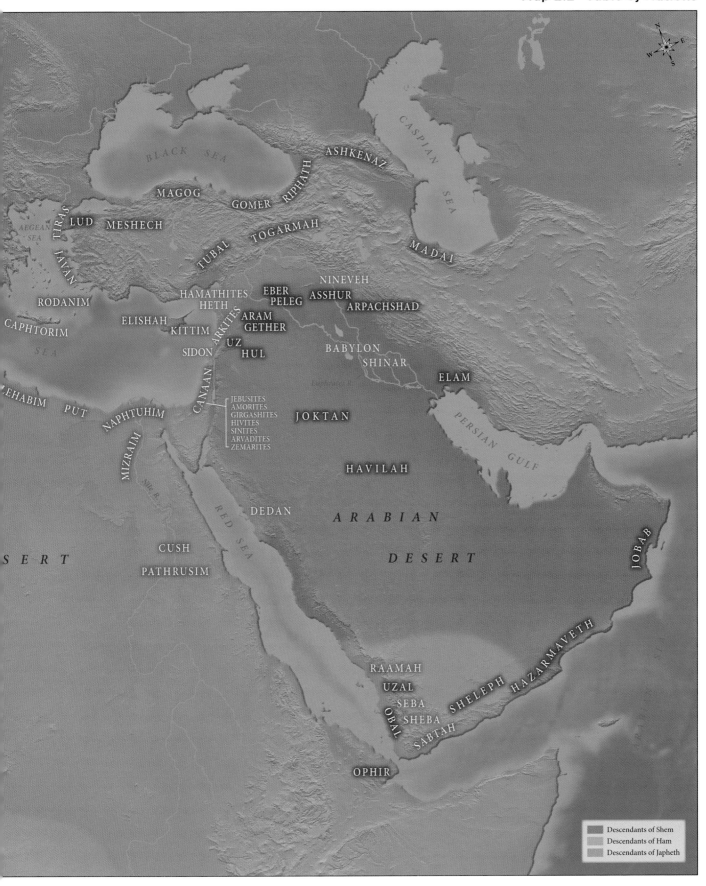

CASPIAN SEA

BLACK SEA

ASHKENAZ

MAGOG

GOMER RIPHATH

AEGEAN SEA

TIRAS LUD MESHECH

TUBAL TOGARMAH

MADAI

JAVAN

RODANIM

NINEVEH

HAMATHITES EBER ASSHUR
HETH PELEG

CAPHTORIM

ELISHAH

ARAM GETHER

ARPACHSHAD

KITTIM ARKITES

SIDON UZ HUL

BABYLON
SHINAR

SEA

ELAM

LEHABIM PUT

JEBUSITES
AMORITES
GIRGASHITES
HIVITES
SINITES
ARVADITES
ZEMARITES

NAPHTUHIM

CANAAN

JOKTAN

PERSIAN GULF

MIZRAIM

HAVILAH

DEDAN

A R A B I A N

SERT

CUSH

RED SEA

D E S E R T

JOBAB

PATHRUSIM

HAZARMAVETH

RAAMAH

UZAL

SHELEPH

SEBA

OBAL SHEBA

SABTAH

OPHIR

Descendants of Shem
Descendants of Ham
Descendants of Japheth

Promised Land

The language of the Table of Nations (Genesis 10) invites us to view a sprawling world filled with the descendants of Noah. By the time we reach Genesis 12, our focus narrows to one man, Abram, and one location—the land of Canaan. This man and this land become the source of hope and a way to communicate that hope for those living during the time of the Old Testament.

We meet Abram, a descendant of Shem and son of Terah, as a man on the move (Genesis 11:31–12:9). With his father Terah and other family members, he moves from Ur of the Chaldeans to Harran. Then after the death of his father and another order from God, Abram moves his family from Harran to Shechem in Canaan (see map 2.3).

The starting point of this two-part journey is Ur. Early in the twentieth century it became popular to associate this biblical city with the large and thriving city of Ur that was the Sumerian capital city on the lower Euphrates River. This identification remains viable.[7] But there is a persuasive alternative. By qualifying the name—Ur "of the Chaldeans"—the writer might be calling our attention to another Ur, one of lesser prominence than the Sumerian capital city. Two reasons favor this other location. First, no sure evidence has been found for a Chaldean presence in the lower Euphrates during the time of Abram like there is in northern Mesopotamia. Second, a pilgrim in the fourth century was shown a city of Ur in northern Mesopotamia. We should at least consider the fact that Abram may have departed from Ur in this other region, only a short distance from Harran.[8]

The second phase of the journey begins when the Lord tells the childless Abram to leave his household in Harran and travel to an undisclosed land (Genesis 12:1; Hebrews 11:8). The route he took likely followed

Map 2.3—Abram's Journey from Ur to Shechem

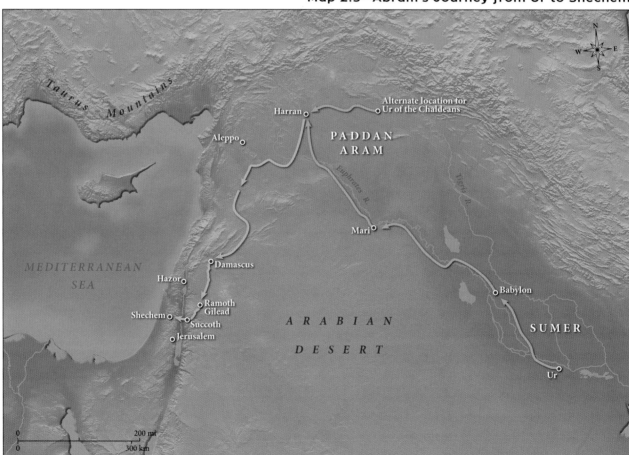

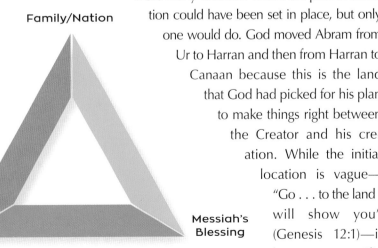

∧ Shechem, the heart of the Promised Land

the natural travel routes of the day. From Harran, Abram would have traveled to Damascus and down the King's Highway to the Jabbok River. Then it was west across the Jordan River and up the Wadi Farah to Shechem (see map 2.3). Once Abram arrived in Shechem, he was in the heart of Canaan, the land we know as the Promised Land.

The Lord appeared to Abram at Shechem and reviewed a set of promises (Genesis 12:1–3), including three that are our focus here. They form three legs of a triangle and are both independent and interconnected. The first leg of the triangle has to do with blessing: "All peoples on earth will be blessed through you" (Genesis 12:3). God blessed Adam and Eve in the Garden of Eden (Genesis 1:28). The same word is repeated in the set of promises made to Abraham. Although this is not apparent from its earlier mention in Genesis 1, by the time we reach Genesis 12, "blessing" becomes the word used to characterize God's promise-plan to bring salvation to

the nations.[9] Abram is now linked to this plan of salvation in a formal way.

The second leg of the triangle addresses Abram's childless state. He is promised that he will have a family. The Lord said to Abram, "I will make you into a great nation" (Genesis 12:2). This would not be just any nation like those described in the Table of Nations, but a nation that would change people's eternal destiny. The hope for eternal restoration that was linked to the offspring of Adam and Eve (Genesis 3:15) now links to the offspring of Abram (Genesis 12:7).

The third leg of the triangle involves land. There were many locations where the plan of salvation could have been set in place, but only one would do. God moved Abram from Ur to Harran and then from Harran to Canaan because this is the land that God had picked for his plan to make things right between the Creator and his creation. While the initial location is vague— "Go . . . to the land I will show you" (Genesis 12:1)—it becomes specific

Family/Nation

Promised Land

Messiah's Blessing

Figure 2.1 Triangle of Promises

once Abram arrives in the heart of Canaan. "To your offspring I will give this land" (Genesis 12:7). Canaan is the Promised Land and now has become the land of hope.

That triangle helps us to remember these three important promises. They can be independently stated and often are by the Bible's authors. God will turn the childless Abram into a nation. That nation will have the Promised Land as its own. From that nation and on that land, an offspring of Abram will restore blessing to the nations. Yet all three promises are interconnected. When we read a direct reference or allusion to any one element of this triangle, we will now picture the whole triangle of promises and hear the message of hope for restored blessing linked to it.

Most Christians find it easier to read the New Testament than they do the Old Testament. This is due in part to the fact that the theological language and images of the New Testament are more familiar to us. Those living in the era of the Old Testament had the same spiritual concerns and needs as those living in the time of the New Testament, but they often expressed their hope for redemption from sin in language and symbols that were common to their own era. Christians will find themselves reading their Old Testament with greater enjoyment and insight when they see that this triangle of promises lies at the heart of Old Testament communication. The hope for forgiveness of sins was linked to the parts and the whole of this triangle.

Abraham In and Out of the Promised Land

The triangle of promises given to Abraham in Genesis 12:1–3 leads us to expect that this man will own property and live in the Promised Land. But Abraham and his family are on the move, shifting locations to obtain the best grazing and water for their animals. During the rainy winter months, they pastured their animals in the southern portion of the Promised Land called the Negev (Genesis 12:9; 13:1), and when the rainless summer months arrived, they progressed north where the more abundant rainfall meant green pastures.

But there is another reason for Abraham's travels through the Promised Land. Abraham was following God's specific direction: "Go, walk through the length and breadth of the land, for I am giving it to you" (Genesis 13:17). This directive, particularly in

∨ *Like Abram, this shepherd moves his flock daily*

Map 2.4—Abraham in the Promised Land

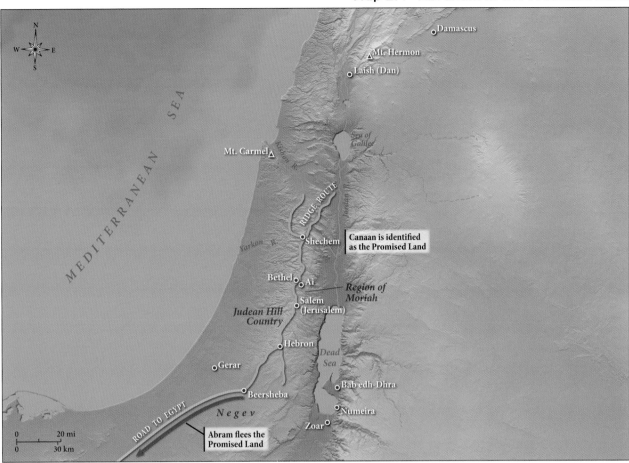

the grammatical form used here, has powerful implications. The ordinary action of walking is presented here with a rather rare Hebrew verb form, *hithpael*, that connects the act of walking with ownership and dominion. This same verb in this rare form is used to describe the Lord walking through his Garden (Genesis 3:8) and to direct the Israelites to walk through the land they had conquered as a sign of its new ownership (Joshua 18:4).[10] Walking was the cultural practice for transfer of property during Old Testament times. The owner and purchaser would walk the boundary of the property prior to completion of the transaction.[11] Thus Abraham's walking through the land becomes a way of marking his rightful claim to the land and heralds the day when this land will be fully claimed and occupied by this "family turned into nation."

So where did he travel when he walked the land? After the Lord appeared to Abraham at Shechem (Genesis 12:6), we read of his presence in the Bethel-Ai area (12:8; 13:3), the Negev, including Beersheba and Gerar

(12:9; 13:1, 3; 20:1; 21:31–33; 22:19), Hebron (Mamre) (13:18; 18:1; 23:2, 19; 25:9), around Salem (Jerusalem) (14:17–18; 22:2), and at Dan (Laish) (14:14). Abraham appears to have spent the most time in the Negev region in the south, traveling north only for improved pastures, and then returning to the Negev. When he traveled, he generally visited places that were along the north-south road in the central mountain range we call the Ridge Route.

But more important is the relationship between his travels and the traditional boundary formula used to define the Promised Land. The common way of describing the north-south extent of the Promised Land was "from Dan to Beersheba" (Judges 20:1; 1 Samuel 3:20; 2 Samuel 3:10; 24:2; 1 Chronicles 21:2; 2 Chronicles 30:5). If Abraham's walking the land is the precursor to the property transfer, then his walking the land from Dan to Beersheba anticipates the extent of the Promised Land as it will be captured in the formula "from Dan to Beersheba" (see map 2.4).

∧ *City gate at Laish (Dan) from the time of Abram*

With the importance attached to Abraham being in this land so that the promises of God might be fulfilled, his move to Egypt seems out of place. The author of Genesis explains that there was a severe famine in the Promised Land (Genesis 12:10). Famines were not unusual in a land that often receives insufficient rainfall or rainfall that is ill timed. The land's fragile ecosystem and agricultural fields are quick to respond. Pastures no longer feed animals and watering stations dry up. One option for Abraham was to retreat from this land with a rain-based hydrology and move to one that had a river-based hydrology like Egypt, where it did not have to rain on agricultural fields so long as it was raining somewhere in the river's larger tributary system. Abra-ham was actually following a well-worn path to Egypt and its more reliable agricultural system (see map 2.4). Over the years whenever the rains failed, many fled Canaan to take advantage of the ecosystem of Egypt.[12]

But Abraham was not just anyone. He was the man God had selected as the father of the world's hope for eternal life. By leaving the Promised Land, famine ridden as it was, and not trusting in God, Abraham put the plan of salvation on hold and even risked the complete undoing of the triangle of God's promises linked to the forgiveness of sin (Genesis 12:14–20). This narrative of Abraham's departure from the Promised Land is not a celebration of Abraham's faith but evidence of how much his faith needed to grow.[13]

Moriah, a Place of Provision and Faith

In time, Abraham did return to the Promised Land, where the Lord's plan to bring salvation to sinners continues with the birth of Isaac (Genesis 17:21). God tells Abraham, "It is through Isaac that your offspring will be reckoned" (Genesis 21:12). This encouraging news only sharpens the horror we feel when we read the opening verses of the next chapter and the Lord asks the unthinkable of Abraham: "Take your son, your only son, whom you love—Isaac—and go to the region of Moriah. Sacrifice him there as a burnt offering on a mountain I will show you" (Genesis 22:2).

The location of this mountain in the region of Moriah is difficult to identify. Moriah is mentioned only once in the story of Abraham.[14] The evidence leads us to a mountain in the greater Jerusalem area. The first clue is the way the Lord presents the place to Abraham. Earlier when the Lord told Abraham to leave Harran, he told him to travel to a "land I will show you" (Genesis 12:1). Abraham had never traveled to Canaan, so the only way for him to know the place was by divine direction. This contrasts with the language we find in Genesis 22. The Lord mentions the region of Moriah as if Abraham is familiar with it, placing Moriah somewhere in Abraham's travels between Dan and Beersheba.

We can narrow our focus to areas within 60 miles (96.5 km) of Beersheba. This is where the biblical author left him at the close of the previous chapter (Genesis 21:33–34) and the place to which he returns at the close of this story (22:19). Genesis 22:4 tells us that on the third day of the journey, Abraham was able to see Moriah. The average distance people walked in a day was about 20 miles (32 km),[15] placing the region of Moriah about 50 miles (80 km) from Beersheba and the Negev.

A Mount Moriah is named in 2 Chronicles 3:1 as the mountain "in Jerusalem" on which Solomon built the Lord's temple. The text does not say that this Mount Moriah is the same mountain in Genesis 22, but it is 50 miles (80 km) from the Negev and reachable within three days of travel. Plus Abraham had been through the area of Jerusalem before, so was familiar with this place (Genesis 14:17–18). It is likely that the "region of Moriah" (Genesis 22:2) to which Abraham traveled is somewhere near the "Mount Moriah" of Jerusalem where Solomon built his temple (2 Chronicles 3:1).

Mount Moriah teaches what it means to trust without reservation. There is nothing in this Bible story that suggests Abraham was anything but ready to follow through with the horrific directions he received from God. But we are given one explanation in a chapter on faith in Hebrews. Since Abraham believed the Lord could raise the dead, he assumed that if he sacrificed Isaac, the Lord would raise him back to life—and in a way God did (Hebrews 11:17–19). That is how Mount Moriah became a place of provision and faith that continued to teach the members of Abraham's family those lessons each time they passed it during their seasonal migration.

⌄ *A view of the region of Mount Moriah, an area associated with the Jerusalem suburbs*

Altars, Tombs, Stone Pillars, and Wells

In the story of Abraham's family, we read again and again about altars, tombs, stone pillars, and wells. Each of these plays an important practical role in the life of this family. And together they work to maintain the spiritual vitality and focus of Abraham's family as they traveled in the Promised Land.

The worship by Abraham's family was done at altars (Genesis 12:6–7; 13:18; 22:9; 26:25; 33:20; 35:1–7). If these altars were built like the standards prescribed later (Exodus 20:24–26; Deuteronomy 27:5–6), they would have been simple structures composed of nothing more than soil or stones gathered from a field and not cut in any way. In some cases animals were sacrificed on them, but in others the altar was built to mark the place where the builder had an encounter with God.

Tombs were built for burial of the dead (Genesis 23:3–20; 25:9; 35:20; 49:29–32; 50:13). The tomb of this period might be a shallow stone-lined pit, a chamber at the bottom of a vertical shaft, or an enhanced natural cave.[16] Occasionally a member of Abraham's family erected a stone pillar (Genesis 28:18–22; 35:14, 20). Some of these simple monuments were built with a tomb; others were built simply to remind those who passed by of an event or agreement linked to the location.[17]

Wells are frequently mentioned in Genesis (21:30; 26:15, 18–22, 25, 32). The well was a vertical shaft dug down to the water table to obtain water. To prevent collapse, the shaft was lined with fieldstones. A cover was placed over the top of the well to prevent contamination. Considering the importance of water in this land, the wells were vigorously defended (Genesis 21:25; 26:19–22). These wells provided a reliable water supply for Abraham's people and herds as they traveled.

All four of these—altars, tombs, stone pillars, and wells—met not only the practical needs of Abraham's family but also served to advance the spiritual well-being of this family that had been promised a land that did not seem to be theirs. At the end of Abraham's life, the land of Canaan was experiencing a rebirth

∨ *Standing stones at Gezer*

Map 2.5—Altars, Tombs, Pillars, and Wells in the Promised Land

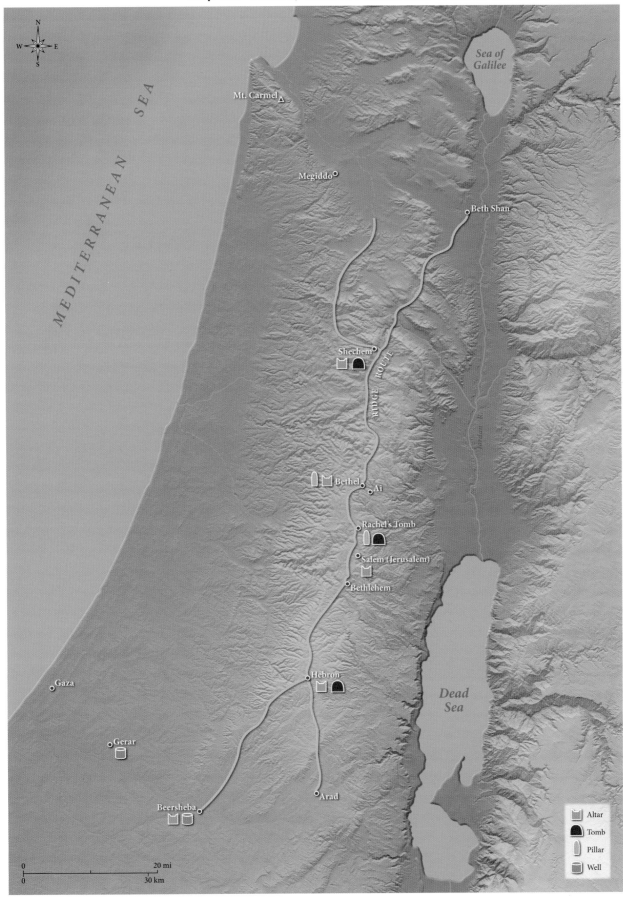

of urbanization. Large city footprints that had gone unoccupied were being built on again with impressive ramparts, walls, and public buildings.[18] But the family of Abraham did not live in any of these cities. They tended flocks and herds that required them to be more mobile than city life allowed. When the dry season imposed its waterless penalty on the southern reaches of the Promised Land, Abraham's family pulled up its tent stakes and folded the tent panels to migrate north toward greener pastures and more certain water. When they walked past the large and imposing cities of this land, they might have wondered about their family's claim on the land. Abraham called himself "a foreigner and stranger" living among locals who controlled the most desirable land (Genesis 23:4). Abraham and Jacob did purchase small parcels of land (Genesis 23:3–20; 33:19), but these did little to change the fact that the land belonged to others in practice. This is precisely where the altars, tombs, stone pillars, and wells came into play. These are the anchors of a seminomadic people, their claim to belong. That is why the author of Genesis mentions them again and again; they are the evidence of this family's connection to the land before the time of Joshua, when God's people will begin to build their own cities here.

These Bedouin anchors in the land were at Shechem (Genesis 12:6–7; 33:18–20; Joshua 24:32), in the Bethel-Ai area (Genesis 12:8; 28:18–22; 35:1–7, 15), the Ramah-Gibeah area (Genesis 35:20)[19], the greater Salem (Jerusalem) area (Genesis 22:9), Hebron (Genesis 13:18; 23:3–20; 25:9; 49:29–32; 50:13), the Gerar area (Genesis 26:15–22), and the area around Beersheba (Genesis 21:31; 26:23–25, 33). With the exception of Gerar, they all were located on or near the Ridge Route in the central highlands of the Promised Land (see map 2.5).

This geography provides an insight into why the

∨ **Below Left:** *Modern reconstruction of a tomb from the time of Abraham's family;* **Below Right:** *Jacob's Well near Shechem*

author of Genesis would so carefully catalog the location of these altars, tombs, stone pillars, and wells. They fall right along the seasonal migration route that Abraham's family used every year. This means that as Abraham's family moved their animals along the Ridge Route, they could stop along the way to get water from the wells, visit the family tombs, and worship and reflect on the promises of God at the stone pillars and altars. Although they walked in the shadow of cities that said otherwise, these anchors to the land were reminders to tell the children and grandchildren of the promises that God had made to Abraham, Isaac, and Jacob about the land they were walking. While Abraham's family was short on land deeds, it was not short on reminders that their family destiny was linked to a land they would one day own.

Jacob's Authorized Departures from the Promised Land

When the Lord told Abraham that the eternal rescue of the world depended on his family and their presence in Canaan (Genesis 12:1–7), it seems highly unlikely that any circumstances might induce them to leave. But twice Jacob does just that. He leaves the Promised Land en route first to Paddan Aram, near Harran, and some years later to Egypt (see map 2.6). But each time, it is at a location—first Bethel, then Beersheba—where he is forced to sincerely think about the trip before he receives divine authorization for his departure.

Jacob's first exit from Canaan was prompted by a problem Jacob and his mother caused. Esau by tradition received special benefits as the firstborn male of the family, and Jacob wanted them. First, for a bowl of stew, he obtained the right of the firstborn from Esau (Genesis 25:27–34). Then, following his mother's plan, he tricked his father, Isaac, into giving him his

Map 2.6—Jacob's Departures from the Promised Land

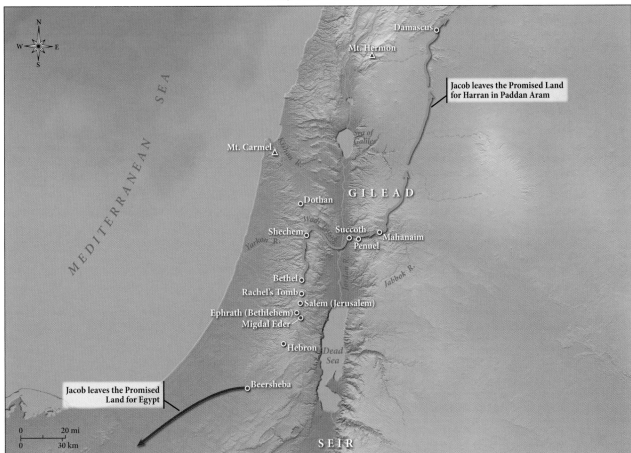

∧ *Jacob traveled north across the Benjamin plateau toward Bethel*

blessing, a blessing that rightly belonged to Esau (Genesis 27:1–45). Esau in his anger threatened to kill Jacob, forcing him to flee from the land to Paddan Aram, to the household of his mother's family, a trip that began with a walk north from Beersheba on the Ridge Route in the direction of Bethel (Genesis 28:10).

Jacob had likely been doing some soul searching in the three days it would have taken him to travel from Beersheba to Bethel, but there is good reason to believe that Bethel caused even deeper reflection. Soon after his grandfather Abraham arrived in the Promised Land, he built an altar to the Lord in this vicinity (Genesis 12:8). Bethel was on the Ridge Route the family would have used during their seasonal migration with their flocks, so Jacob would have been there many times before. It was a place for the family to worship, to remember the Lord's promises that linked them to this land. Jacob might even have thought of how Abraham so many years before left the land without divine authorization during a famine to find food in Egypt (Genesis 12:10–20). These thoughts induced by Bethel likely led Jacob to have reservations about fleeing the Promised Land as he camped there that night. While he slept, the Lord appeared to Jacob in a vision. He saw a stairway stretching between earth and heaven with angelic messengers on the move. The Lord was at the top of the stairs and identified himself as the God of Abraham and

Isaac. He repeated the promises made to Abraham and authorized Jacob's departure from the land with these words: "I am with you and will watch over you wherever you go, and I will bring you back to this land. I will not leave you until I have done what I have promised you" (Genesis 28:15). Thus Bethel becomes the site for the first instance of divine authorization for Jacob's departure from the Promised Land.

The biblical author describes a parallel event from later in Jacob's life, but precipitated by a different problem (Genesis 46:1–5). This time it is not a brother's anger but a seven-year famine that threatened the lives of Jacob and his family. The famine was regional in scope and so intense that the biblical author mentions it repeatedly (Genesis 41:53–57; 43:1; 47:13–26). People fled to Egypt. Even Jacob sent his sons to buy grain, not knowing that Joseph, the son he thought was dead, was actually a high official there who was in charge of the stored grain. After Joseph revealed himself to his brothers, he invited Jacob and the entire family to travel to Egypt and wait out the famine (see map 2.7). Thus driven from the land by a severe famine and drawn by love for a son he had not seen in years, Jacob packed up and began the move toward the Way to Shur, a roadway that began near Beersheba and would take him to Egypt.[20]

Just as Bethel had prompted Jacob to reflect on his plan to leave the Promised Land, so Beersheba did the

^ *The Way to Shur begins in the Negev basin*

same. His father Isaac had built an altar in Beersheba as a memorial to recall the Lord's promises to Abraham (Genesis 26:23–25). Jacob had worshiped there as a child and would certainly have heard his father tell the story of his attempt to leave Canaan during an earlier famine (Genesis 26:1–6). Isaac had been headed for Egypt, but the Lord allowed him to get no farther than Gerar in the land of the Philistines. "The LORD appeared to Isaac and said, 'Do not go down to Egypt; live in the land where I tell you to live. Stay in this land for a while, and I will be with you'" (Genesis 26:2–3). Eventually Isaac moved to Beersheba, where again the Lord appeared to him. Isaac marked the place with an altar. This story of God's message to Isaac would have caused Jacob to wonder if his own plan to leave the Promised Land would meet with the same divine censure. When he arrived at Beersheba, on the traditional southern border of the Promised Land, he stopped and offered sacrifices on the altar

Map 2.7—Joseph and Family Within the Promised Land and to Egypt

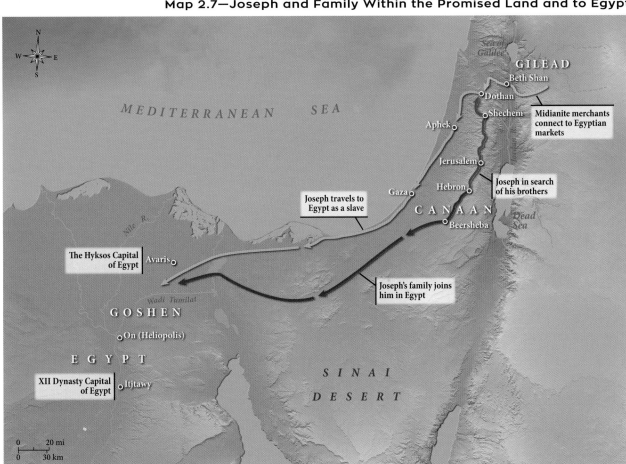

there. He may have wondered whether this was the start of the 400 years Abraham had been told about, a time when his family would be enslaved and mistreated in a foreign land (Genesis 15:13). Should he stay or should he go?

That night, he had his answer. The Lord repeats the triangle of promises given to Abraham and authorizes Jacob's departure. "'I am God, the God of your father,' he said. 'Do not be afraid to go down to Egypt, for I will make you into a great nation there. I will go down to Egypt with you, and I will surely bring you back again'" (Genesis 46:3–4). Jacob would die in Egypt, but as directed, his sons returned his body and buried this faithful man in the Promised Land (Genesis 50:4–14).[21] The author of Genesis gives the details, showing that it was appropriate for Abraham's family to leave the Promised Land. God gave his divine assurance, first at Bethel and then at Beersheba.

The Extended Stay in Egypt

When we consider the theological importance of Abraham's family living in the Promised Land, we assume that any departure would be brief and they would return as quickly as possible. When Jacob and his family leave the Promised Land because of a severe famine that is to last seven years, we expect to read of their return within a few pages of their departure. Not only is their return delayed until we reach the book of Joshua, but a span of more than 400 years has elapsed. This sends us scurrying back into the Scriptures for clues we may have missed that would explain why this family stayed in Egypt for so long. And there we find the answer linked to the pagan worship of the Amorites (Canaanites) who were living in the Promised Land and the unfortunate way in which Abraham's family had been drawn into that worship.

Mention of the Amorites' sin is amid words of reassurance that the Lord gives to Abram as he struggles with the delay in God's promises to him regarding having a son and possessing the land of Canaan (Genesis 15:2–8, 16). In the verses that follow, the Lord assured him that his family, turned into nation, will inherit the land of Canaan, but added that full possession would follow a 400-year stay in a foreign land. In part, this extended stay is attributed to the sin of others, "the sin of the Amorites has not yet reached its full measure" (Genesis 15:16). "Amorites" is the name used here

∧ *Pagan fertility figurine*

for all the non-Israelite people living in the land of Canaan alongside the family of Abraham (Numbers 13:29). The archaeological record shows them to be a people of some sophistication.[22] These cultural advances only thinly veiled ethical problems that disqualified them from continuing to live in the land that the Lord had promised to give to Abraham and his descendants (Genesis 10:15–19).

But it was not just the Amorites who were responsible for this extended stay outside the Promised Land—Abraham's family and their own moral standing before the Lord was at fault. Although a more detailed code of ethics would follow in the books of Exodus, Leviticus, and Deuteronomy, the readers of Genesis expect Abraham's family would stay clear of the local pagan cultures. Both Abraham and Isaac in particular knew that intermarriage with the Canaanites was trouble and so secured wives for their sons from northwestern Mesopotamia (Genesis 24:1–5; 28:1–5).

But Esau and his nephew Judah did not follow this trusted family practice, and instead became involved in a pagan lifestyle and worship. The mention of Esau's transgressions is brief. We are told he married two Hittite women (Genesis 26:34), a source of grief and disgust for his parents (Genesis 26:35; 27:46). Judah's transgressions and their consequences fill a whole chapter, Genesis 38. Judah left the clan to live among the

Canaanites and married a Canaanite woman (Genesis 38:1–2). The messy and sordid details in the rest of the chapter demonstrate just how far from God's plan this led the family of Abraham. The firstborn son of Judah's marriage, Er, is reported to have been so wicked that the Lord put him to death. The Lord's judgment also falls on the second son (Genesis 38:4, 8–10), and he too dies. The loss of two sons who die without producing children is a real tragedy. We might expect that Judah would move quickly to secure a wife for his third oldest son, Shelah, but he doesn't. He does nothing. Then, on his way to the shearing of his sheep, a time of year when the men often overindulged with alcohol and allowed their moral guard to slip, he caused a serious complication for himself and his family.[23] Judah slept with a woman he believed was a shrine prostitute. As it turned out, the woman was his daughter-in-law, Tamar, widow of his second son. When she becomes pregnant and Judah calls for her execution, she reveals that the father of her unborn child is none other than Judah himself. Ironically, it is Judah's daughter-in-law who demonstrates a concern for generating an heir, not Judah. Finally Judah admits his sin. "She is more righteous than I, since I wouldn't give her to my son Shelah" (Genesis 38:26).

The story of Judah in Genesis 38 has been placed right in the middle of the story of his brother Joseph. Genesis 37 recounts the way Joseph's brothers sell him into slavery and trick his father, Jacob, into believing he has been killed by a wild animal. Genesis 39 tells of his imprisonment on false charges of sexual misconduct before his unexpected rise to power in Egypt.

The intrusion of chapter 38 in this narrative of Genesis begs for an explanation. This chapter joins with the language of Genesis 15:16 to explain why Jacob's family spent 430 years in Egypt, away from the Promised Land. Their many years living outside the land of Canaan were necessary to rid Abraham's family of its acceptance and practice of the ideology of the Canaanites. God would take this family out of Canaan and put them in Egypt where Egyptian disdain for shepherds would make it much more difficult for them to marry an Egyptian or join the Egyptians in their pagan worship or even to eat with them (Genesis 43:32; 46:31–34).

∨ *Shepherding was a principal part of life for Jacob's family*

∧ *Makhtesh Ramon in the Desert of Paran*

Chapter 3

EGYPT, EXODUS, AND WILDERNESS

Israel in Egypt

The book of Exodus opens with the family of Abraham living in the same location where we left them when we read the last pages of Genesis—in Egypt. The author of Genesis and Exodus tells us again and again that the Israelites resided in the portion of Egypt called Goshen, in the eastern part of the Nile delta (Genesis 45:10; 46:28–29, 34; 47:4, 6, 27; 50:8; Exodus 8:22; 9:26.).[1] Although this area has limited rainfall, it has rich soil and plenty of water because of its proximity to the Nile River. The Nile gathers the water it delivers to the delta from a large region. Irrigation canals tap into this vital water supply and direct water to agricultural fields. Each year when the Nile floods, these fields receive a fresh coat of topsoil. This river ecosystem also provides fish and waterfowl for local consumption.[2] Joseph called it the best land Egypt had to offer (Genesis 45:18).

The repeated mention of Goshen at the close of Genesis and in the opening pages of Exodus suggests it played an important role in achieving the divine plan—the triangle of promises given to Abraham and his family (see figure 2.1). The part of that promise emphasized in the early verses of Exodus has to do with the growth of Abraham's family into a nation (Genesis 12:2; 17:2, 6; 22:17; 26:4; 28:14; 35:11; 48:4). The small number of people in Jacob's family who went into Egypt "increased in numbers and became so numerous that the land was filled with them" (Exodus 1:1–5, 7). The Lord used the plentiful resources of Goshen as an incubator to allow

Map 3.1—Land of Goshen

the small family of Jacob to become the burgeoning nation of Israelites who left Egypt.

The time to leave Egypt came after changes in Egyptian leadership caused major problems for the Israelites. From 1648–1540 BC, native Egyptian rulers had been displaced by the Hyksos, who established a capital for themselves in the eastern Nile delta at Avaris (see map 3.1).[3] The Israelites likely enjoyed favorable treatment during this period. However, that changed during the Egyptian New Kingdom period (c. 1570–1070 BC). A native Egyptian, Ahmose, expelled the Hyksos from the delta. In the years that followed, multiple Egyptian campaigns into the Middle East, in the region of Syria-Palestine, brought Asian war captives back to Egypt that the state put to work in agriculture and on building projects.[4] This change in the politics of Egypt brought in a "new king" who pressed the Israelites into hard service. This likely took the form of obligatory government service that stripped the Israelites of their autonomy. If their experience was similar to that of the Asian war captives at that time, the Israelites lived in self-contained villages, had their own housing, and tended their own livestock. What they lacked was the freedom to move about at will and to fill their day with tasks of their own choosing.[5]

While the Lord must certainly have recoiled from the social injustice of the Israelites' situation, it is not just social justice but concern for the promises given to Abraham that the biblical authors cite as reasons for the exodus in about 1446 BC (Exodus 2:24–25; 3:8). For everything that Goshen was, it was not the

∧ *A New Kingdom gold signet ring that belonged to Pharaoh Ahmose*

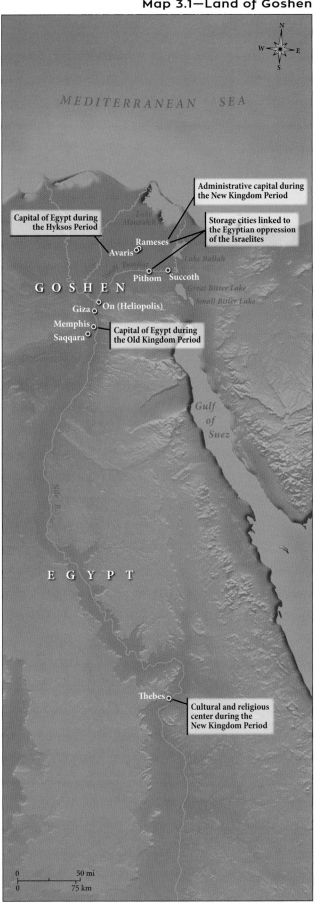

∧ Egypt's prospering ecosystem is a "gift of the Nile" according to Greek historian Herodotus

Promised Land. The Israelites living in Egypt had no memory of life in Canaan. That memory had died with children and grandchildren of Jacob. But the bond between this family and Canaan was not forgotten by the Lord. Because their presence in the Promised Land formed a vital link with God's plan to bless all nations through Abraham's family, the Lord tells Moses, the Israelites, and us that a move from Goshen back to Canaan is necessary (Exodus 3:8, 17; 6:4, 8).

The second leg of the promises given to Abraham, the promise to turn his small family into a flourishing nation, is the opening topic in Exodus. They "became so numerous that the land was filled with them" (1:1–7). But the new king of Egypt saw this differently. He saw them as a threat, yet he did not want to lose their labor. For him the Israelites were too numerous (Exodus 1:9–10), so he began to enact harsh measures. Despite the increasing oppression, the number of Israelites continued to grow. Then the king ordered the execution of Israelite male infants (Exodus 1:22). These policies clearly positioned Egypt as a rival to the Almighty, an opponent doing what it can to block the advance of the divine agenda.

This sent the not-so-subtle message that the Israelite destiny was in Egyptian hands rather than the Lord's, an impression that needed to be corrected. The Lord begins to do it with words, saying again and again that the Israelites are "my people" (Exodus 3:7; 5:1; 6:7; 7:16; 8:1, 20–23; 9:1, 13, 17; 10:3). When the refrain of "let my people go" does not change the will of the Egyptian pharaoh, ten plagues follow, including the final one that "[struck] down every firstborn of both people and animals" (Exodus 12:12), finally freeing the Israelites from the powerful grip of Egypt. Goshen had done its job, providing the environment for Israel's growth into a great nation. Now it was time to leave Egypt and begin the journey to the Promised Land.

The Route of the Exodus

When the Lord broke the resolve of the Egyptians, who had been bent on keeping the Israelites as slave labor, the exodus began. The Israelites had been in Egypt for 430 years (Exodus 12:41). This was not a frenzied flight from Egypt, but an organized departure of 600,000 men, plus women and children, along with all their animals (Exodus 12:37).

Given all the cities, outposts, roads, routes, and the body of water named to describe the exodus from Egypt (Exodus 13:17–14:9; Numbers 33:1–15), we

Map 3.2—Exodus to Sinai and Kadesh Barnea

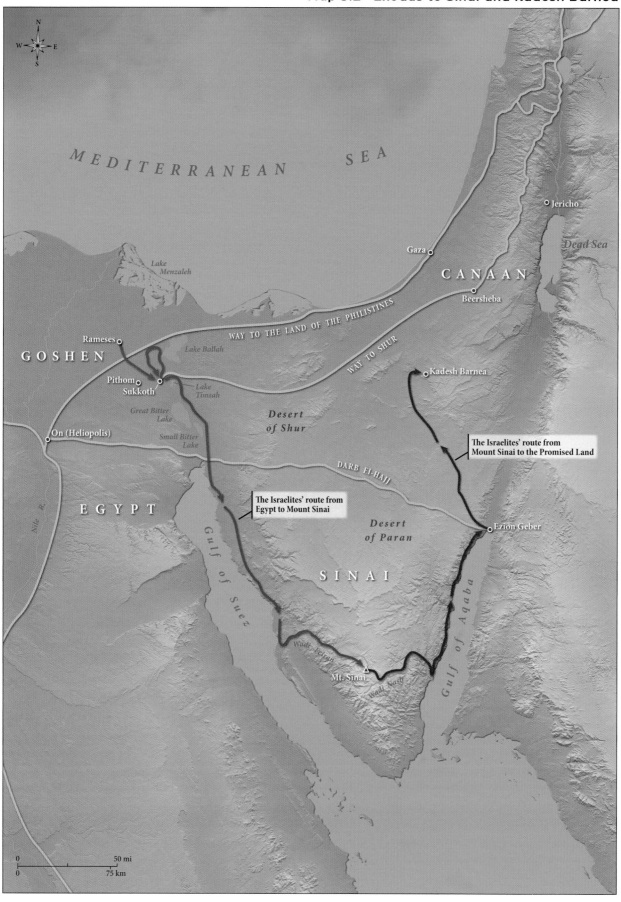

might expect that the route could be placed on a map with relative ease and precision. This is not the case. The list of places is not a complete turn-by-turn list like we might use today to navigate toward a destination. The place names are not all known to us. It seems the Israelites may have named some of the places, making those impossible to trace in other literature. Even when biblical authors include place names more widely used in the ancient world, we still might not be able to pinpoint the location on a map because the archaeological evidence is insufficient.[6] Plus the long-term survival of place names so common in modern Israel is absent in the northern part of the Sinai peninsula, causing us to define the exodus route in a more general way.

The starting point for the exodus was the city of Rameses, on the site of Avaris, the former capital of the Hyksos (Tell el-Dab'a) (see map 3.2). From there the Israelites headed to Mount Sinai, most likely located among the rugged granite mountains of the southern Sinai peninsula, either at or near Jebel Musa.[7] There were three common routes out of the Nile delta. The Way to the Land of the Philistines was the shortest route to Canaan, a route not taken by the Israelites (Exodus 13:17). This important trade and military route was also called the Way of Horus. It bristled with Egyptian logistical bases located in intervals of 15 miles (24 km), designed to support Egypt's military campaigns that regularly took aim at Canaan during the New Kingdom period.[8] The southern route, the Darb el-Hajj, connected Egypt with the Arabian Desert, but the road's distance from Rameses makes this option too far south. That leaves the Way to Shur, a road connected to Canaan via Beersheba. It is the road most likely used by Jacob and his family when they went to Egypt from the Promised Land and used again when they returned (Genesis 16:7; Exodus 15:22).

The Israelites left Rameses on an extension of the Way to Shur that ran to Sukkoth (Exodus 13:20; Numbers 33:5).[9] From this point on, the place names

∨ *Tell el-Dab'a, the location of ancient Rameses, the starting point for the Exodus*

∧ *Lake Timsah in the land of Goshen*

become confusing to us, just as the route was intended to confuse the Egyptians (Exodus 14:1–3). The Israelites camped on the shore of the Red Sea, or Reed Sea, where the Egyptians caught up with them (Exodus 14:9–12; Numbers 33:8).[10] It seems most likely that this body of water would include the Bitter Lakes that were linked by an Egyptian defensive canal that nearly spanned the land gap between the Mediterranean Sea and the Gulf of Suez.[11] After the Lord provided passage through the water on dry ground, the Israelites then would have turned south to travel along the west side of the Sinai Peninsula en route to Mount Sinai (Exodus 15:22; Numbers 33:8–15).

The route of the Israelites that brought them from Egypt to Mount Sinai was anything but serendipitous. The Lord was leading; the route was the one of his choosing (Exodus 13:17–18, 21–22). We surmise that he chose the route for two reasons. First, he sought to reintroduce and redefine himself for people who were generations removed from Jacob. Second, the Lord was calling for the Israelites to step out in faith and trust him.

Consider the role of that route in respect to these two purposes. Exodus 13:17 tells us that the Way to the Land of the Philistines was rejected because the Lord knew the Israelites were not ready for a faith challenge that brought them into contact with a series of Egyptian military installations. Instead the Lord challenged them with a route that was confusing. The Israelites knew the Promised Land of Canaan had a vital theological role to play as the homeland of Abraham's family, so why was the Lord leading them away from it? Aware that the Egyptians could change their minds and pursue the Israelites with their chariots, why select a route that at times reversed course and wasted valuable time (Exodus 14:1–2)? Why camp on the shore of a body of water that allowed the Egyptians to pin them down (Exodus 14:9–12)? And why lead them into the Sinai Wilderness, where the scarcity of food and water made survival of so many unlikely? The answer to each of these questions is the same: So the people would know the Lord and trust him, a trust refined in dire circumstances. He provided a solution that could to demonstrate the unique way his power and love work (Deuteronomy 4:32–35).

Mountain and Wilderness

Places can change the way we think about ourselves and our lives. The Lord took the Israelites from the only place they had known on the Nile River delta and plunged them into the forbidding landscapes of the Sinai Peninsula. In this region of austere mountains and desert wilderness, the Lord would shape the expanded family of Abraham into a nation that would carry on the promise of salvation.

After the dramatic exodus from Egypt, the Lord led his people south toward the mountainous and desert terrain where Moses was when he was called by the Lord to lead the Israelites. God paused the journey at Mount Sinai for about eleven months (Exodus 19:1–2, 23; Numbers 10:11–12). Before taking them to the Promised Land, the Lord defined every aspect of their lives through a set of laws that would mark them as holy, set apart for special service to the Lord. These laws were given on Mount Sinai (Leviticus 19:1). Although a number of different locations for this mountain have been suggested, the area of Jebel Musa

in the southern tip of the Sinai Peninsula is the most likely (see map 3.3). It is located the appropriate distance from Kadesh Barnea (Deuteronomy 1:2), and is the place identified with Mount Sinai in the earliest Christian writings.[12]

Their stay at Mount Sinai accomplished two goals. It isolated the Israelites from all other people, giving them a chance to learn to trust the Lord without interruption or outside interference. In the Nile delta, the ever-present Egyptians imposed a full workweek on the Israelites. They were never alone and they never lacked something to do. Although there was a small Egyptian presence in the Sinai, there were no Egyptians in the area of Mount Sinai. Thus Mount Sinai provided the Israelites with a place of isolation. The mountainous topography aided that isolation, but it also did what mountains do so well: made mortals feel appropriately small, checking the rise of human pride. Here the skyline is punctuated by clusters of steep-sided granite peaks that rise to over 8,000 feet

∨ *Desert of Sinai, near Mount Sinai*

(2,438 m) in elevation and plunge into narrow valleys. While living in the Nile delta, the tallest things the Israelites saw were the massive public buildings that celebrated human accomplishment. Here the towering mountains were God's creation. Long before Mount Sinai began to sway and smoke, the nature of the landscape had prepared the Israelite self-perception to hear God's message.

The Israelites traveled to a variety of wilderness settings whose names are preserved in Scripture. These include the Desert of Shur (Exodus 15:22), the Desert of Sin (Exodus 16:1; Numbers 33:11–12), Desert of Sinai (Exodus 19:1; Leviticus 7:38; Numbers 10:11–12; 33:15), Desert of Paran (Numbers 12:16; 13:26), and the Desert of Zin (Numbers 13:21; 20:1; 33:36). As one might expect, these areas of desert, or wilderness, are not defined by carefully circumscribed borders. Map 3.3 gives their approximate locations.

These wilderness regions join with Mount Sinai in shaping the thinking of God's people. If Mount Sinai was the location where Israel learned to live as the people of God, the wilderness was where they could learn to trust as the people of God. Although each of the wilderness areas has unique qualities, they all are places hostile to human survival. In this landscape, grazing land is sparse. Agriculture is possible only in the vicinity of a few oases, and drinking water is limited.[13] One of the best verbal images of this region was painted by the prophet Jeremiah, who described this as a "barren wilderness," "a land of deserts and ravines, a land of drought and utter darkness, a land where no one travels and no one lives" (Jeremiah 2:6). Here the Israelites are repeatedly faced with a shortage of water and food (Exodus 15:22–17:7). The water and food miracles we read about in Scripture must have been only a small example of the weekly miracles needed to sustain thousands in such a forbidding place.

Map 3.3—Deserts and Road Systems

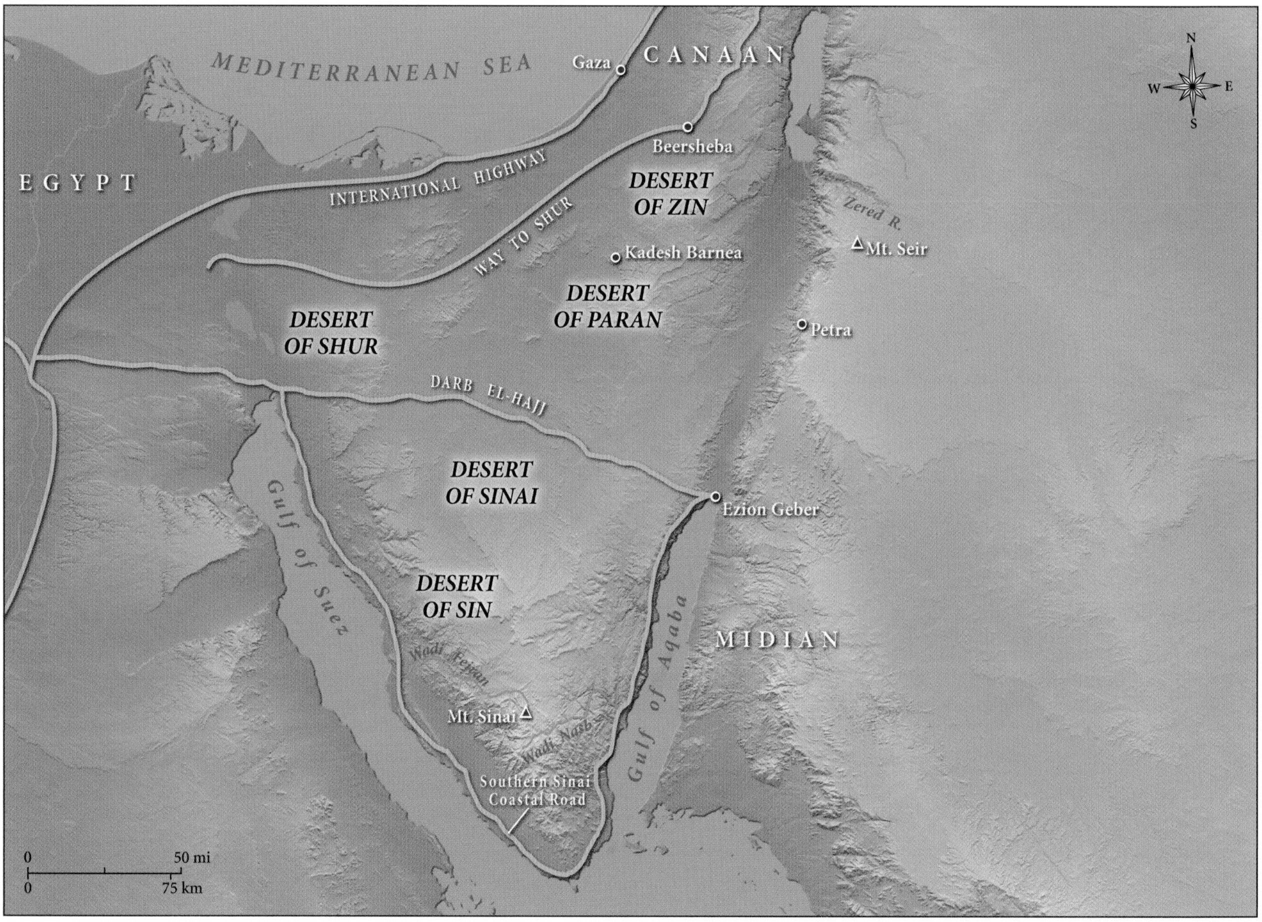

∧ *Makhtesh Ramon in the Desert of Paran*

What did this wilderness have to teach God's people? As a place where mortals could not survive on their own, it could teach them to trust the Lord without reservation. Instead, they remember Egypt, where the supply of food and water was never in question. Egypt, in fact, proves to be the foil of the wilderness experience, a major distraction to the Israelites in their faith development. They remember Egypt as a place where "we sat around pots of meat and ate all the food we wanted" (Exodus 16:3). "We remember the fish we ate in Egypt at no cost—also the cucumbers, melons, leeks, onions and garlic" (Numbers 11:5; see also 14:3). But the Lord had brought them out of that place of secure prosperity to teach that mortals "[do] not live on bread alone but on every word that comes from the mouth of the LORD" (Deuteronomy 8:3). And so it was that Mount Sinai joined with a variety of other wilderness experiences to change the way the Israelites thought about themselves and about their relationship to the Lord, someone who could be trusted even when their very survival seemed in question.

Exploring Canaan

When the Lord had finished his time with the Israelites at Mount Sinai and in the desert wilderness, he led them on toward their ultimate destination, the Promised Land. But as they approached its southern border, a troubling question lingered. Had the wilderness experience done its job and built a solid foundation of trust in the Lord?

Could those following Moses walk the Promised Land with the same faith demonstrated by Abraham, Isaac, and Jacob? The answer to this question comes to us in a geographically detailed narrative about the exploration of Canaan. When the Israelites arrived at Kadesh Barnea, they apparently requested that a delegation be sent

Map 3.4—Exploration of Canaan

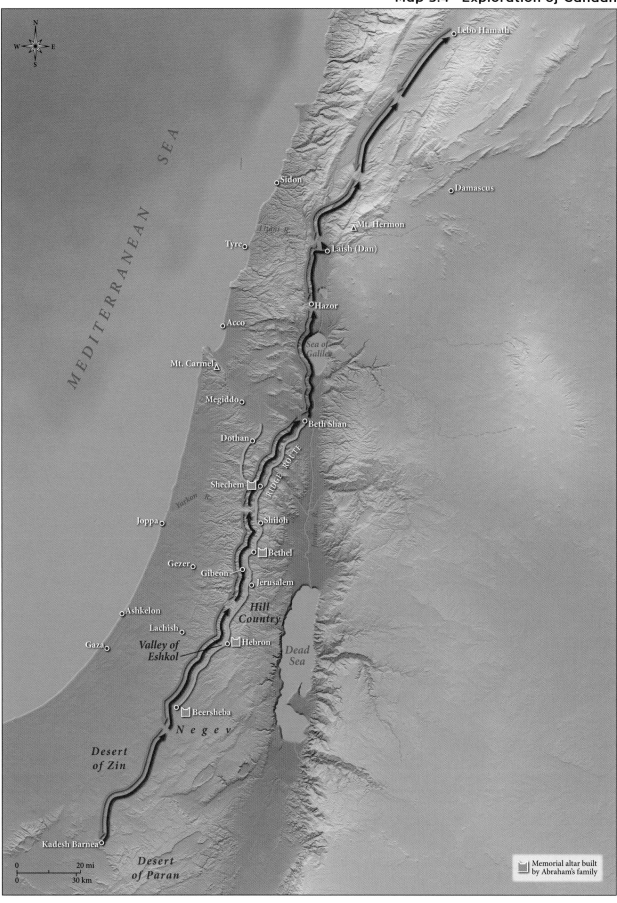

Memorial altar built
by Abraham's family

ahead of the main group to explore Canaan as scouts. The Lord honored this request and transformed it into a command given to Moses (compare Numbers 13:3 and Deuteronomy 1:22–23).[14] Moses identified twelve respected men, each representing his own tribe, to serve in this capacity (Numbers 13:2–16).

Moses sent out these scouts with specific instructions on where to go and what to report on. He told them to travel through the Desert of Zin and enter the Negev, the dry basin that had housed the encampment of Abraham and his family near Beersheba. They were to continue north past the Negev into the central mountain range of Canaan, presumably using the same Ridge Route that had known the footsteps of Abraham, Isaac, and Jacob centuries earlier (Numbers 13:17). These scouts would walk past the same altars, tombs, stone monuments, and pillars that had linked Abraham's family to the Promised Land (see map 3.4).

As they walked they were to keep a record of some specific geographic realities (Numbers 13:17–20). Is the land populated or empty? Is there ample water there?[15] Are the people living in open camps or fortified cities? Does the land have agricultural capability? The answers to these questions could incite enthusiasm in people who had been waiting to enter this cherished land and were ready to trade the wilderness for a land with water and fields suitable for agriculture.

The scouts appear to have done everything they were directed to do. They traveled north from the Desert of Zin all the way to Lebo Hamath in the north before returning to Moses and the Israelites at Kadesh Barnea (Numbers 13:21–26). The one place we know they visited along the way was Hebron, a spot that had a long and meaningful history for the Israelites, including a memorial altar and family tomb that would remind the scouts of the set of promises given to Abraham (Genesis 13:18; 23:9; 35:27). From the Hebron area, they gathered grapes, pomegranates, and figs that demonstrated not only the land's agricultural potential but also showed that water was available even during the driest part of the summer (Numbers 13:20). We expect a glowing report.

But that is not what the scouts gave. Ten of the twelve scouts used the massive cluster of grapes they carried to spring into a description of the massive people who lived in this land, people who lived in large cities that were heavily fortified (Numbers 13:28). The ten scouts list subregions and the people who live in

∨ *Hermon Stream at the base of Mount Hermon near Dan*

them in such a fashion that it makes the land sound full to the brim. "The Amalekites live in the Negev; the Hittites, Jebusites and Amorites live in the hill country; and the Canaanites live near the sea and along the Jordan" (Numbers 13:29). Not only is this verbal report showcasing the more challenging dimensions of the Promised Land that they saw, it also appears to be distorting the reality. The archaeology of this par-

∧ A large cluster of ripe grapes shows the land's potential

ticular period in history suggests that there were only a couple of fortified cities in the central mountain range, and that generally the core of the country had a considerable amount of forested land with a relatively low population density.[16]

Although Joshua and Caleb stepped in to counter this majority report with words of encouragement, the people ignored them. In doing so, they demonstrated that they held the same impoverished faith as the ten who offered the disingenuous report. Geography helps to highlight their lack of faith—a faith the Lord had sought to nurture. The scouts walked the same land that Abraham and his family had walked. They visited the sites Abraham and his family had used in the hope that this family, turned into nation, might one day occupy and own this land. But the faith development of these Israelites was incomplete. They were so frightened by the report of the challenges ahead that they even spoke of returning to Egypt (Numbers 14:3–4). As a result, they were forbidden entry by God. The adults who were responsible for the decision were destined to die in the wilderness. And only after decades more in the wilderness would their children and grandchildren become the people of God who entered the Promised Land.

Moses Barred from the Promised Land

After we meet Moses, we expect him to be the one who will lead Israel into the Promised Land; it is his call and destiny (Exodus 3:8–10). That is what makes his being blocked from ever entering the Promised Land so unbelievable. He disqualified himself from leading the Israelites into the Promised Land when he failed to trust the Lord in the place where trust was to grow, in the Desert of Zin. As a result, he experienced the same penalty as those who decades earlier failed to trust the Lord and never entered the Promised Land, but died in the wilderness (Numbers 14:10–23). The words of the Lord to Moses were clear: "Because you did not trust in me enough to honor me as holy in the sight of the Israelites, you will not bring this community into the land I give them" (Numbers 20:12). But how did Moses break faith with the Almighty?

The Israelites are near the end of their wilderness stay. They have become impatient with the multi-decade wait and are angered by yet another lack of water. They bring their complaint to Moses and use the opportunity to lambaste him for bringing them out of Egypt, only to idle them in a region without grain, figs, grapevines, or pomegranates (Numbers 20:2–5). This was just some of the produce they had been told was in the Promised Land (Deuteronomy 8:7–8). That makes their criticism a clear reminder that Moses failed to deliver what he promised—to lead them to a good land.

Stung by this unfair criticism, Moses turns to the Lord for direction. The Lord tells Moses to take his staff in hand, assemble the people, and speak to the rock, and it will pour out water (Numbers 20:8). But Moses doesn't do that.[17] He takes his staff, assembles the people, speaks harshly to them (Psalm 106:32–33),

⌃ **Above Left:** Water weeping from limestone in the Desert of Zin; **Right:** Red granite characterizes the area near Rephidim

and strikes the rock two times. Water gushes from the rock (Numbers 20:9–11). Striking the rock instead of speaking to it showed Moses' lack of trust in the Lord and his failure to honor him as holy (Numbers 20:12).

The biblical author links this event with the geography of the Desert of Zin because the grave error in judgment demonstrated by Moses is related to the geology and hydrology of this region (Numbers 20:1; 27:14). While the specific geology is not described by the biblical author, it is strongly implied in the Hebrew term that is translated using the more generic English word "rock."[18]

The geology of the region offers an explanation. The Desert of Zin is composed of strata of limestone with softer and more porous layers above hard and dense layers of stone.[19] When it rains, the water percolates down through the softer limestone layers until it reaches one of the hard layers of rock. It then flows laterally along this seam, eventually flowing from the ground as a spring when a seam reaches the surface

of the earth, as on a hillside. This spring water carries with it tiny particles of limestone picked up during its journey through the upper strata of limestone. As the water flows from the rock into the sunshine, some of the water evaporates, leaving behind minerals that collect to form a cap over the water's exit point. This cap "seals" the hole, preventing water from leaking from the rock. Water continues to collect behind the cap under increasing pressure. Someone familiar with this phenomenon can strike such a mineral cap and produce water from rock.[20]

If this entire event sounds familiar, it is because it happened before. When the Israelites were camped at Rephidim, they faced a similar need for water. This time the Lord directed Moses to strike the rock with his staff so that water would pour out for the thirsty throng gathered around him (Exodus 17:1–6). These instructions pertain to the geology of the southern Sinai that is markedly different from the geology of the Desert of Zin. The southern Sinai is composed of

∧ *Ein Avdat Canyon in the Desert of Zin*

water-shedding granite that has no capacity to absorb or hold water in the same way limestone does. There was no expectation that striking the granite rock at Rephidim would produce even a single drop of water. When Moses struck the rock, the unexpected flow of water was a miracle and the Lord received the glory.

In the Desert of Zin, where the geology of the region caused storage of water within its rocky slopes, the Lord specifically directed Moses to use a different tactic here than at Rephidim, one that would work only through the power of the Lord. In the Desert of Zin, Moses was to speak to the rock to make water gush out, clearly a miracle that would direct praise to the Lord. But when Moses struck the rock and broke the cap blocking flow of the water, he ignored the words of God. He directed attention away from the Lord and focused it on himself. Moses was to have been the one to lead Israel into the Promised Land, but he was disqualified for showing a lack of trust in the Lord.

Promised Land Outside the Promised Land

We speak of Canaan as the Promised Land because it is the real estate the Lord promised to give to Abraham's family in conjunction with their role in the divine plan to save the world from sin. But we would be mistaken to think that the Promised Land is the only land that was promised by the Lord. Others also received promised land in a land grant that lay outside the Promised Land, a land grant that came with a specific responsibility.

The Lord gave land not only to the Israelites, but had also given land to their neighbors in the Transjordan Plateau, to Ammon, Moab, and Edom (see map 3.5). By looking at the detailed summary of the land parcels assigned to Reuben, Gad, and Manasseh on the east side of the Jordan River (Numbers 32), we can see the gaps that generally are filled by Ammon, Moab, and Edom. The Ammonites originated with the son born to Lot (Abraham's nephew) and Lot's younger daughter following the destruction of Sodom and Gomorrah (Genesis 19:38). The heartland of Ammon seems to reside around the headwaters of the Jabbok River near the Ammonite capital city of Rabbah and include the tributary system of the Jabbok River (Deuteronomy 2:19; 3:16; Joshua 12:2). The Moabites were descended from the son born to Lot and his oldest daughter (Genesis 19:37). The heartland of Moab extended from the Zered River to the Arnon River (Numbers 21:12–13, 26; Deuteronomy 2:13–14). The region north of the Arnon was given to Reuben (Numbers 32:33; Joshua 13:9–12), but the Moabites often pushed into the agriculturally productive plateau called the Mishor and onto the plain northeast of the Dead Sea that became known as the Plains of Moab.[21] The Edomites were descendants of Jacob's brother Esau (Genesis 25:30; Deuteronomy 2:4–5). The territory the Lord gave to Edom stretched along the rocky plateau-like ridge that stretched from the Zered River to the Gulf of Aqaba (Genesis 36:8). The dramatic elevation of these mountains that in many places exceed 5,000 feet (1,524 m) made it appear to those living at lower elevations as if the Edomites had built their homes among the nests of eagles (Jeremiah 49:16).

When the Lord made these land grants east of the Jordan River, he directed Israel to respect them, and he directed Ammon, Moab, and Edom to do the same for Israel. As the Israelites made their final turn to enter their Promised Land, the Lord told them they were not to provoke a military conflict with Ammon, Moab, or Edom. They were to avoid harassing them. Israel was not to take any of their land, not even a plot the size of a human footprint (Deuteronomy 2:4–6, 9, 19). The land given to Ammon, Moab, and Edom carried with it a sacred responsibility. We do not see it directly addressed to these three groups in the Bible, but we hear echoes of that expectation when the prophets of the Old Testament sharply criticize them for failing in their mission. That mission was to respect the Israelite lands and to encourage and support the family of Jacob in the accomplishment of their divine mission.

Understanding these facts will change the way we read the biblical texts that speak of Ammon, Moab, and Edom. At times we read of events that illustrate

∨ *The citadel of Rabbah (in modern Amman), which became the capital of Ammon*

Above Left: *Rugged mountains near Bozrah, the Iron Age capital of Edom;* **Right:** *Sandstone mountains of Petra, part of ancient Edom*

the mutual respect playing out exactly as the Lord intended. For example, when Moses leads the Israelites into the Transjordan Plateau, the Bible notes that the Israelites did not engage Ammon, Moab, or Edom in any battle, being careful not to target any of the lands divinely assigned to others in the Transjordan. The Israelite conquest of the Transjordan begins north of the Arnon River, north of the land given to Edom and Moab. The Israelites also are careful to avoid targeting Ammonite land to the east (Numbers 20:14–21; 21:24, 26). Four hundred years later when David fled from Saul, the king of the Ammonites offered him sanctuary (2 Samuel 10:1–2). It is just this kind of mutual respect and support that the Lord wanted between Israel and its neighbors in Ammon, Moab, and Edom.

But other times we find just the opposite. We read about Israelites dominating the land of these eastern people, and we read about Ammon, Moab, and Edom fighting against the Israelites and seizing land granted to them. The historical narratives are too numerous to recount here, but every time the biblical authors present us with one of these cases, it ought to make us pause and see the event as running counter to the land grant plan the Lord had for the region. Examples include an Ammonite king attacking and seeking to humiliate the Israelite city of Jabesh Gilead (1 Samuel 11:1–11), the Moabites hiring Balaam to curse the Israelites (Numbers 22–25), and the way the Edomites joined with the Babylonians to harm Israel. An entire book of the Bible, Obadiah, is on the censure of the Edomites.[22]

The promised land outside of the Promised Land came with a set of obligations attached to it.

The Transjordan Conquest and Distribution

The Transjordan conquest and distribution of land east of the Jordan River is described in a number of Bible passages (Numbers 21 and 32; Deuteronomy 2–3; Joshua 13). This suggests it may be deserving of more attention than it often gets.

After Moses led the Israelites around Edom and Moab on their way north to the Promised Land, they camped near the headwaters of the Arnon River (Deuteronomy 2:26). From this location they sent Sihon of Heshbon, king of the Amorites, a request for

Map 3.5—Transjordan Occupation

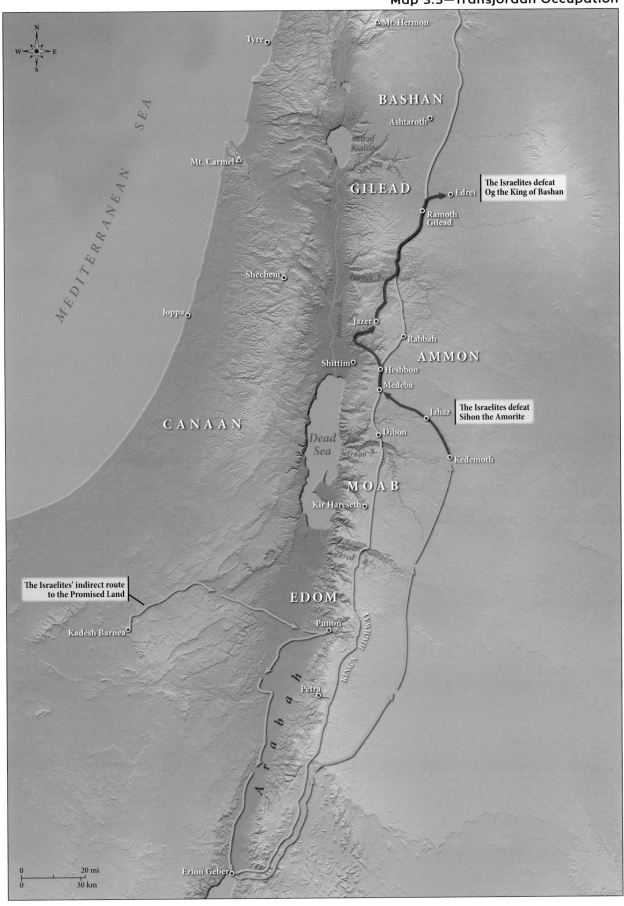

N
W — E
S

Mt. Hermon

Tyre

MEDITERRANEAN SEA

BASHAN

Ashtaroth

Sea of Galilee

Mt. Carmel

Yarmuk R.

GILEAD

Edrei | The Israelites defeat Og the King of Bashan |

Ramoth Gilead

Jabbok R.

Shechem

Jordan R.

Jazer

Joppa

Rabbah

AMMON

Shittim

Heshbon

Medeba

CANAAN

Jahaz | The Israelites defeat Sihon the Amorite |

Dead Sea

Dibon

Arnon R.

Kedemoth

MOAB

Kir Hareseth

Zered R.

| The Israelites' indirect route to the Promised Land |

EDOM

Punon

Kadesh Barnea

KING'S HIGHWAY

Arabah

Petra

0   20 mi
0   30 km

Ezion Geber

safe passage, a request that received a hostile reply. Amorite soldiers mustered at Jahaz and fought the Israelites (Numbers 21:21–31; Deuteronomy 2:24–37). When the fighting ended, Israel was in control of the land between the Arnon and Jabbok Rivers (Numbers 21:24). The next kingdom to fall was that of Og king of Bashan (Numbers 21:33–35; Deuteronomy 3:1–7). This time there is no mention of a request for safe passage. Sensing the Israelite threat, Og marched his soldiers out to fight with Israel at Edrei, where he was defeated. The Israelites now controlled the land that stretched from the Jordan River eastward to the desert and from the Arnon River north to Mount Hermon, including the plateau-like Mishor, all of Gilead, and Bashan (Deuteronomy 3:8–10).

The Israelite tribes of Reuben and Gad quickly saw the value of this land and went to Moses with a request that they might receive their land parcels on the east side of the Jordan River. The half tribe of Manasseh also asked for and received real estate allotments here.

The description of the land each received includes the regional names and the names of cities they rebuilt or founded (Numbers 32:34–42; Deuteronomy 3:12–17; Joshua 13:8–31).

Why do the biblical authors give the conquest and distribution of this land so much attention? First, the value of this land. When we assess all of the land that lies east of the Jordan River, it becomes clear that this is the best land the Transjordan has to offer. Bashan is a high volcanic plateau with rich, dark soil and plenty of rainfall. It excels in producing grain and providing pastures for cattle. Grain does not grow as well in the mountains of Gilead, but here ample rain and elevation foster the growth of grapes and olives. And the rich terra rosa soil of the Mishor can grow everything. The Mishor also has strategic value for those forming a kingdom on the west side of the Jordan River. While the Jordan proved to be an adequate political border, it did not offer any natural defense against invasion. To get that, the people would have to stretch their

∨ *Basaltic highlands of Bashan, home of King Og*

kingdom all the way to Mount Hermon and the Arabian Desert. That is exactly what happened when the Israelites occupied and fortified cities in Bashan, Gilead, and the Mishor. A united kingdom of Israel that included the natural defenses as well as the natural resources of this region was in a much stronger position than one without them.[23]

The biblical authors describe the conquest and division of the area east of the Jordan River because these events help our understanding of how God expected the conquest to look, how the Israelites were to make war as the people of God. The Lord would initiate such a war and clearly direct actions (Deuteronomy 2:24–25, 31; 3:2). With those instructions, there was no room for improvising by Israel. This is emphasized in the early battles, when we see the Israelites follow God's directive to remain clear of the land he had given to the Ammonites (Numbers 21:24; Deuteronomy 2:36–37).

Drawing our attention to the story unfolding east of the Jordan River, the biblical authors show how the Lord has fulfilled the promise he made to Abraham in Genesis. The large herds and flocks that Reuben and Gad spoke of in their request for land east of the Jordan River are evidence that God was making Israel "numerous" and blessing the growth of their herds and flocks (Numbers 32:1–5, 33). It appears that the Lord permitted settlement of land east of the Jordan River in part because the natural resources west of the Jordan were not adequate to provide enough food and water for all of God's people.

Finally, this request for land east of the Jordan illus-

∧ *The Israelites detoured around the travel-friendly plateau of Edom*

trates the change in spirit that had occurred among the people of God since the last time they stood poised to enter the Promised Land. When Reuben and Gad made their request for land, Moses could barely contain his anger because their attitude resembled that of the ten scouts who had discouraged Israel from crossing into the Promised Land decades earlier (Numbers 13:26–14:4; 32:6–15). But the biblical authors show us that this is not the case, for Reuben and Gad offer to take the lead in crossing the Jordan River after they have built pens for their animals and cities to protect their families (Numbers 32:16–19). A new spirit now lives among the people of God.

The Death of Moses on Mount Nebo

We get to know the people we meet in the Bible to different degrees. Many characters walk on and off the pages of our Bible with little more than casual mention, but Moses is not one of them. We get to know Moses in the way we get to know our most intimate of friends. We walk the twists and turns of life with him, sharing in his moments of joy and triumph as well as his moments of failure and despair. So it is not surprising that we feel some grief as we read the last chapter of Deuteronomy, which briefly describes him climbing

Mount Nebo to view the Promised Land before he dies (see map 3.6). The early verses of this chapter are filled with geography that is meant to bring comfort to Moses and to us. The land Moses was shown was meant to ease his passing from this life to the next.

Deuteronomy 34 briefly recalls the highs and lows of Moses' life. He certainly was a man of stellar credentials and experiences. Although it is not physically possible for a human being to look into the face of the Almighty and live (as observed in Moses' own experience in Exodus 33:20–23), the intimate exchanges he had with the Lord are characterized as unique to Moses "whom the LORD knew face to face" (Deuteronomy 34:10). And in service to the divine mission, Moses was enabled to perform one miracle after another, unlike others who claimed the title of prophet (Deuteronomy 34:11–12). But these accolades are dimmed by the failure that disqualified Moses from leading the Israelites into the Promised Land, a failure to do what the Lord told him to do. The Lord had told Moses to speak to the rock in front of the Israelites. He hit the rock instead. And the Lord said, "Because you did not trust in me enough to honor me as holy in the sight of the Israelites, you will not bring this community into the land I give them" (Numbers 20:12). Moses desperately sought a reversal in this judgment, but to no avail (Deuteronomy 3:23–29). Moses died outside the Promised Land not because of physical health (Deuteronomy 34:7), but because of his lack

of trust in that one instance. As a result, his role as leader of God's people ended without ever crossing the Jordan River.

A barrage of geography is contained in the first four verses of Deuteronomy 34. "Then Moses climbed Mount Nebo from the plains of Moab to the top of Pisgah, across from Jericho. There the LORD showed him the whole land—from Gilead to Dan, all of Naphtali, the territory of Ephraim and Manasseh, all the land of Judah as far as the Mediterranean Sea, the Negev and the whole region from the Valley of Jericho, the City of Palms, as far as Zoar. Then the LORD said to him, 'This is the land I promised on oath to Abraham, Isaac and Jacob when I said, "I will give it to your descendants." I have let you see it with your eyes, but you will not cross over into it.'"

It is easy to get distracted by questions connected with this geography. If Moses is viewing the Promised Land from the traditional location of Mount Nebo on

Map 3.6—The Plains of Moab and Mount Nebo

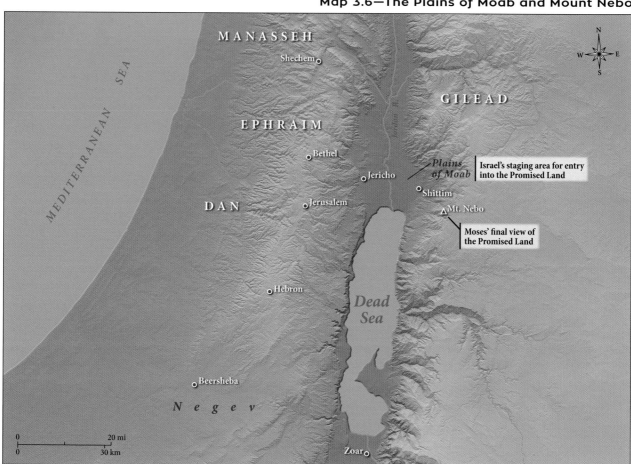

| EGYPT, EXODUS, AND WILDERNESS • The Death of Moses on Mount Nebo

∧ *View from Mount Nebo toward the Promised Land*

the northeast side of the Dead Sea, line-of-sight limitations would have prevented him from seeing all of the locations mentioned. Was Moses allowed to see some of this geography with supernatural assistance? We don't know the answer. It is also easy to get distracted by the Lord's reminder, as if Moses needed one, that he was not permitted to cross the Jordan River (Deuteronomy 34:4).

A closer reading of the text suggests that this geography plays a different and positive role. This look into the Promised Land is coupled with the reminder that this is the land promised to Abraham, Isaac, and Jacob (Deuteronomy 34:4). Moses had written about the important connection between this land and the Lord's plan to save the world. When we see the Promised Land linked to God's promise to save, then this geography becomes a symbol of salvation. Although Moses had sinned, the Lord on the day of Moses' death shows him the land to offer him and the readers of Deuteronomy hope. As Moses' view was turned counterclockwise from north to south on the horizon line, he did not just see Gilead, Naphtali, Ephraim, Manasseh, the Jordan Valley, and the Negev. He saw hope. That is the role of this geography in Deuteronomy 34.

△ The Jordan River

Chapter 4

CONQUEST AND SETTLEMENT

Crossing the Jordan River

The conquest of the Promised Land begins with the march into the Jordan River.[1] The notion of crossing the Jordan River is not new to readers of the Old Testament by the time they read the first verses of Joshua. Moses had stoked the Israelites' anticipation by linking a future crossing of the Jordan with the long-awaited entry into the Promised Land (Numbers 33:50–51; 34:12; Deuteronomy 2:29; 3:27; 4:26; 9:1; 11:31; 12:10; 27:2; 30:18; 31:13; 32:47). The Israelites were camped on the Plains of Moab opposite Jericho (see map 4.1). The moment had come. To enter Canaan, they had to cross the Jordan River. But the swift current of the river at flood stage dampened their enthusiasm for the crossing.

While we give little thought to crossing a river, things were different for people of Bible times. There were no bridges. Travelers crossed a river by wading or floating. Today most children learn to swim. This was not the case in Bible times, a fact that made the crossing of a flooded river a treacherous business. Springtime in Canaan was the time of year when the Jordan River was running at flood stage, a point not lost on the author of Joshua (3:15). This meant that even at a ford like the one opposite Jericho, the river could be 10 to 12 feet (3–3.6 m) deep and up to 1 mile (1.6 km) wide.[2] The riverbanks were muddy, and strong currents threatened to drown even those who knew how to swim.

The Plains of Moab, which lie just northeast of the Dead Sea

The Israelites camped next to the Jordan River for days, wondering what was to come, so it is fitting that the author of Joshua slows our reading of this event, giving us time to reflect on the miraculous nature of the crossing. Two chapters (41 verses) are dedicated to the Jordan River crossing. And lest the reader lose sight of this important river, the Jordan River is mentioned by name 22 times in those 41 verses. The Lord, through Joshua, directed the priests to carry the ark of the covenant to the water's edge and then to stand in the river. When their toes touched the water, the Lord blocked the flow of the Jordan at the town of Adam so that the Israelites could make this crossing on dry ground (Joshua 3:14–17).

But this river crossing was to do more than just get people to the west bank of the river. There were two other goals. The miraculous crossing of the Jordan was to seal the confidence of the Israelites in Joshua as their new leader. Decades earlier, Joshua and Caleb had been among those who explored the Promised Land, and these two alone had encouraged entry (Numbers 14:6–9). Now Joshua is the one who is directing preparations for the crossing, and he is the one who gives the command to advance. A successful military crossing of a river at flood stage was regarded as a mark of honor among military commanders (1 Chronicles 12:15). God's intentions are clear. He said to Joshua, "Today I will begin to exalt you in the eyes of all Israel, so they may know that I am with you as I was with Moses" (Joshua 3:7; see also 4:14).

Assyrian solider using an inflated animal skin to cross a river

But beyond the exalting of Joshua, the crossing of the Jordan River at flood stage addressed another need in Israel, the need for God's people to know that the Lord was with them. Their extended stay in the wilderness had been full of challenges. With the entry into Canaan; they would face new ones. The Israelites were moving from largely unoccupied land into a landscape with cities and villages whose owners would not welcome their arrival. The land of Canaan would become Israel's land, but not without a fight.

The crossing of the Jordan River offers them the assurance that during this fight the Lord will be with them. The nature of the miracle is designed to recall an earlier miracle at the Red (Reed) Sea, when the Israelites left Egypt. There the Lord removed a water barrier so that the Israelites could cross the sea on dry ground. The repeat of this miracle as the Israelites crossed the flooded Jordan River to enter Canaan filled them with confidence. As the Lord had been with the Israelites upon their exit from Egypt, so he was with them on their entry into Canaan (Joshua 3:10; 4:23–24). Lest these two important lessons be lost on subsequent generations, Joshua built a memorial at Gilgal with stones from the Jordan (Joshua 4:7). The memorial would help to preserve the memory of this event and the important lesson it taught God's people about God's presence with them and his power to aid them in their mission.

The Fall of Jericho

The Israelite conquests of Canaan are usually summarized in Scripture. But the fall of Jericho is an exception (Joshua 6). Here the author provides a narrative full of details, inviting us to linger at the story of this city's dramatic fall.

When it comes to the land in the lower Jordan Valley, Jericho has the most to offer its residents. Although this area has a meager annual precipitation of barely 6 inches (15 cm) and sits on the edge of the dry Judean Wilderness, Jericho was a city more than 5,000 years

Map 4.1—Conquest via Jericho

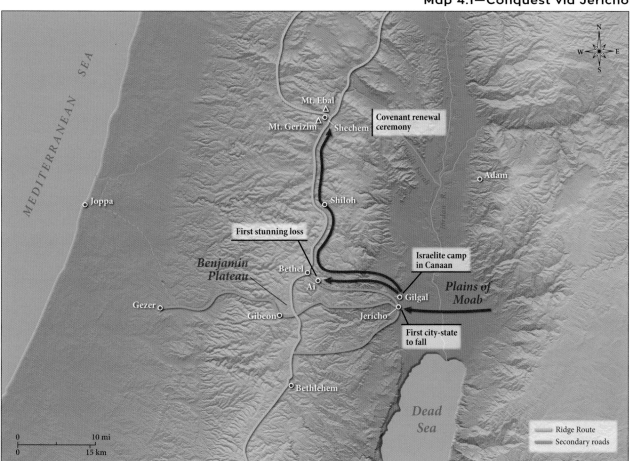

before Abraham was born. The reason is water. Jericho was blessed with a powerful spring that drew its water from the rain-fed west side of the central mountains and poured forth water at the astonishing rate of 1,200 gallons (4,542 liters) per minute.

This spring turned Jericho into a sprawling oasis with economic and strategic value. Part of Jericho's thriving economy was based on agriculture. To this day Jericho's spring gives life to lush vegetable gardens, orchards, and groves of date palms. Jericho was famous for those palms and was often referred to as the "City of Palms" (Deuteronomy 34:3; Judges 1:16; 3:13; 2 Chronicles 28:15). The agricultural industry was complemented by businesses that took advantage of the city's proximity to the Dead Sea. This generally lifeless body of water was a source for salt and bitumen that were harvested and shipped to various markets.[3]

But Jericho's greatest claim to fame and its strategic military value were due to its unique geographic position. It guarded a portion of the east-west corridor that links the King's Highway and the International Highway. To connect these two important parallel trade routes, one has to climb and then descend through the deep Jordan Valley. In most places this is prohibitive.

But opposite Jericho, the terrain softens and allows travelers an easier time moving between the mountains above and the valley below. This natural ramp off the Transjordan mountains leads directly to one of the best natural fords in the lower Jordan Valley, the ford opposite Jericho. Once west of the ford and through Jericho, three natural routes climb westward to the watershed of the central mountains of Judah, then descend to the coastal plain and the International Highway. Thus the unique geographic position of Jericho made it a gateway that controlled entry into Canaan from the east. It was a place to collect trade revenue and a place to defend against military invasion. Because of its water, agricultural land, resources for mining, and military value, Jericho was settled thousands of years before Abraham was born. At the time of the conquest by the Israelites, a fortified city occupied this site.

This geographic background helps to explain why Joshua would report on the fall of this key city in such detail. Although the city did not boast the sprawling defensive works of a medieval castle—Old Testament Jericho had a modest six-acre (2.4-hectare) footprint—this was a fort whose impact had to be neutralized. The Israelites had left family on the east side of the Jordan, and Jericho could have blocked the flow of supplies through this natural corridor. Allowing Jericho to stand would have subjected the Israelite army moving west to harassing attacks.

Jericho had to go; but it was how it went that made it important to record in detail. The attack on Jericho was the first battle waged west of the Jordan River, and it set the manner of how the people of God were to conduct their conquest of the Promised Land. The battles ahead were the Lord's battles. And he called for the Israelites to

∧ Date palm in Jericho, "The City of Palms"

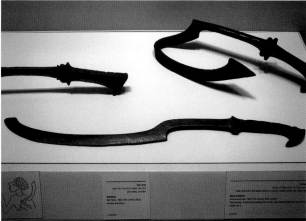

∧ **Above:** *Sickle swords were the "swords" of Joshua's day*

< **Left:** *Defensive structures on the south side of Jericho*

respect the control he insisted on having over where attacks were to be made, when they were to be made, and how they were to be made. The crumbling defensive walls of Jericho illustrated just how successful Joshua and the Israelite army could be when they followed the Lord's directions in conquering Canaan.

Normally, there was no question as to what a conqueror would do with the city of Jericho. Any conqueror would carefully rebuild the walls of this key gateway city and put the city to work for them as it had worked for those from whom they had taken it. This happened repeatedly throughout the history of this city. But after its destruction by the Israelites, the tumbled walls and compromised gates were left in ruins (Joshua 6:26–27). Joshua even issued a curse against anyone who would try to rebuild the city. Those ruins became not only a reminder of the first victory the Lord gave Israel in the Promised Land but also a reminder of the success God gave Israel when they trusted him and followed his commands.

Sacred Assembly at Mount Ebal

After destroying both Jericho and Ai, the Israelites, who were camped near Jericho at Gilgal, traveled north to convene a sacred assembly on Mount Ebal (see map 4.1).

Readers of Deuteronomy have been led to expect this trip. Moses had given clear and specific directions (Deuteronomy 11:29–30; 27:1–26). After the Israelites entered Canaan, they were to make their way to Mount Ebal for a worship experience that was carefully choreographed. They were to set up a monument of large stones coated with plaster on which Joshua was to write the law the Lord had given to Israel through Moses on Mount Sinai. Joshua also was to build an altar of uncut stones on Mount Ebal for offerings of various types. The Israelite tribes were given specific places to stand on Mount Ebal and on Mount Gerizim during the reading of the law of God in this natural amphitheater (Joshua 8:30–35).[4]

The importance of this sacred assembly becomes clear when we realize the role it played in defining the Israelite army and the conquest of the Promised Land. Each time these soldiers picked up their weapons for the next phase of the conquest of Canaan, they did so as representatives of the Lord who had commissioned their advance. The initial defeat at Ai that came as a result of Achan's sin (Joshua 7) emphasized just how important it was for them to see themselves as a people bound to the Lord by covenant.

But why had Moses been so insistent that this sacred assembly occur on Mount Ebal? There is an unmistakable beauty to the setting. Mount Ebal, at 3,044 feet (928 m), is the highest mountain in northern Samaria. Joined with Mount Gerizim, these two mountains create a striking silhouette on the horizon. In the pass between the two is the Ridge Route from which secondary access roads move north, east, and west to connect the Jordan Valley, Jezreel Valley, and the coastal plain. And it is in this pass that the ancient city of Shechem was established.[5] This was a beautiful and relatively convenient place for Israel to travel to for worship, but there is more to the story of Mount Ebal than that.

For the people of God whose identity was built on the words and promises given to Abraham and Moses, this becomes the ideal spot to review the heritage that shaped their identity and their mission. Moses received the laws of God on Mount Sinai, 280 miles (451 km) to the south of Mount Ebal. Although a trip to Mount Sinai would have been meaningful for Joshua and the Israelites, it was not practical. Joshua, following Moses' directions, wrote the words given to Moses on the stones set up as a monument at Mount Ebal. He then read the words written by Moses to the people. Sacrifices were made on the altar that Moses had directed the Israelites to build on Mount Ebal. This unmistakable mountain in Samaria had become the place of worship for a new generation of Israelites, the spot in the Promised Land for them to renew their understanding of their identity

∨ *Mount Ebal as seen from the top of Mount Gerizim*

as God's people—set apart—and to acknowledge acceptance of their role.

At the base of Mount Ebal, in the vicinity of ancient Shechem, the Lord had appeared to Abraham and told him he had arrived in the Promised Land (Genesis 12:6–7). And Abraham too built a memorial altar at this location to commemorate this life-changing event. Shechem, at the base of Mount Ebal, is where it all began. In time there would be a Shiloh that hosted the tabernacle, or the portable tent that the Lord directed the Israelites to build and use as a sanctuary. And in time there would be Jerusalem with its temple. But before either of these two locations became the worship center for God's people, there was Mount Ebal.

△ *Ten Commandments in Hebrew inscribed in stone*

The Pact with Gibeon

If I had been among the leaders of the Israelites at the time of Joshua, I would not have been thrilled to have the pact with Gibeon mentioned, much less its story told in such great detail. But the story of how this nonaggression pact came to be is worth telling not because it serves to embarrass the leaders of Israel, but because it explains how an important geographic location was spared during the Israelite conquest and because it demonstrates that the leaders of God's people learned an important lesson.

Gibeon is an impressive place, on a modest hill that improves its defenses (see map 4.2). It is surrounded by acres of fertile agricultural land. But its greatest value is its relationship to travel within the Promised Land. The Benjamin plateau in the central mountains was not an effortless place to move through, but it was easier to travel there than the alternatives north or south of it. Gibeon sits in the middle of that plateau within sight of the crossroads where the Ridge Route intersects the Jericho-Gezer Road. Thus Gibeon offered oversight of the internal crossroads of the Promised Land. This is a city the Israelites would want to have as their own.

The people of Gibeon knew that. And they, along with other peoples of Canaan, could read the geographic intentions of the Israelites. The Israelites' projected line of march would bring them right through the plateau on which Gibeon sat, and Gibeon would be a key target, given its strategic location. This threat called for a response. Most of the city-states of Canaan that often squabbled with one another were planning a joint counterattack on the Israelites (Joshua 9:1–2). But the Hivites in Gibeon and its satellite villages of Kephirah, Beeroth, and Kiriath Jearim chose a different course of action.

The Gibeonite plan was pure theater, consisting of costumes, props, and well-rehearsed lines (Joshua 9:3–13). The Gibeonites sent men to meet with the Israelite leaders. The men were dressed in old clothing that showed signs of repeated repair. They carried provisions in sacks and wineskins that looked like they had endured weeks of travel. Even the bread they carried was dry and moldy. This pitiful-looking group of men approached Joshua and the Israelites, who were camped at Gilgal near Jericho, with a simple plea: "We have come from a distant country; make a treaty with us" (Joshua 9:6). When the Israelites hesitated, the Gibeonites gushed about the fame of the Israelites' God and their victories of the past, but were careful not to mention the victories over Bethel and Ai that had happened recently and nearby. Instead they spoke of Israel's escape from Egypt and victories won on the east side of the Jordan River.

The Israelite leaders were taken in by the careful manipulation of their history. They did not consult the Lord, maybe because there was a protocol for handling cities that were outside the bounds of the Promised Land. Those cities were to receive an offer of peace that included the stipulation that they would be subject to forced labor (Deuteronomy 20:10–11). A nonaggression pact was struck and ratified by oath that invoked the Lord's name.

All the backslapping and self-congratulations stopped just days later when the Israelites learned that Gibeon was not outside the Promised Land, but within it. These people were not part of the exemption of Deuteronomy 20:10–11. They were Hivites, specifically mentioned by name in Exodus 34:11–12 and Deuteronomy 7:1–2 as among those who were to be removed from the Promised Land. It soon became clear to Joshua and the other Israelites that Gibeon was located at the critical internal crossroads of the Promised Land. What could they do? They had agreed to a treaty of peace. They had sworn an oath in the name of the Lord.

There was more than one solution to the problem. Some wanted to cancel the pact and destroy the Gibeonites. But this is where the true spiritual development of Israel's leaders is becoming clear. Despite the embarrassment they must have felt and the press of those who wanted to attack Gibeon, the leaders knew they had invoked the Lord's name in taking an oath, and they would not go back on their word. Their solution was a creative one. The Gibeonites would be spared and could remain in their city. But because they had asked to be treated as a city outside the Promised Land, that is how they would be treated (Deuteronomy 20:10–11). Their citizens would, for the rest of their lives, be in service as "woodcutters and water carriers" (Joshua 9:23). This embarrassing story explains why Gibeon was spared and how this event shaped the future decisions of Israel's leaders (Joshua 11:19).

Map 4.2—Southern Campaign

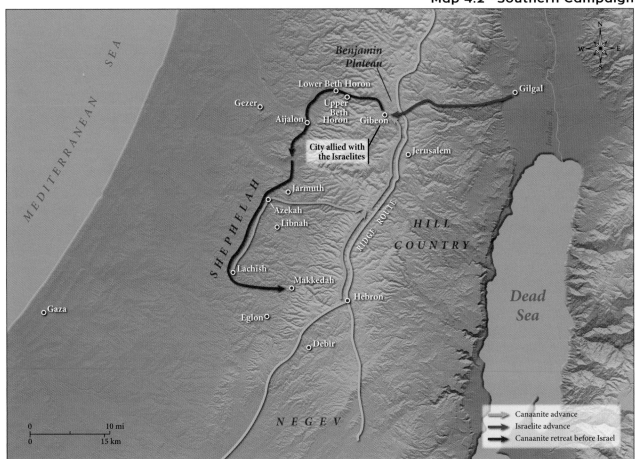

∧ *Gibeon sits on the rounded hill*

The Geographic Story Told in Israel's Conquest of Canaan

Joshua presents the bulk of Israel's conquest of Canaan in two chapters that are followed by a list of conquered kings. Each of these chapters presents a regional campaign provoked by a coalition of city-states, one in the south (Joshua 10) and one in the north (Joshua 11). A closer look at the geography of these campaigns shows that they call attention to both the faithfulness of the Lord and the wisdom of his battle plan.

Alarm bells began to sound in the palace of Adoni-Zedek, king of Jerusalem, when news of the defeat of Jericho and Ai was joined to the defection of Gibeon and its pact with the Israelites. These losses limited Jerusalem's access to the sea, the International Highway to the west, and the King's Highway to the east. The king of Jerusalem appealed to the rulers in the city-states south of Jerusalem for assistance in punishing Gibeon and driving out the Israelites.

These included Hebron in the southern hill country and Jarmuth, Lachish, and Eglon associated with the Shephelah (see map 4.2). At Gibeon, the Lord used Israelite swords below and hailstones from above to win the victory.[6] The geographic summary of the southern campaign (Joshua 10:40–43) indicates that Israel now had control of the mountains, their foothills, and the Negev, stretching south of a line drawn from the Aijalon Valley east to Gibeon and Jericho, and as far south as Kadesh Barnea. The exception to their holdings is the coastal plain.

The northern campaign was provoked by formation of another coalition. When word of the defeat of the southern city-states reached the palace of Jabin, the king of Hazor, he followed the lead of Jerusalem's king. He called for a coalition of regional powers, which included Madon, Shimron, Akshaph, and

Map 4.3—Northern Campaign

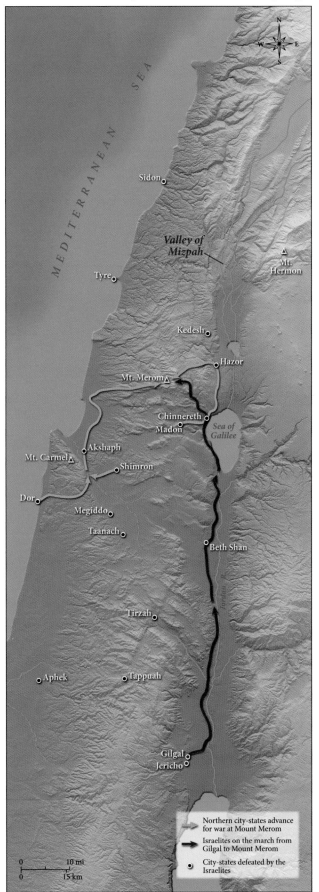

Northern city-states advance for war at Mount Merom

Israelites on the march from Gilgal to Mount Merom

City-states defeated by the Israelites

unnamed others. They assembled for battle against Joshua at the Waters of Merom, which we place in the vicinity of Mount Merom (see map 4.3). Their sheer numbers together with the added advantage of battle chariots (Joshua 11:4) put the Israelites in grave danger. But once again the Lord gave his chosen people success. They now controlled the Jordan River valley and the mountains and foothills north of Gibeon, stretching to the valley systems just west of Mount Hermon (Joshua 11:16–23).

As we read Joshua 10 and 11, it becomes clear that through a variety of battles fought in different regions by opponents with varied technology, the Lord was faithful. He promised victory, and in one instance after another, he provided victory (Joshua 10:42; 11:8, 20). The Israelites' string of victories in the Promised Land is broken only in two instances, Ai and Gibeon. But these two, where an expected victory was not enjoyed by Israel, amplify the point that it was not the Lord who was unfaithful, but Israel. The overall summary makes it clear that God was delivering on his promise to give this land to his people.

The wisdom of the Lord's strategy is clear. He could have directed the Israelites to enter the Promised Land through a number of natural gateways. But by choosing Jericho, the key strategy of "divide and conquer" was put to work. The slashing penetration of Israel through the heart of Canaan meant that subsequent battles involved only a portion of the possible opposition.

We are not able to locate with confidence all the defeated cities mentioned in these two chapters of Joshua. But of those cities we can map, we find that many are located at key points along the international and local transportation systems. Cities like Gezer, Hazor, and Megiddo were along the International Highway. Jericho, Hebron, Lachish, Gibeon, and Bethel controlled access to key local roads. With the defeat of these cities, the Israelites gained control of the communication and movement throughout this region.

The city-states listed in these two chapters appear to have been the strongest military entities

∧ *The northern coalition opposing Joshua included those who lived northwest of the Sea of Galilee*

in the Promised Land. Hazor was called "the head of all these kingdoms" (Joshua 11:10), and its physical footprint supports this title. While many cities of this region occupy only a few acres, the ancient city of Hazor exceeds 170 acres (69 hectares) and at its peak had a population of 40,000.[7] It was the city-states such as this that posed the most serious threat to Israel's capture of the Promised Land. Joshua's defeat of these major centers should have inspired confidence in the tribes who still had to secure their own territories.

Distribution of Conquered Land

Even the most dedicated Bible readers will find themselves challenged by the avalanche of geographic detail in Joshua 13–19, where distribution of the Promised Land among the Israelite tribes is described. Joshua kept the record of each transaction.[8]

After the major power centers of Canaan were defeated, the land was divided into twelve parcels (see map 4.4). Because the Israelites thought of themselves not only as descendants of Abraham but also as members of the twelve tribes who were descendants of Abraham's grandson Jacob, that number makes sense. But this gets a bit more complicated when we learn that the tribe of Levi, which provided the Israelites with their clergy, would not receive a block of land but would be scattered throughout the land. The number twelve is preserved when the tribe of Joseph received not one parcel, but two, for the descendants of Joseph's sons, Manasseh and Ephraim.

Land parcels were formally distributed at three different times. The first was when Moses assigned land to two tribes, the Reubenites and Gadites, who requested that their inheritance be east of the Jordan River. He also gave land to the descendants of Manasseh, who conquered cities in the northern part of Gilead (Numbers 32:33–42). The second land assignments were made at Gilgal when Joshua informed Judah, Manasseh (the portion of the tribe that did not receive their inheritance on the east side of the Jordan River), and Ephraim about the specifics of their inheritance (Joshua 14:6; 15:1–17:11). In the third, Joshua distributed land to the remaining seven tribes at Shiloh (Joshua 18:1–19:48).

Map 4.4—Tribal Land Allotments

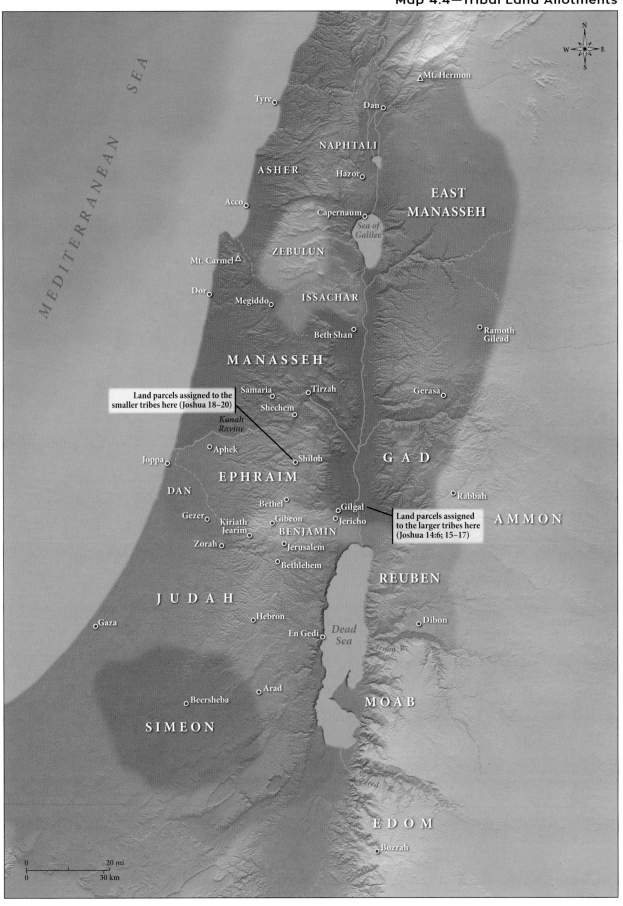

MEDITERRANEAN SEA

Mt. Hermon

Tyre

Dan

NAPHTALI

ASHER

Hazor

EAST MANASSEH

Acco

Capernaum

Sea of Galilee

ZEBULUN

Mt. Carmel

Dor

ISSACHAR

Megiddo

Beth Shan

Ramoth Gilead

MANASSEH

Samaria

Tirzah

Gerasa

Land parcels assigned to the smaller tribes here (Joshua 18–20)

Shechem

Kanah Ravine

Aphek

Shiloh

GAD

Joppa

EPHRAIM

DAN

Bethel

Rabbah

Gezer

Gibeon

Gilgal

Jericho

Land parcels assigned to the larger tribes here (Joshua 14:6; 15–17)

AMMON

Kiriath Jearim

BENJAMIN

Zorah

Jerusalem

Bethlehem

REUBEN

JUDAH

Hebron

Dead Sea

Dibon

Gaza

En Gedi

Arnon R.

Beersheba

Arad

MOAB

SIMEON

Zered R.

E D O M

Bozrah

0   20 mi
0   30 km

The method for determining which tribe would receive which parcel of land was set by the Lord from the time of Moses, when the Lord said the land was to be assigned by the casting of lots (Numbers 26:52–56; 33:54). A slight change in procedure is noted in connection with the distribution at Shiloh, perhaps motivated by the complaint of the tribes of Manasseh and Ephraim about the size of their land grant made at Gilgal (Joshua 17:14).

The last seven tribes received their assignment of land after a survey team had gone into the remaining land to map it, divide it into seven parts, and provide a written description of each parcel (Joshua 18:3–10). We get a sense of what those reports may have looked like in the description of the land in Joshua, where the parcels are described in two ways: The first draws boundary lines demarcated by cities and natural features. The second lists the cities and towns in each land parcel.[9]

A careful record of the specific land allotments is preserved in the pages of Joshua. The extraordinary amount of detail in those descriptions has both practical and theological value. On the practical side, land meant life. The land provided its owner with a place to build shelter, secure water, graze the family's animals, and grow food. For those living in Bible times, being without land was perilous. The formal division of the land and its record brought assurance to families that their practical need for land had been met and guaranteed by divine grant. This formal record of tribal lands would have been relied on to settle any arguments over land rights and defuse any threat of intertribal warfare over land.

At times information about the division of the land is necessary for interpreting later portions of Scripture. For example, the details the author of Joshua provided on the individual tribal land parcels tie in with Isaiah's prophecy on the coming of the Messiah to Galilee. Isaiah promised "a great light" would be seen in the lands of both Zebulun and Naphtali (Isaiah 9:1–2), which were west and north of the Sea of Galilee and included most of the region later known as Galilee. In the New Testament, Matthew says Jesus' move from Nazareth to Capernaum fulfilled Isaiah's prophecy (Matthew 4:12–16). The details we have of the tribal land division allow us to better map the fulfillment of the divine promises from the Old Testament to the New Testament.

For the families who received land, who lived on

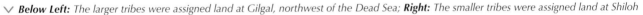

⌄ *Below Left: The larger tribes were assigned land at Gilgal, northwest of the Dead Sea;* **Right:** *The smaller tribes were assigned land at Shiloh*

that land and farmed it and grazed their animals on it, there was a powerful and comforting message in the soil and rock of their inheritance. Ultimately each of these landowners had a need greater than the one for fresh water and food—the need to know that their pangs of guilt for their sins would not lead to the pain of eternal separation from the Almighty. The promise of the Lord to provide forgiveness of sins is found throughout the Old Testament, but is stated differently than in the New Testament. Christians today are prone to visualize the hope they have for eternal life in the symbol of

∧ *Boundary stones mark the border between agricultural fields*

the empty cross and tomb, while believers in the Old Testament saw their hope in the land they lived on. This is one part of the triangle of promises made to Abraham that tied the hope of forgiveness to a descendant of Abraham who would live and die on this land. When people of the Old Testament yearned for a symbol of their forgiveness, they needed to look no farther than the land they walked, the parcel of land deeded to them. The inheritance they received at the time of Joshua was meant not only for the cultivation of field crops and fruit trees but also for the cultivation of spiritual peace.

Levitical Cities and Cities of Refuge

When the last of the land parcels had been distributed among the tribes of Israel, there was one group, the descendants of Levi, with no assigned place to live in the Promised Land. But the descendants of Levi were not left out. They had been given the special privilege of serving as the priests and religious support staff for the people of God. For that reason, they would not be living as a tribe on one parcel of land, but would live in towns scattered throughout the parcels of land received by the other tribes.[10]

Joshua 21 presents the outcome of this special distribution, and once again the amount of geographic detail is almost overwhelming. Forty-eight towns were assigned by lot to the three clans that made up the tribe of Levi. The first clan, consisting of the Kohathites, is split between those who are descendants of Aaron and those who are not. Those who descended from Aaron received thirteen towns in the lands of Judah, Simeon, and Benjamin (Joshua 21:4, 9–19). The other Kohathites received ten towns in the lands of Ephraim, Dan, and the portion of Manasseh on the west side of the Jordan River (Joshua 21:5, 20–26). The

Gershonite clan received thirteen towns in the lands given to Issachar, Asher, Naphtali, and the half-tribe of Manasseh on the east side of the Jordan River (Joshua 21:6, 27–33). And finally the Merarite clan of the Levites received twelve towns in the regions given to Reuben, Gad, and Zebulun (Joshua 21:7, 34–40).

Stepping back from the details to look at the larger geographic picture, three insights emerge. The first is that the towns given to the Levites are not bunched up in one location, but are spread throughout each of the Israelite land parcels. This means every Israelite had access to these towns, a fact made even clearer when we observe that most of the Levitical cities were located on or near the road systems. Second, we note that the Levites who would provide the priests who led worship at the sanctuary—the Kohathites descended from Aaron—were given towns in close proximity to Jerusalem, in the tribal territories of Judah, Simeon, and Benjamin, even though the central sanctuary at this time was in Shiloh rather than in Jerusalem as it would be later in Israel's history. The list also appears to envision an ideal that had not yet been realized. A number of the towns identified in the list, like Gezer and Taanach, were not yet controlled by the Israelites.

The Levitical cities, including the six that doubled as cities of refuge, had specific roles to play in Israel's culture. The Levites were the worship leaders and religious educators among God's people. As each tribe went off to secure their land parcel, they would be met by repeated invitations to take part in pagan ideology and worship. Many would live more than a day's travel from the central sanctuary and would travel to the central sanctuary only three times a year (Exodus 23:14–17). These special towns with Levites were meant to be education centers that imparted a healthy knowledge of and appreciation for the Lord.

The six cities of refuge, placed strategically throughout the land, had a distinct role to offer protection (Joshua 20) (see map 4.5). The life the Lord had given to every person was carefully protected in the laws the Lord gave to the Israelites. Punishment matched the crime: "Take life for life, eye for eye" (Exodus 21:23–24). So anyone who killed another person could be killed by that person's next of kin, called the avenger of blood. But that didn't apply to a death caused accidentally and without clear intention. A system was put in place to prevent the avenger of blood from killing a person who was responsible for an accidental death. That person could flee to one of these cities of refuge and obtain protection there from the avenger of blood. The elders of the city would hear the details of the

The idolatry of Israel's pagan neighbors was a constant threat

Map 4.5—Levitical Cities and Cities of Refuge

∧ Beth Shemesh, one of the Levitical cities

death and rule on whether the death was accidental. To be safe, the person responsible for the accidental death had to remain in the city of refuge until the death of the currently serving high priest. But if the person left the city of refuge before the death of the high priest, then the avenger of blood was free to kill that person (Numbers 35:6–34; Joshua 20:4–6).

These towns for the Levites listed in Joshua 20–21, including the cities of refuge, played an important role in the culture of Israel. The different tribes had to surrender what was otherwise part of their territory for the special use by the Levites and for cities of refuge. And all Israelites who needed the services provided in these towns needed to know the names of the towns and their locations.

But the list of Levitical cities positioned as it is in the book of Joshua has something more to say. As the tribes headed off to their own land parcels, they were in many respects stepping away from one another. There no longer was a unifying figure like Moses or Joshua as their leader. The unifying mission of the conquest was behind them. "All [of] the LORD's good promises to Israel . . . [had been] fulfilled" (Joshua 21:45). Local concerns would soon seize their attention. Conflict among the tribes could erode the national cohesion. But the towns given to the Levites, the worship leaders, served as a reminder that although the tribes split up, they were to remain united as the people of God—not only one nation, but one nation under God.

Promised Land Unclaimed

The "mission accomplished" communicated in Joshua 21:43–45 leaves the reader feeling good about God's people who have rededicated themselves to the covenant and are enjoying the blessings that followed. This quickly gives way to the grim reality check of Judges 1. While the tribes of Israel had been jointly successful in defeating the major power centers within the

Promised Land when they obeyed God, the Lord left more modest opponents in the path of the individual tribes so that the younger generations without any war experience might demonstrate their faith in taking real estate the Lord had promised (Judges 3:1–2). But as the individual tribes try to secure their parcels of land, the stories of success fade. In the first chapter of Judges we find a geographic summary of these failures that doubles as a sad preview of the chapters that follow.

Judges 1 catalogs the successes and failures of each of the Israelite tribes west of the Jordan River in their bid to secure the land parcels assigned to them by Joshua. When we look carefully at the places that were unclaimed by the tribes, we come to these sobering conclusions: The lowlands, in particular the coastal plain and Jezreel Valley, were attacked but not held by God's people (Judges 1:19, 27, 34).[11] Key cities along international routes that linked the Promised Land to the markets of the world were not taken, cities like Beth Shan, Taanach, Dor, Ibleam, and Megiddo (Judges 1:27) (see map 4.6). Cities that guarded east-west access routes to the interior of the hill country where the Israelite tribes settled remained in the capable hands of others, cities like Gezer and Aijalon (Judges 1:29, 35). And for Old Testament readers who know the future importance of Jerusalem to the plan of salvation, it is most disconcerting to hear that Benjamin left this important city in the hands of the Jebusites (Judges 1:21).

In part, the author of Judges lists these geographic failures because of the implications that follow. The subsequent loss of these lowlands meant that the best agricultural land in the Promised Land was unavailable to the plows of the Israelites, requiring them to grow their food in more work-intensive settings. The loss of the lowlands also meant that the potential revenue a tribe could have acquired from taxing trade goods moving through the valleys and plains on the international routes went unclaimed by them. The geography of Judges 1 also tells a story of diminished personal security as key routes to the interior, guarded by places like Gezer, were left outside of Israelite control. But all of that pales when compared with the unsettling news that large Canaanite enclaves remained among the settlements of the Israelite tribes. These Canaanites could and would draw the Israelites away from the Lord, enticing them with the empty but scintillating worship of pagan gods.

˅ *Key cities in the Jezreel Valley—though assigned to Israelite tribes—remained unconquered*

Map 4.6—Unsecured Land in the Promised Land

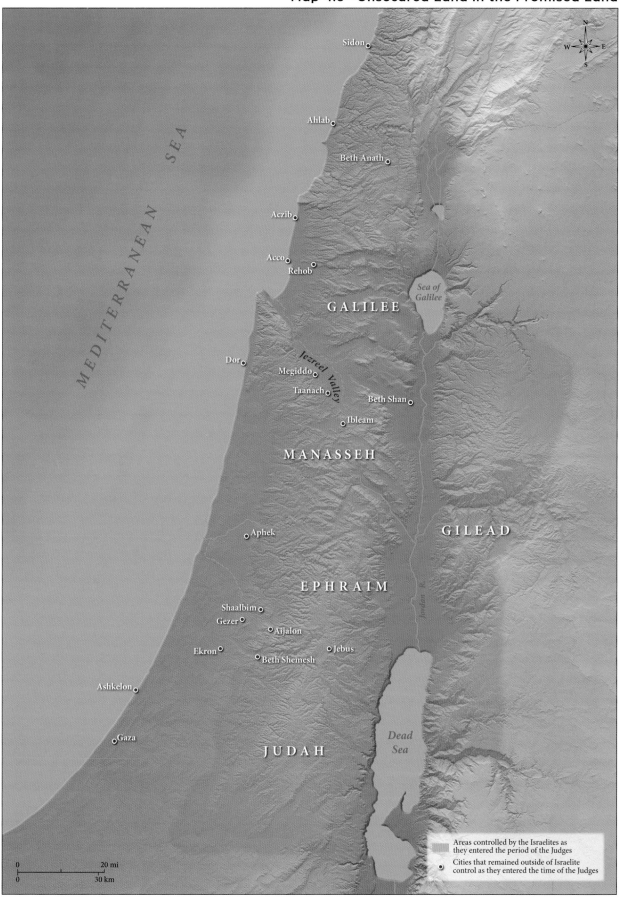

MEDITERRANEAN SEA

Sidon

Ahlab

Beth Anath

Aczib

Acco
Rehob

GALILEE

*Sea of
Galilee*

Dor
Jezreel Valley
Megiddo
Taanach
Beth Shan
Ibleam

MANASSEH

GILEAD

Aphek

EPHRAIM

Jordan R.

Shaalbim
Gezer
Aijalon
Ekron
Jebus
Beth Shemesh

Ashkelon

Gaza

JUDAH

*Dead
Sea*

Areas controlled by the Israelites as
they entered the period of the Judges

Cities that remained outside of Israelite
control as they entered the time of the Judges

0   20 mi
0   30 km

The geographic picture painted in the first two chapters of Judges is a portrait of disappointment. As readers, we may hope that things will improve. But instead we find the realities of Judges 1–2 merely introduced the disappointment that grows worse as we read on.

It is best to start the literary analysis of Judges 1 with a return to Joshua 13. The first verses of this chapter in Joshua become the baseline for reading the geography of Judges 1. After a chest-thumping list of conquered kings is presented in Joshua 12, the author lists the land still to be taken in Joshua 13:2–5 (see map 4.6). What remains untaken is primarily land along the Mediterranean seashore, the coastal plain. We expect that situation to improve as the individual

∧ *The Israelites failed to claim Gezer during the time of the judges*

tribes begin to secure their land parcels. But what we read in Judges 1 states that things do not move forward but backward. There is no progress in securing the coastal plain, and the interior is being compromised as well.

This trajectory from success to failure becomes the profile for the rest of the book. Judah is successful in establishing its hold on its assigned territory (Judges 1:1–20). But the good news of these verses quickly gives way to a catalog of failures. Benjamin tried but failed to hold Jerusalem. Manasseh was not successful in

securing key cities in the Jezreel Valley. Ephraim could not take Gezer. Then two tribes, Asher and Naphtali, not only fail to control key locations in their territories, they are also said to be living in symbiotic relationship with the non-Israelite peoples around them (Judges 1:31–33).[12] Note that this path of success, to difficulty, to failure aptly captures the trend of the narratives in Judges. The book begins with divinely sponsored success, circles back again and again to failure, and then offers witness to the collapse of redeeming spirituality and civility in the closing chapters of the book.

Chariots, Water, and Faith

Difficult times provide the fertile soil in which faith can grow. These were the circumstances faced by the Israelites when they cried out to the Lord for help to free them from the oppression of the Canaanite king in Hazor.[13] Both the narrative and poetic versions of this event (Judges 4–5) employ geography to describe the challenge the Israelites faced and the solution the Lord provided through Deborah and Barak. It is also clear that this event is carefully preserved in a form

that echoes the circumstances faced by the Israelites exiting Egypt as they came upon the Red [Reed] Sea (Exodus 14–15). Both events involve chariots, water, and a call to faith in the Lord.

When the Israelites took on the pagan practices of their neighbors, the Lord used their pagan neighbors to oppress them. At the time of Deborah and Barak, it was Jabin, the Canaanite king who ruled in Hazor, who cruelly oppressed the Israelites for 20 years (Judges

4:1–3). The story of Hazor's rise to power is linked to its geography. Hazor occupied a position along the International Highway where mountains to the west and a forbidding swamp to the east narrowed the corridor for international travel. This allowed Hazor to grow large and wealthy from the trade revenue collected. This revenue subsequently allowed Hazor to purchase and maintain a fleet of 900 iron-enhanced chariots that solidified its dominance in the region.

When the Lord used the capable Hazor to oppress the Israelites, the people repented. It was then that the prophetess Deborah sent for Barak to announce that the Lord recognized the heartfelt repentance of the oppressed Israelites and was poised to deliver them from the hardships imposed by Hazor. For Barak and the Israelites who relied on infantry, the ideal place for battle would be in the mountains. So we find Barak mustering his soldiers on Mount Tabor,[14] near enough to the Jezreel Valley to lure the Canaanite fighters to them but secure from the chariots on steep, wooded slopes that favored hand-to-hand combat (see map 4.7). By contrast, Jabin's general in the field, Sisera, moves his chariots into position on the expansive Jezreel Valley where the level terrain would give his fighters the advantage (Judges 4:13; 5:19). This standoff was resolved when the Lord used Deborah to issue a faith-challenging command (Judges 4:14). In any other circumstance, it was unthinkable for infantry to abandon their advantage on the high ground to charge onto the plain where the Canaanite chariots could do their worst. But that is what the Lord told them to do so that he could turn certain defeat into victory.

Rainfall is not expected in the Promised Land during the summer, the season when kings go to war. But a divinely sponsored storm would become the undoing of the chariot advantage in the plain (Judges 5:4, 21). The Jezreel Valley drains to the west through a small brook called the Kishon. This watercourse is unimpressive during most of the year, a nuisance to the traveler who could cross it in most places with one big step. But when a significant amount of rain enters the Jezreel Valley in a short amount of time, flooding can occur as the valley struggles to drain itself through the confined western portal that empties into the Mediterranean Sea. As the rising terrain pinches shut, the water in the valley starts to back up and the slumbering Kishon becomes a broad, muddy river that floods the valley floor and turns it into a quagmire. This completely changes the battle between the Israelites and the Canaanites. For while chariots have a dramatic advantage over infantry on level terrain, they become a cumbersome hindrance when their wheels get bogged down in gooey mud. Thus the Lord used geography to create a dramatic challenge that summoned the Israelites to trust him. When they do, the Lord provides a water-sponsored victory over the chariots of the Canaanites.

Map 4.7—Deborah and Barak

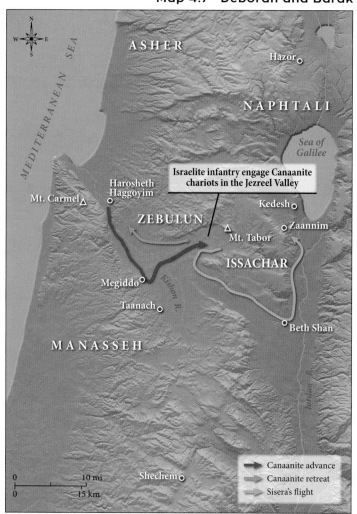

The way the author of Judges communicates this event recalls an earlier challenge that involved geography, chariots, and a water-sponsored victory (Exodus 14:16–28; 15:1–5). When Moses led the Israelites out of Egypt, it was not long before the pharaoh dispatched 600 chariots in pursuit (Exodus 14:7). The chariots, with their speed and maneuverability on the level terrain of the Nile Delta, quickly intercepted

∧ Artifacts from Hazor, the city-state that oppressed Israel during the time of Deborah

God's chosen people and trapped them against the waters of the Red (Reed) Sea (Exodus 14:9). And just when it appeared that things could not get any worse for the Israelites, the Lord told Moses to give the command to advance (Exodus 14:15) and the Lord opened the waters so that they could pass through the sea on dry ground. The emboldened Egyptian charioteers followed, but they had a very different experience. As the Lord had opened the water for the Israelites, so he closed it over the chariots. The author of Exodus and the author of Judges use the same Hebrew word

(*hmm*, המם) to describe the Lord's actions that secured the victories (Exodus 14:24; Judges 4:15).[15]

The parallels in the telling of these two events help the reader of the Old Testament to join the earlier crossing of the sea and the defeat of the Egyptians with the defeat of the Canaanites in the Jezreel Valley. Both individually and jointly, these victories offer examples of how the Lord, who disabled the chariots with miraculous movement of water, gave the Israelites proof of the benefits of having a strong faith in the Lord.

∨ Mount Tabor, the rallying point for Israel in their battle against Hazor

Insights from Ophrah

Unfortunately the powerful lessons taught in the days of Deborah and Barak were all too quickly forgotten. Once again "the Israelites did evil in the eyes of the Lord, and for seven years he gave them into the hands of the Midianites" (Judges 6:1). The Midianites, together with other eastern peoples like the Amalekites, regularly invaded the Promised Land, seizing field crops and animals. The situation was so bad that Israelites abandoned their homes to live in remote locations. After seven years of this, the Israelites were exhausted and impoverished (Judges 6:2–6). The author of Judges moves from this general picture to a close-up look at a small Israelite village, Ophrah. Here the author highlights two perspectives on the invasion, both of which needed to be changed.

In Ophrah, we meet Israelites convinced that pagan deities were worthy of worship and defense. The people of Ophrah had set up an altar for the worship of Baal, the god of rain and dewfall. They kept a sacred bull, the symbol of Baal's fertility and strength. And they had set up a pole associated with the worship of the goddess Asherah. These kinds of pagan shrines had existed in the Promised Land prior to the Israelites' arrival, and the Lord had directed the Israelites to destroy them (Deuteronomy 12:29–13:18). But when we visit the village of Ophrah, we find people emboldened in their pagan worship. When someone dared destroy the altar of Baal, kill the sacred bull, and cut down the Asherah pole, the people demanded the execution of the one responsible (Judges 6:30). This is one perspective that needed changing.

The other is expressed by Gideon, who was from the village of Ophrah. His family had set up the shrine. Gideon loved the Lord but was disillusioned by the Midianite invasion. When the angel of the Lord came to Gideon, he was processing wheat in a winepress. This task was usually done on a large, open threshing floor. It was unthinkable to thresh wheat within the small confines of a winepress, but it was the only way for Gideon to keep his food from the Midianites. The angel of the Lord met Gideon at the winepress and called him a mighty warrior. This was too much for Gideon, and his frustration spilled out: "Pardon me, my lord, . . . but if the Lord is with us, why has all this happened to us? Where are all his wonders that our ancestors told us about when they said, 'Did not the Lord bring us up out of Egypt?' But now the Lord has abandoned us and given us into the hand of Midian" (Judges 6:13). This is not a man who had lost his faith but a man who felt let down by the Lord.

So in Ophrah we find two perspectives: those convinced that Baal was the deity mostly likely to help them and those who believed the Lord was God but were disillusioned by his failure to help them. The story of Gideon addresses both groups. When Gideon is convinced of the Lord's presence and willingness to help, he takes action. Despite the risk to his own life, he destroys the altar of Baal, kills the sacred bull, and cuts down the Asherah pole. This bold action demonstrates the weakness of Baal to Gideon's own extended family. Eventu-

Map 4.8—Gideon

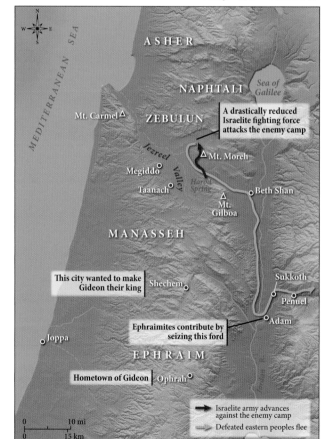

ally they abandon their defense of Baal and become the first to rally to Gideon as he gathers a fighting force to push out the eastern invaders (Judges 6:34).

When not just his clan but fighters from his tribe of Manasseh as well as Asher, Zebulun, and Naptali show up for the fight, the Lord uses the miraculous manipulation of dew to demonstrate that he, rather than Baal, controls the dewfall (Judges 6:36–40). Once again the number of those reclaimed for the Lord increases. Since an Israelite victory involving thousands of soldiers could give rise to the pride of self-accomplishment and deny God's involvement,

the Lord reduced the number of soldiers to a mere 300 fighters. The Lord used this small group to further demonstrate that he alone was worthy of praise as he delivered Israel from its oppressors (Judges 7).

The powerful lessons from the experiences of Deborah and Barak were learned again as the Lord worked though Gideon. In the village of Ophrah, we see the change. People who had been fully convinced of Baal's authenticity were led to see him as a fraud. And those faithful to the Lord, like the previously disillusioned Gideon, were inspired to great acts of faith.

Samson and Fading Hope

The book of Judges can be frustrating to read. By the time readers arrive at the story of Samson (Judges 13–16), they are ready to hear of an enduring remedy to the cycles of rebellion and oppression that characterize the narrative. But no remedy is to be found in the story of Samson; in fact, the Israelites' story grows more troubling. Samson seeks affection and love with three different Philistine women in three different places. These relationships provoke conflict with the Philistines in five places. But for all of our work to trace the movements of Samson across the landscape, we are rewarded with nothing but a fading hope.

When the Israelites did evil in the eyes of the Lord, he gave them into the hands of the Philistines (Judges 13:1). These coastal residents, with roots in the Aegean world, were now settling in along the Mediterranean coastline at about the same time the Israelites were settling into the mountain interior of Canaan.[16] The Philistines exercised control of the coastal plain and foothills in connection with five cities that rose from the rubble of the Canaanite cities they displaced. The cities are Gaza, Ashkelon, Ashdod, Ekron, and Gath.

We are led to believe Samson will be the answer to the Philistine problem (Judges 13:5; 14:4), so we follow his movements about the country with great anticipation (see map 4.9). Samson's story begins in the Israelite village of Zorah, where he is born into a family from the tribe of Dan (Judges 13:2). We read that Samson tears up the usual social contract that would have him marry a member of his own clan, or tribe,

or at least an Israelite. Instead Samson travels west in the Sorek Valley to Timnah, where a young Philistine woman catches his eye. The marriage week did not go well and left Samson owing 30 linen garments to members of the wedding party who had figured out his riddle. Samson acquires those garments in a way

Map 4.9—Samson

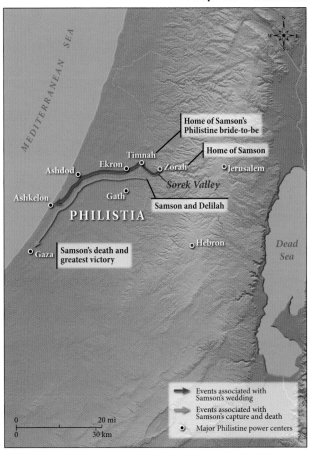

that seems sure to provoke conflict with the Philistines. He travels to the Philistine city of Ashkelon, kills 30 men, and takes their garments to pay the debt (Judges 14:12–20). There is no response from the Philistines.

Samson returns to Timnah, planning to spend time with his wife, only to find that she has been given to another member of the wedding party. With all the malice he could muster, Samson responded by destroying agricultural fields in the Sorek Valley between Timnah and Zorah (Judges 15:1–5). This does produce a response. Angry Philistines pursue Samson to the mountain interior of Judah. Surrounded by his countrymen, Samson certainly could have expected assistance. But instead we learn that his fellow Israelites have come to bind Samson and hand him over to the Philistines. When they deliver him to the Philistines, Samson breaks the bonds and kills hundreds of Philistines using the jawbone of a donkey (Judges 15:9–17).

From Judah, it is off to the Philistine city of Gaza, where Samson spends the night with a prostitute. When the locals learn of his presence, they plan to ambush him before he gets up the next morning. But Samson got up early, dismantled the city's main security system, the city gate, and carried it off in the direction of Hebron (Judges 16:1–3). This again does not produce a Philistine response.

The conclusion of this narrative sweeps us back to the Sorek Valley where Samson has fallen in love with Delilah, a third Philistine woman. Thinking he is only engaged in loving banter with his new significant other, Samson teasingly speaks of the way in which his special strength would be compromised. And then he reveals to her the connection between his unshorn hair and his strength. Moments later, the man no one was able to defeat has his eyes put out and is led to Gaza as a prisoner.

In time, the Philistines of Gaza thought a victory party was in order. They brought their prize prisoner to the temple of Dagon and used the disability they had imposed on him to make fun of him. The story closes as Samson, whose hair had grown, is filled one last time with the power of God. He presses against the pillars of the pagan temple, collapsing it on himself, taking not only his life but the lives of thousands of Philistines with him (Judges 16:4–30).

If the complexity of the geography has left you a bit confused and in need of a map to trace the movements of Samson, that is part of the role of the geography in this story. While many of the other narratives in Judges take us to one location for one decisive battle, the story of Samson whisks us along on seven different trips. And although we seem to be constantly on the move, we never get anywhere. We move from place to place, from woman to woman, from one conflict to the next, but never read about that ultimate victory that frees the Israelites from the oppression of the Philistines. We never see other Israelites rallying to his side when Samson does achieve a victory. We are not told that the land enjoys a time of rest even after the

∨ *Bichrome pottery of the Philistines who oppressed Israel during the time of Gideon*

∧ *The Sorek Valley between Zorah and Timnah hosted many events in Samson's story*

death of so many Philistines in Gaza. And in Judges 18, we read that things got so bad, most of the tribe of Dan picked up their goods and moved away from the land given to them by divine inheritance to settle instead in Laish, north of the Sea of Galilee. There's lots of geography, but so little satisfaction in the life of Samson. As we travel with him, back and forth through the land, through his relationships and conflicts, our pursuit of resolution is never rewarded. It is a story that makes us work hard without receiving any sort of good news at the end. And that is the point. No matter where we travel with Samson, his story is that of the Israelites of that day—a story of fading hope.

Israel Had No King; Everyone Did as They Saw Fit

As we close out the book of Joshua, everything appears to be headed in the right direction. The conquest of the Promised Land was successful, the tribes of Israel each received their land parcel, and the system of Levitical cities scattered throughout the tribes laid the foundation for national unity based on loyalty to the Lord's covenant relationship with the Israelites. But at the end of the book of Judges, nothing seems to be headed in the right direction. The stories in the final chapters of Judges are so shocking and scandalous that we might be tempted to check the book binding to be sure we are still reading the Bible. Judges ends with this sober assessment: "In those days Israel had no king; everyone did as they saw fit" (Judges 21:25).

There are three instances in Judges 18–21 where we see tribes of Israel operating with an extremely partisan perspective, doing as they saw fit. The first has to do with the tribe of Dan that had been unable to establish itself on the land it had been given at the time of Joshua (Joshua 19:40–48). Instead of redoubling their efforts against the opposition, a portion of the tribe moved north and seized land around Laish (Judges 18) (see map 4.10), land that had been assigned to the tribe of Naphtali (Joshua 19:32–39). Rather than seeing themselves as a part of the larger Israel, they showed a lack of respect for the land rights of other Israelites.

The second example of partisan thinking involved a violation of hospitality (Judges 19). A Levite from Ephraim married a woman from Bethlehem in Judah. She was his concubine. She was unfaithful and returned home to her parents. Four months later, the man went to get her. The two left Bethlehem, traveling north toward Ephraim. As daylight faded, they looked for an overnight stop, but avoided the city of Jebus (Jerusalem) because Jebusites were not of Israelite

Map 4.10—Judges

Sidon

Mt. Hermon

Dan (Laish)

MEDITERRANEAN SEA

ASHER

Hazor
NAPHTALI
Shamgar

EAST MANASSEH

Sea of Galilee

Elon | ZEBULUN

Deborah and Barak | Mt. Tabor
ISSACHAR
Mt. Moreh
Gideon

Kamon | Jair

Jezreel Valley

Megiddo

Beth Shan

MANASSEH

Tola | Shamir

GILEAD | Jephthah

Shechem

Abdon | Pirathon

EPHRAIM

GAD

DAN

Ophrah | Gideon
Shaalbim | Bethel

Rabbah

AMMON

Jericho | Ehud

Heshbon

BENJAMIN

Zorah

REUBEN

Samson | Sorek Valley

Bethlehem
Ibzan

JUDAH

Hebron

Gaza
Othniel

Dead Sea

Arnon R.

Beersheba

MOAB

SIMEON

Zered R.

Bozrah

0   20 mi
0   30 km

→ Tribe of Dan migrated north to seize Laish

• Cities opposed to Israel during the time of the Judges

AMMON Regions opposed to Israel during the time of the Judges

stock. The man instead chose to stay in Gibeah, a town a few miles north (about 5 km) in the tribal territory of Benjamin, where he expected to be offered lodging by fellow Israelites. The code of hospitality in the ancient world gave him reason to believe that one of the local residents, when he saw them sitting in the town square, would invite them into his home for the night.[17] But no Benjamite extended an invitation. It was only when another Ephraimite who lived in Gibeah came by that shelter was provided for the two travelers (Judges 19:16–21). The biblical author is careful to state the tribal relationship of the individuals, which highlights the partisan attitude of the citizens of Gibeah.

The third example of partisanship grows from the events in Gibeah when the tribe of Benjamin becomes involved. A group of men from Gibeah made extreme sexual demands, putting themselves in the company of Sodom (compare Judges 19:22–26 with Genesis 19:4–5). Then they so badly violate the concubine of the Levite after he sends her out to them that by morning she is dead. The Levite returns home with her body, then sends a piece of the concubine's body to each of the twelve tribes of Israel. That sparks a national gathering the likes of which we do not see

∧ *Israel had no royal crown or king during the time of the judges*

elsewhere in Judges. All Israel, from Dan to Beersheba and from Gilead (except those from Benjamin), gathered at Mizpah, about 7 miles (11 km) north of Gibeah (Judges 20:1–3). Word was sent to the tribe of Benjamin demanding that those from their tribe who

∨ *Territory of Benjamin*

were responsible for the death be handed over for punishment. We expect the tribe to punish the sinful behavior of the men at Gibeah. But the Benjamites rallied to the defense of Gibeah, ready to fight against the coalition of the other tribes seeking retribution for the crime (Judges 20:12–13).

In all three cases of partisanship, we see a world very different from the one envisioned by Joshua. Rather than twelve tribes who respect one another and cooperate to accomplish their national mission, we see isolation and a lack of cooperation. We see an Israel where everyone does as they see fit.

The author of Judges links the breakdown in national unity to inadequate national leadership. There was no king in Israel (Judges 17:6; 18:1; 19:1; 21:25). There had been leaders like Deborah, Gideon, and Samson, but there had not been the equivalent of a Joshua or Moses. Even when the author of Judges describes the operation undertaken by the tribes against Gibeah, we find no mention of a single national leader whose voice directs the joint activity of the tribes. We read only about a collection of nameless leaders who appear to be functioning as a committee (Judges 20:2).

Two striking errors that highlight the lack of leadership get our attention as the operation gets under way. First, despite a nearly fifteen-to-one advantage in the number of soldiers available for battle (Judges 20:15–17), the eleven tribes were defeated in two successive engagements with the soldiers of Benjamin (Judges 20:19–25). And second, when the eleven tribes were successful in the third battle, they acted in such unrestrained fashion that they nearly wiped out the entire tribe of Benjamin (Judges 21:46–48). Only two unusual and extreme actions by the eleven tribes prevented the extermination of all Benjamites (see Judges 21). This illustrates that even when the Israelite tribes attempted to band together in a righteous cause, the lack of effective leadership compromised their success. And so we close the book of Judges on this grim note: "In those days Israel had no king; everyone did as they saw fit" (Judges 21:25).

∧ *The heights of Moab, home of Ruth, lie east of the Dead Sea*

Ruth, Bethlehem, and Moab

The book of Ruth offers one of the most engaging stories in the Bible. While it is a story that revolves around the challenges and joys of Naomi, Ruth, and Boaz, who lived during the time of the judges in Israel, it is chiefly a story told in the interests of Israel's most famous king, David. And because it is a story about David, it becomes a story that is vitally concerned with Bethlehem and Moab.

Naomi and her family enjoyed living in the village of Bethlehem. It was the kind of place that had much to offer. It was one of the few places in Judah's hill country where the narrow V-shaped valleys that are so difficult to farm give way to broader valleys where more grain can be grown with less effort. Good soil and plenty of rainfall promised healthy grain harvests, a fact that turned Bethlehem into a place known for its baked goods. In Hebrew, Bethlehem means "house of bread."

But in the time of Naomi, trouble came to Bethlehem in the form of a famine. Things got so bad that her family moved from Judah to the east side of the Dead Sea to land controlled by Moab. This region receives rain and dew even when the mountains of Judah are dry because the air moving upslope into the higher mountains produces more rain. The stay of the family in Moab stretched into ten years. This was not home, but it may have started to feel like home for this displaced Bethlehem family. After Naomi's husband died, her sons married Moabite women. Then tragedy struck again. Both of Naomi's sons died. Naomi and her two daughters-in-law faced serious hardships. Learning that the famine was over in Judah, Naomi and one of her daughters-in-law, Ruth, returned to Bethlehem. Upon their arrival, we watch the Lord provide one solution after another for this family, chiefly through Boaz, the man who would become Ruth's husband. Despite all that was lost at the beginning of the story, there is a happy ending: food, marriage, a home, and a son.

Map 4.11—Ruth and Naomi

The story is worth reading even if it were to stop there, but for the author, the story is not over until it includes the connection of King David to this family. The book of Ruth concludes with a genealogy that shows David is a great-grandson of Ruth and Boaz (Ruth 4:22). Even to this day in the Middle East, where you are from and into which family you were born defines who you are. For that reason, the author of Ruth gives particular attention to two places, Bethlehem and Moab (see map 4.11).

Bethlehem is named seven times in this story and, after the first chapter, is the setting for the rest of the chapters.[18] Places can carry special meaning. And through the story of Ruth, Bethlehem becomes the place where the Lord provides solutions for seemingly impossible problems. So when the nation of Israel has been disturbed by the deteriorating reign of Saul and the Lord sends Samuel to Bethlehem to anoint the king who will replace Saul, we feel good about David even before we meet him. That is because he is from Bethlehem, the place where the Lord provided a solution for Naomi and Ruth.

The author of Ruth names Moab twelve times,[19] once again providing a connection to David, this time a Moabite connection because Ruth, his great-grandmother, is from Moab. This could have been a problem for David. Moab and Moabites are cast in a negative light in the Old Testament, from Genesis through Judges. They are related to the Israelites through

Possible routes used to travel between Bethlehem and the territory controlled by the Moabites

Jericho · Jerusalem · Bethlehem · **Home of Naomi's family** · JUDAH'S HILL COUNTRY · Hebron · Dead Sea · Arnon R. · **Home of Ruth's family** · MOAB · Zoar · Zered R.

0 · 20 mi
0 · 30 km

∨ *Ruth proposed marriage to Boaz on a threshing floor near Bethlehem*

∧ *Bethlehem, on the ridge in the distance, provides the setting for much of the book of Ruth*

Abraham's nephew Lot (Genesis 19:37) and were given a land parcel of their own that the Israelites were not to violate (Deuteronomy 2:9). This is about the nicest thing the biblical authors have to say about Moab. The Moabites hired Balaam to put a curse on the Israelites who had camped on the Plains of Moab opposite Jericho (Numbers 22:1–7), an event Joshua urged the Israelites to remember (Joshua 24:9). When Balaam's efforts failed, Moabite women coaxed Israelite men into sexually immoral practices associated with the Moab worship of Baal (Numbers 25:1–3). During the time of the judges, Eglon of Moab invaded Israelite land and occupied the key city of Jericho for 18 years before being dispatched with a sword by Ehud (Judges 3:12–30). The author of Judges labels Moab "your enemy" (Judges 3:28) and lists the gods of Moab among the deities the Israelites served at the time of Jephthah (Judges 10:6).

These negative events connected with Moab cer-

tainly could have created a public-relations problem for David. We might expect the author of Ruth to downplay rather than emphasize David's family connection, but just the opposite is the case. The story of Ruth refurbishes the Moabite image. She is so easy to like. She shows no pretention and is loyal to Naomi and to the God she has come to know through Naomi. She is industrious, hardworking, and thoughtful. Ruth becomes the new standard for what a Moabite can be.

The story of Naomi, Ruth, and Boaz occurs during the days of the judges, but the story directs our attention to the coming days of King David. The story prepares us to meet him by reinforcing the positive connotations of Bethlehem and by softening our negative feelings about Moabites. David is from Bethlehem, the place where the Lord provides solutions, and he has a Moabite heritage—one made rich through Ruth, his great-grandmother.

∧ *The desert oasis of En Gedi, one of David's hideouts when he fled from Saul*

Chapter 5

SAMUEL AND THE UNITED KINGDOM

Samuel at Mizpah

At the close of the period of the judges, no one appeared to be listening to the Lord. And dismal reports from the tabernacle at Shiloh concerning the worship leaders did nothing to inspire hope that things would change (1 Samuel 2:12–17, 22–25). That is, until we hear the voice of the Lord calling Samuel's name and the young man responding: "Speak, for your servant is listening" (1 Samuel 3:10). This humble sentence breathed new hope into God's chosen people, who looked to Samuel as both a judge who could fight the Philistines and a prophet who would share the very thoughts of God with them. His accomplishments are many and most of them are closely connected to the town of Mizpah.

Mizpah's most likely location is the archaeological site of Tel en-Nasbeh in Benjamin. *Mizpah* is the Hebrew word for "watchtower," and as expected we find this village on a hill, 2,500 feet (762 m) above sea level. Mizpah is situated in the center of Israel near the intersection of the Jericho-Gezer Road and Ridge Route. This became a convenient point for the tribes of Israel to meet—as they had most recently to deal with the problems in Gibeon (Judges 20:1, 3; 21:5, 8).

Map 5.1—Events in the Life of Samuel

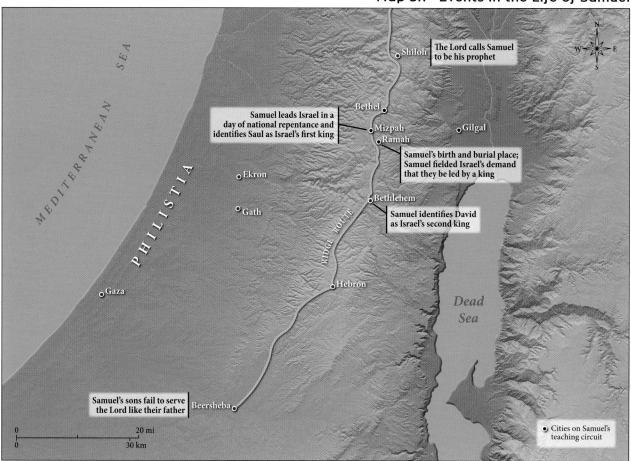

Mizpah is mentioned eight times in 1 Samuel. The cycle of spiritual disasters in the era of the judges comes to a sudden and dramatic end at Mizpah when Samuel summons all Israel to this location for a national day of repentance and a service of rededication to the Lord (1 Samuel 7). We have not read of such a day since Joshua 24 when Joshua challenges the people to join him in declaring allegiance to the Lord: "As for me and my household, we will serve the LORD" (verse 15). When all Israel gathered at Mizpah, they renounced allegiance to any other god but the Lord.

However, as the rededication service was under way, trouble rose on the horizon. The Philistines, who had been oppressing Israel, used this occasion to assemble their soldiers for an attack. This became a moment of testing for Israel. Rather than abandon their time in worship, they urged Samuel to continue the service of rededication, trusting that the Lord would save them. He did. "That day the LORD thundered with loud thunder against the Philistines and threw them into such a panic that they were routed before the Israelites" (1 Samuel 7:10). So generations would remember this important moment in Israel's history and trust God, Samuel constructed a memorial named "Ebenezer" near Mizpah. It continued as a memorial and place of prayer into the period between the Old and New Testament (1 Maccabees 3:46).

Mizpah, mentioned six times in this story above, is mentioned twice more in Samuel's life. Samuel is described as a prophet on the move. He regularly walked a circuit that took him from Bethel to Gilgal and to Mizpah before returning to his home in Ramah (1 Samuel 7:15–17). This circuit that frequently brought him to Mizpah had two important advantages. First, it meant that Samuel was at a convenient location for those who wanted to travel to see him. Second, it placed whatever he had to say at Mizpah in the context of the day when Israel declared its full allegiance to the Lord and the Lord demonstrated his commitment to Israel.

The final mention of Mizpah in 1 Samuel is the critical moment of Saul's coronation. It is interesting to note that the people who came to Samuel to request a king (8:19–20) did not meet Samuel at Mizpah but Ramah, removed from the memorial and the faithfulness they had shown at an earlier time. Despite Samuel's reservations with their request, he moved forward at the Lord's direction to appoint a king. He anointed Saul, an event that likely took place at Ramah (9:6–10:1). We might wonder if we will ever get back to Mizpah and the positive tone set there. It happens within a few verses. After the request for a king at Ramah and the king's anointing at Ramah, Samuel calls for all Israel to join him in Mizpah once again. Here he will announce Saul's selection as king and introduce him to the people he will rule (10:17–24). In Mizpah, where God's people had repented before, they are met with an invitation to repent again. And in this place where the Lord has rewarded faithful obedience with blessing, they are invited to return to an earlier time when their trust in the Lord was more apparent.

The Changing Reputation of Shiloh

Events can change the way we think about a place and teach the lessons we take from it. The Old Testament city of Shiloh is that kind of place, a place that experienced a dramatic change in reputation during the life of Samuel, which in turn changed the lesson the city continues to teach.

Shiloh became the Israelites' worship center after Joshua put the tabernacle on this site (Joshua 18:1). Joshua likely chose Shiloh as the location for the tabernacle because it offered both access and security. Shiloh was located in the mountainous interior of the Promised Land near the central north-south road, the Ridge Route. This gave the tabernacle a higher level of security. With the tabernacle placed here, the city was seen in a positive light as home to the "house of the Lord" (1 Samuel 1:7). This portable sanctuary, built at the time of Moses, had traveled from place to place with the Israelites as they wandered in the wilderness after their exodus from Egypt. The tabernacle was not like a church with pews where people came to sit and worship, but a tent sanctuary that contained the ark of the covenant. God's people could go to this place to worship, to learn, and to pour out their troubles before the Lord. We see it function in just that way in 1 Samuel 1–2. People felt good about going to Shiloh and felt good thinking about it.

But the positive feelings about Shiloh begin to fade when we meet the sons of Eli. Eli is a descendant of Aaron and the high priest at Shiloh. His sons, Hophni and Phineas, are priests responsible for maintaining the worship and sacredness of the place. But they did wrong. "Eli's sons were scoundrels; they had no regard for the LORD" (1 Samuel 2:12). The people criticized them for their attitude toward worship and their sexual behavior, a censure that culminates in the stunning statement that it was the Lord's will to put them to death (1 Samuel 2:13–17, 22–25). Lest we miss the fact that the reputation of Shiloh had been badly tarnished, we learn that on two separate occasions the Lord sent a message to Eli to make clear his displeasure and warn that a punitive response was imminent (1 Samuel 2:27–36; 3:11–14).

∧ *Mountains form a protective barrier around Shiloh and the tabernacle*

△ *The Philistines destroyed Shiloh at the time of Samuel*

The city itself would feel the pain of this divine judgment. When the Israelites became embroiled in a fight with the Philistines at Aphek and endured a staggering loss, the elders decided to move the ark of the covenant from Shiloh to the battlefront so the Lord would be with them (1 Samuel 4:3). In the early chapters of Joshua, the Lord directed the Israelites to use the ark of the covenant in the battle against Jericho, but there is no divine sanction for a similar military use of the ark in this case. In fact it further tarnishes the priestly leadership because this action resembles Canaanite ideology that used means like this to magically manipulate deities into doing what the people wanted the deities to do.[1] The Lord responded by permitting the precious ark of the covenant to be captured by the Philistines, and Eli's two sons, who had traveled with the ark, were killed.

Eventually even the sanctuary city of Shiloh itself was destroyed. The destruction of the city is not men-

tioned in 1 Samuel, but is alluded to in Jeremiah 26:6. The archaeology of Shiloh gives evidence of a violent and horrendous destruction during this particular era.[2] Although Shiloh enjoyed a positive reputation as the host city for the tabernacle, that reputation was destroyed by the wicked acts of Eli's sons and by Eli's failure to correct them.

For those who passed by the ruins of Shiloh as they walked along the Ridge Route, the change in reputation taught an important lesson about the Lord's sanctuary and the city where it had been placed. If a sanctuary of the Lord became sodden with wickedness and corruption, it was far better for that sanctuary and the city to lie in ruins than for it to endure in a corrupt state. This is part of the literary legacy of Shiloh, a place with a once-glowing reputation, now a symbol of divine judgment. In Psalm 78, the poet refers to Shiloh: "He abandoned the tabernacle of Shiloh, the tent he had set up among humans. He sent the ark of his might into captivity, his splendor into the hands of the enemy. He gave his people over to the sword; he was furious with his inheritance" (verses 60–62).

Jeremiah uses the soiled reputation of Shiloh to overcome the misperception associated with the temple in Jerusalem. With the Babylonian destruction of Jerusalem looming, many were of the mind-set that the Lord would never allow the divine sanctuary and the holy city where it resided to be destroyed, even if the Israelite moral compass had fallen off its pivot point. Their argument is captured in this language: "This is the temple of the Lord, the temple of the Lord, the temple of the Lord!" (Jeremiah 7:4). In reply, the Lord urged those espousing this perspective to take a field trip. "Go now to the place in Shiloh where I first made a dwelling for my Name, and see what I did to it because of the wickedness of my people Israel. Therefore, what I did to Shiloh I will now do to the house that bears my Name" (Jeremiah 7:12, 14).

The Ark of the Covenant at Ashdod and Beth Shemesh

Readers of the Old Testament frequently read about people who are on the move. However, 1 Samuel 4–6 is distinct in that it is not focusing on people but on an object on the move—the ark of the covenant. There are two places on its itinerary that call for closer inspection, Ashdod and Beth Shemesh (see map 5.2).

During the Israelites' battle with the Philistines near Aphek, the Israelites had foolishly brought the ark of the covenant into battle. The Philistine soldiers captured the ark and immediately transported it to Ashdod, one of the five city-states through which the Philistines controlled their region (1 Samuel 4:1–11; 5:1). Apparently the Philistines chose to take the ark to this city because this special worship piece of the

Map 5.2—Movements of the Ark

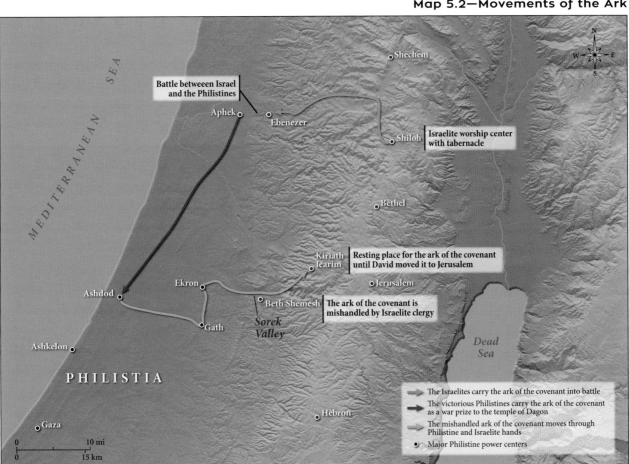

Israelites was to be placed in the temple of Dagon, the chief deity of the Philistines. People in the ancient Near East did not consider war to be merely a battle between two human armies. They believed that the deities of the warring nations were battling one another in the fight right alongside the soldiers of the respective nations. When there was a victory, the deity of the victorious nation was regarded as the victor. When defeated, the losing deity was subject to all the indignities and abuses met by the defeated soldiers in the field. The ark of the covenant was transported to Ashdod because this is where it could be housed in the temple of Dagon to illustrate how Dagon had defeated the God of the Israelites in combat.

But the Lord had his own reasons for allowing the ark of the covenant to be transported to Ashdod. There in the temple of Dagon he demonstrated that there was no connection between Israel's defeat at Aphek and weakness on his part. The morning after the Philistines put the ark of the covenant in Dagon's temple, the statue of Dagon through which Dagon was thought to express himself fell facedown before the ark in a submissive posture. The embarrassed priests quickly put the statue of Dagon back into its place. The next day the same thing happened, but this time the head and hands had broken off, symbolic of Dagon's total defeat and submission before the Lord (1 Samuel 5:2–5).[3]

When the humiliation of their deity was joined by the development of terrible tumors, the people of Ashdod sent the ark of the covenant off on the next stage of its journey. The Philistines moved the troublesome box inland to the city-state of Gath. While this move put distance between Dagon and the ark, the outbreak of tumors followed. In time, the people of Gath had had enough and the ark was moved to Ekron, where the locals received it with fear and panic (1 Samuel 5:7–12).

After seven months of this, the Philistine leaders developed a plan to move the ark of the covenant back into the hands of the Israelites (1 Samuel 6:1–12). They needed to do this in a way that did not make matters worse, so the Philistine priests and diviners huddled and came up with a plan they hoped would both appease the Lord and confirm that their gift was accepted. They prepared five gold rats and five gold tumors. The plan was to use these as models of their problems that would magically carry their afflictions, along with the ark, from them.[4] To confirm that their offer was accepted, the Philistines used two cows that had recently given birth but had never before pulled

∨ **Left:** *Replica of the tabernacle;* **Right:** *Replica of the ark of the covenant*

∧ *Ruins at Beth Shemesh from the time of Samuel*

a cart. Every inclination would be for these cows to resist the yoke and return to their calves, so if they walked away from them pulling the cart carrying the ark and the guilt offering, it would confirm the success of the plan. And that is exactly what the cows did, pulling the cart and its sacred cargo east down the Sorek Valley toward the city of Beth Shemesh (1 Samuel 6:10–12).

The reception that the ark of the covenant received in Beth Shemesh is important, but so is the city itself. Lest we fail to observe the destination, the biblical author formally repeats the city name, Beth Shemesh, nine times in nine verses. What is there about Beth Shemesh that is so important to the author? The answer lies in the nature of this city and the larger purpose in telling this story the way it has been told. Beth Shemesh was no ordinary Israelite city; it was a Levitical city (Joshua 21:16). The Levites were the clergy and religious educators among the Israelites who had not received a single land parcel but had been distributed throughout the other tribes in special cities. As the ark moved toward Beth Shemesh, it was moving to the doorstep of those who would best know what to do with it. The Lord had warned the Levites who were responsible for the daily care and keeping of the holy object never to look at the ark of the covenant, much less look into it (Numbers 4:20). But some of the people of Beth Shemesh did just that. They looked into the ark of the covenant and paid a terrible price. Seventy died (1 Samuel 6:19–20).

The repeated mention of Beth Shemesh in this narrative plays a larger role in the early chapters of 1 Samuel as we are being prepared to read about the dramatic religious reformation among the Israelites led by Samuel (1 Samuel 7). Before we get to this important turning point, we are led to appreciate just how much of a need there was for this reformation. That becomes clear when we read how Israel's religious leaders mishandle the ark of the covenant both at Shiloh and at Beth Shemesh.

∧ *The Sorek Valley looking west from Beth Shemesh toward Ekron*

Saul's Geographic Hurdles En Route to the Throne

When the sons of Samuel failed to show the promise the Israelites were looking for in a leader, the elders asked Samuel to appoint a king (1 Samuel 8:5, 19). Saul was their first king, but his journey to acceptance was not an easy one. Geographically, two places, Gibeah and Jabesh Gilead (see map 5.3), became hurdles he had to negotiate en route to his confirmation as king.

Saul was born into the tribe of Benjamin, and his family had a strong connection to Gibeon (1 Samuel 9:1; 1 Chronicles 9:35–40). But it is Gibeah that is called Saul's home (1 Samuel 10:26). The city of Gibeah was the site of a horrible gang rape and murder of a Levite's concubine (Judges 19:22–26; 20:4–7). This act was so heinous, so egregious that the Levite sent word to each of the tribes of Israel to gather at Mizpah for a punishing attack against this city. The tribe of Benjamin should

∧ *Philistine bichrome jug*

have taken the lead in punishing those responsible for the crime. That's what they were asked to do. Instead the entire tribe of Benjamin rallied to fight on behalf of Gibeah and against the other tribes of Israel (Judges 20:13–14). At the end of this story, Gibeah and the rest of the towns of Benjamin lay in ruins. Only 600 men of Benjamin survived the punishing assault brought against them, putting this tribe on the brink of extinction. Success in political office is in part making sure there are no skeletons in the family closet that might cause people to refuse to support you. Given Saul's heritage as a member of the tribe of Benjamin and his hometown of Gibeah, it is not surprising that there were those who recoiled from the notion that Saul would be their king (1 Samuel 10:27).

Jabesh Gilead also brought problems to Saul. Jabesh Gilead is

Map 5.3—Saul's Kingdom

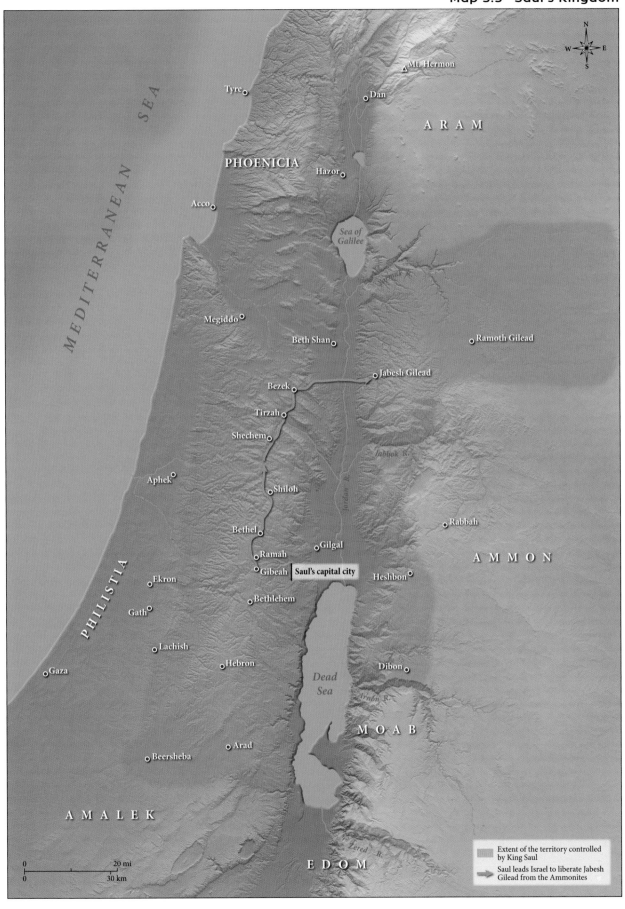

N
W   E
S

MEDITERRANEAN SEA

Mt. Hermon

ARAM

Tyre

Dan

PHOENICIA

Hazor

Acco

Sea of Galilee

Megiddo

Beth Shan

Ramoth Gilead

Jabesh Gilead

Bezek

Tirzah

Shechem

Jabbok R.

Aphek

Shiloh

Jordan R.

Rabbah

Bethel

Gilgal

Ramah

AMMON

Gibeah   **Saul's capital city**

Ekron

Heshbon

PHILISTIA

Bethlehem

Gath

Dead Sea

Lachish

Hebron

Dibon

Gaza

Arnon R.

MOAB

Arad

Beersheba

AMALEK

Zered R.

EDOM

0   20 mi
0   30 km

Extent of the territory controlled by King Saul

Saul leads Israel to liberate Jabesh Gilead from the Ammonites

a city east of the Jordan River. Nahash of Ammon had been pushing farther and farther out from his heartland near the headwaters of the Jabbok River, seeking to gain better agricultural land and to control trade revenue on the King's Highway.[5] This push brought Nahash as far as Jabesh Gilead, where he threatened the city with a punishing siege. A treaty was discussed with the men of Jabesh, but the Ammonites required a brutal codicil. "I will make a treaty with you only on the condition that I gouge out the right eye of every one of you" (1 Samuel 11:2), an act designed to disgrace the city and disable its fighters.[6]

∧ *The Philistines (Sea People) portrayed as captives on an Egyptian relief*

Jabesh Gilead was willing to agree to these horrific terms of surrender but asked for a delay of seven days. They then sought rescue from the Israelite tribes west of the Jordan (1 Samuel 11:1–3). When their plea for help reached Saul, he immediately called out the tribal militias to join him in a rescue operation on behalf of Jabesh Gilead.

Saul would be doing his nation a favor by securing the well-being of a key city strategically located along an important secondary road connecting the Jezreel Valley and International Highway with the Transjordan Plateau and the King's Highway. The mission to free Jabesh Gilead had merit. But there are reasons why Saul might well have considered taking a pass on this request to intervene. The rescue would not bring Saul into combat with the Philistines. By all accounts, the Philistines were the larger and more pressing problem the Israelites faced. The people had asked for a king

∨ *Tribal territory of Benjamin, Saul's homeland*

to lead them who would go out and fight their battles for them because the Philistines had proven to be so aggressive and had penetrated deep into Benjamin territory (1 Samuel 8:19–20; 10:5). If Saul was going to war, the more popular war and the one people were expecting him to wage was against the Philistines, not the Ammonites.

Jabesh Gilead also carried negative political baggage that ironically was linked to Gibeah. Jabesh Gilead was the only city (other than those in the territory of Benjamin) that had failed to join the Israelite tribes in punishing Gibeah for the rape and death of the Levite's concubine. Because Jabesh Gilead had linked itself to the sins of Gibeah, refusing to join in the battle to punish the city, the Israelites had turned on this city as well, sparing only 400 unmarried girls who could become wives for the surviving tribe of

Benjamin that had nearly been wiped out (Judges 21:5–14). Considering the pressing need to address the Philistine problem and the negative history of the city of Jabesh Gilead, we can only imagine that Saul might well have considered ignoring this city's plea for help.

But he did not. Saul's home in Gibeah and his decision to make his first military campaign one to rescue the reputation-tarnished city of Jabesh Gilead created some hurdles for this man seeking the support of the masses. He had associated himself geographically with some very dark days in Israel's history. And this may be exactly why the author of 1 Samuel wanted us to learn about these events from Saul's life. His acceptance as king despite these obstacles says something about the political acumen of this man who so often stands in the shadow of his successor, David.

The Philistines Highlight Saul's Failures

Saul led all of Israel for more than 40 years, but during those years his competence as the leader of God's chosen people diminished. The author of 1 Samuel uses two incursions by the Philistines to review the performance of the first king of Israel and demonstrate this decline. God wanted a king who would be a man after his own heart (1 Samuel 13:14); the people wanted a king who would fight battles on their behalf (1 Samuel 8:19–20). The two Philistine invasions early in Saul's reign demonstrated that he was not the king the Lord or the people of Israel wanted.

The Philistines were a non-Israelite people who controlled the western portion of the Promised Land along the Mediterranean coast (see map 5.4). As Saul comes to the throne, the Philistines had penetrated deep into the central mountains of the Promised Land. We first read about a Philistine incursion that finds them camped at Mikmash (1 Samuel 13:5–14:23). They apparently had displaced the 2,000 soldiers Saul had positioned there (1 Samuel 13:2) and had begun conducting operations from Mikmash in the direction of Ophrah, Beth Horon, and the Valley of Zeboim (1 Samuel 13:16–18). The Philistine objective was obvious. They intended to cut the kingdom of Saul in half in the same way Joshua cut Canaan in half

when he began to divide and conquer this land. The geography of the plan is clear, stirring panic in the Israelites (1 Samuel 13:6–7).

This is exactly the situation the Israelites had in mind when they demanded that a king lead them. We can almost feel the eyes of everyone turn to Saul for an answer to this Philistine invasion. But the response from Saul fails. He began to gather soldiers at Gilgal, but fumbled the pre-battle sacrifice (1 Samuel 13:8–14).

∨ *Mikmash and the Suweinit Canyon negotiated by Jonathan and his faithful armor-bearer*

His fighting force, first reported at 3,000, shrinks to 600 in just a few verses (1 Samuel 13:2, 15). And instead of positioning his men at Geba across the canyon from the Philistine camp at Mikmash, we find Saul lingering farther south at Gibeah (1 Samuel 13:5; 14:2).[7]

In the end, it is not Saul but Jonathan, Saul's son, who plays the role of king. Jonathan advances north toward Geba (see map 5.4) and sets his sights on a small Philistine outpost just east of the main Philistine camp at Mikmash.[8] The geography does not favor his plan. Moving from south to north, Jonathan must descend the sheer southern cliff into the valley and then climb the northern face of the canyon wall to get to the outpost (1 Samuel 14:4–5). Outnumbered and facing an exposed climb that can only be made using both hands and feet (1 Samuel 14:13), Jonathan's courage joins with his words of faith to reveal a leader everyone wishes Saul could be (1 Samuel 14:6). Faith and courage are rewarded as Jonathan's successful attack on the outpost prompts the rest of the Israelite army to join the fight and drive the Philistines from the Israelite interior (1 Samuel 14:46). Saul becomes involved only after the battle's outcome is assured, leaving us less than impressed with his performance as king.

Saul gets another chance to prove his worth when the Philistines invade the Elah Valley. Once again the biblical author uses geography to highlight the grave nature of the Philistine invasion. "Now the Philistines gathered their forces for war and assembled at Sokoh in Judah. They pitched camp at Ephes Dammim, between Sokoh and Azekah. Saul and the Israelites assembled and camped in the Valley of Elah" (1 Samuel 17:1–2). This was yet another national crisis for the Israelites. The enemy had taken over one of the important agricultural valleys in the foothills just west of the central mountain spine. This meant not only a loss in agricultural goods for the Israelites but a real threat to national security since this valley served the two main roadways that linked the coastal plain with the interior and places like Bethlehem and Hebron.[9]

Map 5.4—Jonathan at Mikmash and David in the Elah Valley

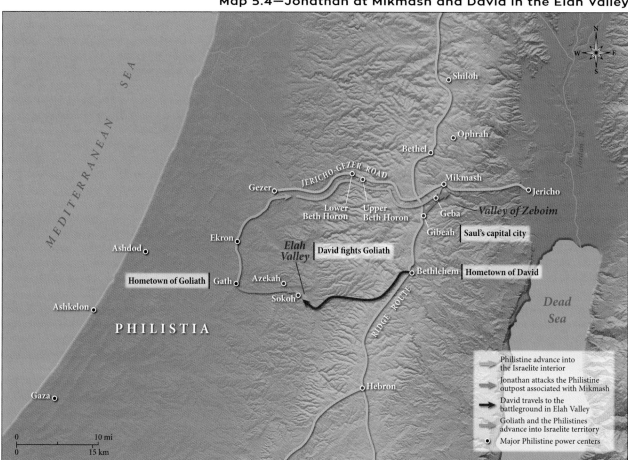

∧ *Elah Valley was the site of David's fight with Goliath*

Once again all eyes turn to Saul, hoping he has a word of encouragement, an act of courage, a plan of action. But as Goliath, the massive Philistine warrior, spews his invectives morning and evening for 40 days, challenging the Israelites to send a man to fight and kill him, Saul remains silent. And his failure to act or inspire action in his soldiers is evident in the paralyzing fear that gripped the Israelite soldiers (1 Samuel 17:11, 24).

This time it is not Jonathan but David who supplies what Saul has failed to deliver. David had already been anointed as Israel's next king (1 Samuel 16:13), but we have yet to see him in action until now. With faith born from experience, David steps out to face Goliath and makes one of the most powerful declarations of trust in the entire Bible. He shouts to the menacing Philistine warrior, "You come against me with sword and spear and javelin, but I come against you in the name of the LORD Almighty, the God of the armies of Israel, whom you have defied" (1 Samuel 17:45). Goliath headed toward David. Then David, taking his sling in hand, runs at the aggressor, fells him with a slingstone, and ends Goliath's life. With the warrior's own sword, David cuts off his head. David's words and actions inspire the Israelite army. Gone is their fear as they pursue the fleeing Philistine soldiers who have no fight left in them. The Philistines head west down the Elah Valley only to have their escape slowed by the ridge of Azekah in the western part of the valley. Hours later, the valley that had been so full of Philistines when the story began had been purged of the threat (1 Samuel 17:52–53).

The national crisis for the Israelites by these two Philistine threats is shaped by the geography—by the richness of the valley and by the barriers of the cliffs. In both cases, it is not Saul but another promising leader who speaks and acts like the king the Lord and the people wanted. These Philistine incursions serve as a performance review for Saul, a review he fails miserably.

David Flees from Saul

The amazing victory over Goliath and the Philistines propelled David into the public eye as a hero. But as his fame spread, the jealousy of Saul grew (1 Samuel 18:7–9). This jealousy of Saul's eventually spilled over into attempts on David's life that caused David to live life on the run for upwards of ten years. The author of 1 Samuel reports on these days in some detail, tracing David's flight with the stories and an abundance of geographic data designed to shape our understanding of the man who would succeed Saul as king of Israel (1 Samuel 21–26).

The nature of David's evasive travels becomes clear when we extract them from the text and attempt to put his path on a map to follow his movements (see map 5.5). David flees to Nob (1 Samuel 21:1), then Gath (21:10), the cave of Adullam (22:1), Mizpah of Moab (22:3), Masada (22:4),[10] the forest of Hereth (22:5), Keilah (23:5), Horesh on the hill of Hakilah in the Desert of Ziph south of the barren plateau of Jeshimon (23:14–15, 19), in the Desert of Maon south of Jeshimon (23:24–25), then En Gedi (23:29; 24:1), Desert of Paran (25:1), and back to the hill of Hakilah in the Desert of Ziph (26:1). There are a couple of striking things about this list. First, most of the places are not well known. Only the first two, Nob and Gath, are likely to be on any Bible reader's mental map of the area. The strange place names leave us with the unmistakable impression that David is spending most of his time in places that are off the normal travel routes.

Second, when we put these place names on a map, we can see that David's movements are erratic, even desperate. The first stop at Nob seems logical, as David is looking for provisions and a weapon from the priests at Nob whom he presumes will be neutral during this time of tension. But after that, the route appears to be more than a little desperate. He flees

Map 5.5—Saul's Pursuit of David

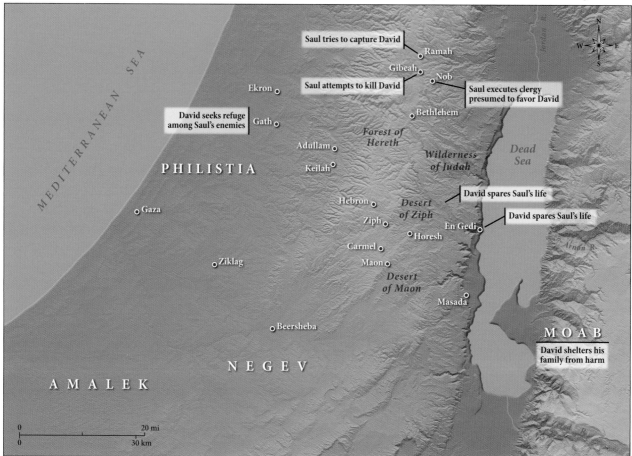

The desert oasis of En Gedi used by David

The fact that David lingered here is reported to us in 1 Samuel to show his development as the man God needs him to be. The confusing maze of valleys and the low population of the wilderness made it possible for David to disappear, to evade Saul, and to avoid those who seemed so ready to betray his location to Saul. But the isolation also gave David time for reflection and growth. Set against this desolate and threatening landscape, the goodness of God and his provision and protection can strengthen faith.

We see the faith of David developing both in what he wrote and how he responded to Saul. The extended weeks of isolation in the wilderness are likely the time when some of David's most heartfelt poetry was written. His poetry seizes on the images of the wilderness. "You, God, are my God, earnestly I seek you; I thirst for you, my whole being longs for you, in a dry and parched land where there is no water" (Psalm 63:1). He learned what it meant to trust. "In you, LORD, I have taken refuge; let me never be put to shame; deliver me in your righteousness. Turn your ear to me, come quickly to my rescue; be my rock of refuge, a strong fortress to save me"

The austere wilderness of Judah in which David hid from Saul

to Gath, the hometown of Goliath, seeking asylum among the Philistines. But he doesn't trust the Gath king, so pretends to be insane so as not to be a threat. Once past that location, the helter-skelter route that slashes across the landscape allows us to feel the extreme tension of this time in David's life. There was no time to settle in and grow food, no quiet time with family, only the unrelenting strain of days on the run. David said, "There is only a step between me and death" (1 Samuel 20:3). Thus the report of David's flight to places we hardly know along an erratic route that is difficult to trace re-creates the fear that was part of this time in David's life.

Another thing that becomes clear in the itinerary of David is how much time he is spending in the greater Judean Wilderness. This is a hauntingly beautiful place but one that is a challenge because of its extreme heat and the lack of water. The terrain is as rugged as you will find in the Promised Land with upwards of 20 east-west gorges whose slopes pitch steeply into narrow valley floors. The chalky slopes are too steep and too barren to suit the farmer even if there were sufficient rain, which there is not. In David's travels, we read of subregions in the wilderness, places like Ziph and Maon. During the rainy season, places like these did offer meager pastureland compared to the barren and even more rugged wasteland of Jeshimon.[11]

(Psalm 31:1–2). We see David's faith not only in his words but also in his actions.

On two occasions, the isolation of the wilderness gave him an opportunity to do to Saul what Saul was trying so desperately to do to him. But in both instances David spared Saul's life, refusing to take advantage of the perilous circumstances in which he found Saul (1 Samuel 24 and 26). Thus the geography of David's flight from Saul allows us to experience those days on the run and see how David's extended stay in the wilderness shaped the faith and language of the man who would become Israel's next king.

Once Again There Is No King in Israel

The Philistines were a non-Israelite people who occupied the coastal plain of the Promised Land, ruling it through five powerful city-states. Early chapters in 1 Samuel tell of Philistine incursions into the mountainous interior of the Promised Land where the Israelites lived, but nothing like the invasion we read about in the closing chapters of this book. The ambitious Philistine effort begins with their forces gathering at Aphek, along the International Highway at the point of transition between the Philistine Plain and the Sharon Plain, where the farmland of the south gives way to swampland in the north (see map 5.6). From here they march along the International Highway into the Jezreel Valley, where they set up camp at the base of Mount Moreh near Shunem (1 Samuel 28:4; 29:1). The goal is clear. The Jezreel Valley offered the most travel-friendly east-west passage through the mountains of the Promised Land. Every trade caravan and every army moving through this arena used this travel corridor, this bridge connecting Africa, Europe, and Asia. The Philistines would graduate to international player if they held this valley, and in the process, they

Map 5.6—Saul's Final Battle

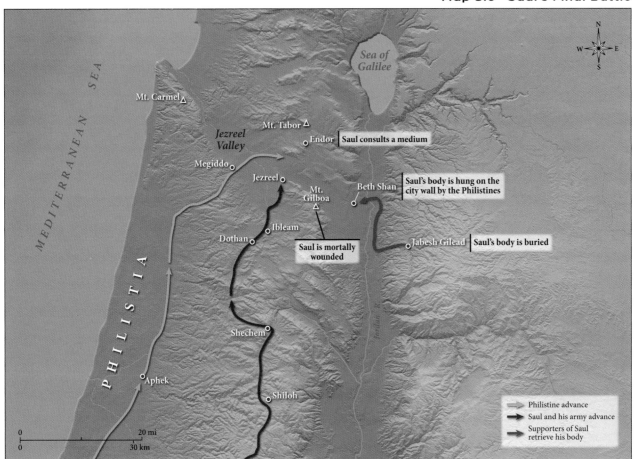

^ *Mount Gilboa, the setting of Saul's death*

would effectively cut the Israelite kingdom of Saul in half.

This was the perfect stage for King Saul to demonstrate his value to the nation. Saul moves the Israelite soldiers to the base of Mount Gilboa, south of the Philistine position, near the spring of Jezreel (1 Samuel 28:4; 29:1). Ironically these encampments of Philistines and Israelites mirror those of the Midianites and Israelites at the time of Gideon (Judges 7:1).[12] But the nature of these two leaders and the outcome of the battle could not be more different. Both a fearful Saul and Gideon go up onto the slopes of Mount Moreh above the enemy camp to obtain insight into how the battle will go on the next day (Judges 7:8–14; 1 Samuel 28:4–25). Faithful Gideon creeps to a spot near the Midianite camp and hears a word of encouragement. Saul travels to Endor to consult a medium and is told that his army will be defeated and he will die. Gideon defeats the enemy gathered in the Jezreel Valley; Saul will witness a devastating loss in the same location. The day after Saul consulted the medium, the Philistines rout the Israelites, leaving in their wake a decimated Israelite army dying on Mount Gilboa. Saul's sons are killed, and Saul is mortally wounded on the same mountain

and takes his own life (1 Samuel 31:1–3, 8). In a crude and gruesome display of total dominance, the Philistines take the bodies of the king and royal princes and suspend them from the city walls at Beth Shan for all to see (1 Samuel 31:10). There is no longer a king in Israel.

Throughout the book of 1 Samuel, we have been led to look to David for hope, but where is he now when Israel appears to need him the most? David has joined the Philistines! As the battle with the Philistines evolves, our eyes wander to the ridges expecting to see David and his soldiers coming to the rescue. It does not happen. Saul's relentless pursuit led David to take a drastic step. Long before the battle in the Jezreel Valley, David had approached the Philistine king of Gath, Achish, to offer him his allegiance (1 Samuel 27:1–3). Achish accepted the offer and initially David took up residence in Gath. Soon afterward he received a Philistine village, Ziklag, that he and his men call their own (1 Samuel 27:6). David then makes it look like he is making raids against the Israelites, though he targets other peoples, in a move designed to enhance his credibility and stature among the Philistines (1 Samuel 27:8–12). This worked so well that

Achish elevated David's status to make him his "body-guard for life" (1 Samuel 28:2). And when it came time for the Philistines to advance into the Jezreel Valley for war against Saul and the Israelites, David appeared ready to join in the battle but was prevented from doing so only when other Philistine rulers questioned his loyalty (1 Samuel 29:4–9). David was turned back, but before he left he delivered this protest: "Why can't I go and fight against the enemies of my lord the king?" (1 Samuel 29:8). There certainly were advantages to David joining ranks with Gath and the Philistines,[13] but it leaves the reader of 1 Samuel wondering where his loyalties lie. He is the anointed king of Israel; but for the moment, he is bonded to the Philistines, not the Israelites.

With Saul dead, there is no king in Israel, a reality that takes us back to the final verse of the book of Judges. The Philistines, the archenemy of God's people, have taken possession of the most valuable land in the Promised Land. Panic set in among the villages and even in the lands across the Jordan River. The Israelites abandoned their homes, which the Philistines soon occupied (1 Samuel 31:7). The Promised Land had been split. The northern and southern Israelite landholdings are no longer connected. Once again, hope seems lost.

Civil War Geography

When Saul died, we expected that David, his divinely anointed successor, would quickly assume the throne of Israel, but David did not become the king of all Israel for more than seven years. Civil war erupted. The author of 2 Samuel presents this part of Israel's history (1:1–5:5) as a quickly changing political map that is shaping the story of David's rise to power as king of all Israel.

David's song of lament was composed after the deaths of Saul and Jonathan (2 Samuel 1:17–27). The Philistines had won a major victory over Saul and now controlled an important stretch of the Promised Land, reaching through the Jezreel Valley to Beth Shan just west of the Jordan River (1 Samuel 31:7, 10). This valley is where the International Highway traveled east and west through the Promised Land. Every trade caravan was in view for a great distance, making it the ideal place to collect the tax revenue that would now pour into Philistine coffers. And by seizing this east-west strip of land, the Philistines had cut off the northern tribes of Saul's kingdom from the rest of the tribes to the south.

The map of the Promised Land becomes even more complicated by the fact that the area south of the Jezreel Valley was further divided by a civil war. With Saul dead, the commander of his army, Abner, quickly put Saul's son Ish-Bosheth on his father's throne to rule Israel (2 Samuel 2:8).[14] Abner claimed to have established him as king over "Gilead, Ashuri and Jezreel, and also over Ephraim, Benjamin and all Israel" (2 Samuel 2:9), but there is little to suggest this list of places is anything more than political propaganda, considering the extent of the Philistine control throughout the Jezreel Valley area and the loyalty of at least Judah to David. Abner claims control of "all Israel" but does not name any tribe north of the Jezreel Valley.[15] Abner houses Saul's son as king in Mahanaim, east of the Jordan River in Gilead on a secondary road system that connects the Jordan Valley with the north-south King's Highway (2 Samuel 2:8–9). It is far from the territory Abner claims Ish-Bosheth rules and far from Saul's capital at Gibeah.

The southern one-third of the Promised Land, the land of Judah (which included the land allotted to Simeon), comes under the leadership of David after he is anointed their king in a ceremony at Hebron (2 Samuel 2:4, 10–11). David is bound to these tribes by strong tethers. David's family was from Bethlehem in Judah. He married into the local clans of Judah with wives from both Carmel and Jezreel (2 Samuel 2:2).[16] And true to the expectation of what a family member would do, David had a history of defending these southern clans against raiding peoples who infiltrated from the south (1 Samuel 27:8). David had shared the plunder seized from his raids on the northern portion of the Sinai Peninsula with those who recognized him as their king (1 Samuel 30:26–31).[17] This includes Hebron, the centrally located city in Judah that would

⌃ **Left:** *Following Saul's death, the Philistines seized the Harod Valley, cutting the kingdom in half;* **Right:** *Saul and his sons were impaled on the city wall of Philistine Beth Shan, which was built on the far hill*

become his capital for seven and a half years (2 Samuel 2:11). The map of this time period is that of a Promised Land divided into three parts: Philistine control in the north, nominal control of the center by Saul's family, and a south firmly in the hands of David.

These divisions diminish the hope of a reunited kingdom of Israel. The Philistines have plowed an east-west swath clean through Saul's old kingdom, dividing the northernmost tribes from those in the south and occupying some of the most desirable land in the region. The southern portion of what remains of Saul's old kingdom is claimed by Saul's son Ish-Bosheth, but much of it is loyal to David.

David was not ready to settle for a kingdom limited in this way. His hope and plan become apparent in the geography. David started with a stronger geographic hand than Ish-Bosheth. He controlled the country's internal crossroads located on the Benjamin plateau. Abner and Ish-Bosheth appear intent on claiming this geographic prize as their own, but they fail to do so in a battle that begins at the key city of Gibeon located at the heart of this plateau (2 Samuel 2:12–17). To this geographic advantage, we add David's diplomatic skills in negotiating a relationship with Jabesh Gilead (2 Samuel 2:4–7) and in using marriage to build a bridge to the king of Geshur, to the east and northeast of the Sea of Galilee (2 Samuel 3:3).

David was clearly growing stronger, a fact that led Abner to see David as the solution for the Philistine problem in the north. Near the end of the civil war, this general who had served Saul elected to throw his lot in with David rather than Ish-Bosheth, allowing David to assume rule over Israel from the Jezreel Valley to Judah (2 Samuel 3:17–19). During David's early years, this energetic king reduced the Philistine holdings and reclaimed the land that Saul, in his early days as king, had held in the north. David could focus his attention elsewhere when the tribes loyal to Ish-Bosheth ended the civil war by going to Hebron to make David their king, starting his rule over "all Israel" that continued for 33 years (2 Samuel 5:1–5).

Jerusalem, a City of Healing and Hope

As David began the process of reuniting an Israel that had experienced more than seven years of civil war, he selected his capital city carefully. The three leading contenders for the capital of Israel were Hebron, Gibeah, and Jerusalem. Each had its advantages and disadvantages. David certainly would have considered

Map 5.7—David's Jerusalem

Threshing floor of
Arauna the Jebusite

*Mount
Moriah*

*Western
Hill*

Royal
Palace

Millo

Jebusite
Tunnel

Spring Tower

Possible access
route for Joab

*Gihon
Spring*

CITY
OF
DAVID

Pool Tower

*Mount Zion
(Byzantine)*

Central Valley

*Siloam
Channel*

*Mount of
Olives*

Hinnom Valley

Siloam Pool

King's
Garden

En Rogel Spring

Defensive wall of David, 10th century BC
Wall built by Suleiman, 16th century AD

0   500 ft
0   150 m

continuing with Hebron as his capital, a role this city had played for more than seven years during the civil war that followed the death of Saul (2 Samuel 2:11). Of the three, Hebron had the best water supply and the strongest agricultural capability. It enjoyed the strongest economic advantages, located at a crossroads between those with agricultural products to sell, those with pastoral products to sell, and those with desert products to sell.[18] Hebron also had become familiar to David; he trusted the loyalty of those living there. But Hebron had two disadvantages: It was too far south of the country's natural center and had been David's capital during the civil war. It would be hard for those in the north to accept this city as the capital.

Those who lived in the north under the reign of Saul would have preferred Gibeah. Although its food and water supplies were more modest than those of Hebron, it too occupied an important location on the Ridge Route close to the natural crossroads of the country where the Ridge Route and Jericho-Gezer Road intersected. It was centrally located with access to markets on all four compass points. But the fact that those in the north favored Gibeah caused problems for those in the south. Gibeah had been the home of Saul and his capital city. For those who had shown David loyalty during the civil war, this icon of the north was not a welcome choice.

∧ *Part of the water system Joab used to capture the Jebusite fortress*

Then there was Jerusalem, or Jebus, as it was called at that time. This city had more than a few disadvantages. It had only modest springs for water and only difficult land for growing grain and fruit. It was two ridgelines away from the Ridge Route and 20 or 30 miles (32 to 48 km) from the nearest harbor or international road system. But of the three choices, the city had the best natural defenses. People had first settled there more than a thousand years before Abram met Melchizedek, king of Salem there (Genesis 14:18). The Jebusite city sat on a finger ridge that rose dramatically above deep valleys to the east, south, and west—a highly secure location. The city was on the border between lands given to Judah and Benjamin, but had

∨ *Left: The Jebusite fortress sat atop this ridge, which rises sharply from the Kidron Valley; **Right:** David's palace was built on this sloped stone foundation*

been assigned to the tribe of Benjamin (Joshua 15:8; 18:28). Despite the efforts of both of these tribes, the non-Israelite Jebusites had resisted all efforts to dislodge them from the ridge (Judges 1:8, 21). So the Jebusites were confident that David too would fail. But David didn't fail. He moved in and made it his capital city, naming it the City of David (2 Samuel 5:6–8) (see map 5.7).

The author of 2 Samuel directs our attention both to the capture of this city as well as the events that immediately follow because they illustrate something about David. The years of civil war that followed Saul's death had left wounds that were slow to heal. The choice of Hebron or Gibeah as David's capital would have fanned old partisan flames, so David captured a city that was centrally located and had been neutral during the country's civil war. It had historic connections with both Saul, Benjamin (Joshua 18:28), and Judah (Joshua 15:63). David is careful to give the city a neutral name. It will not be Jerusalem of Benjamin or Jerusalem of Judah, but "the City of David" (2 Samuel 5:9).[19]

Jerusalem was not only to become a capital of healing but also a capital of hope. For the first time in Israel's history, David seeks to link the political and religious centers by bringing the ark of the covenant from Kiriath Jearim to Jerusalem (2 Samuel 6). The ark symbolized the uniqueness of Israel and recalled the special role the Israelites were to play in restoring hope to the people of a fallen world. God's plan of redemption takes another significant step forward when the Lord informed David that his family would be the one through which the Lord would bring the Messiah into the world.[20] David longed to build a "house" (a "temple") for the Lord, but it was the Lord who would build a "house" (a "dynasty") for David that would last into eternity (2 Samuel 7:16). In this set of promises, the Lord tells David that his blood will run in the human veins of the Messiah. With the hope of the promised Savior linked to both David's family and his capital city, Jerusalem became not just a healing capital but a place of hope as well.

Israel Expands Under David

With superpowers of the ancient world like Egypt and Assyria temporarily weakened and unable to impose their influence on the Promised Land, David seized the opportunity to expand the landholdings and influence of his kingdom (see map 5.8). The account of this expansion in 2 Samuel does not seem to be presented in chronological order.[21] But we can take what the biblical author tells us to construct a map of Israel's changing circumstances that will help us to see the practical and theological implications of Israel's expanding geography under David.

The land described in this expansion falls into three categories: land that was annexed, land that was subjugated, and land that was merely managed.

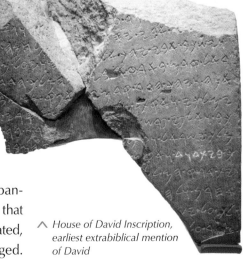

∧ *House of David Inscription, earliest extrabiblical mention of David*

The lands that were annexed are those portions of the Promised Land that had been in question following the civil war. We find this annexed land when we trace the route of the census takers whom David dispatched to determine how many men he had available for military conscription (2 Samuel 24:1–8). Because this census would be conducted only in areas that were part of David's kingdom, we can see just what lands David had claimed following the death of Saul. All of Galilee, the Jezreel Valley, and the Shephelah have been fully annexed to Israel (see map 5.9).

Some land was merely subjugated to Israel by military conquest. The author of 2 Samuel uses expressions like "became subject" and

Map 5.8—David's Battles Expand the Kingdom

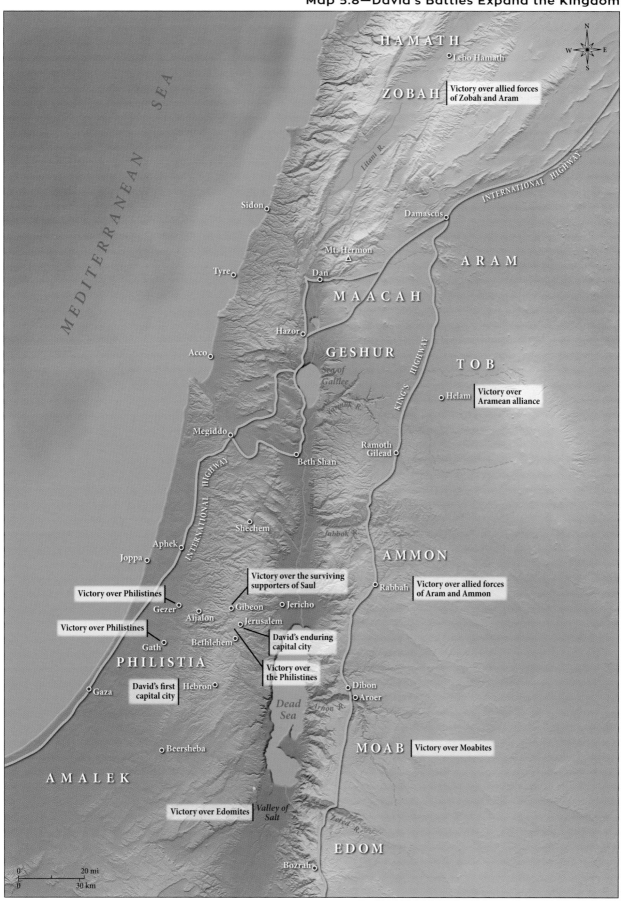

HAMATH

ZOBAH

Lebo Hamath

Victory over allied forces
of Zobah and Aram

MEDITERRANEAN SEA

Litani R.

INTERNATIONAL HIGHWAY

Sidon

Damascus

ARAM

Mt. Hermon

Tyre

Dan

MAACAH

Hazor

GESHUR

Acco

Sea of
Galilee

TOB

KING'S HIGHWAY

Helam

Victory over
Aramean alliance

Yarmuk R.

Megiddo

Ramoth
Gilead

Beth Shan

INTERNATIONAL HIGHWAY

Shechem

Jabbok R.

AMMON

Aphek

Joppa

Victory over the surviving
supporters of Saul

Rabbah

Victory over allied forces
of Aram and Ammon

Victory over Philistines

Gezer

Gibeon

Jericho

Aijalon

Jerusalem

Victory over Philistines

Gath

Bethlehem

David's enduring
capital city

PHILISTIA

Victory over
the Philistines

Gaza

David's first
capital city

Hebron

Dibon

Aroer

Dead
Sea

Arnon R.

Beersheba

MOAB

Victory over Moabites

AMALEK

Victory over Edomites

Valley of
Salt

Zered R.

EDOM

Bozrah

0   20 mi
0   30 km

"brought tribute" to describe the subjugation of these states that include Moab (2 Samuel 8:2, 6); Aram including Zobah, Damascus, Maacah, and Tob (8:3–8; 10:6–19); Ammon (8:12; 10); Edom (8:12–14); and territory occupied by Amalek (8:12).

The states managed in other ways included Philistia, Geshur, Hamath, and Phoenicia. After David reunited Israel, the Philistines responded with multiple invasions directed at Jerusalem (2 Samuel 5:17–25).[22] Each was repulsed by David. But careful reading of the text reveals that the Philistines were "humbled" (כנע, kn') after the battle (2 Samuel 8:1). It appears that Philistine landholdings were reduced (for example, David took Metheg Ammah) and their influence was confined to a smaller space, but they retained more autonomy than other nations listed above. The kingdoms of Geshur and Hamath both made overtures of peace to Israel either through marriage, in the case of Geshur, or financial gift, in the case of Hamath (2 Samuel 3:3; 8:9–10). Phoenicia depended on Israel's land for its food and established a nonaggression pact with David, offering materials and craftsmen to build his palace in Jerusalem (2 Samuel 5:11).

By redrawing the map of Israel to define its core holdings as well as the lands over which it imposed considerable influence, practical insights come to light. David dramatically improved the security of Jerusalem. David's walled city had strong natural defenses on all sides but the north. Those wishing to attack Jerusalem from the north would typically arrive on this vulnerable side of the city after entering the interior via the Jericho-Gezer Road. When David is finished with the Philistines, the biblical author tells us that David controls the stretch of land from Gibeon to Gezer (2 Samuel 5:25). Israelite control of these two cities on the Jericho-Gezer Road means the user-friendly attack route has now been secured by David and is no longer available to those attacking Jerusalem. The second practical benefit has to do with the security of all the Promised Land. A look at map 5.9 shows David has arranged a buffer zone that extends to the north, east, and south of his core landholdings. This ring of protection would make it much more difficult for invaders to attack his kingdom from any of these quarters. The third practical advantage of Israel's new map has to do with collecting tax revenue from those using the international trading routes between the Syrian Desert and the Mediterranean Sea. For the

∨ *David subjugated Maacah, south of Mount Hermon*

Map 5.9—David's Kingdom

MEDITERRANEAN SEA

PHOENICIA

Kadesh on
the Orontes

Tadmor

INTERNATIONAL HIGHWAY

Sidon

Damascus

Tyre

Dan

ARAM

Hazor

Acco

Sea of
Galilee

KING'S HIGHWAY

Megiddo

GILEAD

Beth
Shan

Ramoth
Gilead

Shechem

GAD

Joppa

Jazer

Rabbah

Ashdod

Jerusalem

AMMON

INTERNATIONAL HIGHWAY

Gath

Gaza

Hebron

Dibon

Aroer

Arnon R.

PHILISTIA

Dead
Sea

Beersheba

MOAB

River of Egypt

NEGEV

EDOM

Bozrah

Kadesh Barnea

Petra

Ezion Geber

Gulf of
Aqaba

0	30 mi
0	40 km

Core territory of the Kingdom
of Israel in which David conducted
his military census (2 Samuel 24)

Areas strongly influenced by
the kingdom of Israel following
David's wars

The International Highway descended through this valley between the cliffs of Arbel

had promised Abram that his family, turned into kingdom, would exert an influence over a broad stretch of land from the river of Egypt to the Euphrates (Genesis 15:18–21). Joshua had urged the Israelites to press ahead and finish the conquest of the Promised Land he had begun (Joshua 23:4–11). But Israel had never taken the Promised Land to these promised limits until the time of David.

David's faithfulness to God's direction is also clear in how he managed his conquests. In those instances where he was making contact with land the Lord had promised to give to the Israelites, his policy was annexation. However in regards to Ammon, Moab, and Edom, where the Lord had clearly said that these nations had divine land grants that were not to be taken from them (Deuteronomy 2:2–19), David did not attempt annexation, but practiced only subjugation. Thus in all that David did in expanding the landholdings and influence of Israel, he was careful to honor the Lord's direction, thereby linking himself more closely with the faithful Joshua and distinguishing himself from the faithless Saul.

first time in their history, Israel will have the chance to collect tariffs along the entire stretch of the King's Highway and over a substantial stretch of the International Highway as well.

In addition to these practical benefits derived from David's expansions, we can add the ever-critical theological components that illustrate just how faithful David has been in doing the Lord's work. God

Solomon's Golden Age

The age of King Solomon dawned with growing hope and grand expectations. The author of 1 Kings communicates the positive spirit that filled this golden age. It shows that the Promised Land was delivered as promised, that the Promised Land was being managed as needed, and that key cities within the Promised Land were being fortified as required.

The promises the Lord had made to Abram (Genesis 12:1–3) were slowly realized over time and recorded on the pages of our Bible between Genesis and 1 Kings. By the time we arrive at the age of Solomon, two important things have happened. Abram's family has become as numerous as the sand on the seashore (Genesis 22:17; 1 Kings 4:20). And this nation's sphere of influence has grown to extend from the Euphrates

River to the River of Egypt or Wadi el-Arish (Genesis 15:18). While the fulfillment of this land promise was implied in the ever-expanding conquests of King David, it is stated in 1 Kings 4:21: "Solomon ruled over all the kingdoms from the Euphrates River to the land of the Philistines, as far as the border of Egypt." The language in 1 Kings parallels the promises given in Genesis, demonstrating that the age of Solomon was an age of fulfilled prophecy (see map 5.10).

Before the time of Solomon, the focus had been on conquest rather than on management. But when Solomon took the throne, there was a need for an administrative plan. Solomon divided the Promised Land into twelve administrative districts and assigned an administrator for each district who was responsible

Map 5.10—Solomon's Kingdom

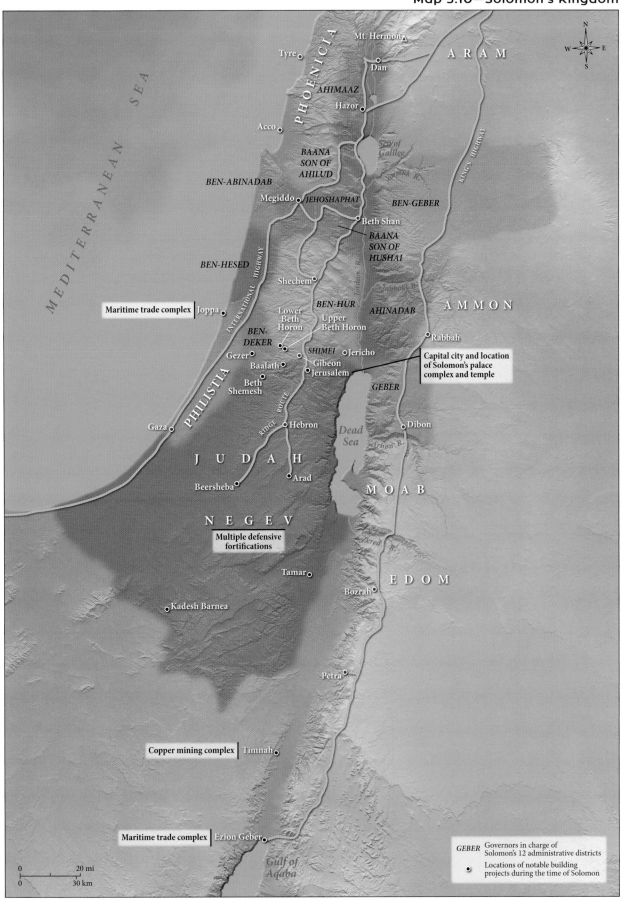

N
W · E
S

Mt. Hermon △

ARAM

Tyre ○

PHOENICIA

Dan ○

AHIMAAZ

Hazor ○

Acco ○

Sea of Galilee

BAANA SON OF AHILUD

BEN-ABINADAB

King's Highway

Megiddo ○ *JEHOSHAPHAT*

BEN-GEBER

Beth Shan ○

BAANA SON OF HUSHAI

MEDITERRANEAN SEA

BEN-HESED

INTERNATIONAL HIGHWAY

Shechem ○

BEN-HUR

AHINADAB

AMMON

| Maritime trade complex | Joppa ○

Rabbah ○

Lower Beth Horon

Upper Beth Horon

BEN-DEKER

Gezer ○
Baalath ○

Beth Shemesh ○

SHIMEI

Gibeon ○
Jericho ○

Jerusalem ○

| Capital city and location of Solomon's palace complex and temple

PHILISTIA

RIDGE ROUTE

GEBER

Gaza ○

Hebron ○

Dead Sea

Dibon ○

Arnon R.

JUDAH

Beersheba ○

Arad ○

MOAB

N E G E V

| Multiple defensive fortifications |

Zered R.

Tamar ○

E D O M

Bozrah ○

Kadesh Barnea ○

Petra ○

| Copper mining complex | Timnah ○

| Maritime trade complex | Ezion Geber ○

Gulf of Aqaba

| 0 — 20 mi |
| 0 — 30 km |

GEBER Governors in charge of Solomon's 12 administrative districts
● Locations of notable building projects during the time of Solomon

for providing the royal household with the necessary supplies for one month during the year (1 Kings 4:7–19). At times an administrator's territory is defined using an old tribal land label and at other times with a list of key cities in a district. But in no way does this list provide us with enough detail to draw an accurate map of these districts.[23]

So why did the author of 1 Kings include such a list? Some point to a more nefarious role for this list, allowing it to cast a negative shadow over Solomon's rule. They point to his apparent lack of regard for matching the size of an administrative district with its capability to provide the resources required for the assigned month. They also suggest that it was Solomon's goal to break up loyalty to the tribes by splitting them into multiple administrative districts.[24] But just the opposite has been suggested using the same data. Here Solomon's wisdom is showcased by retaining many of the tribal names in an effort to cement a connection with Israel's past.[25]

This interpretive stalemate can be resolved by broadening our view to the general context of 1 Kings 3–4. In 1 Kings 3, the biblical author impresses us with a new king who values wisdom more than wealth and insight more than power. We are even given an illustration of that wisdom at work in the closing verses of the chapter when two women approach Solomon with one child, both claiming to be its mother, and Solomon quickly gets to the truth. In the next chapter, Solomon does what so many other ancient Near Eastern leaders did—he established an administrative structure for his large and diverse kingdom.[26] Thus the districting plan illustrates not a failure of Solomon but part of the success that attends the early years of his reign. Combined with other events, it demonstrates Solomon's wise rule.

A note of celebration also surrounds the fortifying of key cities in the Promised Land. Three stand out because of their strategic importance: Hazor, Megiddo, and Gezer (1 Kings 9:15). These cities have all undergone extensive archaeological investigation, and the evidence from this period of history links these three locations in an interesting way. Hazor, Megiddo, and Gezer all have similar structural defenses. Each city has a large six-chambered gatehouse as its primary entrance, and each of these cities is surrounded by a casemate wall.[27] The fortifying of these cities with the latest in structural technology certainly is because two are along the International Highway and the third is in a strategic location overlooking east-west travel. Hazor is just north of an important split in the International Highway north of the Sea of Galilee. Megiddo is

∨ **Left:** *Model of Solomon's gate at Megiddo;* **Right:** *Steps associated with Solomon's entrance to Megiddo*

∧ *Foundation of Solomon's six-chambered gatehouse at Gezer*

just east of a critical narrowing of this road system by the Mount Carmel range that restricts travel options. And Gezer is on the most easily traveled route from the coastal plain to Jerusalem. By fortifying these three cities, Solomon achieved the highest level of national security achieved to this point and obtained access to trade revenue from merchants traveling the International Highway.

Temple in Jerusalem

Of all Solomon's significant accomplishments, none is more important to the author of 1 Kings than the building and dedication of the temple in Jerusalem. Of the eleven chapters, four cover the temple, ending with moving the ark of the covenant from the City of David to the temple and the dedication of the temple (1 Kings 5–8). This attention is merited, given the massive size of this public building, its unique composition (1 Kings 5:8–9, 17–18; 6:7), and the fact that it is where the Lord chose to meet his people and receive their worship (1 Kings 6:13; 8:27–29). But there is another reason why the building of the temple in Jerusalem merits this kind of attention. It ends the times when the Lord's sanctuary and the ark of the covenant were separated. We will better grasp the importance of building the temple by tracing the history of the Lord's sanctuary from Sinai to Jerusalem.

At Mount Sinai, the Lord commissioned Moses to build a sanctuary. It would not be a building made of stone, but a portable cloth tent called the tabernacle, or Tent of Meeting. This tent was constructed to specifications from the Lord along with the altar for burning incense, the ark of the covenant, and other components needed to worship the Lord as he directed (Exodus 26–27, 30). At this point in Israel's history, it is easy to know the whereabouts of the divine sanctuary because it went wherever the people went, always located in the same position within the line of march and set up in the same location among the tribes when camp was made (Numbers 2:17; 10:17). Eventually the time for traveling from place to place came to an end after the Israelites moved into the Promised Land. That's when Joshua set up the tent sanctuary in Shiloh (Joshua 18:1). This is where Hannah went to pray for a son and where her son, Samuel, first served the Lord (1 Samuel 1:3; 3:3). Thus from the time the sanctuary was commissioned at Mount Sinai through the time we find it at Shiloh, Bible readers pretty much know where it is.

Map 5.11—Solomon's Jerusalem

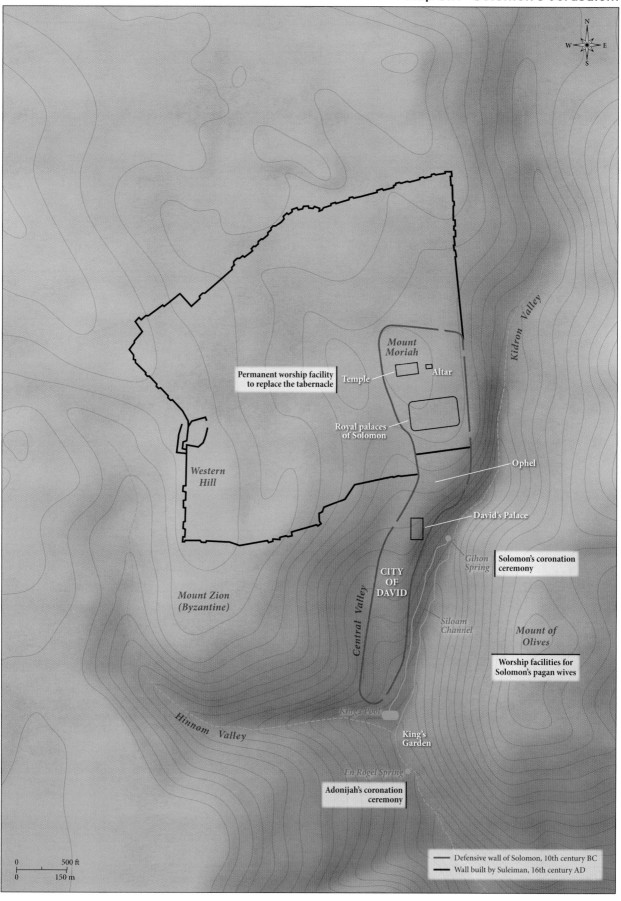

Permanent worship facility
to replace the tabernacle

Mount
Moriah

Temple

Altar

Royal palaces
of Solomon

Ophel

Western
Hill

David's Palace

Kidron Valley

Gihon
Spring

Solomon's coronation
ceremony

Mount Zion
(Byzantine)

CITY
OF
DAVID

Central Valley

Siloam
Channel

Mount of
Olives

Worship facilities for
Solomon's pagan wives

Hinnom Valley

King's Pool

King's
Garden

En Rogel Spring

Adonijah's coronation
ceremony

| 0 | | 500 ft |
| 0 | | 150 m |

Defensive wall of Solomon, 10th century BC
Wall built by Suleiman, 16th century AD

That is not the case in the years that follow. In a desperate bid to defeat the Philistines, the Israelites removed the ark of the covenant from the tabernacle at Shiloh and took it into battle with them. The Israelites were defeated and the city of Shiloh, including the tabernacle, was destroyed (Psalm 78:60; Jeremiah 7:12–15). The ark of the covenant was captured and began a tour of Philistine cities before returning to Israelite hands in Beth Shemesh (1 Samuel 4–6). It then was moved to Kiriath Jearim, where it remained for the next 20 years (1 Samuel 7:1–2).

The priests who survived the Philistine attack on Shiloh moved south to Nob, near Jerusalem. We read about them when David began his flight from Saul. Although no sanctuary is mentioned, its presence in Nob is strongly implied because the priest at Nob gave David some of the sacred bread that would have been associated with the sanctuary (1 Samuel 21:6). And King Saul, after hearing about it, ordered the massacre of all the priests at Nob, raising questions about what then happened to the sanctuary (1 Samuel 22:18). The next time the tabernacle and altar show up in the same place is when Solomon goes to worship the Lord at Gibeon on the day he received the gift of wisdom. He offered his sacrifices on the altar there (1 Kings 3:4–5). But we would not know that the altar and tabernacle

were at Gibeon at the time of Solomon without the assistance of 2 Chronicles 1:5. There we are told that the altar was in front of the tabernacle at Gibeon. After Solomon finished at Gibeon, he returned to Jerusalem where the ark of the covenant was located (1 Kings 3:15). It had been moved there by his father, David, who had gone to Kiriath Jearim to bring the ark of the covenant to Zion, the City of David, placing it in a "tent" within his capital city (2 Samuel 6:2, 12, 16–17). The ark would remain in that tent until Solomon completed the temple and had the ark brought into its new home (1 Kings 8:1; 2 Chronicles 5:2).

As you can see, once we get past the early chapters of 1 Samuel, it becomes difficult for readers of the Bible to trace the location of the sanctuary of the Lord, its incense altar, and the ark of the covenant because they often are not located in the same place. This mystery on the location of the sanctuary, or Tent of Meeting, helps readers to appreciate why David longed to build a permanent sanctuary for the Lord in Jerusalem. Readers also can feel relief when the altars, ark, and sanctuary are together in one place—safe.

When that time comes, the author of 1 Kings lavishes details on the reader (1 Kings 5–8). The location for the temple had already been determined. North of the City of David was a hill on which a man named

∨ *The ark of the covenant remained at Kiriath Jearim for 20 years*

Araunah had a threshing floor. David purchased this hill from Araunah, making it the property of the state (2 Samuel 24:18–25). This was in the same mountain range where the Lord had tested Abraham by asking him to sacrifice Isaac (Genesis 22:2). The name of the region, "Moriah," became attached to the hill on which the temple would be built (2 Chronicles 3:1) (see map 5.11).

For the first time in the history of God's people, the Lord had chosen a specific city for the building of an enduring sanctuary where the Lord would make his presence known to his people (1 Kings 8:16). But there was one more problem that needed solving. The ark of the covenant had not been in the Lord's sanctuary since the time of Eli and Samuel at Shiloh, preventing God's people from fulfilling the worship rites prescribed for the Day of Atonement. King Solomon brought together all the elders of Israel to watch as the priests brought the ark of the covenant from the City of David to the new temple on Mount Moriah (1 Kings 8:1, 3–5).

∧ Solomon's temple was built on the site now occupied by the Dome of the Rock

Jerusalem and the Songs of Ascents

The Bible's authors spent a great deal of time outdoors, so it was natural for them to comingle geography with what they wrote. We see it not only in Bible stories but in poetry as well. A good example of this is Jerusalem and its relationship with a collection of psalms known as the songs of ascents, Psalms 120–134. It seems that this collection of psalms was composed in connection with the three annual travel festivals that brought men, and likely their families as well, to worship in Jerusalem (Exodus 23:14–17; Deuteronomy 16:16).[28] Even if these travelers began their journey at an elevation higher than that of Jerusalem, the road systems connecting them to this holy city would eventually require them to climb the final stretch to Jerusalem, hence the label attached to each of these travel psalms, "a song of ascents."[29] Here we examine portions of Psalms 122 and 125 to see how geography is employed by these poets.

We begin with Psalm 125 because its language reflects the en route phase of the trip to Jerusalem. Walking time became a time for reflection and, in this case, the poet was reflecting on the security believers enjoyed because of the divine protection that encompassed them. Both Mount Zion (another name for the Jerusalem of David and Solomon) and the mountainous terrain around it become part of this poetic reflection.

"Those who trust in the LORD are like Mount Zion" (Psalm 125:1). The believer's personal security is likened to the security enjoyed by Mount Zion. This is a rather puzzling statement given the topography of Jerusalem. Standing either on the City of David or on the Temple Mount, we do not feel like we are on much of a mountain, nor do we feel particularly secure. The Jerusalem of David and Solomon sits at the bottom of a geographic bowl with rising terrain all around. It is true that two deep valley systems protect Zion from below, but when an enemy is present on the mountains above, they are able to see everything going on in the city and can fire their weapons into the city from the high ground. To see the connection between security and Mount Zion, we need to travel on the roads being used by the Jewish pilgrims en route to the holy city.

Those making their pilgrimage to Jerusalem, particularly those coming into Jerusalem from the coastal plain, found the going pretty tough. Mount Zion is surrounded by a shield of mountains, characterized by high, steep ridges and narrow V-shaped valleys. From the perspective of those living in Jerusalem, these mountains were like a protective barrier making invasion difficult. The Lord plays a similar role in the lives of his own. "As the mountains surround Jerusalem, so the LORD surrounds his people both now and forevermore" (Psalm 125:2). The long-standing nature of the protection deserves comment as well. Because the mountains that surround Jerusalem are composed of a hard limestone that erodes at a rate of .4 inches (1 cm) every one thousand years, these mountains and their physical protection never seem to change. Just as the mountains are unchanging, so the Lord provides an unfading and unchanging layer of security for his people "now and forevermore."

Psalm 122 carries our journey to Jerusalem to its conclusion, celebrating the moment we enter the city, a moment when life feels right. The lives of Jewish pilgrims, like our own, are often filled with the mundane and difficult. Festival time was a time to escape all of

^ *The ever-enduring Cenomanian limestone of Jerusalem's city wall*

that and to feel life as it was meant to be. This is captured by the poet both when stepping into the gates of the city and when walking its narrow streets. The joy expressed in Psalm 122 is palpable. "I rejoiced with those who said to me, 'Let us go to the house of the LORD.' Our feet are standing in your gates, Jerusalem" (verses 1–2). Lest we miss the power of the moment, we are invited to pause and take it all in, just as many Christian pilgrims do today when they walk through the gates of Jerusalem's Old City for the first time. It

∨ *Travel to the temple in Jerusalem required climbing*

feels good to reach our travel goal. It is a moment to be captured. Flush with joy, excitement, and emotion, the tired travelers experience a rush of feelings when they step through the gates of the city where the Lord has promised to meet his people.

With the next steps, the Jewish pilgrims find themselves hemmed in by the architecture of the city. It is so different from the wide-open country they have traveled through to get here, where views ran to a distant horizon line. Now visibility is reduced to feet as the walls of the city press in and confine movement in the narrow streets. But rather than balk at the confined space, the poet celebrates: "Jerusalem is built like a city that is closely compacted together. That is where the tribes go up—the tribes of the Lord—to praise the name of the Lord according to the statute given to Israel" (Psalm 122:3–4). Pressing together out of necessity to negotiate the narrow streets, the pilgrims excitedly move as one toward the temple. The poet then expresses his concern that this experience might be taken away because of war. "Pray for the peace of Jerusalem: 'May those who love you be secure. May there be peace within your walls and security within your citadels.' For the sake of my family and friends, I will say, 'Peace be within you'" (Psalm 122:6–8).

∧ Jerusalem's Old City still has narrow streets

Solomon's International Network

For most of Israel's history, its kings influenced a rather modest realm, often limited to a portion of the central mountain range. This makes the expansive map needed to chart Solomon's international network stand out from the norm (see map 5.12). The author of 1 Kings offers lavish details on this dimension of Solomon's influence not only because it is unique in its breadth, but also because it creates some interesting opportunities for this king that sadly went unclaimed.

The extent of Solomon's international network is presented in 1 Kings by describing the lands he ruled or had substantial influence in, his maritime accomplishments, and his many international alliances. Control of this expanse of land would not be replicated by any of Israel's future kings. Thanks to the work of King David, Solomon's early years are distinguished

as a time of peace on all sides with no significant adversary challenging his authority (1 Kings 4:24; 5:4). His kingdom dominated the Promised Land from Dan to Beersheba and from Gilead to the Mediterranean Sea (1 Kings 4:21, 24). Although the perimeter states of Aram, Ammon, Moab, and Edom were not annexed to his kingdom, even they were subordinate to him. This assured Solomon control of overland international trade between the Syrian Desert and the Mediterranean Sea on the International Highway, the King's Highway, and all the east-west feeder routes in between. The author of 1 Kings specifically mentions two outcomes of this control. He observes that Solomon became a middleman in the exchange of horses and chariots between Egypt, Arabia, and Asia (1 Kings 10:28–29), and he offers an extended account of the visit of the Queen of Sheba. The queen had come some 1,400 miles (2,253 km) from the southwest side of Arabia to Jerusalem to negotiate access to the routes she needed to move her country's aromatics to market (1 Kings 10:1–13).[30]

Solomon's international network is also associated with harbors on both the Mediterranean and the Red Sea. The Israelites had never developed a strong maritime culture of their own because they rarely found themselves in control of any sections of the Mediterranean coast. Solomon changed that. He went to some of the most sophisticated shipbuilders and sailors of the ancient world, the Phoenicians, to acquire building materials, shipbuilders, and sailors.[31] His ships sailed from Joppa and Ezion Geber (1 Kings 9:26–28; 10:22; 2 Chronicles 2:16). Markets as far away as Europe and Africa were accessed via these trading fleets.

Finally, Solomon's international network is marked by his many marriages. Ancient diplomatic relationships were often secured by the intermarriage of the royal families. The more such marriages one had, the more influential one was. Solomon had 700 wives and 300 concubines, some of which would have strengthened international treaties that Solomon had

∧ Boats in the modern harbor of Jaffa, site of Solomon's harbor at Joppa

with countries like Egypt, Moab, Ammon, Edom, the Sidonians, and the Hittites (1 Kings 11:1, 3).

This international network provided Solomon with two unprecedented opportunities. First, wealth flowed into the kingdom of Israel. The amount of precious metals, precious stones, and luxury items that fueled the economy was staggering. Silver was so plentiful it was said to assume the value of stone (1 Kings 9:28; 10:10–12, 14, 22, 27). At no other time in Israel's history would we read of a more thriving economy.

The second international opportunity Solomon had was to speak to an international audience on behalf

∨ The Red Sea near Solomon's seaport at Ezion Geber

of the Lord. Representatives from all over the world were coming to Solomon to bask in his famous wisdom (1 Kings 4:34; 10:24). What an opportunity, hundreds of years before Pentecost, to tell the world all that God had made known in his Word.

But alongside these opportunities we find some yawning traps. Israel had been warned about getting entangled in foreign alliances. And long before Israel had a king, Moses had warned that Israel's kings were not to bring large numbers of horses into their stables, or marry many wives, or accumulate large amounts of silver and gold, or be drawn into pagan ideology (Deuteronomy 17:14–20). These words of warning appear to form the outline with which the author of 1 Kings presents Solomon's tumble into the trap. He filled his stables with horses and his household with wives and concubines. He amassed large quantities of silver, gold, precious stones, aromatics, and other luxury items. And he allowed pagan ideology to take over his thinking. He even had pagan temples built on the ridge to the east of the temple (1 Kings 11:3–7). What a squandered opportunity! The world was coming to Solomon to see what made him different. Instead of changing them, Solomon allowed himself to be changed by the pagan world he had taken into his own household.

Map 5.12—Solomon's Trade Network

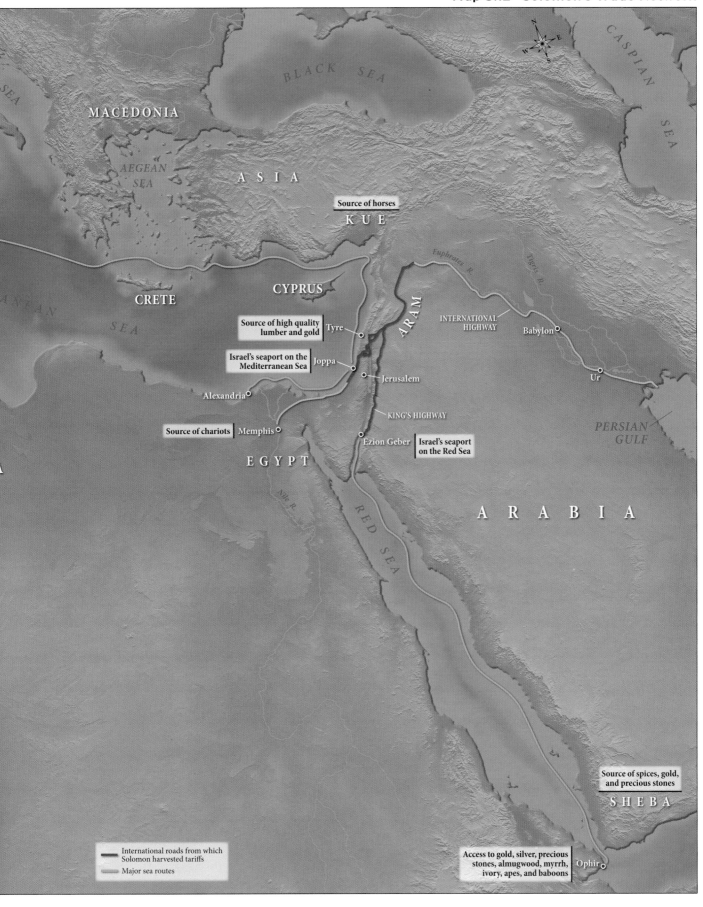

BLACK SEA

MACEDONIA

CASPIAN SEA

AEGEAN SEA

ASIA

KUE

Source of horses

Euphrates R.

Tigris R.

CYPRUS

CRETE

ARAM

INTERNATIONAL HIGHWAY

Babylon

Source of high quality lumber and gold | Tyre

Israel's seaport on the Mediterranean Sea | Joppa

Jerusalem

Ur

Alexandria

KING'S HIGHWAY

PERSIAN GULF

Source of chariots | Memphis

Ezion Geber

Israel's seaport on the Red Sea

EGYPT

Nile R.

ARABIA

RED SEA

Source of spices, gold, and precious stones

SHEBA

International roads from which Solomon harvested tariffs

Major sea routes

Access to gold, silver, precious stones, almugwood, myrrh, ivory, apes, and baboons | Ophir

∧ *Megiddo overlooks the Jezreel Valley*

Chapter 6

THE DIVIDED KINGDOM

The Kingdom Divides

During the days of David and Solomon, Israel was united as one nation. However, when Solomon's son Rehoboam was set to succeed his father as king, the northern tribes balked at offering him their allegiance. A meeting was arranged to discuss the matter. This meeting took place at Shechem (see map 6.1). When the northern tribes did not receive the concessions they demanded, they announced their departure from the union. The kingdom of Israel divided at Shechem (1 Kings 12:1–17).

Shechem would seem to be a good choice for the gathering. It, like many convention centers today, is located at an important transportation hub. The Ridge Route connecting the Promised Land north to south joins with east-west secondary roads at Shechem.[1] Easy to get to, it offers a large outdoor meeting space and excellent acoustics. Shechem is in a narrow valley below the slopes of Mount Gerizim and Mount Ebal that forms a natural amphitheater. But Shechem was not Jerusalem.

To this day, public figures carefully choreograph the backdrop for important announcements. They plan events to coincide with cities that will be helpful to their message. Our expectation is that any meeting with Rehoboam about the future status of the kingdom would occur in Jerusalem, the nation's capital. David had founded the city as the capital of all Israel. Solomon had constructed public

∧ *Shechem sits between Mount Ebal and Mount Gerizim*

buildings there, including administrative palaces and the Lord's temple. Plenty of historical precedent suggests that the appropriate place to meet a king or a king-to-be is in the nation's capital. Earlier when the northern tribes wished to acknowledge David as their king, they traveled to Hebron, which was his capital city (2 Samuel 5:1–2). When dignitaries from foreign lands wanted a serious sit-down with Solomon, they met him in his capital city of Jerusalem (1 Kings 10:1–13, 24–25). That is what makes the geographic language in this Scripture so attention grabbing. "Rehoboam went to Shechem, for all Israel had gone there to make him king" (1 Kings 12:1). Shechem was not Jerusalem. And this fact highlights the lack of power and prestige wielded by Rehoboam in contrast to his father Solomon and his grandfather David.

We also note the lack of religious language in the exchanges between Rehoboam and his would-be subjects in this sacred space. Shechem is a place with a powerful theological history. When Abram entered the Promised Land and God told him that he had arrived in the land he had been promised, he is at Shechem, where he built an altar to remind himself and others of what God had promised there (Genesis 12:6–7). When Jacob returned from Paddan Aram, he entered the city of Shechem and secured the

family connection to the place by purchasing property there and building his own altar. And in this location

Map 6.1—Schism at Shechem

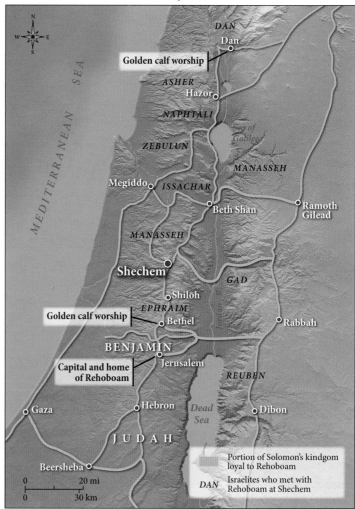

where Jacob commemorated his return to the Promised Land, the bones of Joseph were buried, fulfilling the request Joseph made in Egypt (Genesis 33:18–20; Joshua 24:32). After the initial victories of Joshua's campaign to secure the Promised Land for the Israelite tribes, he brought the people to Shechem. After constructing an altar on Mount Ebal and copying the law of Moses on stone monuments, this site is the setting for a worship service in which the Israelites rededicate themselves to the Lord (Joshua 8:30–35 in obedience to Deuteronomy 27–28). At the close of his life, Joshua brought the people back to Shechem to deliver his final words of encouragement, including these unforgettable words: "But as for me and my household, we will serve the LORD" (Joshua 24:15).

Considering the history of Shechem and the powerful language of faith this place had known, it is unthinkable that God's people could go there, conduct a meeting on the future of the kingdom, and not once mention the Lord or give voice to matters of faith in God. But that is exactly what we find in 1 Kings 12. The northern tribes asked for concessions related to their concerns about high taxes and harsh labor practices.[2] Rehoboam played political hardball. He ignored advice from elders and instead followed the advice of young men he had grown up with. He declared his intention to demand more rather than less of the people. We do not hear the kind of conversation we are used to hearing at Shechem. There is absolutely no mention of the Lord, of Israel's religious responsibilities, or of the glorious moments of the past at Shechem. The conversation does not fit the place. The readers of 1 Kings know division is coming (1 Kings 11:9–13, 29–39). The fact that the split happened at Shechem illustrates just how bad things had become.

Shechem, Bethel, and Dan

The founding of the Northern Kingdom of Israel had God's approval, and the first king, Jeroboam, had a promise from the Lord that his dynasty would endure (1 Kings 11:37–39). From this point on, the Southern Kingdom of Judah and the Northern Kingdom of Israel would coexist. The divided kingdom was not a temporary glitch, but the new normal, creating a new map of the Promised Land that would last for centuries (see map 6.2). The lingering question was whether Jeroboam and his successors could form an independent state of Israel in the north without destroying the all-important religious unity of God's people and their subjects' connection to the temple at Jerusalem in Judah, ruled by King Rehoboam. The answer to this question takes shape quickly and involves three cities: Shechem, Bethel, and Dan.

King Jeroboam needed a capital city that would give his government credibility and become the counterpart to Jerusalem. Shechem was that city (1 Kings 12:25). It offered a number of advantages. The land around the city is fertile and good for producing grain and fruit harvests. It was well connected by roads to the regions Jeroboam ruled. The Ridge Route brought north-south traffic right past his capital city

∧ *Rich agricultural fields near Shechem*

Map 6.2—Divided Kingdom

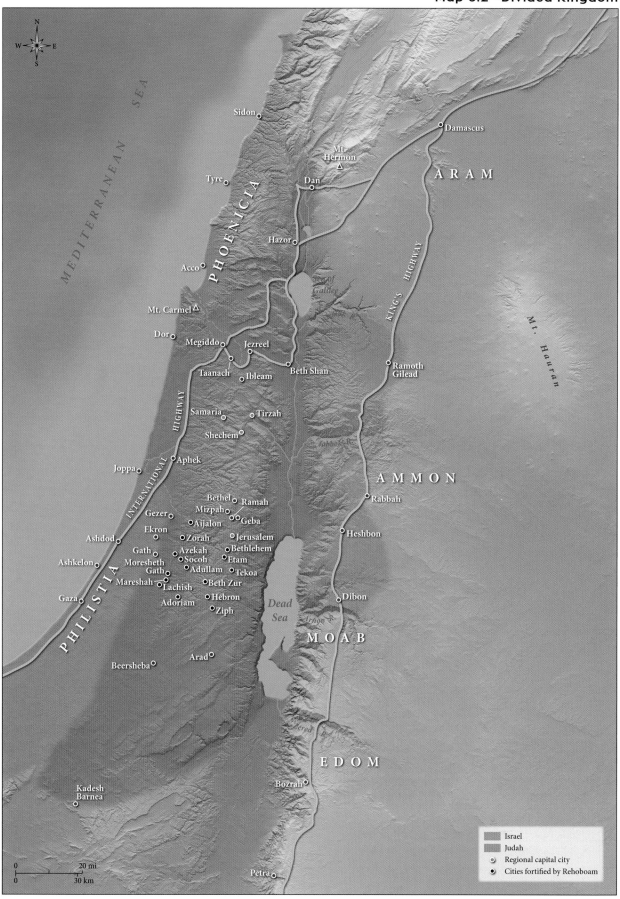

MEDITERRANEAN SEA

Sidon

Damascus

Mt. Hermon

ARAM

Tyre

Dan

Hazor

Acco

PHOENICIA

Sea of Galilee

KING'S HIGHWAY

Mt. Carmel

Mt. Hauran

Dor

Megiddo

Jezreel

Taanach

Ibleam

Beth Shan

Ramoth Gilead

Samaria

Tirzah

HIGHWAY

Shechem

Jabbok R.

Joppa

Aphek

AMMON

INTERNATIONAL

Bethel

Ramah

Rabbah

Mizpah

Geba

Gezer

Aijalon

Ekron

Zorah

Jerusalem

Heshbon

Ashdod

Azekah

Bethlehem

Gath

Socoh

Etam

Ashkelon

Moresheth

Adullam

Tekoa

Gath

Mareshah

Lachish

Beth Zur

PHILISTIA

Adoriam

Hebron

Dibon

Gaza

Ziph

Dead Sea

Arnon R.

MOAB

Beersheba

Arad

EDOM

Zered

Kadesh Barnea

Bozrah

	Israel
	Judah
◉	Regional capital city
●	Cities fortified by Rehoboam

Petra

0   20 mi
0   30 km

and east-west roads connected the city with those who lived on the east side of the Jordan River. Jeroboam's interest in maintaining a strong relationship with tribes east of the Jordan River is illustrated by the building up of Peniel, a site along the secondary road that connected Shechem with the Transjordan (1 Kings 12:25). Shechem had the further advantage of being the city where the people of the north declared their independence from King Rehoboam and David's dynasty (1 Kings 12:16).

The bull calf was a symbol for Baal

But the hardest task Jeroboam faced was controlling his subjects' religious relationship with Jerusalem. Any attempt to disconnect them from the temple there would be a violation of divine law (Deuteronomy 12:1–14). Yet this is exactly what Jeroboam set out to do. His plans take on an unwholesome and desperate tone. "Jeroboam thought to himself, 'The kingdom will now likely revert to the house of David. If these people go up to offer sacrifices at the temple of the LORD in Jerusalem, they will again give their allegiance to their lord, Rehoboam king of Judah'" (1 Kings 12:26–27). His solution to what he saw as a problem involves the cities of Dan and Bethel.

To keep his subjects from worshiping in Jerusalem, Jeroboam invented a hybrid religion of calf worship[3] and built worship facilities with golden calves at Bethel and Dan (1 Kings 12:28–33).[4] These sites had certain practical advantages that advanced Jeroboam's harmful goal. Both are easily accessed by worshipers because they are located along the Ridge Route, the main north-south road that runs through the heart of the Northern Kingdom. Dan is a major city on the International Highway and so serves as a watch station against northern invasion and a place to collect taxes from traveling merchants. This is particularly critical given the rising power and ambitions of Aram, which was due east of Dan. Its companion city, Bethel, just north of Jerusalem, had religious significance even before Jeroboam built a sanctuary there.

It was where Jacob received the vision that likely gave Bethel its name (Genesis 28:10–19). It also had a strategic role in intercepting and redirecting religious pilgrims headed for Jerusalem because travelers from the north would literally travel through Bethel on the Ridge Route en route to the temple in Jerusalem.

Establishing sanctuaries at Dan and Bethel had one more important role to play in affirming the independence of the Northern Kingdom. When the biblical authors speak of the Promised Land, they often describe it as a land that extends from Dan to Beersheba (Judges 20:1; 1 Samuel 3:20). This expression finds frequent mention when the biblical authors define the extent of the kingdom ruled by David and Solomon. During the civil war that followed Saul's death, Abner went to David, promising to deliver a kingdom that extended from Dan to Beersheba (2 Samuel 3:10). David took a census of his kingdom that extended from Dan to Beersheba (2 Samuel 24:2, 15). "During Solomon's lifetime Judah and Israel, from Dan to Beersheba, lived in safety, everyone under their own vine and under their own fig tree" (1 Kings 4:25). "From Dan to Beersheba" celebrated

Jeroboam's calf-cult sanctuary at Dan

the extent, unity, and ideal of a united kingdom, an ideal that did not fit the desires of King Jeroboam. He wanted to end the use of this expression, so he built worship sanctuaries at Dan and Bethel, marking the north-south extent of his kingdom. It was something rulers of the day did to define their political boundaries.[5] He hoped to retire the traditional phrase "from Dan to Beersheba" and replace it with a new slogan more in tune with his aspirations—Israel, the state that extends "from Dan to Bethel."

We do not know how well this slogan worked, but we do know that the biblical authors came to see Bethel and Dan as emblematic of Jeroboam's failure as king. Subsequent kings of the Northern Kingdom are evaluated on the basis of their relationship to these abhorrent sanctuaries, the so-called "sins of Jeroboam." And these kings are censured for continuing in the sinful ways of Jeroboam (e.g., 1 Kings 15:34; 16:2, 19; 22:52; 2 Kings 3:3; 10:29; 13:11; 15:9, 18; 17:22).

Omri and Ahab, the Best and Worst of Times

Israel was teetering on the edge of collapse when Omri came to the throne of the Northern Kingdom. His was the third ruling family in three years. Yet he and his son Ahab established an enduring dynasty that brought a strong economy to Israel. It was again the best of times. But the author of 1 Kings focuses on the negative side of this father-son team, emphasizing

that this best of times was also the worst of times. The geography helps communicate both realities.

The events associated with three locations help to explain why this was the best of times. The first is Phoenicia. Omri built the same kind of economic ties with Phoenicia as David and Solomon had with this seaside country (see map 6.3). Evidence for this is

Map 6.3—Omri and Ahab

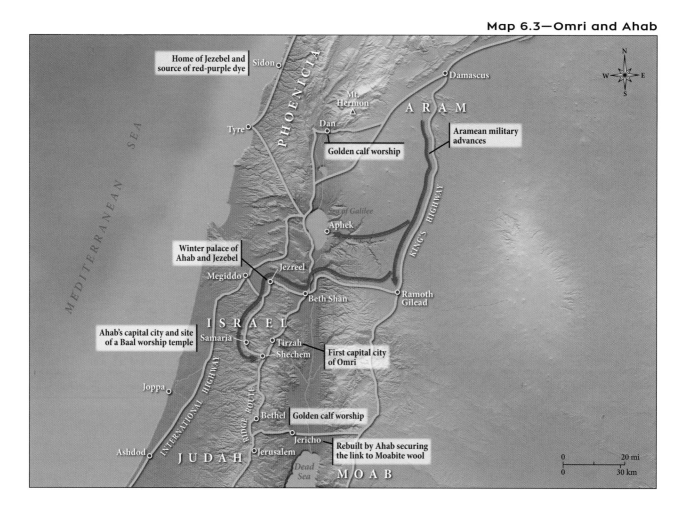

∧ *Ruins of Ahab and Jezebel's palace at Samaria*

found in the marriage of Omri's son Ahab to a Phoenician princess, Jezebel (1 Kings 16:31). This marriage secured an alliance with Phoenicia that allowed Israel to tap into the international markets accessed by the Phoenician trading fleet that touched the shores of Spain and Africa.[6] It also gave Omri and Ahab access to the famous dye industry associated with Phoenician cities like Tyre and Sidon.[7]

The second location is Jericho. When this city was rebuilt (1 Kings 16:34), it opened Israel's access to the King's Highway via a natural route that lay just northeast of the Dead Sea. By employing this gateway, Israel could become a trading partner in connection with the highly pursued aromatics of Arabia as well as the wool of Moab that now would move through Israel en route to the dye facilities in Phoenicia.[8]

The third location is Ramoth Gilead. Ahab would die in battle at this remote location in the Transjordan, but not before confirming the larger economic agenda of Israel we have been painting.

The battle at Ramoth Gilead is the third battle with Aram mentioned by the author of 1 Kings (Samaria, 20:1; Aphek near the Sea of Galilee, 20:26; and Ramoth Gilead, 22:29). The first two battles were initiated by Aram because Omri and Ahab had worked to reroute international trade so that it would bypass Damascus and flow through Israel. The battle at Ramoth Gilead was initiated by Israel to further isolate Damascus by

∨ *Jericho was rebuilt at the time of King Ahab*

∧ *Ramoth Gilead near the King's Highway was the site of battles between Israel and Aram*

16:32). The Lord had put his people on notice with regards to the worship of other gods. There is no command more aggressively and regularly articulated than the one we find in the first commandment. While other deities of the ancient world seemed less distressed by competitors so long as their needs were met, the Lord was not among them. "Do not worship any other god, for the LORD, whose name is Jealous, is a jealous God" (Exodus 34:14). The grand trade connections made by Omri and Ahab gave them the opportunity to share their understanding of this unique God with others, but the flow of influence went in the opposite direction. When Jezebel packed up her Phoenician belongings and moved to Samaria to become the wife of Ahab, she brought along her love for Baal and deeply influenced Ahab's spiritual views. Israel's leadership became so compromised by foreign ideology that Ahab built a temple for Baal in his capital city, a move that essentially recognized Baal as one of, if not the sole, national deity. The paganism of Samaria is characteristic of the leadership of Ahab.

The second city is Jericho, and it too characterizes the stunning abandonment of faith in God (1 Kings 16:34). The rebuilding of Jericho during the time of Ahab helped to accomplish the economic goals of this dynasty. But Jericho had a history that demanded the respect and attention of God's chosen people. Following Jericho's capture and destruction at the time of Joshua, the Lord commanded that this important gateway city to the east remain in ruins as a way of demonstrating trust in the Lord (Joshua 6:26). This command is recalled in 1 Kings 16:34 not just because it explains the death of the builder's sons but because the rebuilding of Jericho becomes emblematic of the careless and reckless manner in which Ahab ran his faith life. So while the time of Omri and Ahab was among the best of Israel's economic times, as far as the biblical authors are concerned, it ranks among the worst of times in light of Israel's spiritual fiascoes.

seizing control of the northern segment of the King's Highway just south of Damascus. The biblical author does not describe the economic plan in detail, but the tantalizing mention of Phoenicia, Jericho, and Ramoth Gilead betrays an economic strategy that provided unprecedented wealth and influence to Israel (note the mention of imported ivory in 1 Kings 22:39). The time of Omri and Ahab had a corner on international trade, making theirs among the best of times.

But the author of 1 Kings emphasizes that these were also the worst of times (16:25–26, 30). The author is much more concerned about the spiritual well-being of this country than its economic strength. Once again two locations help tell the story. The first is Samaria. When Omri became king, he initially ruled from the capital city of Tirzah. That changed in the seventh year of his reign when he purchased the hill of Samaria and established his capital city of Samaria (1 Kings 16:24). This building site had a number of important advantages. As a hill rising some 300 feet (91 m), it offered better natural defenses. It also was a westward-looking place. On a clear day the Mediterranean Sea is visible from Samaria as are all the routes that lead west and north, aptly capturing the trade aspirations of Omri and Ahab, who sought to connect their land to the deepwater ports of Phoenicia. But it is the darker side of this city that gets our attention in 1 Kings.

King Ahab built a temple to Baal in this city (1 Kings

THE DIVIDED KINGDOM • Omri and Ahab, the Best and Worst of Times

Baal Proven a Fraud at Mount Carmel

The construction of a temple for Baal in the Northern Kingdom's capital city of Samaria provided the Canaanite deity Baal with more credibility than was his due. In response, the language of 1 Kings 17–18 becomes a necessary corrective that mocks Baal by describing a sustained famine and a contest between Elijah and the prophets of Baal that took place on the slopes of Mount Carmel.[9]

While there are many manifestations of Baal in the ancient world, the common denominator among them is that this deity is perceived to provide the moisture in the form of rain and dew that people need to survive. The actions of Ahab and Jezebel helped to validate this fraudulent claim. By building a sanctuary for Baal in their capital city of Samaria, they identified Baal as the national deity of the Northern Kingdom (1 Kings 16:32). In addition, this royal couple used royal funds to pay 450 prophets of Baal and 400 prophets of Asherah (the female consort of Baal). This royal sponsorship of Baal sent a powerful message to subjects of the kingdom, leaving them either uncommitted or uncertain about whether the Lord or Baal or both were authentic deities worthy of their worship (1 Kings 18:21).

The actions of Ahab and Jezebel offered Baal so much credibility that two chapters of 1 Kings are used to address it. The author of 1 Kings 17–18 presents both a severe famine and an embarrassing failure on Mount Carmel that dismantle the credibility of Baal. Nothing could be as harmful to the public-relations campaign of Baal as a famine, and this is exactly what the Baal worshipers of the Northern Kingdom get. The Lord sends a multiyear famine on Israel during which neither rain nor dew would fall (1 Kings 17:1). The failure of Baal would quickly become apparent as grain could not be grown, fruit trees would not ripen, pastures would not green, and the water supply did not recharge. The more persistent the famine, the worse the news was for Baal.

In the first verse of 1 Kings 18, we learn that the famine is entering its third year. This is crisis time because of the grain storage strategy of the people. The people ate the previous year's harvest and stored the current year's harvest for consumption the following year. The first year of the famine, much of the reserve would have been eaten. The second year, the remainder of the reserve and any meager harvest from

Statue of Elijah erected on Mount Carmel

A bull sacrifice lay at the heart of Elijah's contest with the prophets of Baal

Map 6.4—Elijah and Elisha

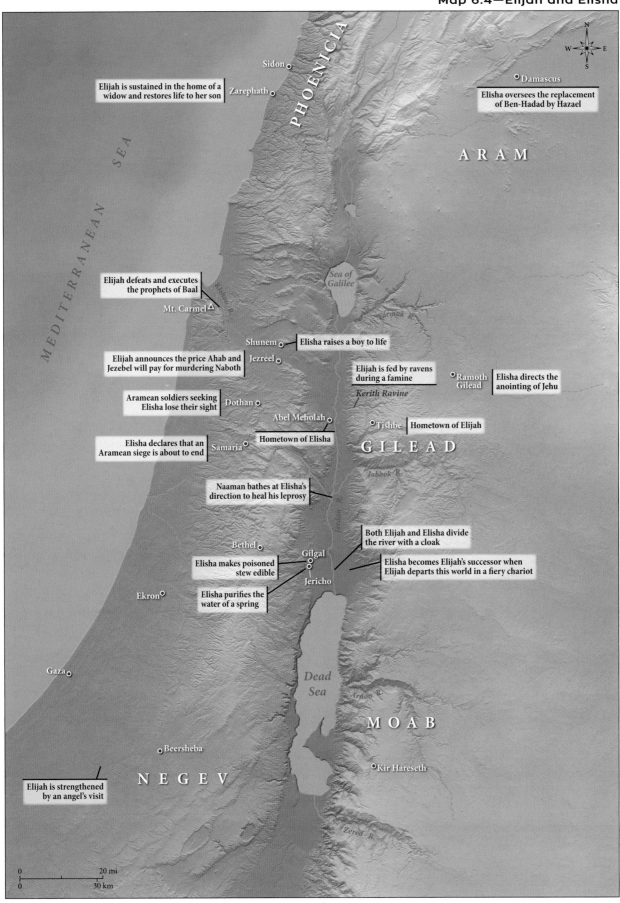

Elijah is sustained in the home of a widow and restores life to her son

Elisha oversees the replacement of Ben-Hadad by Hazael

Sidon

Zarephath

PHOENICIA

Damascus

A R A M

MEDITERRANEAN SEA

Sea of Galilee

Elijah defeats and executes the prophets of Baal

Mt. Carmel

Shunem

Elisha raises a boy to life

Jezreel

Elijah announces the price Ahab and Jezebel will pay for murdering Naboth

Elijah is fed by ravens during a famine

Ramoth Gilead

Elisha directs the anointing of Jehu

Kerith Ravine

Aramean soldiers seeking Elisha lose their sight

Dothan

Abel Meholah

Tishbe

Hometown of Elijah

Hometown of Elisha

G I L E A D

Elisha declares that an Aramean siege is about to end

Samaria

Jabbok R.

Naaman bathes at Elisha's direction to heal his leprosy

Bethel

Both Elijah and Elisha divide the river with a cloak

Gilgal

Elisha makes poisoned stew edible

Jericho

Elisha becomes Elijah's successor when Elijah departs this world in a fiery chariot

Ekron

Elisha purifies the water of a spring

Gaza

Dead Sea

Arnon R.

M O A B

Beersheba

Kir Hareseth

Elijah is strengthened by an angel's visit

N E G E V

Zered R.

0   20 mi
0   30 km

the current year would be eaten. When the famine entered the third year, things would come to full crisis because all grain—apart from what may have been reserved for the new growing season—had been consumed, putting even the royal animals at risk (1 Kings 18:5). People would be questioning the ability of Baal to deliver rain.

Entry into the third year of famine moved Elijah to summon the prophets of Baal to a contest of sorts that would give Baal a chance to redeem himself. The contest required both Elijah and the prophets of Baal to set up a sacrificial altar complete with wood and meat from a bull. The exception to the standard protocol was that no one was to ignite the tinder. Elijah and the prophets of Baal would ask their respective deities to provide the ignition miraculously. And the deity who responded would demonstrate his authenticity.

This contest takes place on Mount Carmel, a detail important enough for the author of 1 Kings 18 to mention three times (18:19–20, 42) (see map 6.4). Mount Carmel was a water-rich place whose green presentation was its defining feature (Song of Songs 7:5; Isaiah 35:2; Jeremiah 50:19; Amos 1:2). The healthy and dense foliage was a product of this mountain's size and location. Mount Carmel is an extended 30-mile (48 km) ridge set on a northwest-southeast line, rising 1,790 feet (546 m) above the Mediterranean Sea just to its west. The prevailing westerly winds bring air brimming with moisture against the flanks of this mountain that force the air masses to rise and cool as they cross this natural barrier. Rain falls and dew settles so that the water totals on Mount Carmel exceed those of the surrounding area by more than 30 percent.[10] For those interested in worshiping a rain deity, Mount Carmel becomes an ideal setting. The Egyptians knew the place as the "Holy Headland." The Assyrians called it "Baal of the Headlands."[11] The author of 1 Kings 18 emphasized the location for this demonstration because it is the one place where we might expect Baal to perform at his peak. Elijah had

∨ *Chapel at Mukhraka, the traditional location of Elijah's contest with the prophets of Baal*

not chosen a neutral site for this contest; he chose a location that offered the Baal prophets home-field advantage.

That makes what follows all the more harmful to the reputation of Baal. The Baal prophets summoned their deity to respond with fire. They danced with increasing intensity around the unlit altar. By noon, Elijah began to taunt them to shout louder because their deity appeared to be asleep or traveling far from Mount Carmel. The prophets began to cut themselves and use their own blood to stimulate Baal's response. But when evening came, the unlit sacrifice mocked

their efforts and their god. The Bible is clear on the fact that there is only one God who controls the rain and dew (Deuteronomy 11:11–15; 28:12, 24). When Elijah finally invokes the name of the Lord, fire descends from heaven, consuming everything—the sacrifice, the wood, the surrounding water that had been poured over the sacrifice, and even the stones. And what was to become of Baal? Baal was completely discredited because if Baal could not perform on Mount Carmel, then Baal had no claim to legitimacy even if Ahab and Jezebel had built him a temple in Samaria.

Translation into Glory and Transition in Leadership— Elijah and Elisha

The time of Elijah's transfer into eternal glory is also the time of Elisha's transition into leadership (2 Kings 2:1–18). The striking image of the chariot of fire rising within the turbulent folds of a whirlwind gets our attention. But what happened on the ground is just as meaningful.

This story, told in a small amount of reading space, unfolds over a long stretch of roadway. We move quickly from Gilgal, to Bethel, to Jericho, to the Jordan River, to the Plains of Moab, and then back to the Jordan River.[12] This route follows the roads that connected the mountainous interior of Samaria and

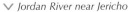
∨ *Jordan River near Jericho*

Judah with the Jordan Valley, eventually linking to the King's Highway on the Transjordan Plateau. But these places in the order they are mentioned ignite a memory. They are among the same places used to describe the entry of the Israelites into the Promised Land at the time of Joshua, but in reverse order (Joshua 1–8).

This has two important implications for the way we understand the story of Elijah and Elisha. The list of places given in this order gets our attention. We have been here before. We have traveled this same route and met the same places at the time of Joshua. This list of places also gives us the impression of movement toward a destination. We are not just strolling with Elijah and Elisha; we are moving in a purposeful way toward a climactic moment. The foreboding sense that something dramatic is about to happen is communicated by the question Elijah's students directed at Elisha both at Bethel and at Jericho. "Do you know that the LORD is going to take your master from you today?" (2 Kings 2:3, 5). It is also communicated by the route they are traveling.

The climactic moment comes after they cross the Jordan River. Elijah and Elisha arrive at the ford opposite Jericho. Rather than wade through the water, Elijah removes his outer cloak and strikes the water with it. When he does, the water divides and the two men cross on dry ground (2 Kings 2:6–8). Once they are on the east side of the Jordan River, Elijah is near the place where his earthly sojourn will end. He was standing on the Plains of Moab below the impressive mountain façade of the Transjordan Plateau when a fiery chariot and horses and a whirlwind combine to carry him into glory (2 Kings 2:11–12). Elisha picked up the cloak dropped by his mentor and walked back to the Jordan River. He struck the water with the garment and crossed the Jordan River on dry ground, repeating the miracle that happened just a short time before (2 Kings 2:13–14).

This combination of place and event ignites another memory. The Lord brought Moses to his eternal rest on Mount Nebo just above the Plains of Moab (Deuteronomy 34:1–6). The Israelites prepared to enter the Promised Land from this plain, and it was on this plain that the transition in leadership from Moses to Joshua took place. Joshua's first task as the new leader of

^ Medeba Map showing Jericho and the Jordan River

God's people was to lead them across the Jordan River opposite Jericho. Two chapters of the book of Joshua are dedicated to the telling of this momentous story. At the Lord's direction, Joshua directed the priests carrying the ark of the covenant to step from the shoreline into the river. As soon as their feet touched the water, the flowing water was cut off and the Israelites were able to cross into the Promised Land on dry ground (Joshua 3:14–17; 4:22–24).

These geographic parallels enhance our reading of 2 Kings 2 in two important ways. First, it appears that the Lord brought Elijah to a place just below Mount Nebo so that his entry into eternity would be geographically linked to that of Moses. Certainly there is already symmetry between the two stories because their end-of-life accounts are different from all the other end-of-life accounts we read in the Old Testament.

The geographic symmetry between them invites us to compare the two more closely. When we do, the second element of symmetry becomes clear. The place of Moses' and Elijah's passing is also the place that marks transition in leadership. Towering figures like Moses and Elijah leave such deep and enduring marks on Bible history that they can be seen as irreplaceable. To build the people's confidence in their successors, the Lord uses specific actions to confirm the authenticity and integrity of these new leaders.

The Lord does this with Joshua by having him lead the people of God through the dry Jordan River bed with a miracle, which in part is designed to confirm him as Moses' successor. "That day the LORD exalted Joshua in the sight of all Israel; they stood in awe of him all the days of his life, just as they stood in awe of Moses" (Joshua 4:14; see also 3:7). Although we do not have parallel language in 2 Kings, it really becomes unnecessary. Just as Joshua succeeded Moses on the Plains of Moab, so Elisha succeeded Elijah. And as Joshua was exalted before the eyes of Israel when the Lord used him to perform a miracle drying up the water of the Jordan River, so Elisha was exalted by doing the same miracle his mentor Elijah had done at exactly the same Jordan River ford opposite Jericho.

Jezreel, Jehu, and Justice

As Elijah's successor, Elisha continued the Lord's work, which included anointing Jehu as the leader who would destroy the Baal-loving dynasty of Ahab and Jezebel. The biblical author names several places that explain Jehu's rise to power, his faithful service, and his failures and the unfortunate consequences. One location is more important than any other in the story of Jehu—the city of Jezreel. This city was linked to a royal crime awaiting justice too long delayed.

The first place of importance to the story of Jehu is Ramoth Gilead. Israel and Aram had been fighting over the city for years. It began when King Omri and his son Ahab tried to control the upper reaches of the King's Highway south of Damascus to divert trade west from Ramoth Gilead toward the Jezreel Valley, bypassing Aram and benefiting Israel (1 Kings 22). Ahab's successor, Joram, was similarly occupied (2 Kings 8:28). During the time Joram was at war

Map 6.5—Jehu's Revolt

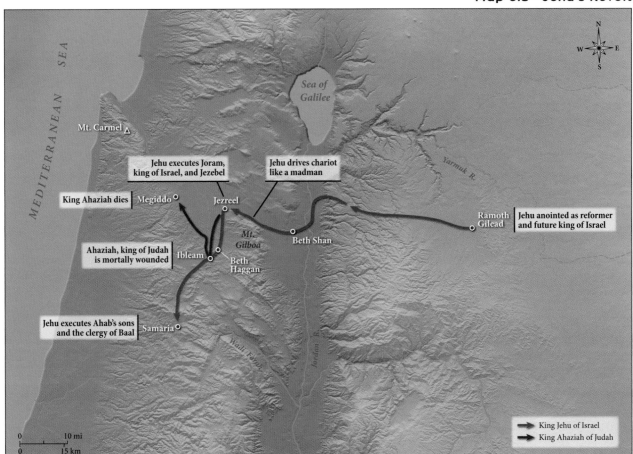

∧ *This view east from the location of the fortress of Jezreel shows how visible Jehu's reckless driving was*

with Aram, the prophet Elisha sent a student from the school of prophets to Ramoth Gilead to anoint Jehu, Joram's commander in the field, as the Northern Kingdom's next king (see map 6.5). The prophet charged Jehu not with continuing the attack on the Arameans but with annihilating Ahab's family and their propensity for Baal worship (2 Kings 9:4–13).

Our attention is next turned to Samaria, the capital of the Northern Kingdom. In this city, Ahab had constructed a temple to Baal, raising Baal worship to an officially sanctioned form of worship in his kingdom. Jehu used a ruse to gather all the prophets and priests and servants of Baal to this temple in Samaria. All were executed and the temple was destroyed. The people used the site as a public toilet (2 Kings 10:18–27).

So far so good for Jehu. But even King Jehu was not fully faithful to the Lord, and the author of 2 Kings turns our eyes to a third location, the homeland of Reuben, Gad, and Manasseh. In summary fashion, we read that all of this land from Aroer on the Arnon River, through Gilead and Bashan was lost to the aggression of the ruler of Aram, King Hazael (2 Kings 10:32–33).[13] These losses had profound implications for the economic well-being and the security of the Northern Kingdom.

Gone was control of the King's Highway, the international north-south trade route of the Transjordan. Jehu's rise to power at Ramoth Gilead and his faithfulness in Samaria stand in sharp contrast to the economic decline his country would know due to the loss of the Transjordan lands, a loss linked to his spiritual failings.

By contrast to the other places mentioned in 2 Kings 9–10, the city of Jezreel is mentioned 14 times in just two chapters. This calls for us to learn why this city would have become so important. Jezreel is located on the east side of the Jezreel Valley where the narrower Harod Valley begins at the base of Mount Gilboa and connects the Jezreel Valley to the Jordan River valley to the east. This city appears to have gained prominence during the time of King Ahab. The 11-acre (4.5-hectare) compound was defended by a dry moat some 20 feet (6 m) deep and 30 feet (9 m) wide, a casemate wall, and a six-chambered gate.[14] Because Jezreel enjoyed a more temperate climate in the winter season than Samaria, it functioned as a winter palace for Ahab (see map 6.3). Its location on the direct route to Aram made it an important staging area for launching campaigns in the direction of Ramoth Gilead.

Jezreel, according to the biblical authors, was a city where justice was missing. King Ahab and Queen Jezebel enjoyed spending time in Jezreel and wanted a vineyard owned by a local citizen named Naboth. The king tried to purchase the vineyard to turn it into a vegetable garden since it was near the palace. Faithful to the Lord's instructions regarding land ownership, Naboth declined the offer. While Ahab sulked over the refusal, Jezebel crafted a plan to have Naboth unfairly accused of a capital crime and executed. Naboth's death was followed by royal seizure of the property (1 Kings 21:1–16).

The Lord promised to deliver justice in response to this heinous act, and Jehu would be the one to dispense it. The fulfillment of no less than three prophecies depended on Jehu taking action in Jezreel. The first is fulfilled when Jehu kills Ahab's son Joram and has the body thrown on the plot of ground that had belonged to Naboth (2 Kings 9:21–26). Elijah

had gone to Ahab to tell him that dogs would lick up the blood of his son on the same ground where they licked up the blood of Naboth (1 Kings 21:19, 29). The second describes the death of Jezebel (1 Kings 21:23). When Jehu rode into Jezreel, Jezebel taunted him from a window. She then was thrown from the window and the horses pulling his chariot trampled her. Again we are reminded that this event had been foretold (2 Kings 9:30–37). The third prophecy may be the most gruesome of the lot. Elijah had promised that the male descendants of Ahab would be "cut off" (1 Kings 21:21, 24). Jehu did just that by ordering the men of Samaria to cut off the heads of Ahab's 70 male relatives and send them to Jezreel. He had those heads put in two piles outside the gates of Jezreel, creating a grizzly memorial (2 Kings 10:7–8). The sins of Ahab and Jezebel at Jezreel had been awaiting justice. That justice was delivered when Jehu came to Jezreel.

Geography and Israel's Spiritual Vulnerability

The uprooting and exile of the Northern Kingdom is an unexpected intrusion in the story line of the Bible. The author of 2 Kings spends the greater part of a chapter delivering a two-tiered explanation of this exile that takes into account both world politics and the spiritual health of Israel. On the political side, the world of the eighth century BC was changing. The imperial aspi-

∨ *Pagan incense altars should have had no place in the Promised Land*

rations of Assyria led to multiple campaigns designed to dominate the Fertile Crescent. During this process, Shalmaneser V invaded Israel and imposed payment of tribute (see map 6.6). When Hoshea, the last king of the Northern Kingdom, withheld payment and joined Egypt in a revolt against Assyria, Shalmaneser responded with yet another invasion and the deportation of Israel's citizens (2 Kings 17:1–6). But this invasion and deportation was about more than the imperial aspirations of Assyria; this disaster was precipitated by the spiritual failure of the Northern Kingdom. "All this took place because the Israelites had sinned against the LORD their God" (2 Kings 17:7). Their sins are the subject of the rest of this chapter with its repeated emphasis on their worship of other deities and adoption of pagan ideology (2 Kings 17:7–23).

Geography played a critical role in the spiritual vulnerability that led to the rapid demise of the Northern Kingdom of Israel. The geography of the Northern Kingdom is distinct from the geography of the Southern Kingdom in a number of ways. While both Israel and Judah lay within the central mountain range, the mountains of Israel in the north are somewhat lower

∧ *The terrain of Samaria opened the Northern Kingdom to foreign markets and ideology*

in elevation with less severely pitched slopes than the mountains of the Southern Kingdom. The valleys of the north are broader and not as deeply cut into the terrain as those in the south. This topography allows the rain-bearing westerly winds to penetrate deeper into the mountain interior, bringing more precipitation to Israel's arable farmland. The wider valleys were easier to farm and allowed for easier access. There was more to sell and easier access to the markets outside Israel because both the International Highway and the King's Highway ran through this kingdom. It also had larger cities and a higher percentage of non-Israelites who continued to live in the northern stretches of the Promised Land.

The Lord had directed that these pagan families and their worship practices be removed from his holy land (Deuteronomy 7:1–6). But when the Israelites failed to drive paganism from their midst at the time of the judges, the Lord resolved to leave these pagan families to test the Israelites' faith (Judges 2:20–23). Unfortunately Israel failed this test repeatedly, allowing their own worship to become so pagan that it was indistinguishable from their Gentile neighbors. This influence was felt all the way to the top (2 Kings 17:8, 21–22). As part of his plan to consolidate his subjects

under his rule, Jeroboam invented a religion with sanctuaries at Bethel and Dan. These sanctuaries and the priests who ran them were designed to draw people away from the Lord and into a new national religion. Even reforming kings like Jehu, who had success in diminishing the worship of Baal, failed to undo the influence of these sanctuaries and the damage they did (2 Kings 10:31).

And it was not just the paganism of those nearby but the paganism of those more distant that intruded as the Northern Kingdom "imitated the nations around them" (2 Kings 17:15). The open topography of the Northern Kingdom eased not only the invasion by foreign armies but the invasion of foreign ideology. The travel-friendly openness of the topography brought trade goods of every kind into the Northern Kingdom. The imported spices, beautiful woods, and ivory carvings were accompanied by foreign ideologies that the residents of the Northern Kingdom adopted. They were repeating their ancestors' failure to trust the Lord (2 Kings 17:14).

The Northern Kingdom had become a place of trade wealth and agricultural surpluses. There was more than a little money to be made by associating with the overland traders who moved through the

Northern Kingdom. While difficult times turn our eyes upward, easier times can cause us to forget the Lord. The geography of the Northern Kingdom helped to create self-sufficient, self-satisfied people who failed to honor the Lord and put their faith in him.

The prophets had been warning the Northern Kingdom to repent of its sins (2 Kings 17:13). And what better place for spiritual correction and restoration to occur than in Jerusalem, home of the

∧ *Imported ivory furniture inlay*

Lord's temple and the priests who taught his Word? But geography again conspired against the people of the Northern Kingdom. Not only was Jerusalem outside the boundaries of their state, it had been the practice of the northern kings to prevent their subjects from going there (1 Kings 12:26–29). So while the geography of the Northern Kingdom cannot be used to excuse the errant behavior of its citizens, it did play a role in increasing their spiritual vulnerability.

Jonah and Nineveh

Jonah was a prophet from the rural village of Gath Hepher (see map 6.7), called to speak on the Lord's behalf (2 Kings 14:25). The messages the prophets of the Old Testament delivered included powerful words of rebuke, encouraging words of comfort, and often revelations of God's purposes behind unfolding events. Jonah conveys his message by writing about his life experiences. His actions and words illustrate his errant thinking. And at the center of it all is Nineveh, a city mentioned twenty-one times in the Old Testament, including nine times in just forty-eight verses of Jonah. There is no missing the author's emphasis on this location and its people. It is the subject of chapter 1 and both the subject and the setting for chapters 3 and 4.

Nineveh was a massive urban complex that at a later date would become the capital of Assyria's empire. During the time of Jonah, it was an Assyrian administrative center by the Tigris River with a population of at least 120,000 (Jonah 4:11), but not the city of 300,000 it would become. By contrast, the population of the Israelite capital city of Samaria was 30,000.

The frequent mention of Nineveh in Jonah is due to the fact that it was

typical of those least likely to benefit from the grace of God delivered through the nation of Israel. It was a Gentile city. It was far away, more than 500 miles (805 km) from Samaria. It had posed a serious threat to the Promised Land and the Israelites. Just before the time of Jonah, Shalmaneser III had conducted a campaign (841 BC) that brought Assyrian soldiers through the Jezreel Valley and onto Mount Carmel, forcing Jehu, the king of Israel, to pay tribute (see map 6.6).[15] A piece of ancient art called the Black Obelisk pictures Jehu bowing to kiss the feet of Shalmaneser III to show the full submission of his country to Assyria.

∨ *Black obelisk showing Jehu of Israel bowing before the Assyrian king Shalmaneser III*

Map 6.6—Assyrian Invasions of the Northern Kingdom

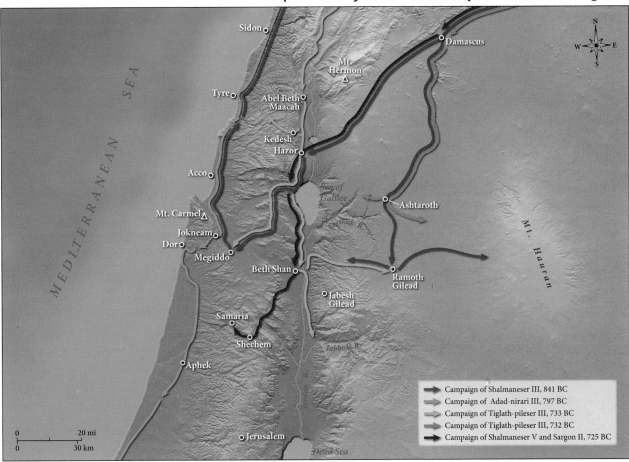

By the time of Jonah and Israel's Jeroboam II in about 760 BC, things had changed. The Assyrian influence in the west had diminished and Israel was enjoying a heady renaissance during which its regional influence extended north as far as it had during the time of Solomon (2 Kings 14:25, 28).[16] The result of diminished Aramean and Assyrian threats was a resurgence of Israelite nationalism.

In this age, there is no passion for delivering special favors to Gentile nations, especially not to Assyria. Jonah is a child of this age. When the Lord calls him to "*Rise* and go to Nineveh" (Jonah 1:2, author's translation), Jonah begins a series of *descents* in elevation that begin with descending in altitude to the seaport city of Joppa and descending into the innermost hold of a ship.[17] A ship was no way to get to Nineveh from the Promised Land, but Nineveh was not where Jonah was headed. He was going to Tarshish, a city that represented the westernmost horizon of shipping in the ancient world.[18] It was where one

went to get away, and that is what Jonah planned to do. When the Lord reversed his course with the aid of a large fish, Jonah ended up in Nineveh. Upon arriving, he performed his duty to minimum standards. Jonah 3:4 may simply represent the theme of Jonah's message, but it suggests that Jonah's message was intentionally terse, harsh, and unlikely to produce a change in his listeners. However, when he spoke, the Holy Spirit changed Gentile hearts. And when that happened, Jonah, God's prophet, threw an angry fit, lamenting the effectiveness of his preaching (Jonah 4:1–3).

How can we make sense of this? Jonah explains why he was upset. "Isn't this what I said, LORD, when I was still at home? That is what I tried to forestall by fleeing to Tarshish. I know that you are a gracious and compassionate God, slow to anger and abounding in love, a God who relents from sending calamity" (Jonah 4:2). This Israelite prophet did not want to see the grace of God turning the hearts of Gentiles, particularly not in

^ *Jonah intended to escape his mission by fleeing on a ship departing from Joppa*

Nineveh. In saying this, he gives voice to a misperception that the book of Jonah addresses. When Abram and his family are designated as the chosen people of God, the Lord states that Gentiles will be included in the legacy of spiritual blessing they will bring (Genesis 12:3). The prophets Elijah and Elisha exemplify that inclusive ministry by aiding Gentiles in their times of distress (1 Kings 17:7–24; 2 Kings 5:1–14). Their acts of kindness and the spiritual conversion of Gentiles—like the widow at Zarephath, Naaman who was healed of leprosy, and the people of Nineveh—are all mentioned by Jesus when he speaks to Jews of his day who persisted in the errant thinking that Gentiles were not part of God's plan of salvation (Matthew 12:40–41; Luke 4:24–27).

The people of Nineveh were among those in Jonah's day who seemed most likely to be condemned. Jonah did not want them to benefit from God's grace. But when the Lord includes them, the message is clear. If the residents of Nineveh are in, then no one of any era, of any nationality, or burdened with any kind of sin is outside God's gracious forgiveness. That is the message of the city of Nineveh in the book of Jonah. This city and its response to Jonah's message illustrate just how pervasive the forgiveness of God is in reaching deep into the darkest corners of all the world.

The Prophets Look East for Hope

The labeling of the cardinal compass points of north, south, east, and west is not an invention associated with GPS, the magnetic compass, or a printed map. The ancients oriented themselves to their world using this language because it is related to the rising and setting of the sun as well as the positioning of the celestial bodies in the night sky. As the prophets of the Old Testament encouraged, directed, and warned the people, they mentioned the cardinal compass directions. What Bible readers will benefit from knowing is that each of these directions has its own set of distinctive meanings. Here we focus on the prophet's use of "east," particularly as it is linked to hope.

East is where God is. The omnipresence of God does not prevent the biblical authors from speaking of God as locally present either "above" the plane of mortal existence or to the "east." This is the most likely explanation for why the Lord's sanctuaries are physically oriented so that the front is facing east (Numbers 3:38; Ezekiel 11:1, 47:1). Ezekiel pays particular attention to this in his vision regarding the movement of the glory of the Lord. Before the Babylonians invaded the city of Jerusalem and destroyed the temple, Ezekiel sees the glory of the Lord rise from the city and move just to the east to what we know today as the Mount of Olives (11:22–23). Upon Israel's return from captivity in Babylon, Ezekiel sees this glory of the Lord return to Jerusalem from the east (mentioned three times in 43:1–4). Thus when the presence of God is envisioned, he is pictured as above the plane of mortals and to the east.

Because east is linked to the presence of God, it is natural that the Messiah would come from the east. The prophets use this compass direction in speaking of both his first and second entry into the realm of mortals. Although Isaiah does not formally use the term "east" in describing the first coming of the Messiah,

each of the geographic indicators he employs turns our attention to the east. In Isaiah 40, we find mention of the "desert" and "wilderness" through which the Messiah will travel to bring the comfort this holy city so desperately needs. The "desert" and "wilderness" lie to the east of Jerusalem. It is from the inhospitable terrain and rugged topography of the Judean Wilderness that the voice of the Messiah's forerunner announces his coming and encourages preparation for his arrival. "In the wilderness prepare the way for the Lord; make straight in the desert a highway for our God. Every valley shall be raised up, every mountain and hill made low; the rough ground shall become level, the rugged places a plain. And the glory of the Lord will be revealed, and all people will see it together" (Isaiah 40:3–5). Because the Messiah will come from the east to save his people, the east becomes the direction of hope. "The sun of righteousness will rise with healing in its rays" (Malachi 4:2; compare Isaiah 60:1).

The second coming of the Messiah is also pictured in the Old Testament as starting in the east. This fact is not stated but strongly implied through the use of geography. Because Edom not only failed to support the Israelites during the difficult days of the Babylonian invasion of the Promised Land but even contributed to the hardships visited on them (Obadiah 1–21), Edom and Bozrah, its capital city, become symbols for all

▽ *Model of the temple at Jerusalem, which faced east*

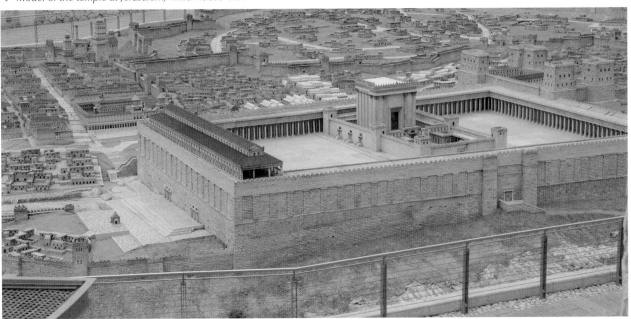

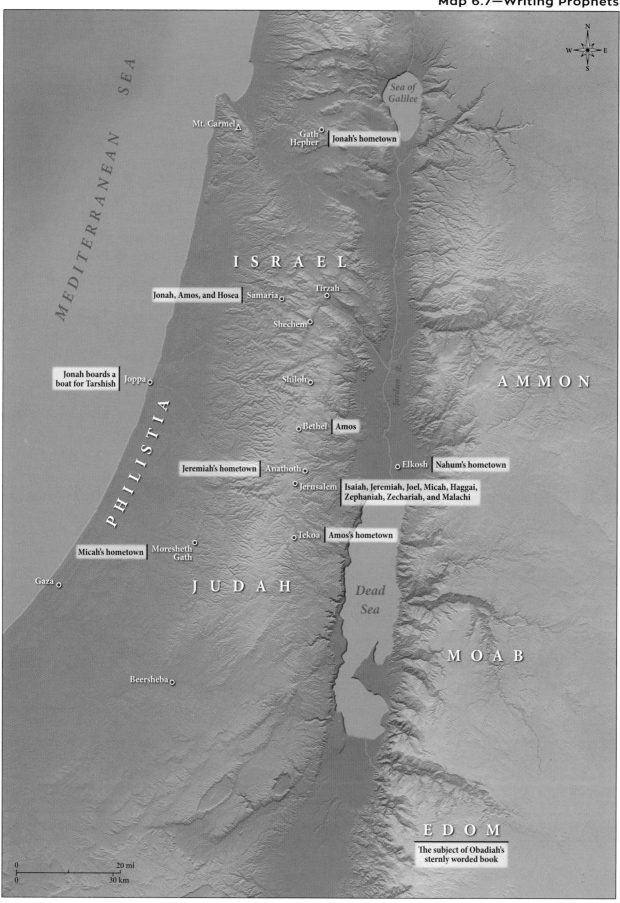

Map 6.7—Writing Prophets

MEDITERRANEAN SEA

Sea of Galilee

Mt. Carmel △

Gath Hepher ○ | Jonah's hometown

I S R A E L

Jonah, Amos, and Hosea | Samaria ○   Tirzah ○

Shechem ○

A M M O N

Shiloh ○

Jonah boards a boat for Tarshish | Joppa ○

P H I L I S T I A

Bethel ○ | Amos

Jeremiah's hometown | Anathoth ○   Elkosh ○ | Nahum's hometown

Jerusalem ○ | Isaiah, Jeremiah, Joel, Micah, Haggai, Zephaniah, Zechariah, and Malachi

Jordan R.

Tekoa ○ | Amos's hometown

Micah's hometown | Moresheth Gath ○

Gaza ○

J U D A H

Dead Sea

M O A B

Beersheba ○

0   20 mi
0   30 km

E D O M

The subject of Obadiah's sternly worded book

∧ *Bozrah, the capital of Edom, lies east of Jerusalem*

the capital cities and nations that chose to oppose the divine agenda. That is how we understand the language in Isaiah's question: "Who is this coming from Edom, from Bozrah, with his garments stained crimson?" (Isaiah 63:1). It is the Messiah directing judgment against nations, starting with those "east" of the Promised Land.

Prophets Joel and Zechariah picture the day of divine judgment occurring within the mountain and valley context of Jerusalem. Joel speaks of the nations gathered for judgment in the Valley of Jehoshaphat (Joel 3:2, 12). The label for this valley aptly fits the nature of the event; Jehoshaphat is Hebrew for "the Lord judges." This is the only place in the Old Testament where the Valley of Jehoshaphat is mentioned, so its identification is challenging. By the fourth century AD, it was identified with the Kidron Valley.[19] This is no doubt related to the fact that Zechariah speaks of the judgment of the second coming in connection with the Mount of Olives, which, like the Kidron Valley, lies just east of Jerusalem (Zechariah 14:4). Thus the Old Testament prophets linked both the first and second coming of the Messiah with the compass heading of east.

This has an impact on how the authors of the New Testament present Jesus' life. Whenever the Gospel writers speak of Jesus' approach to the city of Jerusalem, they mention that he is doing so from the east.[20] This is particularly evident in the reporting of Jesus' last entry into Jerusalem that begins in Jericho and contin-

ues through Bethany and Bethphage en route to the descent from the Mount of Olives, a route that brings him on a sustained journey from the east through the wilderness to Jerusalem. And this also explains why Matthew preserves the quote of Jesus that describes his return to this earth at the end of time. Jesus said, "For as lightning that comes from the east is visible even in the west, so will be the coming of the Son of Man" (Matthew 24:27). The biblical authors use the cardinal compass directions in what they write, and they expect us to be aware of the significance of them. In that regard, we can see that east is linked with the promise of hope.

∨ *Tombs in the Kidron Valley, the Valley of Jehoshaphat, east of Jerusalem*

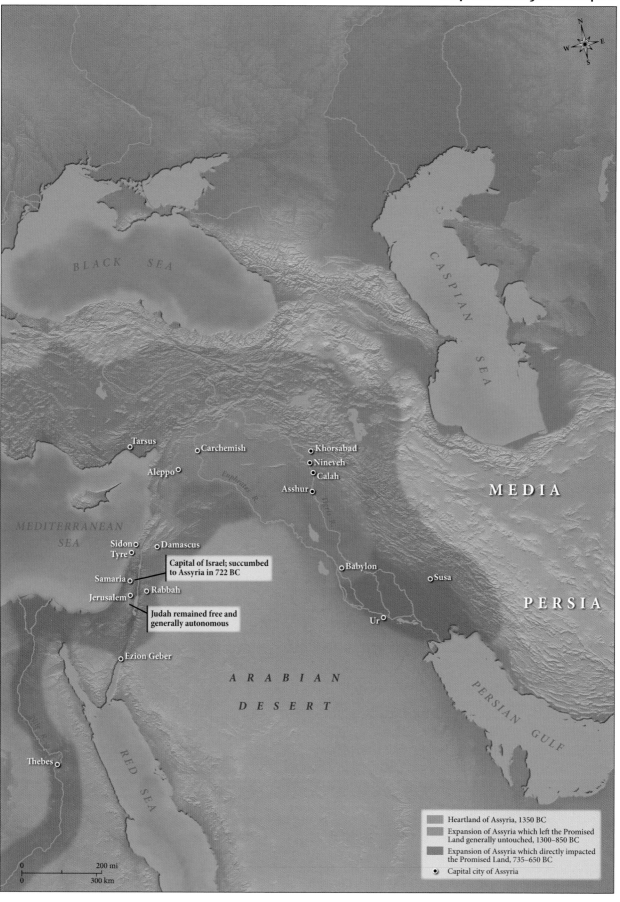

Map 6.8—Assyrian Empire

BLACK SEA

CASPIAN SEA

MEDITERRANEAN SEA

MEDIA

PERSIA

Tarsus

Carchemish

Khorsabad
o Nineveh
o Calah

Aleppo

Asshur

Sidon o
Tyre o

o Damascus

Babylon

o Susa

Samaria o

Capital of Israel; succumbed to Assyria in 722 BC

Jerusalem o

o Rabbah

Judah remained free and generally autonomous

Ur o

Ezion Geber

A R A B I A N

D E S E R T

PERSIAN GULF

Thebes o

RED SEA

	Heartland of Assyria, 1350 BC
	Expansion of Assyria which left the Promised Land generally untouched, 1300–850 BC
	Expansion of Assyria which directly impacted the Promised Land, 735–650 BC
•	Capital city of Assyria

0   200 mi
0   300 km

Map 6.9—Southern Kingdom Conflicts

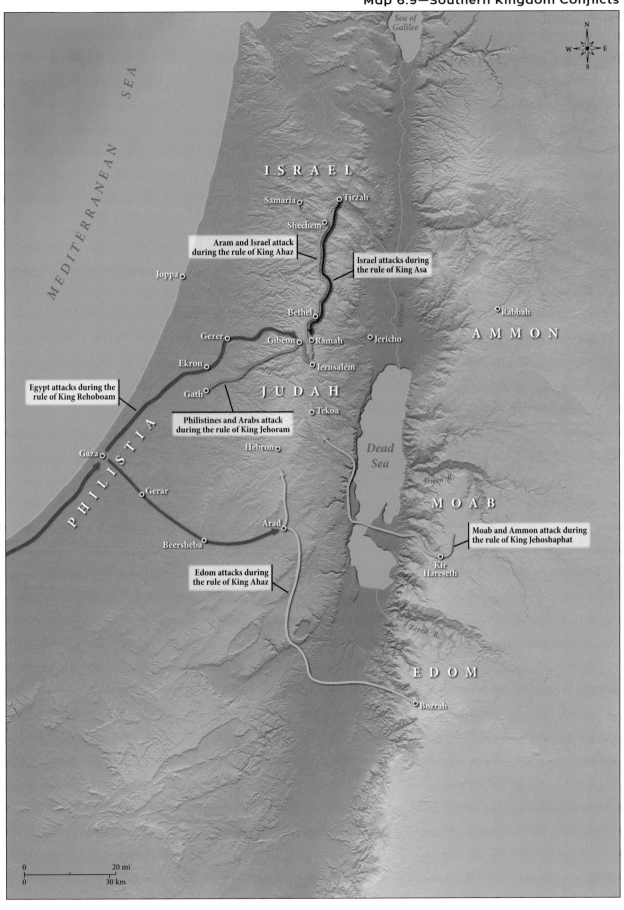

Sea of Galilee

MEDITERRANEAN SEA

ISRAEL

Samaria ○   ○ Tirzah

Shechem ○

Aram and Israel attack during the rule of King Ahaz

Israel attacks during the rule of King Asa

Joppa ○

Bethel ○   ○ Rabbah

AMMON

Gezer ○   Gibeon ○ ○ Ramah   ○ Jericho

Ekron ○   ○ Jerusalem

Egypt attacks during the rule of King Rehoboam

Gath ○   JUDAH

Philistines and Arabs attack during the rule of King Jehoram

○ Tekoa

Dead Sea

PHILISTIA

Hebron ○

Arnon R.

Gaza ○   MOAB

Gerar ○

Moab and Ammon attack during the rule of King Jehoshaphat

Arad ○

Beersheba ○

Kir Hareseth ○

Edom attacks during the rule of King Ahaz

Zered R.

EDOM

○ Bozrah

0   20 mi
0   30 km

Jerusalem and the Assyrian Threat

Assyria's sustained assault on the land of Judah occurred during the reign of King Hezekiah. The Northern Kingdom and its capital, Samaria, had fallen 21 years before (see map 6:6). Hezekiah knew that the religious reforms he championed would be seen as mutiny by the Assyrians, so he planned for the defense of Jerusalem and the safety of its citizens. As the author of 2 Chronicles describes this preparation in chapter 32, we are given fascinating insights into the strategy of Hezekiah as he built walls and water systems. The success of Hezekiah and the enduring lesson he teaches us is found not only in his actions but in his perspective on life. He did what he could and then trusted the One who could do more.

The challenges Hezekiah faced began during the reign of his father, King Ahaz (see map 6:10). Ahaz had suffered the loss of key fortifications in the Shephelah, the foothills just west of the central mountain range (2 Chronicles 28:18). This represented a major security problem for Jerusalem, because the Shephelah was the buffer zone that prevented invasion of Judah's mountain homeland from the coastal plain. Rather than looking to the Lord, Ahaz looked to Assyria to solve this problem and made an alliance with them. This saddled Hezekiah with tribute payments that strained the royal budget and forced the king to maintain pagan worship in the temple itself. Ahaz replaced the Lord's altar with a model of an Assyrian altar and virtually shut down proper worship of the Lord in Jerusalem (2 Kings 16:10–18; 2 Chronicles 28:22–25).

After Hezekiah took possession of the throne in Jerusalem in 715 BC, he did everything he could do to prepare for attack. First he recaptured the Shephelah from the Philistines (2 Kings 18:8). He then established a system of forts along invasion routes that threatened

Map 6.10—Syro-Ephraimite War and Ahaz

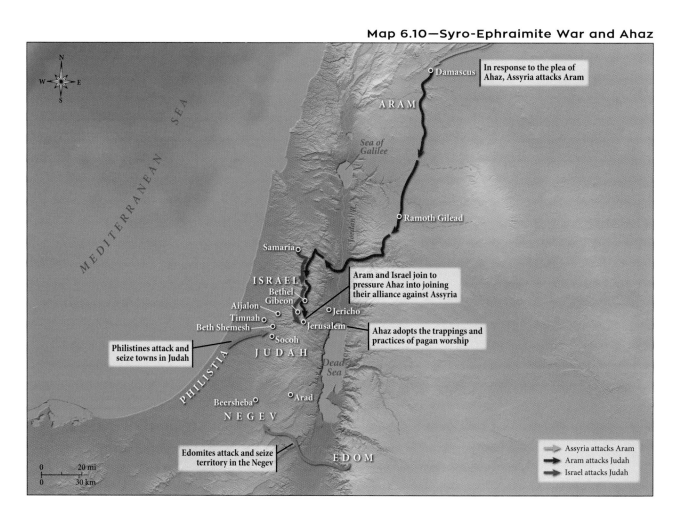

∧ **Left:** *Hezekiah's Tunnel brought much-needed water within Jerusalem's defensive walls;* **Right:** *The Broad Wall shows that Hezekiah expanded Jerusalem onto the Western Hill*

Jerusalem and made sure those forts were stocked with weapons and provisions (2 Kings 18:13).[21]

During this time, he also expanded the city wall and improved the water system (see map 6.12). The last time Jerusalem's defensive walls had received significant attention was during the expansion of the city under King Solomon. Hezekiah knew that this walled city of 32 acres (13 hectares) would be insufficient to protect the citizens of Jerusalem much less the influx of refugees that the Assyrian invasion would bring to the city. Consequently he extended the defensive wall of Jerusalem west beyond the Central Valley so that the Western Hill would be included in the secure city of Jerusalem (2 Chronicles 32:5). The added space became known as the New Quarter or Second District (2 Kings 22:14). This addition dramatically increased the secure zone behind the city walls of Jerusalem from 32 acres to 125 acres (13 to 50.6 hectares).[22]

Water was another issue that required urgent attention. Hezekiah directed the blocking and concealing of all water sources outside the city walls of Jerusalem that might be used by the Assyrians (2 Chronicles 32:3–4). He then directed the excavation of a water

tunnel that would connect the Gihon Spring with an excavated pool, the Siloam Pool, in the Central Valley (2 Kings 20:20; 2 Chronicles 32:30). This would bring water from outside the city walls at the bottom of the Kidron Valley to the Siloam Pool within the new city wall. This required excavation of a tunnel 1,750 feet (533 m) through the solid limestone ridge of the City of David. Because the project's completion was urgent, two excavation teams went to work, one on either side of the ridge, tunneling toward one another until they broke through and water began to flow.[23]

Then Hezekiah waited for an opportune moment. He maintained the tribute payments and kept up appearances of loyalty to Assyria until 705 BC when Sargon II died (see map 6.11). During the transition in the Assyrian monarchy from Sargon to Sennacherib, there was a period of several years during which the new king was distracted with affairs at home. This was just the opportunity Hezekiah needed. He withheld tribute and the revolt began.

Eventually King Hezekiah had reached the limits of what a mortal could do to prepare for the Assyrian arrival. He urged his subjects to trust the One who

Map 6.11—Assyria Invades Judah

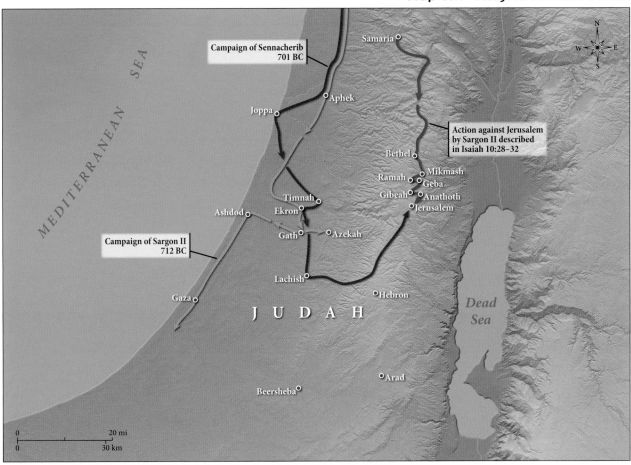

could do more. He had laid the foundation for that trust by repairing the temple and reinstituting orthodox worship (2 Chronicles 29). Hezekiah spoke words of encouragement to those who knew that the arrival of the Assyrians was imminent. "Be strong and courageous. Do not be afraid or discouraged because of the king of Assyria and the vast army with him, for there is a greater power with us than with him. With him is only the arm of flesh, but with us is the LORD our God to help us and to fight our battles" (2 Chronicles 32:7–8).

And that is how Jerusalem and the surviving archaeology from the time of Hezekiah still

∧ *Relief depicting the Assyrian siege of Lachish*

speak to us. We can visit a segment of the extended wall he built and we can walk through the water system he excavated, marveling at the technical skills demanded by such projects. Those public works projects give powerful testimony to the fact that King Hezekiah truly did all that he could to prepare the city. When we are faced by life's circumstances that shake us to the core, this wall and water system remind us to do all that we can. But then what? When we have done all we can, like Hezekiah, there is one more thing we can do, "for there is a greater power with us." Do all you can, and then trust the One who can do more.

Map 6.12—Hezekiah's Jerusalem

N
W • E
S

Mount Moriah

Temple ☐ ☐ Altar

Kidron Valley

Broad Wall

Western Hill

NEW

QUARTER

Over 90 acres added to the walled city by King Hezekiah

Gihon Spring

Mount Zion (Byzantine)

Central Valley

CITY OF DAVID

Hezekiah's Tunnel

Mount of Olives

Siloam Channel

Siloam Pool

King's Pool

King's Garden

Hinnom Valley

En Rogel Spring

0   500 ft
0   150 m

——— Defensive wall of Hezekiah, 8th century BC
——— Wall built by Suleiman, 16th century AD

Josiah's Fatal Choice at Megiddo

Hezekiah's faithful leadership was followed by yet another time of rampant disobedience as Manasseh and Amon, son and grandson of Hezekiah, reversed many of Hezekiah's religious reforms. This deterioration in faithfulness was finally halted when Hezekiah's grandson Josiah came to the throne. Josiah made many honorable choices during his reign as king of Judah, restoring the temple and removing pagan worship sites from the land. But it was an unfortunate choice at the age of 39 that brought Josiah's life to an end; that choice was to intercept and fight the Egyptian army near Megiddo (2 Kings 23:29–30; 2 Chronicles 35:20–24). A look at the historical setting and geographic backstory will sharpen our understanding of Josiah's fatal choice at Megiddo.

The biblical authors occupy most of their accounts with the honorable choices Josiah made. He systematically cleared the country of pagan worship (2 Kings 23:4–20; 2 Chronicles 34:3–7). He repaired the temple in Jerusalem and restored worship of the Lord in that place (2 Kings 22:3–7; 2 Chronicles 34:9–13). When a written copy of God's law was discovered in the temple, he took its message to heart and led his subjects in rededicating the nation to its founding religious principles (2 Kings 23:1–3; 2 Chronicles 34:29–32). And he initiated a celebration of Passover unlike any since the time of Samuel (2 Chronicles 35:1–19). The Lord blessed these positive moves and gave Josiah an opportunity to extend his territorial control and his religious reforms beyond Judah into the lands of Benjamin (including Bethel), Manasseh, Ephraim, and Naphtali (2 Kings 23:8; 2 Chronicles 34:6, 9). Both in terms of its geographic extent and its religious demeanor, the days of King Josiah were looking more and more like the glory days of David and Solomon.

These heady and exciting days in Judah were

Map 6.13—Assyria's Defeat at Carchemish

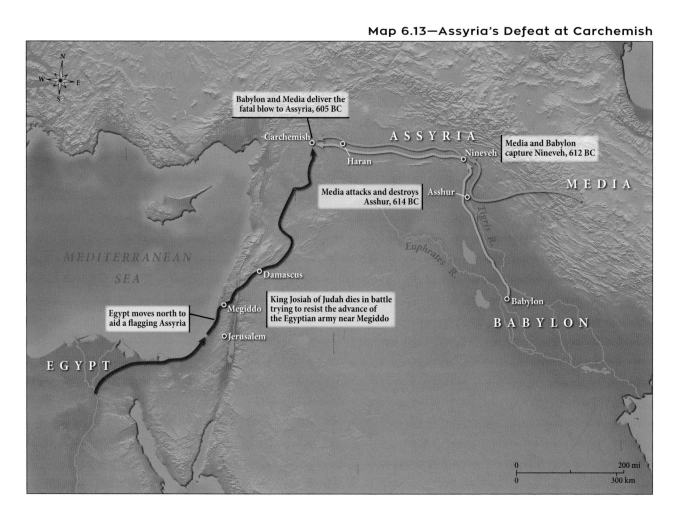

∧ *Carchemish, site of a critical battle involving Babylon, Egypt, and Assyria*

occurring at the same time that profound changes were happening in the power distribution of the larger Fertile Crescent. The mention of Carchemish on the Euphrates River (2 Chronicles 35:20) opens the historic floodgates. The events and participants may best be summarized with timeline and map in hand. Assyria had risen to the top of the pyramid, having conquered the lands from the Persian Gulf to Egypt. However their conquests had exceeded the amount of territory they could effectively rule. By 626 BC, Nabopolassar the Chaldean had taken Babylon from Assyria. In 614 BC, the Medes took Asshur, the old religious capital of Assyria. In 612 BC, a combined force of Medes and Babylonians seized the Assyrian political capital of Nineveh, forcing the army to flee to the west end of the Fertile Crescent in the direction of Carchemish. And that is where Pharaoh Neco II was headed in 609 BC. His Egyptian army would join the flagging Assyrian forces to push back against Babylonian forces. Apparently his goal was to preserve the stalemate in the northern and eastern portions of the Fertile Crescent so that he could impose Egyptian dominance on its west side.

This brings us to Josiah's fatal choice. The urgency of Neco's mission led him to take the quickest route toward Carchemish. This meant he headed north on the International Highway along the Coastal Plain of the Promised Land, through the pass west of Megiddo, and onto the Jezreel Valley (see map 6.13). Josiah decided to impose himself in these larger affairs of the Fertile Crescent. And despite Neco's pleading that his fight was not with Israel and that Israel's God had sponsored his mission (2 Chronicles 35:21), Josiah decided to intercept and fight the Egyptians at Megiddo.

An awareness of the historical setting and geography illuminate this ill-fated decision. Josiah knew the Egyptians were on their way to aid Assyria. Because of the recent history between Assyria and God's people, Josiah did not feel kindly disposed toward them.

∧ *Egyptian Pharaoh Necho II with goddess Hathor*

And his recent territorial expansions would be at risk if the balance of power changed in the region to favor Egypt.[24] But dare he proceed with this plan after Neco's declaration that he was on a divine mission?

The geography proved too tempting for Josiah. There were two places where the larger Egyptian army would have an advantage over the more modest forces of Josiah: on the level Coastal Plain and in the Jezreel Valley. Josiah chose to take on the Egyptian army at Megiddo because it was the one place where geography gave him an advantage. As the International Highway moved between the Coastal Plain and Jezreel Valley, it coursed through Mount Carmel via narrow passes. The narrowest pass into the Jezreel Valley lay just west of Megiddo. If Josiah positioned his army at this location, then the Israelites would have to fight only a small number of Egyptian soldiers at one time.

But it is likely that more than the narrowness of the pass gave Josiah confidence. The biblical authors show that Josiah brought a strong religious passion and perspective to all he did. That made Megiddo appealing in yet another way. From Megiddo, we can see many of the locations where the Lord provided victory in improbable circumstances. For example, he gave Deborah and Barak victory over Canaanite chariots on the eastern side of the Jezreel Valley. He gave Gideon victory over the Midianites in virtually the same spot. He gave Elijah victory over the prophets of Baal on Mount Carmel. And he gave Elisha the ability to raise a boy from the dead at Shunem. The Megiddo vicinity had witnessed some of the most stunning acts of divine intervention in the lives of mortals. Josiah positioned himself for what he believed would be the next in a string of improbable victories. But faith is doing more than what we think God wants; it is doing what he clearly has told us to do. Admittedly the Egyptian pharaoh is an unlikely messenger of God (2 Chronicles 35:21). Nevertheless, God had spoken. And no matter how Josiah might have felt about Egypt aiding Assyria, he was to stand down. It is this failure to honor God's plan that led Josiah to make a choice that proved fatal for him at Megiddo.[25]

∨ *King Josiah died in battle near Megiddo*

Jerusalem in Ruin

Josiah was the last of Judah's kings who cared about the spiritual health of the nation. Israel's failure to heed the prophets' warnings and its failure to sustain Josiah's reforms brought about a stunning divine judgment. The Lord exiled his people from the Promised Land and used Babylonian soldiers to destroy Jerusalem completely. Authors of the Bible are justifiably proud of the city of Jerusalem. Their writing is rich with details on the nature of the city's most prominent public buildings (1 Kings 5–7). With Jerusalem in ruins, we might expect them to go silent, hiding our eyes from the harm that has come to their beloved

Zion. But that is not the case. The inspired poet of Lamentations urges us to step in for a closer look. "Is it nothing to you, all you who pass by? Look around and see" (Lamentations 1:12). The Babylonian destruction of Judah's capital made it almost unrecognizable, a sentiment captured in the cruel question of the scoffer: "Is this the city that was called the perfection of beauty, the joy of the whole earth?" (Lamentations 2:15). Just when we are inclined to avert our eyes, the Lord calls for us to get a good look at the ruins because they have an important lesson to teach.

The destruction of Jerusalem came about 19 years after the Babylonian general Nebuchadnezzar defeated a coalition of Egyptian and Assyrian soldiers at Carchemish. His vision was to create an empire that stretched from one end of the Fertile Crescent to the other. En route to finishing off any further trouble from Egypt, he stopped in Judah and forced King Jehoiakim to pledge his allegiance to Babylon and agree to pay annual tribute (2 Kings 24:1; Jeremiah 25:1). This was a difficult decision, but there is nothing to suggest that the city of Jerusalem endured any physical harm. Within a few years, a rebellion by Jehoiakim and Jehoiachin brought Nebuchadnezzar back to the city, placing it under siege for three months (2 Kings

∧ *The Babylonian Chronicle mentions Nebuchadnezzar's capture of Jerusalem*

Map 6.14—Babylon Invades Judah

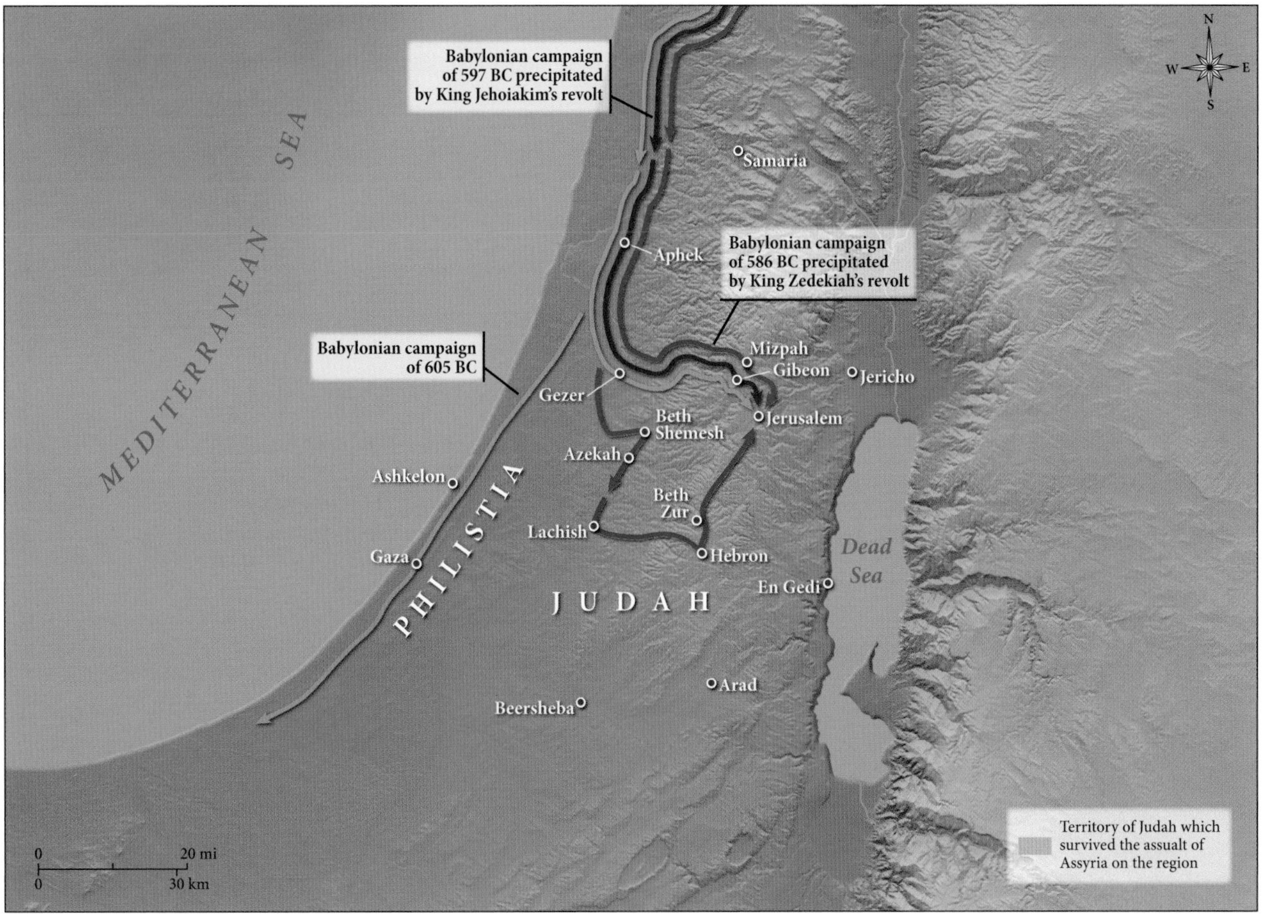

Babylonian campaign of 597 BC precipitated by King Jehoiakim's revolt

Babylonian campaign of 586 BC precipitated by King Zedekiah's revolt

Babylonian campaign of 605 BC

MEDITERRANEAN SEA

Samaria

Aphek

Gezer

Mizpah
Gibeon   Jericho

Beth Shemesh   Jerusalem

Azekah

Ashkelon

PHILISTIA

Beth Zur

Lachish

Gaza

Hebron   En Gedi   Dead Sea

JUDAH

Arad

Beersheba

0   20 mi
0   30 km

Territory of Judah which survived the assault of Assyria on the region

^ *Quarried blocks of hard limestone were vulnerable to destruction by fire*

24:10–11). Again no specific damage to the city is mentioned, although Jehoiakin (son of Jehoiakim) was taken as a prisoner to Babylon and the public buildings were looted. Nebuchadnezzar put Jehoiakin's uncle Zedekiah on the throne as a puppet ruler and went on his way. By 587 BC, Zedekiah followed a familiar script in Israel's history. Trusting that Egypt would come to his aid, he rebelled against Babylon. Once again the Babylonians entered Judah and put Jerusalem under a siege that lasted for 18 months during the years 587–586 BC (see map 6.14). The Egyptian army did come to the aid of Judah but was successful in creating only a small window of relief before the siege resumed (Jeremiah 37:5–8). In the end, food in the city gave out and the Babylonians breeched the walls (2 Kings 24:20–25:7). This time Jerusalem's public buildings and walls did not survive.

The Babylonians directed their destructive energy at the temple, the royal administration buildings, homes of high public officials, defensive towers, and the city's encircling defensive wall (2 Kings 25:9–10; Lamentations 2:2, 5–7). Fire appears to have been their tool of choice, mentioned repeatedly by the biblical authors. While there was some organic material in all of these structures, they were composed primarily of limestone. The limestone used to construct the public buildings and defensive walls of Jerusalem is a durable building material, impervious to the erosion of wind or rain. But it has a weakness. Moisture can penetrate its porous structure, and when a fire is built against these stones, the moisture inside them turns to steam. As the steam aggressively expands, the pressure built up within the stone can literally cause it to burst. Fire creates a dramatic and permanent way of ruining both the building and the building stone.

The Babylonians wanted people to look at the ruined buildings for a variety of reasons. The destruc-

^ *Foundations of Jerusalem homes destroyed in 586 BC*

tion of the citadels and the defensive walls of the city ruined its ability to defend those who lived there. The shattered stones gave testimony to the power of the Babylonian war machine. The destruction of the public buildings sent another message. A country's public buildings become a symbol of a nation's political autonomy. Think of the message sent by a building like the White House, Buckingham Palace, or the Kremlin. The eradication of such a symbol is equivalent to the eradication of the state it served. Judah lost its identity as a nation when its architectural identity was removed. Rather than a thriving state, Judah had become little more than a large estate attached to the nation of Babylon. A few workers were left in place to manage the flocks and tend the agricultural fields, but they did so to benefit the well-being of Babylon.[26] And the Babylonians' destruction of the temple in Jerusalem more than any other destruction challenged the Israelites' beliefs about the Lord. The Israelites were forced into exile knowing their temple had been destroyed. They could not ignore the message about their God sent by Babylon's ravaging of the temple.

Were the deities of Babylon actually more real and more powerful than the Lord?[27]

The reason the Babylonians wanted people to look at the ruins of Jerusalem were different from why the Lord wanted people to look at them. For the Lord, the ruins were not a symbol of divine weakness, but a symbol of the reliability of the Lord's words, spoken shortly after the temple in Jerusalem was dedicated. The Lord had said the future of the building was linked to the behavior of those who worshiped there. If they persisted in worshiping other gods, "then I will cut off Israel from the land I have given them and will reject this temple I have consecrated for my Name. Israel will then become a byword and an object of ridicule among all peoples. This temple will become a heap of rubble. All who pass by will be appalled and will scoff and say, 'Why has the LORD done such a thing to this land and to this temple?'" (1 Kings 9:7–8).

"Look around and see," the poet wrote after the destruction. "Is it nothing to you, all you who pass by?" (Lamentations 1:12). A ruined Jerusalem was a call to repentance.

﹀ *Homes destroyed by Babylon in Jerusalem in 586 BC*

⌃ *The austere Edomite highlands lie above and east of the Dead Sea*

Chapter 7

EXILE AND RETURN

The Remnant Flees to Egypt

King Josiah proved to be the last hope for Jerusalem and Judah. The kings that followed pursued a spiritual and political course that assured divine judgment. It came like a tempest in 586 BC when the Babylonians ransacked Jerusalem and took most of its remaining citizens to Babylon (2 Kings 25:1–21). The poet of Lamentations captures the grief and horror of Jerusalem's empty, smoldering streets with thought-provoking questions: "Is any suffering like my suffering that was inflicted on me, that the LORD brought on me in the day of his fierce anger?" (Lamentations 1:12). The one ray of hope in this sorry scene shines on a small group of impoverished Israelites the Babylonians left behind (Jeremiah 40:7; 42:19). But this hope that God's plan of salvation will survive among them is extinguished when they flee to Egypt.

From 2 Kings and Jeremiah, we learn the details of the remnant's retreat (see map 7.1). The Babylonian destruction of Jerusalem and the exile or death of the leaders created a leadership vacuum that needed to be filled. Babylon appointed a Jewish governor, Gedaliah, who ruled from Mizpah. Gedaliah assured his small band of Jewish subjects that things would go well for them if they would simply settle in, harvest their food, and serve the king of Babylon (2 Kings 25:22–24). This arrangement lasted a few scant months before Ishmael, a Jewish descendant of David who had political

Map 7.1—Jeremiah Taken to Egypt

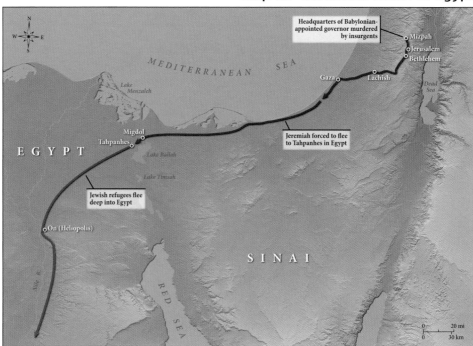

aspirations of his own, assassinated Gedaliah and killed the men of Judah and the Babylonians who were with him at Mizpah (2 Kings 25:25; Jeremiah 41:1–3). Johanan, a Jewish general who believed it was best to allow Gedaliah to be governor, had warned of this assassination attempt. After it was done, he raced after Ishmael to capture him and fix the problem with Babylon. But Ishmael escaped, leaving Johanan and the rest of the Jewish remnant to face the Babylonian response (Jeremiah 41:11–15).

Johanan and the remnant of Jews thought seriously about putting distance between themselves and the Babylonian army. They needed a safe place to flee that could be reached in a reasonable amount of time, a place with a reliable supply of food and water among a people who were opposed to the Babylonian expansion that had swallowed up the Promised Land. Only one place met these criteria—Egypt.[1] And in time, the Jewish remnant fled deep into the core of Egypt, traveling as far as Migdol, Memphis, Pathros, and Elephantine (Jeremiah 44:1). The prophet Jeremiah was compelled to travel with a contingent of the Jewish refugees who established themselves at Tahpanhes in the eastern part of the Nile River delta (Jeremiah 43:4–7).[2]

When Jeremiah presents this event in which he is a key player, he makes sure we see it as a grave violation of God's plan that extinguishes the hope that had lingered while the Jewish remnant remained in the Promised Land. While the flight to Egypt appears to be a reasonable response, it is in fact an egregious act of disobedience. Jeremiah communicates that fact to Johanan and the others when they approach him seeking divine direction following the escape of the assassin, Ishmael. They pledged to obey whatever God would say to them, no matter how favorable or unfavorable it appeared at the human level (Jeremiah 42:1–6). Jeremiah told them to remain in the Promised Land and said the Lord would soften the Babylonian response to Gedaliah's assassination so they would

∨ *With Jerusalem in ruins, many Israelites left for Egypt*

∧ A large community of Jews settled on Elephantine Island in Egypt

receive Babylonian compassion rather than revenge (Jeremiah 42:9–12).

What follows is one of the most emphatic geographic directives we read in the entire Bible. Jeremiah repeats the word "Egypt" six times in six verses in dismissing the flight to Egypt for refuge (Jeremiah 42:14–19). The pounding repetition and clear language leave no room for misunderstanding or uncertainty regarding this dimension of divine instruction. This confirms our hope in the remnant of Jews right up to the moment they ignore God's instructions. They first seek to discredit the message of Jeremiah and then boldly set out for Egypt, apparently forcing Jeremiah to go with them (Jeremiah 43:2–7).

This hope-robbing decision stands on its own but is further amplified in two ways. It reverses one of the great national moments of Israel's past and links the Jewish remnant with the rebels in the wilderness. The Israelite exodus from Egypt remains a stellar landmark in the history of Israel. It is frequently mentioned by the biblical authors and is commemorated by an annual festival, the Passover, designed to keep the memory of the exodus alive. A return to Egypt was like turning back the clock and reversing one of the great national moments of God's people. This demand to return to Egypt makes those advocating it sound like the rebels in the wilderness during the day of Moses. Their question from old becomes the one advanced by the remnant: "Wouldn't it be better for us to go back to Egypt?" (Numbers 14:3; see also Exodus 16:3; 17:3; Numbers 11:5, 20:5; 21:5). Thus the hope that the Jewish remnant left by the Babylonians might be the bridge to the coming of the Messiah is extinguished in the Promised Land.

Map 7.2—Babylonian Empire

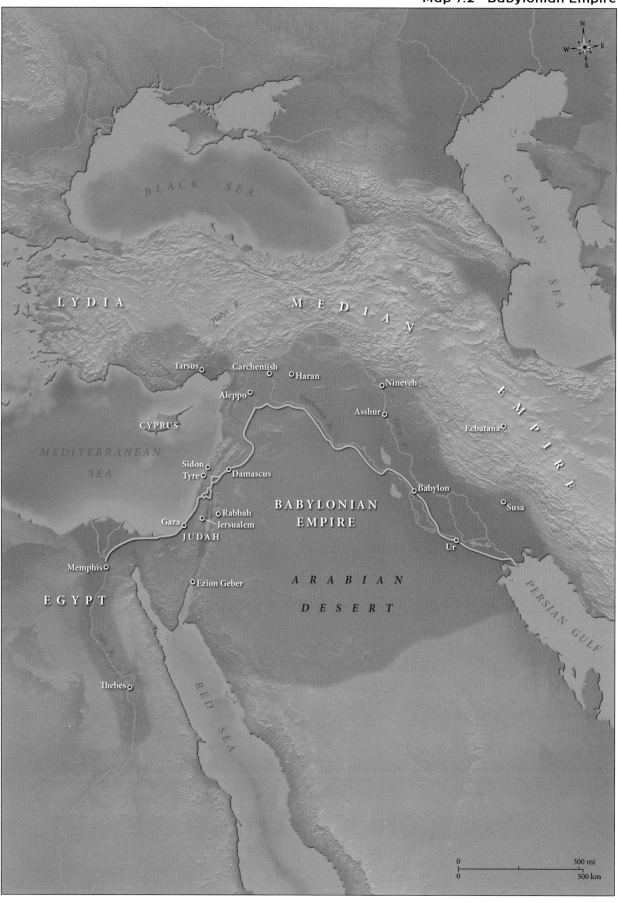

△ Lion from Babylon's Processional Way

△ Replica of the Ishtar Gate of Babylon

Obadiah and the Edomites

Where we live plays a role in how we live and how we think about ourselves. Knowing this helps us to understand who the Edomites were and why Obadiah includes so much geography in describing their character and their failures.[3] The heartland of Edom stretches from the Zered River southward for 75 miles (121 km) down the plateau that provides a scant 15-mile-wide (24-km-wide) living space. To the east of the plateau is forbidding desert, and to the west is the dramatic drop from Edom's mountains of more than 5,000 feet (1,524 m) into the valley of the Arabah. From the perspective of those traveling the valley, craning their necks upward, the Edomites did seem like a people nesting with the eagles (Jeremiah 49:16). The northern and western portions of the Edomite homeland received just enough precipitation to plant grain and pasture animals. But these were not the mainstays of Edomite life. The geography that limited the viable living space also narrowed the travel options for international traders. Merchants who used the King's Highway on the plateau or those who traveled in the Arabah Valley below had to pass through land con-

trolled by Edomites. Cargo loads of aromatics, gold, and other exotic goods of southern Arabia and eastern Africa became a resource the Edomites could exploit through taxation of those goods.

The geography of Edom encouraged in Edomites a frontier-like independence, brimming with overconfidence.[4] In an era when soldiers did without mechanized travel and gunpowder, the high ground was a

∨ "Though you soar like the eagle and make your nest among the stars, from there I will bring you down," declares the Lord (Obadiah 4)

Map 7.3—Edom's Incursions

powerful Edomite ally that hampered invasion by enemy soldiers forced to fight while climbing rock walls. The geographic security the Edomites enjoyed led to an overconfidence that Obadiah sharply criticized: "'The pride of your heart has deceived you, you who live in the clefts of the rocks and make your home on the heights, you who say to yourself, "Who can bring me down to the ground?" Though you soar like the

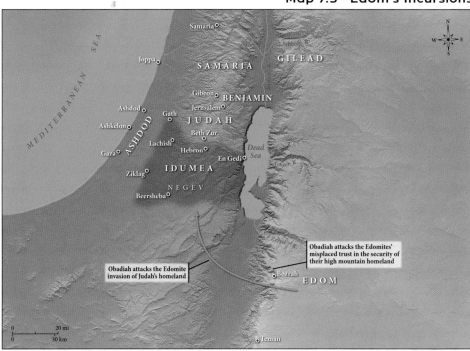

eagle and make your nest among the stars, from there I will bring you down,' declares the Lᴏʀᴅ" (Obadiah 3–4).

The high-handed pride of Edom led them to commit a variety of sins, each of which will become clearer in light of the special relationship Edom was to have with Israel. While the Edomites were not descendants of Jacob, they were family. The Edomites were

The Negev of Israel became part of Idumea

descendants of Jacob's brother Esau (Genesis 25:24–26; 36:8).[5] Like the Israelites, the Edomites received a land grant that was not to be violated (Deuteronomy 2:2–6). Although the Edomites did not have primary responsibility for bringing the Messiah into the world, they were to foster the well-being of Israel and, in a supporting role, facilitate the advance of God's plan of salvation.

It is this understanding of Edom's unique status and responsibility that makes their attitude and actions so heinous. When the Lord allowed the Babylonians to invade the Promised Land and even destroy the city of Jerusalem, the Lord expected Edomites to offer compassion and support. Instead Edom adopted a hostile attitude toward beleaguered Israel and looked for ways to take advantage of its misfortune. They "stood aloof" as family members lost their personal belongings to plunderers. They gloated over Israel's misfortune and celebrated the destruction of Jerusalem. They even participated in the looting themselves, harassed fugitives attempting to flee, and handed some of the survivors over to the enemy (Obadiah 11–14).

After the Babylonian invasion of the Promised Land, the Edomites fashioned an invasion of their own. Remember that these relatives of the Israelites were to respect the land grant given to Israel. But seeing an opportunity to expand their commercial reach to the road system that extended from Bozrah, through the Negev, and on to the Mediterranean seaport of Gaza, the Edomites took possession of the southern portion of the Promised Land. They appear to have remained in this area well into the Hellenistic (Greek) era (332–165 BC), when the southern extent of the Promised Land was called Idumea.[6]

The book of Obadiah not only censures the Edomites for these sins but also announces divine judgment against these pride-filled highlanders. The coming "day of the LORD" (Obadiah 15) would be felt by all nations who opposed the advance of God's kingdom, especially Edom. We note in particular the geographic reversals that go along with this divine justice. Although Edomites invaded and occupied the lowlands of the Negev, things would be reversed. "People from the Negev will occupy the mountains of Esau" (Obadiah 19). These "people from the Negev" are Israelites who had been exiled by the Babylonians. "The exiles from Jerusalem . . . will possess the towns of the Negev" (Obadiah 20). The holy mountain of Zion on which the Edomites caroused would again be occupied by descendants of Jacob who "will go up on Mount Zion to govern the mountains of Esau" (Obadiah 21). Thus the mountain-dwelling Edomites who came down to occupy the Negev would be driven back up into the mountains, there to be ruled by the lowlanders whose misfortunes the Edomites had enjoyed.

Ezra Describes the Return from Exile

The prophets had warned the people of Judah that their worship of pagan deities had made them a target of divine judgment. That judgment fell quickly and unmistakably when the Babylonian Empire invaded the Promised Land, destroyed the temple in Jerusalem, and forced the exile of many citizens of Judah. The last two, destruction of the temple and the exile, created a theological crisis. If we understand the extreme theological crisis the exile introduced, we will better understand the way Ezra describes the return from exile in the first two chapters of his book.

When the Babylonians forced Judah's citizens to leave their homes, we can only imagine the anguish Israelite families must have felt as they caught a last look at their homes, farm fields, and all that was familiar. Only uncertainty lay ahead in a land five-months travel away from all they had known as normal. Walking time became reflection time. *Will we ever see our homes again? What is to become of us as a nation? Will God forgive us for the grave sins we have committed?*

This is more than a personal crisis for those in exile; it becomes a theological crisis of worldwide proportions when we recall how God's plan to redeem the world from sin was bound to his chosen people being in the Promised Land. Ever since Genesis 12:1–3, Bible readers had expected that the key figure in the plan of salvation, the Messiah, would be Jewish and would be born in the Promised Land. No single event in our Bible reading creates such a threat to God's promise of forgiveness as the exile of Israel from the Promised Land. It makes us look for any word from God that addresses a return of the exiles and an end to the horrible circumstances they endured.

∨ *An Assyrian relief depicting the misfortune of exile*

The first two chapters of Ezra address both why there was a return to the Holy Land and who returned. Ezra makes it clear that the return is the result of Cyrus the Great who, after defeating the Babylonians, established Persian dominance across the Fertile Crescent that lasted from 539–332 BC. He immediately enacted a policy toward those displaced by the Babylonians that looks completely different from the policies of Babylon and Assyria. These two nations did all they could to break down former national and religious identification to create a new homogenized culture. Persian policy was the opposite. It recognized the ethnic, cultural, and religious diversity of those who had been conquered. Cyrus encouraged the exiles of many nations to move back to their homelands and reestablish their national culture and religious practices.[7] Ezra records the proclamation given by Cyrus that clears the way for Israel's return to the Promised Land and authorizes reconstruction of the temple in Jerusalem (Ezra 1:2–4) (see map 7.4).

But before we read this proclamation, Ezra is careful to let us know that there is more going on here, for the Lord is at work fulfilling the promise he made to the displaced Israelites through the prophet Jeremiah. He had told them that their time in exile would be for 70 years (Jeremiah 25:11–12). Then the Lord himself would bring the people of the promise back to the Promised Land (Jeremiah 27:22; 29:10). Ezra affirms

⌄ *The Cyrus Cylinder that mentions Persia's policy of returning exiles to their homeland*

Map 7.4—Exile and Return

the Lord's role in fulfilling that promise by starting his account this way: "In the first year of Cyrus king of Persia, in order to fulfill the word of the LORD spoken by Jeremiah, the LORD moved the heart of Cyrus king of Persia to make a proclamation throughout his realm and also to put it in writing" (Ezra 1:1).

Ezra then moves from the question of why the return happened to the question of who was going back. He identifies nearly 50,000 people who will be part of this first return from exile, some by clan name, some by the role they will play in the new temple, and others by the village to which they will return (Ezra 2:1–61). The group mentioned in Ezra 2:21–35 helps us draw a map of resettled Judah.

The Persians, in setting up the administration of and tax collection in their new empire, divided it into larger satrapies and smaller provinces. The province of Yehud (Judah) in the satrapy of "Beyond the River" ("Trans-Euphrates" in NIV) is defined in part by the village list in Ezra 2:21–35, enhanced by the list in Nehemiah 3:1–22, and confirmed by the archaeology of this period.[8] This allows us to draw a map of post-exilic Judah that is strikingly smaller than the pre-exile kingdom (see map 7.5).

The organization of Ezra's list of villages also provides an important theological gem that is easily missed. Ezra's list is chiefly comprised of villages north of Jerusalem in the older tribal territory of Benjamin. Only the first two villages are in Judah, and the first one mentioned is Bethlehem.[9] While the list of villages does not give us a clear picture of Yehud's southern border, it emphasizes the area and village that Micah 5:2 names in regards to the coming of the Messiah. "But you, Bethlehem Ephrathah, though you are small among the clans of Judah, out of you will come for me one who will be ruler over Israel, whose origins are from of old, from ancient times." Thus Ezra organizes the village list to call our attention to the most important village in Judah. If there was one place exiles from Judah had to get back to, this was it!

Map 7.5—Restored Province of Judah

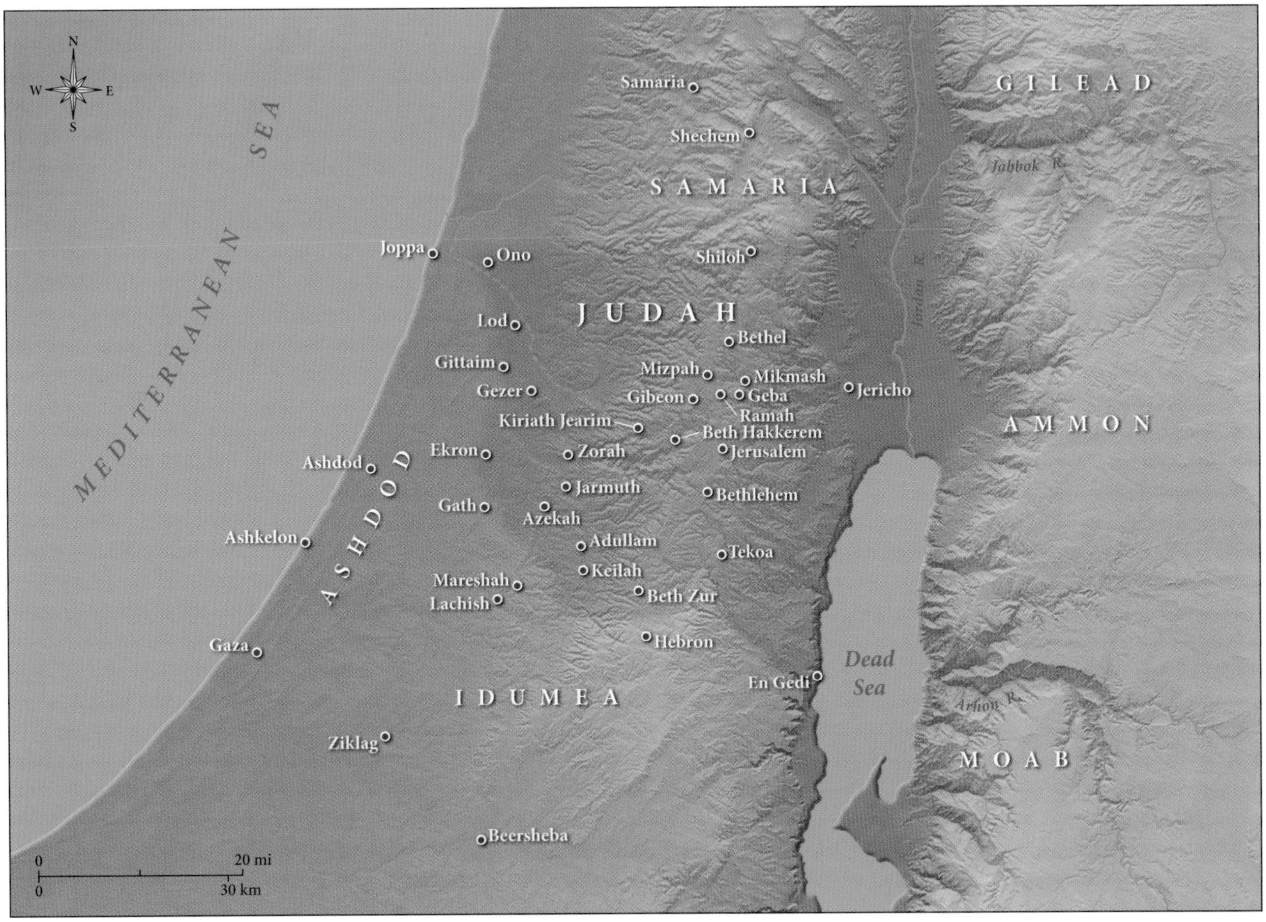

The Jewish Diaspora

The attention the Bible gives to the returns from exile at the time of Zerubbabel (538 BC), Ezra (458 BC), and Nehemiah (444 BC) could easily give us the impression that virtually all of the Jewish families who left the Promised Land during the Assyrian and Babylonian invasions returned (see map 7.4). The reality is that only a small percentage did. This means that when we draw the map of the Jewish presence in the world at the close of the Old Testament, we need to draw a map that is much larger than the small Persian province of Judah, one that shows the extent of the Jewish diaspora, or dispersion.

The map of the diaspora is hard to draw because the biblical authors were much more interested in the geography involving the returning exiles than of those who stayed away. But when we assemble the scattered comments, we get a sense of where Jewish families were taken or fled during the time of the Assyrian and Babylonian invasions. To destroy old national identities, the Assyrians permanently moved entire people groups from one part of their empire to another. In the case of Israel, we are told that they were taken to the heartland of Assyria (2 Kings 15:29) and settled in Halah and Gozan on the Habor River as well as in the towns of the Medes on the east side of the Fertile Crescent (2 Kings 17:6; 18:11).

During the Babylonian exile, Jews were moved into the vicinity of Babylon (2 Kings 24:15–16; 2 Chronicles 36:20; Daniel 1:1–7).[10] Ezekiel mentions that exiles lived at Tel Aviv near the Kebar River, though its exact location remains a mystery (Ezekiel 3:15). Many Jews fled ahead of the Babylonian threat, retreating deep into Egypt. Jeremiah is given a message for Jews living in Tahpanhes, Migdol, and Memphis as well as for others who had migrated up river into Upper Egypt (Jeremiah 43:7; 44:1).[11] The diaspora has a Persian

Map 7.6—Persian Empire

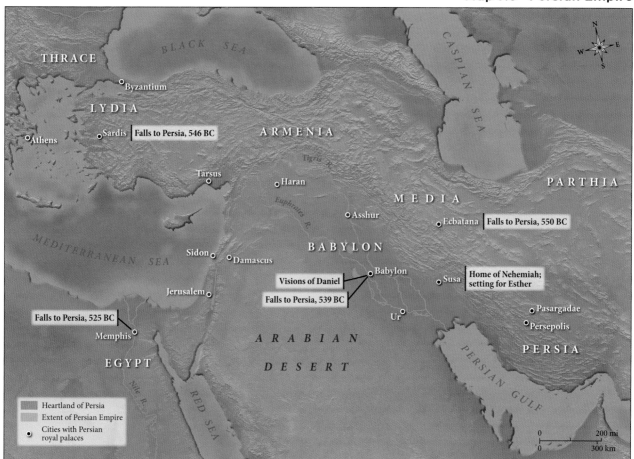

face too. Both Nehemiah and Esther were living in Susa when the Bible begins to tell their stories (Nehemiah 1:1; Esther 1:2). Assuming that these texts provide a representative picture of the diaspora, we can see that the family of Abraham was dispersed from one end of the Fertile Crescent to the other at the close of the Old Testament era.

Clearly some members of this community struggled with their separation from the Promised Land, joining in the mournful question of the psalmist, "How can we sing the songs of the LORD while in a foreign land?" (Psalm 137:4). For others, the 70 years that passed had muted their passion for return. They had built homes, businesses, and friendships in lands that did not seem so terribly foreign anymore. For

∧ *Persian column capital from Persepolis*

the majority of Jewish families who elected to remain abroad, one question emerged. How can we maintain our Jewish heritage when living away from the Promised Land? The books of Daniel and Esther provide an answer and role models to follow.

The diaspora Jews could maintain their Jewish identity by maintaining the lifestyle defined for them in the covenant law. We see Daniel and his friends doing just that in Babylon when they ask to be exempted from the meals provided for them in the royal court because those meals would "defile" them (Daniel 1:8–9). This may have been either because the food being served was from unclean animals or animals that were improperly drained of their blood. In either case, Daniel and his friends retained their Jewish identity by observing the Old Testament food law.

Maintaining their Jewish identity also meant not taking part in pagan worship even when this meant putting one's life at risk. We see two examples of this in the book of Daniel. Shadrach, Meshach, and Abednego are thrown into a fiery furnace for refus-

ing to acknowledge Babylonian gods. And Daniel is thrown into a den of hungry lions (Daniel 3; 6:13–23). In both cases, the Lord intervenes to save the lives of these faithful men who refused to accept a theological mind-set that was foreign to their Jewish heritage.

Seeking the well-being of God's chosen people in prayer and through actions also maintained the Jewish traditions and lifestyle. Daniel prayed three times a day while facing Jerusalem (Daniel 6:10). The direction and number of times one prayed per day are nowhere mandated in the Old Testament. But Daniel's example of seeking the well-being of his people in prayer is offered as an example of Jewish living.

Esther too was able to use her position to save her people. This young Jewish woman was in Susa (see map 7.6) when the king of Persia selected her to be his bride. As queen, she initially kept her Jewish identity a secret. But when her people were threatened by a

∨ *Persian fallow deer were among the clean animals that Daniel and his friends could eat*

plot that would exterminate Jews throughout the Persian Empire, she had to make a decision. It was at this critical moment that Mordecai, her uncle, challenged her to see that her rise to the throne was providential. "And who knows but that you have come to your royal position for such a time as this?" (Esther 4:14). She acted bravely to save her people.

Most Jewish families who left the Promised Land would never see it again. At the end of Old Testament times, Jews had been dispersed from one end of the known world to the other. When we see the map of where the Jewish people were living at that time, we are less surprised by the Magi coming from the east seeking the Christ child, Jews descending on Jerusalem from far-flung places to hear Peter on Pentecost, and Paul preaching in Jewish synagogues in Asia Minor and Europe.

Nehemiah's Jerusalem

While not all the Jewish families returned to the Promised Land following their exile, it was absolutely imperative for some to return. The rebuilding of Jerusalem was fundamental to obeying Old Testament law and advancing God's plan of salvation. When families returned to Jerusalem under the leadership of Zerubbabel, they set about rebuilding the worship center (Ezra 3; 6:13–18). We expected to read about that.

But what we didn't expect to read about in such great detail is the rebuilding of the defensive walls of Jerusalem at the time of Nehemiah.

We meet Nehemiah not in Jerusalem, but a four-month journey away from the Promised Land in Susa (see map 7.6), where he is serving in the Persian court as the high-ranking social director of palace affairs.[12] When word reached Nehemiah regarding the sorry

∨ *Foundation of the Water Gate (Fountain Gate) in Jerusalem*

∧ *The sixteenth-century Lion's Gate located near where Nehemiah built the Muster Gate and Sheep Gate*

condition of Jerusalem's defensives (Nehemiah 1:3), he used his influential position to get a hearing with King Artaxerxes and soon found himself traveling toward Judah as its new governor.[13] Before he left, Nehemiah obtained permission to access royal resources so that he could rebuild the walls and gates of Jerusalem (Nehemiah 2:5–9).

In the third chapter of Nehemiah, we learn how the city's walled perimeter was divided into sections and how multiple crews went to work simultaneously on all the sections. We are given a virtual avalanche of details describing the ten gates and more than twenty other identifying features of the city in the work areas.[14] Archaeological evidence allows us to say with increasing certainty where to put architectural structures like the Broad Wall (Nehemiah 3:8) and the Water Gate (Nehemiah 3:26). But in most cases, the trowel of the archaeologist has not provided a solid link between ground and text. We surmise the location of other features listed in Nehemiah because they are mentioned in other Bible texts. We place the Sheep Gate associated with the Bethesda Pools on the north side of the city (Nehemiah 3:1, 32; John 5:2). The fact that Nehemiah lists the gates and features in order, starting with the Sheep Gate and moving counterclockwise around the city, allows us to estimate the location of the other gates (see map 7.7). Our map may not be exact, but Nehemiah did provide enough detail to develop a general map of Jerusalem from his day.

The big picture looks like this. The Jerusalem of Nehemiah's day was considerably smaller than the Jerusalem of King Hezekiah's day, which is not surprising since the population of Jerusalem was significantly smaller (Nehemiah 7:4). The Jerusalem of Hezekiah incorporated the Western Hill of Jerusalem and enclosed approximately 125 acres (50.6 hectares). The Jerusalem of Nehemiah's day was reduced to the area of Solomon's Jerusalem, which at 32 acres (12.9 hectares) enclosed the City of David and the Temple Mount. Archaeology from the Persian period clearly supports this general picture, matching where Nehemiah describes the boundary of the city and providing no evidence of occupation on the Western Hill.[15]

Map 7.7—Ezra/Nehemiah's Jerusalem

Tower of the
One Hundred

Sheep
Gate

Muster
Gate

Tower of
Hananel

*Mount
Moriah*

Fish Gate

East Gate

Temple · Altar

Kidron Valley

Ephraim Gate

Horse
Gate

Broad Wall

Tower of
the Ovens

*Western
Hill*

Water Gate

Valley Gate

*Gihon
Spring*

*Mount Zion
(Byzantine)*

*Jackal's
Well*

**CITY
OF
DAVID**

*Mount of
Olives*

Dung
Gate

Fountain Gate

*Siloam
Pool*

Hinnom Valley

King's Pool

**King's
Garden**

En Rogel Spring

⎯⎯⎯	Defensive wall of Nehemiah, 5th century BC
⎯⎯⎯	Wall of Hezekiah, 8th century BC, in ruin
⎯⎯⎯	Wall built by Suleiman, 16th century AD

0   500 ft
0   150 m

∧ *Foundation of the Broad Wall mentioned in Nehemiah*

"The wall of Jerusalem is broken down, and its gates have been burned with fire" (Nehemiah 1:3). This information drove Nehemiah to grieve and weep for days (verse 4). It is what led him to realize that the city itself was in deep "trouble" (2:17). If the Jews in Jerusalem were disappointed that the rebuilt temple was not as impressive as the earlier structure (Ezra 3:12), imagine their reaction at seeing this city that was so badly ravaged by the Babylonians still in ruins, defenseless, with broken down walls and ruined gates.

This may be why Nehemiah provides so many details regarding the rebuilding of the city's defensive walls and gates. Certainly it would have been a more modest defensive system than its predecessor not only in scope but also in quality (Nehemiah 4:3). Many of those building the wall were not masons, and it was done quickly, in just 52 days. But even this modest wall lifted Jerusalem from the status of village to city. Jerusalem once again became a fit setting for the temple in which the Lord of all creation met his people, a *city* like the one envisioned by the psalmists (see, for example, Psalms 48 and 125). Thus the details Nehemiah provided helped his first readers see that God was moving Jerusalem back to its rightful status, from village to holy city.

While we are greatly indebted to Nehemiah for providing the details that allow us to draw this picture of post-exile Jerusalem, we suspect the primary purpose for these descriptions in Nehemiah 3 was for the benefit of Nehemiah's first readers. Modern readers are likely to miss the meaning because we do not think of living spaces in the same categories as those living in Bible times. For Nehemiah's first readers, there were villages and there were cities. Villages tended to be small, rural, and lacking in defensive walls and other structures. They provided simple living spaces for their residents. But this is not what comes to mind when you think of a royal city that doubles as a worship center. Such a city would be considered incomplete without defensive walls and gates. Yet that is how Jerusalem looked when the first exiles returned, and that is how the governors who ruled provinces around Judah wanted it to stay (Nehemiah 2:10; 4:1–9). When a delegation arrived in Susa from Jerusalem, it reported,

∧ *Wall dating to Nehemiah's rebuilding efforts*

∧ *Near Paneas, the Seleucids decisively defeated the Ptolemies in 198 BC*

Chapter 8

BETWEEN THE TESTAMENTS

Alexander the Great

The biblical authors are quiet with regards to events occurring during the 400 years between the Old and New Testaments. But an understanding of the important people, events, and cultural changes in the Promised Land during those years prepares Bible readers to cross the bridge between the Old Testament and the New Testament eras.[1]

The amazing achievements of Alexander the Great of Macedonia were propelled by both his love of learning and his passion for conquest. The former was stimulated by his teacher Aristotle, who imbued the impressionable Alexander with a love of Greek culture and a curiosity about what life might hold just beyond the horizon. This curiosity about life joined with a passion for conquest instilled in him by his father, King Philip II of Macedonia. Feeling both the threat of a Persian invasion and realizing that the once-great Persian Empire was beginning to weaken, Philip united Macedonia behind a strong army geared to conquest rather than just defense of the home front. When Philip was assassinated in 336 BC, Alexander inherited his father's throne and his vision for conquest. By the end of his life, he had built a Greek empire that stretched from Asia Minor to India.

Alexander's success was a result of his aggressive spirit, his flair for leadership, and his intelligence. He took the reins of his father's kingdom at the age of 21 and boldly charged in when others would have turned back. He enhanced the organization and weapons of his father's army. But where Alexander excelled was as a field tactician who had a way of sniffing out weakness in an opposing army's position or capabilities that he then exploited en route to victory.

Among the highlights from his campaigns was his crossing of the Hellespont, leaving Europe for Asia Minor in 334 BC. With a flair for the dramatic, Alexander is said to have thrown his spear into the Asian shore, claiming victory over it. Once all were ashore, he burned the ships they had used for the crossing, denying his soldiers the thought of return. His first battle with the Persians followed quickly at the Granicus River, where he used an unexpected early morning crossing of the river and uphill charge to catch the superior forces of the Persians by surprise. Following this victory, he methodically moved south down the western coast of Asia Minor to secure the seaports

the Persian navy might otherwise have used to land soldiers on his flank.

The year 333 BC found Alexander engaged in a decisive battle against King Darius of Persia at Issus, in what is now Turkey. After the Macedonian victory, Alexander moved south again, securing the seaports of the Mediterranean along the coast of Phoenicia and through the Promised Land toward Egypt. It was during this time that Alexander reportedly traveled to Jerusalem. The high priest is said to have shown the Greek general passages in Daniel 2 and 7 that spoke of a Greek leader defeating the Persian Empire.[2] Alexander was appreciative and quick to identify himself with those texts. There is no record of Jewish resistance to the arrival of Alexander, and they appear to have simply accepted the new situation.

Egypt had always intrigued Alexander, so he pressed on to the south, where he was welcomed as the Egyptian liberator from Persia and even identified as the offspring of Amon-Re, hence linking him with the long line of pharaohs who had ruled Egypt. It was here he founded Alexandria, the ancient Greek

∨ **Left:** *Bust of Alexander the Great;* **Right:** *Greek vase depicting the ideals that Alexander instilled wherever he traveled*

city destined to become a major commercial center and seat of academic learning. But a restless Alexander had to move on, so he returned to the north, moving around the top of the Fertile Crescent for the next and final battle in 331 BC against Darius and the Persians. Alexander's army faced the Persians with their cavalry, chariots, and war elephants poised for action in the plain west of Arbela. Once again Alexander designed a battle plan that sent Darius fleeing east. The Persian leader would not live to fight again. He was assassinated near the Caspian Gates, a mountain pass on the western shore of the Caspian Sea. Without a leader, Persia's capital cities of Susa and Persepolis were open to the pillaging hands of the Greeks. Payday at last. New life was breathed into the soldiers.

∧ *The Hellespont separates Europe from Asia*

Alexander pressed eastward, defeating all opposition on the way to India. By 326 BC he had defeated the Indian forces, but he now faced a different problem. The wet climate and a longing for home were taking a toll on Alexander's soldiers. The Greek troops refused to follow Alexander any farther east, so he returned to Babylon, where he hoped to revive his forces for an Arabian campaign. It was not to be. Alexander died in Babylon in 323 BC just short of his thirty-third birthday, ending an amazing story, one that had a lingering impact on all the regions he touched.

It is hard to imagine anyone other than Alexander the Great accomplishing what he did on the battlefield while bringing about the cultural changes that defined the region for centuries. Alexander was a great assimilator who adopted Asian dress and married an Asian, blending his personal life in a Greek-Asian fashion that portrayed the world he wished to leave as his legacy. Greek cities, architecture, art, culture, and technology were sewn into the fabric of Alexander's empire. Greek became the language of commerce and also of the ideas that shaped the worldview of the people. Alexander shaped the world that centuries later Jesus and Paul would enter, walking the paths he trod.

The Ptolemies and Seleucids

Alexander the Great displayed remarkable talent during his eleven years of conquest. We wonder what the ancient world might have become had he had the chance to govern the lands he conquered. Instead we are left with the violent tug of war that defined the struggle to succeed him. Alexander had not named a successor, leaving his generals to fight and claw for control. Each took hold of whatever he could. This summary is from the pages of 1 Maccabees, written by Jews during the second century BC.[3] "Then his officers began to rule, each in his own place. They all put on crowns after his death, and so did their sons after them for many years; and they caused many evils on the earth" (1 Maccabees 1:8–9).

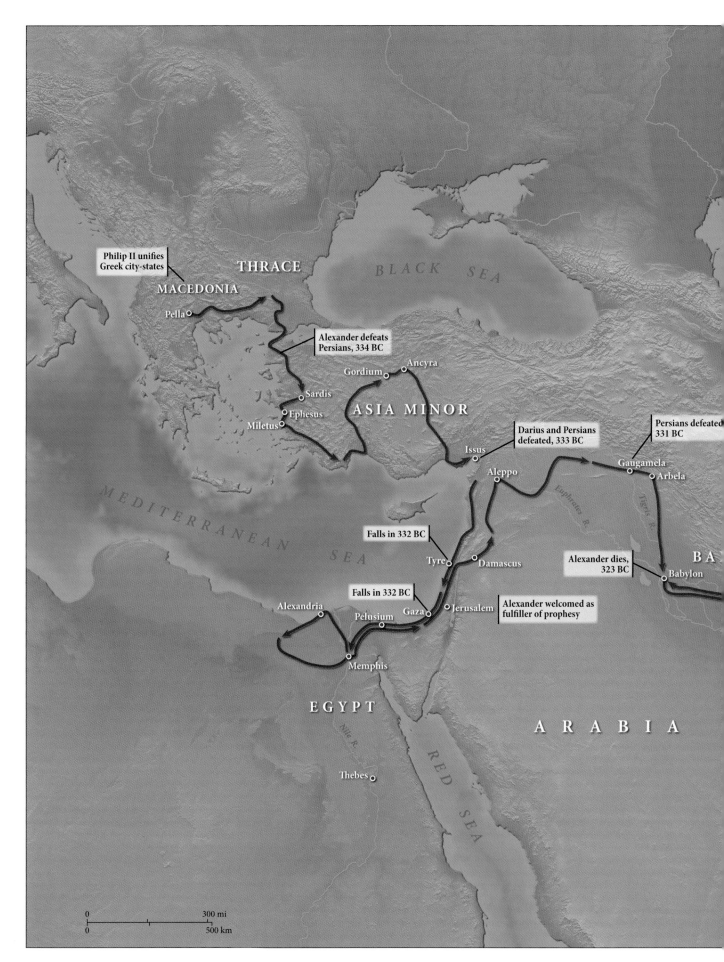

Philip II unifies
Greek city-states

THRACE

MACEDONIA

BLACK SEA

Pella

Alexander defeats
Persians, 334 BC

Ancyra

Gordium

Sardis

ASIA MINOR

Ephesus

Miletus

Darius and Persians
defeated, 333 BC

Persians defeated
331 BC

Issus

Gaugamela

Aleppo

Arbela

Euphrates R.

Tigris R.

MEDITERRANEAN SEA

Falls in 332 BC

Alexander dies,
323 BC

BA

Tyre

Damascus

Babylon

Falls in 332 BC

Alexander welcomed as
fulfiller of prophesy

Alexandria

Pelusium

Gaza

Jerusalem

Memphis

EGYPT

ARABIA

Nile R.

RED SEA

Thebes

0   300 mi

0   500 km

Map 8.1—Empire of Alexander the Great

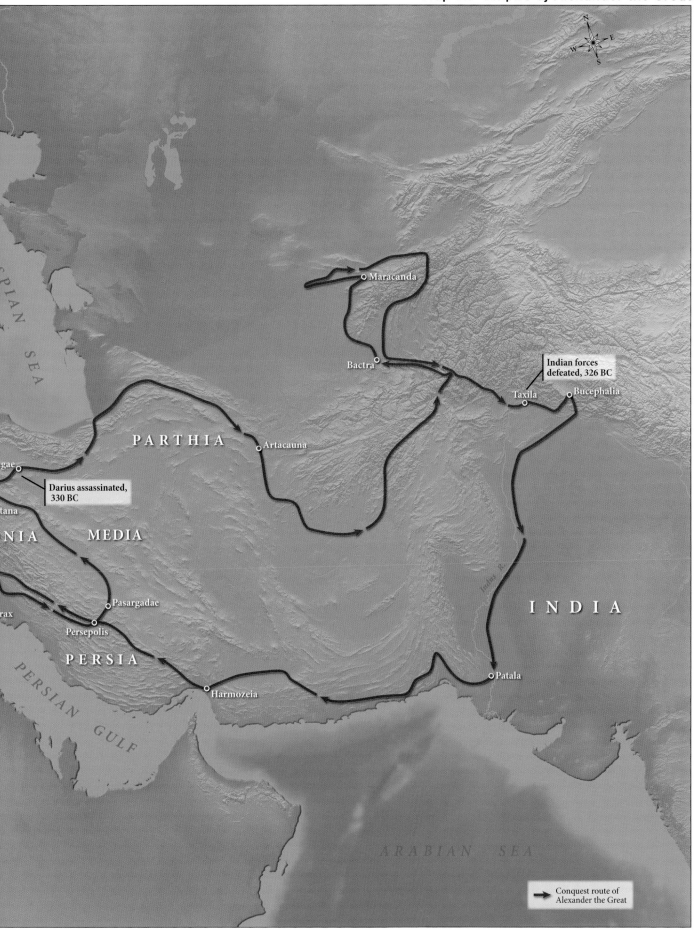

Conquest route of
Alexander the Great

Two of the ruling families rose to the top, the Ptolemies and the Seleucids (see map 8.2). Ptolemy I took control of Egypt, Cyrene, Cyprus, Phoenicia, and Palestine.[4] He ruled from Alexandria in Egypt. Seleucus I took control of Asia Minor, Syria, and most of Mesopotamia east to India. His capital city was Antioch on the Orontes River. The book of Daniel, chapter 11, touches on the struggle that went on between these two ruling houses, a period known to historians as the "Syrian Wars." Because the Promised Land is between these two political entities and is of economic value to both, much of the fighting was over control of this land bridge. The struggle impacted the Jews not only physically but culturally. Among God's people were those who favored the Ptolemies, while others favored the Seleucids. Because both Ptolemies and Seleucids were interested in imposing Greek culture on the Jews, there was another division among the Jews between those who wanted to be a part of the Greek world and those who wanted to maintain their Jewish cultural identity (1 Maccabees 1:11–15, 43; 2 Maccabees 4:9–10, 14–17).

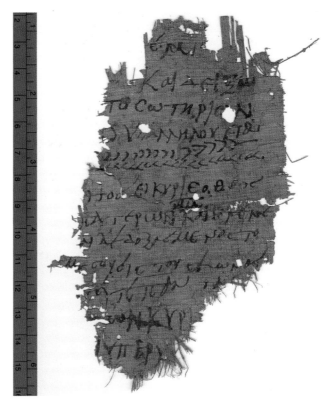

∧ *Fragment of Psalm 90 from a fifth-century Septuagint manuscript*

There were two general periods in the Promised Land: 304–198 BC when the Ptolemies held control of the Promised Land, and 198–142 BC when the Seleucids held that role. For the Jews, the Ptolemaic period was a time of greater cultural autonomy under the leadership of Ptolemy II. He worked to advance the intellectual well-being of his kingdom by building a library and a zoo in Alexandria as well as a scholarly learning center called the Museum where thousands came to study. The Letter of Aristeas (second century BC) says that the king of Egypt (presumably Ptolemy II) wanted the Hebrew Old Testament translated into Greek for his library. Thus 72 Jewish scholars went to Alexandria to produce what we now call the Septuagint. The Ptolemies were practical people and saw value in maintaining the Promised Land as a buffer between themselves and the opposing Seleu-

cids.[5] The downside for the Jews was the Ptolemies' rigorous system of taxation that caused more than a little hardship on the average Jewish family. This included a 33.3 percent tax on grain and a 50 percent tax on fruit.[6]

A major change occurred in 198 BC when the Seleucids defeated the Ptolemies in a decisive battle near Paneas, giving control of Jerusalem and the Promised Land to the Seleucids. The Jewish leaders of this era were quite facile in changing allegiance and offered logistical support to the Seleucid army. Antiochus III showed his gratefulness by granting a three-year tax exemption, offering assistance in repairing the temple, providing subsidies for keeping the temple in operation, and safeguarding the desire of those who wished to live an orthodox Jewish lifestyle.[7]

∧ *Coin bearing the image of Antiochus IV Epiphanes*

Map 8.2—Ptolemies and Seleucids

Things changed dramatically for God's people in the Promised Land with the rise to power of the Seleucid ruler Antiochus IV Epiphanes. Rome, having gained power, threatened to reduce the size of the Seleucid holdings and the income the Seleucids received. In response, Antiochus IV taxed and took as he could, even robbing the temple treasury in Jerusalem (1 Maccabees 1:21–24). When his efforts met with resistance, Antiochus started down a path of high-handed control and forced Hellenization, which guaranteed a permanent scar to his reputation among the Jews. The priesthood, which had become the key political position, was sold to the highest bidder without regard for maintaining an association with the family of Aaron (2 Maccabees 4:7–24). The high priest became the one responsible for collecting the taxes. To put down any revolution in Jerusalem associated with the temple complex, Antiochus built a citadel on the temple grounds that housed a Syrian garrison, defiling the sanctuary itself (1 Maccabees 1:33–37).

Further resistance on the part of the Jews was met by even more aggressive Hellenization. Antiochus Epiphanes appears to have tried to destroy each component of Jewish identity in the land. He banned worship at the temple, banned circumcision, and banned observance of Sabbath. He ordered destruction of Torah scrolls and placed an altar to Zeus in the temple complex, then sacrificed unclean animals on the most holy ground known to the Jewish faith. Jews were forced to participate in pagan worship or die (1 Maccabees 1:41–63; 2 Maccabees 6:1–11). Some Jews yielded to the social changes imposed by Antiochus, but many died resisting. These were dark days in the Promised Land. The prophet Daniel saw this terrible time coming and spoke of it. "His armed forces will rise up to desecrate the temple fortress and will abolish the daily sacrifice. Then they will set up the abomination that causes desolation. With flattery he will corrupt those who have violated the covenant, but the people who know their God will firmly resist him" (Daniel 11:31–32).

The Maccabees and Hasmoneans

The aggressive Hellenization by the Syrian king Antiochus IV was bent on eradicating traditional Jewish life in the Promised Land. As extremism often does, it met with a violent response. Jewish freedom fighters, the Maccabees, and subsequent Jewish political leaders, the Hasmoneans, championed a quest for religious freedom. This in turn became a quest for political autonomy that led to wars of conquest intended to increase the amount of territory ruled by the Hasmoneans.[8]

The Syrians started this chain of events when they demanded that an elderly Jewish priest from the village of Modiin, Mattathias, make a pagan sacrifice. They offered to make his life easier if he would make their lives easier, using his influential example to get his village to adopt pagan sacrifice as the new normal. When he refused, another Jewish elder stepped forward to make the sacrifice. Mattathias set an example for the village, but not the one they had expected. He killed the Jewish elder who was willing to offer the sacrifice and the Syrian official. And with that, the Maccabean revolt seeking religious freedom was under way.

Mattathias died shortly after this, but not before appointing his son, Judas Maccabaeus ("Hammerer")

▽ *Model depicting Jewish soldiers guarding Jerusalem*

Map 8.3—Maccabean-Hasmonean Period

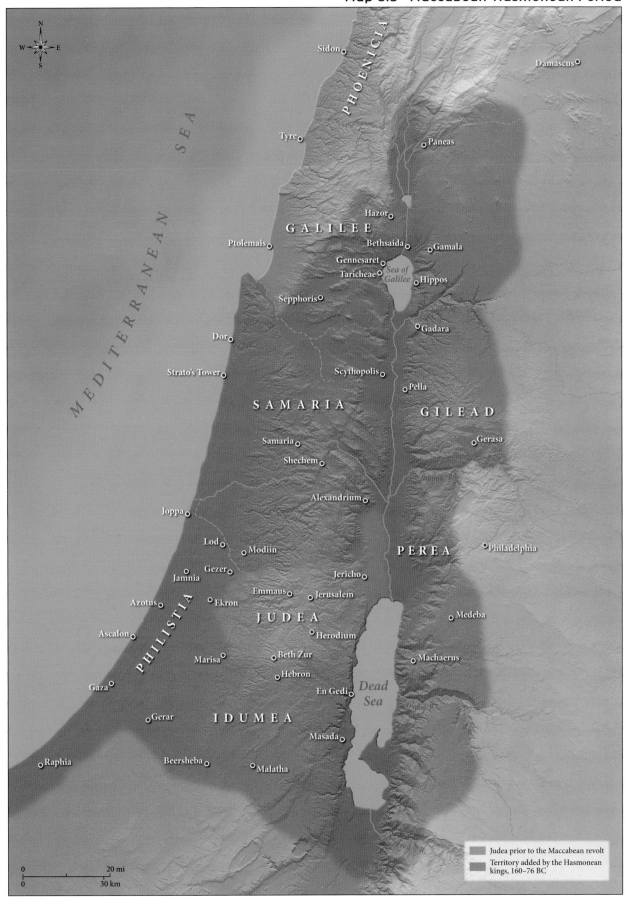

N
W — E
S

MEDITERRANEAN SEA

PHOENICIA

Sidon

Damascus

Tyre

Paneas

Hazor

GALILEE

Ptolemais

Bethsaida

Gamala

Gennesaret

Taricheae

Sea of Galilee

Hippos

Sepphoris

Dor

Gadara

Strato's Tower

Scythopolis

Pella

SAMARIA

GILEAD

Samaria

Gerasa

Shechem

Jabbok R.

Alexandrium

Joppa

PEREA

Lod

Philadelphia

Modiin

Gezer

Jericho

Jamnia

Emmaus

Jerusalem

Azotus

Ekron

JUDEA

Medeba

Ascalon

Herodium

PHILISTIA

Marisa

Beth Zur

Machaerus

Hebron

Gaza

En Gedi

Dead Sea

Gerar

IDUMEA

Masada

Jordan R.

Raphia

Beersheba

Malatha

Salt R.

Judea prior to the Maccabean revolt

Territory added by the Hasmonean kings, 160–76 BC

0   20 mi
0   30 km

to lead the movement. He was the right man for the job. Although the forces he came to lead were small in number, not properly trained, and poorly armed, Judas found success against the Syrians again and again (1 Maccabees 3–9). His accomplishments can be traced to a number of things he did well. He chose to fight using hit-and-run tactics employing speed, surprise, and his knowledge of the local terrain. He acquired the support of a faction within Judaism called the Hasidim. Among the most conservative group of the Jews in this era, the Hasidim had already demonstrated their willingness to die rather than yield to the pagan practices imposed by Antiochus IV. They would fight to the death, and Judas spoke their language. "It is not on the size of the army that victory in battle depends, but strength comes from

∧ *Tomb of Maccabees at Modiin*

Heaven. They come against us in great pride and lawlessness to destroy us and our wives and our children and to despoil us; but we fight for our lives and our laws" (1 Maccabees 3:19–21). Though he advocated for orthodox Judaism, he was quick to set aside conservative practices that were hurting the chances for success. When he saw that the Syrians attacked Jews on the Sabbath, knowing the most conservative factions would refuse to defend themselves, he insisted that fighting on the Sabbath to defend oneself was not a violation of Moses' law (1 Maccabees 2:40–41).

Judas led the Jewish resistance fighters for four years (165–161 BC). During that time he coerced Jews into repudiating Hellenism and came to the rescue of countless villages attacked by the Syrians. His signature accomplishment was the retaking of the temple complex in Jerusalem so that it could be ritually purified and put back into operation. This historic moment in Judaism is marked by the annual celebration of Hanukkah (1 Maccabees 4:36–59). Judas's brother Jonathan was the next resistance leader (160–142 BC). While he too aggressively attacked the Syrians, he is better known for his diplomacy. The death of Antio-chus IV produced a power vacuum many wished to fill. Jonathan used this to his advantage, courting first one, then another Syrian wannabe leader. It was also during the time of Jonathan that the Jewish military agenda underwent a significant shift. With religious freedom achieved, operations were now conducted with a view toward obtaining political freedom.

Ironically, Jonathan the negotiator died while attending a negotiation, double-crossed by another aspiring Syrian leader. Jonathan was succeeded by the third of Mattathias's sons, Simon (142–134 BC). Feeling the need to have Simon as an ally, the leader of Syria released the Jews from payment of taxes and gave them political independence in hopes that this Jewish state would support him in his bid to lead Syria. And so in 142 BC, Simon ushered in a life the Promised Land had not known since 586 BC. Judea acquired political autonomy. This was cause for great celebration that included the waving of palm branches signifying the liberation of the land (1 Maccabees 13:51–52).

This age of the Maccabees was succeeded by the Hasmonean period, the time when Jewish kings again ruled the land.[9] Many of these kings had their sights set on adding territory to the land they ruled and taxed. John Hyrcanus I (134–104 BC), the son of Simon, was the first of the Hasmonean leaders. He expanded Judea southward, adding Idumea to the land he controlled and forcing conversion of those living in that province (see map 8.3). He did the same in the north, incorporating Samaria. When the Samaritans resisted, Hyrcanus destroyed their worship complex on Mount Gerizim (128 BC), creating the bad blood between Jews and Samaritans that persisted to Jesus' day (John 4:9).

Hyrcanus's son Aristobulus ruled for only two years (104–103 BC). He added Galilee to the land under Jewish control and again forced those in the north to undergo circumcision and conversion to Judaism. Suspicions many held about the integrity of Galilean Jews can be traced to this event. Alexander Jannaeus, a brother-in-law of Aristobulus, ruled next (103–76 BC). He ruled a Judea that encompassed the land from Dan to Beersheba and from the Mediterranean Sea through the Transjordan (see map 8.3). Control of the trade routes made for a financial boon akin to that enjoyed during the time of Solomon. However, his sympathies were toward Hellenism, causing him to favor the Sadducees over the Pharisees (who owed their origin to the Hasidim). Jannaeus was responsible for the deaths of thousands of Pharisees who opposed him. Thus the discord between Sadducees and Pharisees we read about in the New Testament had deep and bloody roots.

The era of the Maccabees and Hasmoneans was an era of significant religious and political change. The temple was back in operation, the Hasmonean kingdom had been greatly expanded, and Judea had once again become an independent state. That would last until the Romans took over in 63 BC.

Rome and the Promised Land

During the Hasmonean era, the menacing shadow of Roman domination edged closer and closer to the Promised Land. In 63 BC, it arrived, bringing to a close the independent Jewish state of 142 BC.[10] Roman domination of the Promised Land would remain a part of the historical landscape throughout the New Testament era (see map 8.4).

We begin the story of Rome's arrival with the final years of the Hasmonean kingdom and the death of Alexander Jannaeus. His widow, Salome Alexandra, ruled from 76–67 BC. Most notably she reversed her husband's policy of treating the Pharisees harshly. This allowed them to become more firmly entrenched in the Jewish ruling council, the Sanhedrin, where the Pharisees continued to play an important role in the New Testament era. Alexandra's two sons, Hyrcanus II and Aristobulus II, both wanted to succeed her. Hyrcanus was supported by the Sadducees and was Alexandra's choice—this despite the fact that he was widely considered the weaker leader of the two brothers. Aristobulus had the support of the Pharisees and was of no mind to surrender this position without a fight. In 67 BC when Alexandra died, quiet maneuvering gave way to open conflict, and civil war broke out in the Promised Land.

The civil war and the sibling rivalry for leadership in Judea drew the attention of two non-Jewish players, Antipater and Pompey. Antipater had been appointed to govern in Idumea by Alexander Jannaeus. This Idumean ruler is characterized as rich, seditious, and ambitious.[11] His goal was to get the weaker brother, Hyrcanus, confirmed as high priest because he knew that Hyrcanus could be manipulated

∧ *A Roman soldier's helmet*

Map 8.4—Roman World First Century BC

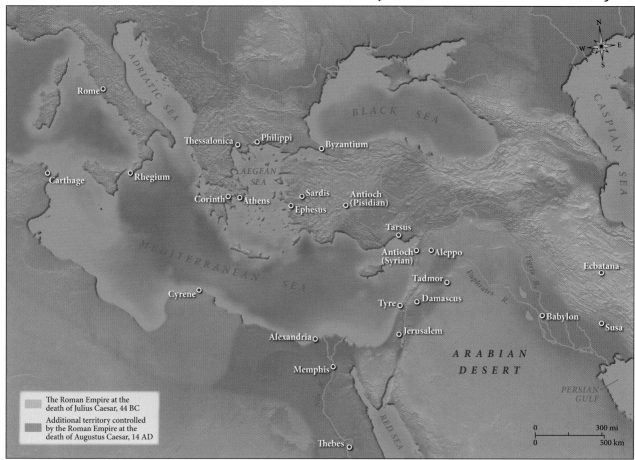

The Roman Empire at the death of Julius Caesar, 44 BC

Additional territory controlled by the Roman Empire at the death of Augustus Caesar, 14 AD

to facilitate Antipater's own quest for power. It seems unlikely that Hyrcanus would have persisted in the civil war without the dogged encouragement offered by Antipater.

Pompey was a Roman military and political leader during the time of the late Roman Republic. In 64 BC, he conquered Syria and made it a Roman province. Standing at the threshold of the Promised Land, he could not resist involving himself in the Jewish civil war. Hyrcanus and Aristobulus recognized the value of Pompey's support. They both traveled to Damascus for a meeting with him and presented their case. Pompey threw his support behind Hyrcanus. Just like Antipater, Pompey identified the weaker brother as the man he could more successfully exploit. Aristobulus fled to Jerusalem to prepare for the fight he knew the Romans would bring. Pompey obliged, putting Jerusalem under a three-month siege during which thousands of Jews died. Finally, the supporters of Hyrcanus opened the city to the Roman general, who then designated Hyr-

canus as high priest and ethnarch, or Roman ruler of the Jewish people in and around Jerusalem. Pompey also carefully dissected and redistributed the landholdings of the old Hasmonean kingdom to further weaken the capabilities of Hyrcanus.[12] Josephus captures the consequences of it all in one sentence: "We lost our liberty, and became subject to the Romans."[13] In 63 BC, the independent Jewish state was no more.

∨ *Bust of Pompey*

The next major changes occur with the eclipse of Pompey and the rise of Julius Caesar. By 49 BC, civil war had broken out in Rome. Julius Caesar marched on the historic city, forcing Pompey and many Roman senators to flee. Pompey sought asylum in Egypt, but while his request for asylum was being processed, assassins ended his life. Caesar then decided to intervene in the civil war brewing in Egypt. With the aid of Antipater, Julius Caesar left Egypt as victor in 47 BC. When his attention turned to Jerusalem, Julius Caesar confirmed ever-malleable Hyrcanus as high priest and ethnarch. But the man who received the plum promotion was Antipater, the man who had proven his worth to Rome. Caesar granted Roman citizenship to Antipater and made him proconsul of Judea, which meant he was responsible for managing the finances of this district for the benefit of Rome. No sooner had Caesar departed from Syria than Antipater went to work exploiting his position. He appointed his son Phasael as governor of Judea and his son Herod as tetrarch of Galilee. The latter would become the powerful and infamous figure known to Bible readers as Herod the Great.

Bust of Julius Caesar

This final political shift sets the stage for understanding the world of the New Testament. Mary and Joseph traveled from Nazareth to Bethlehem just before Jesus' birth in connection with a Roman census.

"In those days Caesar Augustus issued a decree that a census should be taken of the entire Roman world" (Luke 2:1). Jesus stood trial before Pontius Pilate, "the Roman governor" (John 18:28). Paul was arrested in Jerusalem by Roman soldiers and stood trial before two Roman governors, Felix and Festus (Acts 24–26). Considering the powerful role the empire of Rome played in the Promised Land during the time of the New Testament, we might well ask, Where is the Lord in all of this?

The book of Daniel helps us understand that the evolving stream of empires exerting control over the Promised Land were simply executing a dance choreographed by the Lord and revealed in two striking visions to Daniel (Daniel 2 and 7). In each vision, the final empire he saw appeared more menacing than those that preceded it. But it is precisely during the time of this final kingdom that "the God of heaven will set up a kingdom that will never be destroyed" (Daniel 2:44; see also Daniel 7:26–27). It would be during this time of Roman domination that the true King of the world would arise. Paul captures the precision of it all in these memorable words: "But when the set time had fully come, God sent his Son, born of a woman, born under the law, to redeem those under the law, that we might receive adoption to sonship" (Galatians 4:4–5).

∧ *Modern Nazareth and the small valley where first-century Nazareth, Jesus' hometown, was situated*

Chapter 9

BIRTH AND EARLY YEARS OF JESUS

Herod the Great

As the New Testament era dawned, Herod the Great became the face of Rome in the Promised Land. He and his sons cast a long shadow into the events of the Gospels, even threatening the life of Jesus. Herod's rise to power required careful negotiation. After Julius Caesar was assassinated in 44 BC, the Roman Republic fell into the hands of Octavian, who ruled in the west, while Marc Antony ruled in the east. Antony oversaw events in the Roman district of Judea until 31 BC, when Octavian defeated him in the naval Battle of Actium in the Ionian Sea between Italy and Greece.

With the passing of Antony, the Roman Empire began in earnest. The Senate quickly escalated the position of Octavian to "first citizen" and gave him the title by which he would be best known, "Augustus Caesar." Augustus set about reorganizing the political structure within the provinces to expedite the flow of tax revenue. He appointed leaders in revolt-prone regions like Judea whom he trusted would quash any form of rebellion quickly and efficiently. This is the world where Herod rose to power, and this is why Herod became Rome's man in Judea.[1]

As the son of Antipater, Herod had already seen public life as the military commander in Galilee. When the Parthians, Rome's great eastern enemy, invaded, they sought a local alliance with Antigonus, who had hopes of reviving the glory days of his Hasmonean family. Outmatched, Herod sheltered his family at the Herodium, an isolated butte along the western shore of the Dead Sea—the future site of his sprawling palace-fortress—while he fled to Rome, where the Roman Senate designated him "King of Judea" in 40 BC. As Rome's trust in Herod grew, so did his territory. Eventually his rule extended well beyond Judea, and his kingdom came to include Idumea, Perea, Judea, and Samaria. But his first job was to quell the revolt against Rome in Judea. Only then could he begin to function as the "king of Judea."

Against all odds, Herod was successful not only in living up to his title but doing so with such distinction as to be acclaimed Herod the Great. He achieved that status by fighting well and marrying well, and for his strategic political maneuvering and his flare for architecture. Herod returned to the Promised Land with a license to raise an army and reclaim this land bridge for Rome. He did just that, defeating the Parthians and Jewish resistance handily. He recaptured Jerusalem in 37 BC.

Herod used marriage as a tool in establishing his credibility. This is particularly evident in his marriage to the beautiful Mariamne, a Jew with Hasmonean blood in her veins. Herod was born into an Idumean family that had been forced to convert to Judaism during the time of the Hasmoneans. Jews considered him little more than a "half-Jew."[2] Herod felt the sting of this criticism and so married a Jewish princess to give himself the Jewish credibility he lacked. In addition to fighting and marriage, Herod was also a shrewd political operative. As things were heating up between Octavian and Mark Antony, moving toward the decisive Battle of Actium, Herod had been supporting Antony. We might expect this to be the last step in Herod's political career, if not his life. But when Herod met with the victorious Octavian, the soon-to-be Augustus Caesar reconfirmed Herod's position and in time added the area northeast of the Sea of Galilee to his kingdom.

⌄ **Left:** *Herod's palace/fortress, the Herodium;* **Right:** *A model of Herod's northern palace at Masada*

Map 9.1—Herod's Kingdom and Its Division

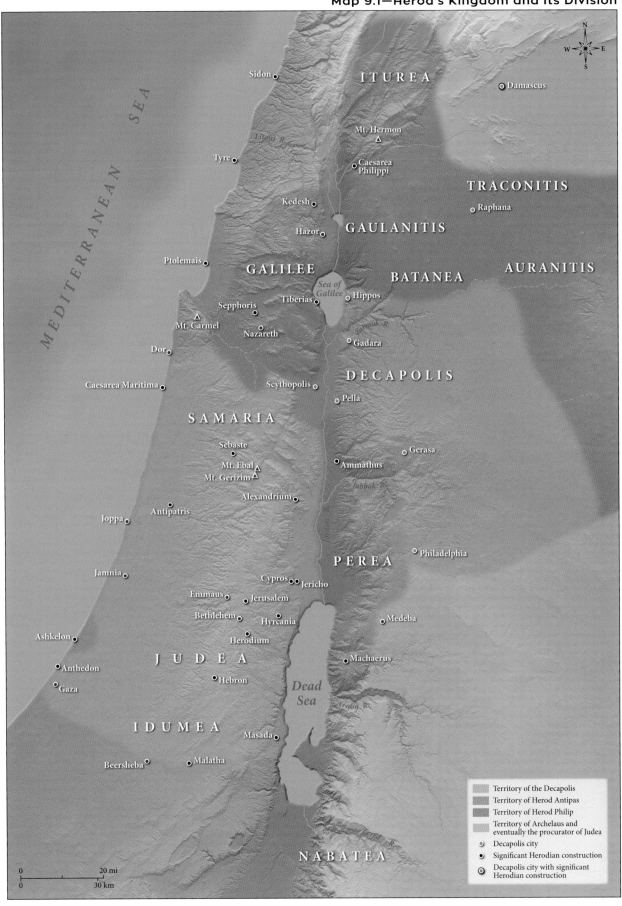

MEDITERRANEAN SEA

Sidon

ITUREA

Damascus

Litani R.

Mt. Hermon

Tyre

Caesarea
Philippi

TRACONITIS

Kedesh

Raphana

Hazor

GAULANITIS

Ptolemais

GALILEE

BATANEA

AURANITIS

Sea of
Galilee

Hippos

Sepphoris

Tiberias

Mt. Carmel

Nazareth

Yarmuk R.

Dor

Gadara

Caesarea Maritima

Scythopolis

DECAPOLIS

Pella

SAMARIA

Sebaste

Mt. Ebal

Gerasa

Mt. Gerizim

Ammathus

Jabbok R.

Alexandrium

Joppa

Antipatris

Jamnia

PEREA

Philadelphia

Cypros

Jericho

Emmaus

Jerusalem

Bethlehem

Hyrcania

Medeba

Ashkelon

Herodium

Anthedon

JUDEA

Hebron

Dead
Sea

Machaerus

Gaza

Arnon R.

IDUMEA

Masada

Beersheba

Malatha

Territory of the Decapolis

Territory of Herod Antipas

Territory of Herod Philip

Territory of Archelaus and
eventually the procurator of Judea

Decapolis city

Significant Herodian construction

Decapolis city with significant
Herodian construction

NABATEA

0   20 mi
0   30 km

Finally we come to Herod's great building legacy that is indicative of his creativity and administrative ability. During the relatively short period from 37–4 BC, Herod had major construction under way in some 25 locations.[3] He built showplaces like his harbor at Caesarea Maritima—a seaport to rival any in the ancient world and a city with a thoroughly European feel. He built luxury palaces in the desert, places like Jericho, Masada, and the Herodium, with colonnaded gardens, swimming pools, and lavish dining halls. While these ambitious projects fed Herod's love of all things Roman, he also invested considerable energy in Jerusalem, including a complete renovation of the temple complex. His goal was to win the loyalty or submission of all the people in his kingdom, whether Roman or Jewish.[4] Toward the end of his life, Herod the Great, his paranoia taking hold, used yet another tool to hold on to power—murder. He had used this tool before in executing perceived rivals like Antigonus, but came to use it against his sons and even his beloved wife Mariamne.[5] We can imagine how news of a "Jewish king" born in Bethlehem reported by those coming from the "east" (like the Parthians) must have triggered Herod's paranoia. The innocents in Bethlehem paid the price. Mary, Joseph, and Jesus fled to Egypt (Matthew 2:1–18). While they were there, Herod died and was buried in the tomb he had prepared for himself at the Herodium (4 BC). The historian Josephus wrote, "A man he was of great barbarity towards all men equally, and a slave to his passion; but above the consideration of what was right; yet was he

∧ *Foundation of Herod's tomb at the Herodium*

favored by fortune as much as any man ever was, for from a private man he became a king; and though he were encompassed with ten thousand dangers, he got clear of them all, and continued his life until a very old age."[6]

Upon his death, the kingdom ruled by Herod the Great was divided among his three surviving sons (see map 9.1). Archelaus ruled in Judea, Samaria, and Idumea until 6 AD, when he was banished to Gaul for his violent abuse of power (see Matthew 2:19–23). Subsequently Rome elected to rule Judea via a Roman prefect of whom Pontius Pilate was the fifth. Herod Antipas ruled in Galilee and Perea (Luke 13:31–32; 23:6–12). And Herod Philip ruled the share of his father's former kingdom that lay north and east of the Sea of Galilee.

Geography and John the Baptist

As the authors of the Gospels take us to the early years of Jesus, they introduce us to John the Baptist. Almost everything about this man is unique: his birth, his manner of dress, his diet, and where he lived. It seems that everyone wanted to hear him speak, in part because of what geography says about who he was. The Gospels pay particular attention to where John was teaching and baptizing. *Where* John was says something important about *who* John was.

During the first years of his life, John the Baptist lived in the hill country of Judea (see map 9.2). This is where John's parents had their home and where John was born (Luke 1:39, 65). A late eighth-century Christian tradition is more precise, putting the home of his parents Zechariah and Elizabeth just west of Jerusalem in the small village of En Kerem. Because it was typical in the first century for a person to be born, grow up, raise a family, and die in the same village, we can expect that John's life followed this rule, at least for a while. He likely followed in the footsteps of his father, living as priest in his village and traveling to the temple in Jerusalem when selected to perform

Map 9.2—Life of John the Baptist

his sacred duties, just as his father had before him (Luke 1:8–9). But things were not all they should have been at the temple, and John knew it. He saw the corruption the aristocratic priests had introduced in this sacred space, running the temple like a business meant to produce a profit rather than profiting those who came to worship. We get a sense for how deeply this offended John when we hear the sharp, even biting tone of the language he used when he addressed the Pharisees and Sadducees whose curiosity brought them to the place where John was baptizing (Matthew 3:7–10). John would leave the Judean hills in search of something better. We don't know how many years John called the hill country his home, but the gospel writers put the spotlight on his time in the wilderness of Judea (Matthew 3:1; 11:7; Mark 1:4; Luke 7:24).[7] In the rugged and forbidding topography of this wilderness, John grew up physically and spiritually before he began to speak publicly (Luke 1:80).

The emphatic association of John with wilderness tells us something about who he was. When the Old Testament announces the coming of the Messiah, it speaks of a forerunner who will prepare the world for his arrival. "I will send my messenger, who will prepare the way before me. Then suddenly the Lord you are seeking will come to his temple" (Malachi 3:1). It is not just that the forerunner is coming but where his voice is expected that becomes important to notice. "A voice of one calling: 'In the wilderness prepare the way for the LORD; make straight in the desert a highway for our God'" (Isaiah 40:3). The gospel writers leave nothing to chance. When they speak of John being in the wilderness, they quote Isaiah 40:3 to make sure we see the connection (Matthew 3:1–3; Mark 1:1–4; Luke 3:1–6). John may have moved into the wilderness because he was weary of the corruption occurring in Jerusalem, but John had to move into the wilderness because this was where he was destined to be. That is why the Gospels are so insistent that we get John's geography right. Where he was says something important about who he was—the Messiah's forerunner.

The Old Testament also speaks of the forerunner as a new Elijah, and this opens the door for an even more refined geographic connection. Elijah lived

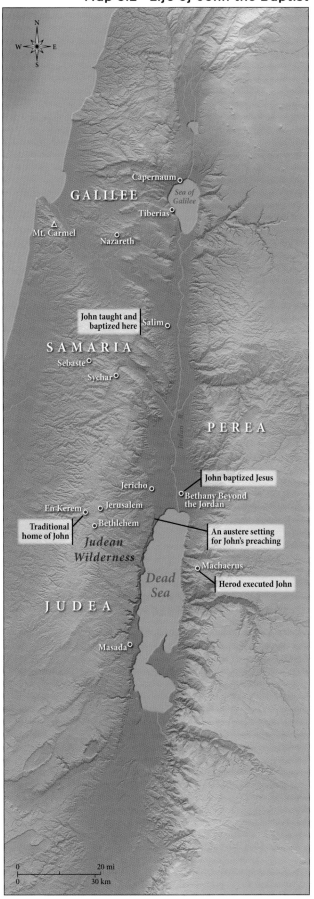

some 900 years before the time of John the Baptist. Elijah was, without a doubt, one of the most powerful spokesmen of his time, calling the corrupt kingdom of Ahab and Jezebel to repent. Malachi refines his description of the forerunner by noting that he will be Elijah-like. "See, I will send the prophet Elijah to you before that great and dreadful day of the LORD comes" (Malachi 4:5). When John arrives, the Gospels identify him as the prophet anticipated in Malachi 3:1 (Matthew 11:10; Luke 1:76; 7:26). In even more precise language, the angel who announced John's birth to Zechariah talks about John moving "in the spirit and power of Elijah" (Luke 1:17). And Jesus confirms in unambiguous fashion that John is the new "Elijah who was to come" (Matthew 11:14).

The geographic connection between John the Baptist and Elijah follows when we correctly place Bethany Beyond the Jordan "where John was baptizing" on our maps (John 1:28). The majority of geographic references to the ministry of John the Baptist put him in the southern end of the Jordan River valley in the wilderness just north of the Dead Sea. The expression "wilderness of Judea" (Matthew 3:1; 11:7; Mark 1:4; Luke 7:24) puts him on the west side of the Jordan River, while the language of Luke 3:3, "into all the country around the Jordan," allows for his presence on the east side of the Jordan River as well. When John the gospel writer speaks of a "Bethany on the other side of the Jordan" River as the place John was baptizing,[8] it is best for us to look for this location east of Jericho near the traditional location of Jesus' baptism by John, near the Wadi el-Kharrar ford. This location allows for a striking geographic connection to Elijah (see map 9.2). When Elijah went up into the heavens in a fiery chariot, he did so east of Jericho and just east of this location for Bethany Beyond the Jordan (2 Kings 2:4–12). The old Elijah left the stage of history precisely where the new Elijah took the stage to fulfill his role as Jesus' forerunner.[9]

En Kerem, the traditional home of John the Baptist

Solutions Abound in Bethlehem

We all need places that offer solutions to life's problems. If our vehicle stops working, we look for a solution at a repair shop. If our child becomes seriously ill, we look for a solution at a doctor's office. When we trace the different times that Bethlehem is mentioned in the Bible, we find that it too is a place where solutions abound.

Bethlehem is located in Judea about 5 miles (8 km) southwest of Jerusalem (see map 9.3). It is alongside the Ridge Route that connects all the important population centers of Judea and Samaria, about 9 miles (4.8 km) south of the important internal east-west crossroads of the country. Given the importance of its location, Solomon's son Rehoboam fortified Bethlehem to guard the southern access to Israel's capital city, Jerusalem (2 Chronicles 11:5–6). Bethlehem was also an agriculturally productive place. Most of the Judean hill country, with its steep, eroded mountainsides and narrow valleys, presents a challenge to farming. It is difficult to coax much of a grain harvest from this stingy landscape even when terraces are built. Bethlehem is the exception. Here the harshness of the slopes softens

∧ *A broad agricultural valley near Bethlehem*

and the valleys widen to create more friendly agricultural land for the farmer. This grain-friendly place may well be reflected in the name given the village. In Hebrew, Bethlehem means "house of bread."[10]

The most frequent mention of Bethlehem involves three people, all related to one another: Naomi, David, and Jesus. In each story, Bethlehem provides a critical solution. The story of Naomi is presented in a book that carries the name of her daughter-in-law Ruth. In the first chapter of Ruth, Bethlehem is mentioned five times (of the seven times in this short book). Naomi and her husband, Elimelek, were from Bethlehem, but were forced to seek refuge in Moab during a famine that had gripped the Promised Land (Ruth 1:1–2). First Elimelek died. Then ten years later, Naomi's two sons, who had married Moabite women, died. Eventually Naomi and her daughter-in-law Ruth returned to Bethlehem (Ruth 1:19, 22). As Ruth set about doing all she could to support them by gleaning, the Lord was providing a solution for their problem. Ruth was gleaning in the fields of Boaz of Bethlehem (Ruth 2:4). And in time, Boaz married Ruth and provided both her and Naomi with the physical and financial security they needed. People from Bethlehem blessed the marriage

(Ruth 4:11). Bethlehem provided the solution for this family in need.

In the next book of the Bible, we meet descendants of Ruth and Boaz who are living in Bethlehem (Ruth 4:22) when the Lord sends the prophet Samuel to anoint a new king (1 Samuel 16:1). The first king of Israel, who initially had shown promise, failed to be the king the people wanted or the Lord demanded. Saul was from Gibeah, a place with a dark reputation (Judges 19:12–20:48). Bethlehem was a place with a more positive reputation. When Samuel arrived in Bethlehem (1 Samuel 16:4), he worked his way through all of Jesse's older sons, but not one was the man the Lord wanted. In desperation, Samuel asked if these were all the sons Jesse had. There was one more, David, who was outside the village taking care of the family animals. When he joined the others, Samuel knew he was the one God had chosen. "Then the LORD said, 'Rise and anoint him; this is the one'" (1 Samuel 16:12). To erase any lingering uncertainty about David's qualifications, the author of 1 Samuel shows David at work on the battlefield in his fight with Goliath. His faith-filled words, courage, and intelligence confirm his credentials. And lest we

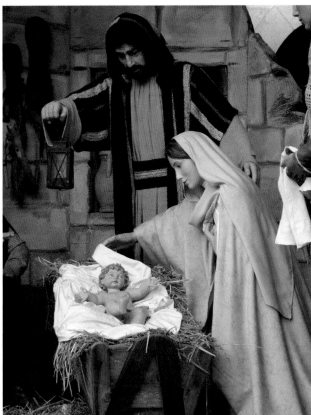

Main entry to the sixth-century Church of the Nativity in Bethlehem; **Right:** *Nativity scene in Bethlehem's Manger Square*

forget where he is from, we are reminded three times in this story that David came from Bethlehem (1 Samuel 17:12, 15, 58). The little village that had provided a solution for Naomi when she and her daughter-in-law were in trouble would now provide the solution for a nation that was in trouble.

But the best was yet to come. The world lay in sin's strong grip in desperate need of an eternal solution. David had been promised that one of his descendants would provide the solution (2 Samuel 7:12–16), and Micah was clear that Bethlehem would once again be the place that would provide the solution. "But you, Bethlehem Ephrathah, though you are small among the clans of Judah, out of you will come for me one who will

be ruler over Israel, whose origins are from of old, from ancient times" (Micah 5:2). This expectation so lingered around the little village of Bethlehem that it became widely accepted that the Messiah would come from this village (Matthew 2:4–6; John 7:42).[11] Once again the biblical authors call on geography. When Jesus is born, they make it clear that his birth took place in Bethlehem, a detail they repeat again and again to confirm the connection (Matthew 2:1, 6, 8; Luke 2:4, 15). This village that provided a solution at the level of family during the days of Naomi, and for a kingdom during the days of David, now provided the best solution of all: "Today in the town of David a Savior has been born to you; he is the Messiah, the Lord" (Luke 2:11).

The Flight to Egypt

When Christians list their favorite stories from the life of Jesus, the flight to Egypt is unlikely to be among them. It is less well known, presented only in the gospel of Matthew (2:13–18). And its value is not readily apparent. But as we will see, Matthew offers this event

from Jesus' life because it has something important to say about the Savior who saves by substitution.

The need for this dash south starts with a question asked by the Magi. There is uncertainty with regards to whether these men were Persians, Nabateans, or

Map 9.3—Jesus' Early Years

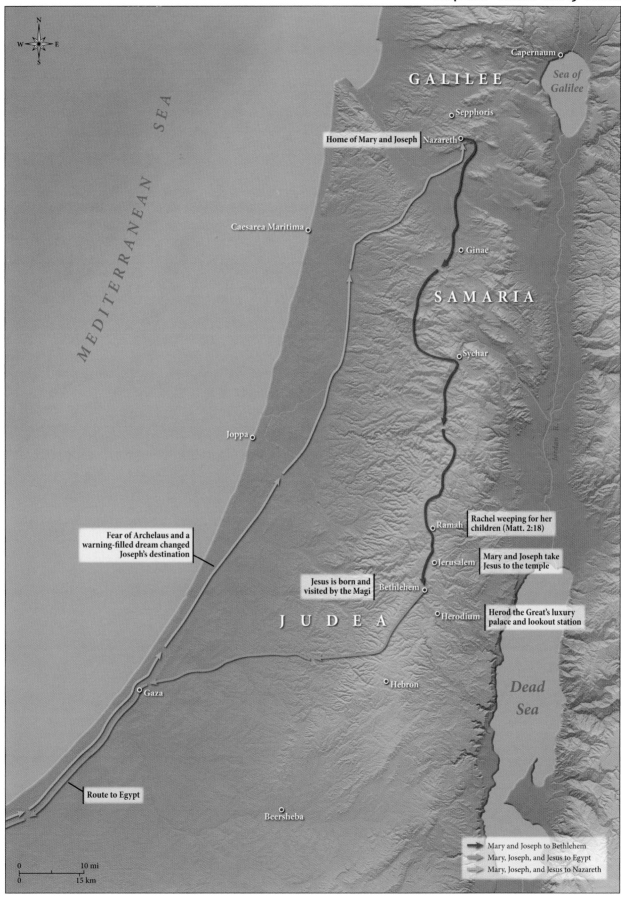

GALILEE

Capernaum

Sea of Galilee

Sepphoris

Home of Mary and Joseph | Nazareth

Caesarea Maritima

Ginae

SAMARIA

Sychar

MEDITERRANEAN SEA

Joppa

Ramah | Rachel weeping for her children (Matt. 2:18)

Jerusalem | Mary and Joseph take Jesus to the temple

Fear of Archelaus and a warning-filled dream changed Joseph's destination

Jesus is born and visited by the Magi | Bethlehem

Herodium | Herod the Great's luxury palace and lookout station

JUDEA

Dead Sea

Hebron

Gaza

Route to Egypt

Beersheba

0   10 mi
0   15 km

→ Mary and Joseph to Bethlehem
— Mary, Joseph, and Jesus to Egypt
— Mary, Joseph, and Jesus to Nazareth

members of the royal court in Babylon, but the important detail we don't want to miss is that they had come from the "east." Observing an aberration, "his star" (Matthew 2:2), in the evening sky, they set out on a quest to find the new king born among the Jews. Their quest brought them to Jerusalem, where they delivered this question: "Where is the one who has been born king of the Jews?" (Matthew 2:2). Combining this question, the eastern heritage of the Magi, and Herod the Great presents a volatile mix. Herod the Great had been named "King of Judea" by the Roman Senate in 40 BC, but before he could become the king, he first had to fight and defeat the Parthians, who were from the "east" and had laid claim to Judea. When men from the east asked about a new king of the Jews, they dialed up all the paranoia brewing in Herod. He had already killed family members he perceived as a threat. It was a short step to unleash the soldiers of the Herodium on little Bethlehem.

Feigning interest in worshiping this new king, Herod tried to use the wise men to find him. When an angel redirected the wise men to avoid any further contact with Herod, the king sent soldiers into Bethlehem with orders to kill all infant males two years of age and younger (Matthew 2:16–18).[12] It was because of this threat that an angel came to Joseph in a dream and told him they had to flee to Egypt.

While the reason for their flight to Egypt is clear, the route and destination in Egypt are not (see map 9.3). There are two routes that Mary, Joseph, and Jesus could have taken. The first is down the Ridge Route to Beersheba and then via the Way to Shur. This is the route Jacob and his family used when they left the Promised Land for Egypt during a severe famine (Genesis 46:1–7). The second is the more likely choice, since it is less rigorous and had better food and water resources along the way. It would take them out of the hill country to Gaza and then via the International Highway to Egypt. The destination in Egypt is unknown, although there is no shortage of Christian traditions that link Jesus to specific locations.[13] It is likely that Mary and Joseph sought the company of other Jews who were already living in Egypt.[14] For Matthew it is enough to say that they were in Egypt, out of Herod's reach.

The theological importance of this event is linked to Jesus' role as Savior-Substitute for all people and for Jewish people in particular. For Jesus to identify himself as the substitute for the Jewish people, he experienced life on earth, living the trials, threats, and

∨ *View from the Herodium, where Bethlehem is clearly visible on the opposite ridge*

temptations that the Israelites experienced. Matthew calls our attention to this part of Jesus' life to remind us of three experiences the Israelites had in the Old Testament: time in Egypt, threat of execution, and an exodus.

The first experience shared by the Israelites of the Old Testament and Jesus was that they both spent time in Egypt. With a famine clutching the farm fields and pastureland of their homeland, Jacob's family went to Egypt. Jesus' family did the same, but for a different reason. Matthew does not say where Jesus was in Egypt. More details on where they stayed could distract our attention from the most important point: Jesus spent time in Egypt just as the Israelites did.

The second experience Jesus and God's chosen people shared was the threat of execution. The family of Jacob traveled to Egypt voluntarily, accepting the invitation of Joseph to live in the land of Goshen while a famine gripped the world around them. At the close of 400 years, God's chosen people faced another threat. The Pharaoh of Egypt felt endangered by the growing Israelite population and began to address it using extreme measures. He severely oppressed the Israelites, and when that did not stem their population growth, he called for the murder of every Israelite male child who was born (Exodus 1:16, 22). Jesus faced this same threat. Bathed in fear and paranoia, Herod the Great ordered the execution of every male child in Bethlehem two years of age and younger in hopes that he would kill the newborn "King of the Jews." The order to kill all newborn boys in Egypt was the same as the order that threatened Jesus in Bethlehem.

The third experience that Jesus and the Israelites shared was an exodus, both from Egypt. The risk to

^ *An artist captures Jesus' early life in Bethlehem*

God's people in Egypt became so great that the Lord arranged for their departure, finally causing a series of plagues that devastated the economy of Egypt and broke Pharaoh's resolve. The exodus followed. For Jesus, the threat to his life ended after Herod the Great died. God then led Mary, Joseph, and Jesus out of Egypt. Matthew quotes the prophet Hosea (11:1) when he writes, 'And so was fulfilled what the Lord had said through the prophet: 'Out of Egypt I called my son''' (Matthew 2:15). Just as the Israelites had experienced time in Egypt, threat of execution, and an exodus, so Jesus as the Savior promised by God had the same experiences, highlighting his role as substitute.

Jesus of Nazareth

Jesus, Mary, and Joseph left Egypt and appeared to be planning a return to Bethlehem. But because the new leader of Judea, Herod the Great's son Archelaus, was known to be exceptionally cruel,[15] a warning dream redirected Jesus' family to Galilee and their former home in Nazareth (Matthew 2:22–23) (see map 9.3). This is the village where Jesus spent the majority of his time on earth. Because hometowns help shape who we become, we expect Nazareth to shape Jesus' personality, passions, and view of life. And because people evaluate us on where we are from, we expect that the views of Jesus' contemporaries will be molded, in part, by the fact that Nazareth is his hometown.

The first-century village of Nazareth was tucked

Caves were incorporated into many first-century Nazareth homes

into a small valley that sits on a high ridge in Lower Galilee. The archaeology suggests Jesus grew up in an agricultural village that had little more than 400 residents.[16] It is a place where you knew everyone and maybe felt that everyone knew a bit too much about you. Culturally Nazareth was a traditional, or orthodox, Jewish community, where the people eat kosher, keep Sabbath, and keep to themselves as a community. As far as the larger world was concerned, Nazareth was out of sight. No one significant had come from there, and nothing important ever seemed to happen there. It is unmentioned in the Old Testament, in the writings of Josephus, and in the Jewish traditional writings.

The gospel writers have almost nothing to say about the decades Jesus spent in this village, but Matthew does make one important observation: "[Jesus] went and lived in a town called Nazareth. So was fulfilled what was said through the prophets, that he would be called a Nazarene" (Matthew 2:23). Matthew keeps showing us how Jesus fulfilled prophecies from the Old Testament. But when we try to find this specific language in any of the books of the Old Testament, it simply is not there.

To decode this challenging text, we need to look

Map 9.4—Jesus and the Nazareth Ridge

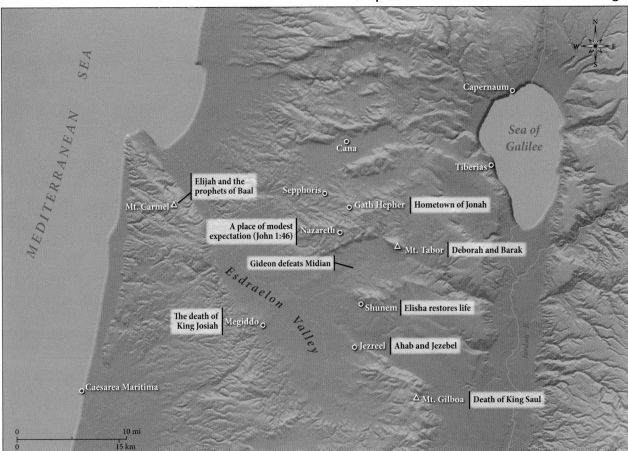

∧ *View from the Nazareth ridge includes the settings of many Old Testament stories*

for an Old Testament theme found among the prophets rather than a direct quote of one passage. That is because Matthew does not say Jesus is fulfilling something said by a "prophet" but by "the prophets." This is the only place Matthew introduces an Old Testament quote with the plural "prophets." By doing so, Matthew implies that he does not have a single text in mind but an idea or theme reflected in multiple places.[17]

To find that theme, we need to decode the word "Nazarene." Two options seem best, given the typical pattern of vocalizing Hebrew words in Aramaic, the commonly spoken language of Jesus' day. Either "Nazarene" should be connected with the Hebrew word *nezer*, which means "branch," or it is simply a reference to someone who comes from Nazareth, a Nazarethite. Since Matthew presents this word right after telling us that Jesus "went and lived in a town called Nazareth," the latter seems the most likely choice.

This leads us right back to the village of Nazareth and its first-century reputation. To get that first-century perspective, we need to go to Nathanael, who was from Cana, a small village just a short distance north of Nazareth. When Philip, who had just become an apostle, told Nathanael he had found "the one Moses wrote about in the Law" (John 1:45) and he was from

Nazareth, Nathanael replied, "Nazareth! Can anything good come from there?" (John 1:46). That spells out the first-century impression of the place, one the Romans were quick to pick up on and use during the crucifixion of Jesus. To mock Jesus and the Jews, they posted a sign above his head on the cross that placed the two facts side by side: "Jesus of Nazareth, the King of the Jews" (John 19:19).

People back then did not think much of those who came from Nazareth. And that is exactly how the authors of the Old Testament characterize the Messiah. Isaiah 11 in particular picks up on the idea of the unassuming branch: "A shoot will come up from the stump of Jesse; from his roots a Branch will bear fruit" (verse 1). And Isaiah 53 speaks of the low public profile that will characterize the Messiah: "He had no beauty or majesty to attract us to him, nothing in his appearance that we should desire him. He was despised and rejected by mankind, a man of suffering, and familiar with pain. Like one from whom people hide their faces he was despised, and we held him in low esteem" (verses 2–3). These texts and others in the Old Testament (Psalm 22:6; 69:8; Isaiah 49:7; Daniel 9:26) indicate that the Messiah will call attention to himself by the fact that he calls so little attention to himself—the definition of someone from Nazareth.

The First Miracle in Cana

Wedding couples dread any problems that can complicate their special day. At the center of John 2 is just such a glitch. During the seven-day wedding celebration, attention had been given to every detail except the wine. Much to the embarrassment of the host family, the wine ran out. This gaffe would have become the talk of Galilee even if Jesus had not stepped in to turn water into wine. But it really became the talk of the region after the miracle was done in Cana of Galilee. The location of the miracle is so important to our understanding of the story that John mentions it twice, both at the beginning and at the end of the narrative (John 2:1, 11).

Three different locations have been suggested for the Cana that hosts the first miracle of Jesus. The first is the least likely candidate, Kanah of Asher (Joshua 19:28). This spot is favored by church historian Eusebius but is much too far to the north to be the village mentioned in this story.[18] The second is the modern Kafr Kana located on the Nazareth Ridge. It has long been the traditional location of the miracle, filled with churches, souvenir stands, tour buses, and stores that specialize in wedding wine![19] But the best evidence takes us farther north. Eight miles (13 km) north of Nazareth, just above the Beit Netofa Valley on the lower flanks of the Jotapata Ridge, is the site we favor (see map 10.1). A long hike is required to get to this spot today, but during the New Testament era, this village sat on the important road that extended from Acco to Tiberias in the region of Lower Galilee.[20]

Cana is mentioned twice by John as he tells the story because the location of the miracle helped address a major obstacle to Jesus' credibility—the fact that he hailed from Nazareth in Galilee. To appreciate the problem, it will help to see that this story follows the calling of the first disciples, Andrew, his brother Simon (Peter in Greek), Philip, and Nathanael (John 1:35–43, 45). The first three disciples were from the fishing town of Bethsaida (John 1:44). Nathanael was from Cana (John 21:2). This creates the geographic bridge between the calling of Jesus' first disciples and his first miracle. Both stories are Galilee stories.

We are prone to celebrate the village of Nazareth

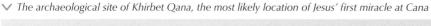

∨ *The archaeological site of Khirbet Qana, the most likely location of Jesus' first miracle at Cana*

∧ *The Beit Netofa Valley and Jotapata Ridge of Lower Galilee*

and the region of Galilee because we have the Gospels that describe things Jesus did there. But for those living during the 400-year bridge between the Old and New Testaments, the center of theological interest was Jerusalem in Judea because this was where the temple was located. And Bethlehem rates attention because this was where the Messiah was to be born (Micah 5:2). By contrast, Galilee was perceived to be a backwater. It was an area that had lost its orthodox Jewish character until the Hasmonean king Aristobulus (104–103 BC) reconquered it and forced its residents to assume a Jewish identity and lifestyle. No wonder there were questions about the commitment to the Jewish faith of those who lived in Galilee. Nathanael, who was from the same region and faced the same harsh presuppositions, gives us the insider's view. When confronted with the possibility that the Messiah had surfaced in Nazareth, Nathanael replied, "Nazareth! Can anything good come for there?" (John 1:46). The impressions people had in the first century of someone coming from Nazareth created a problem that impacted not only the way the general public viewed Jesus but the way his new special students, the disciples, viewed him as well. While this general perception of Galilee would change over time, Jesus did not have the luxury of time. He

needed the full confidence of his disciples now. Jesus was in the process of asking these men to engage ideas that would sound foreign to the ears of orthodox Jews. He would ask them to put themselves at odds with the power of Rome and at odds with the Jewish authorities in Jerusalem. A Messiah from Galilee was a problem, and the turning of water into wine would begin to address it.

∨ *First-century stone water containers*

John tells us that Mary, Jesus, and his disciples had come to Cana in Galilee for a wedding celebration (John 2:1–11). When trouble erupted with the wine supply, Mary called this to Jesus' attention. From what we know, Mary had been keeping Jesus' special identity to herself, reflecting, pondering, and treasuring all these things in her heart (Luke 2:19, 51). But she must have been anxious for others to know more, perhaps in no small part to remove the moral questions that lingered around Jesus' birth. It is unlikely that everyone in Galilee bought the idea of an angel telling Mary that she would have a miraculously conceived child. So she urges Jesus to respond to this opportunity in Cana among extended family and friends. Jesus initially deflects her request, noting that his time for a broad revelation of his identity had not yet come. But he then changes water into wine, miraculously producing the best wine of the week.

"What Jesus did here in Cana of Galilee was the first of the signs through which he revealed his glory" (John 2:11). Combining location with outcome, we see why John tells the story the way he does. The Nazareth-Galilee public-relations problem was real. Jesus' need for the disciples to have full confidence in him—to believe he was the Messiah—was real. So he performs a miracle in Cana of Galilee that answers any misgivings the disciples may have about his and their Galilean heritage. The result: "And his disciples believed in him" (verse 11).

Jesus Had to Be in His Father's House

Our teenage sons and daughters absolutely "have to be" somewhere so often that we grow numb to any sense of urgency these words suggest. Consequently we are at risk of missing the spectacular gravity of the first words that spill from Jesus' lips in the gospel of Luke. In 2:49, he says to his parents, "Didn't you know *I had to be* in my Father's house?" (emphasis added).[21] This story from Luke opens with Mary, Joseph, and Jesus traveling to Jerusalem in the company of friends and family. They left their home in Nazareth to fulfill one of the explicit directives in the Old Testament Law that required every responsible male to travel to Jerusalem to celebrate the eight-day festival of Passover, also called the Feast of Unleavened Bread (Exodus 23:14–17; Deuteronomy 16:16). At the age of twelve, Jesus was not required to go, but it was not unusual for eleven- and twelve-year-old boys to make the trip so they would learn what their responsibilities would be as Jewish males accountable for obeying this law when they turned thirteen.[22] So it was off to Jerusalem and the temple, where Jesus' family looked forward to worshiping.

To understand why it was necessary for Jesus to be at his "Father's house," we would do well to determine what Luke wants us to be thinking as we read the story. It appears that the theme of "searching" to achieve "understanding" is at the heart of what Luke is saying. Notice how frequently key words occur that direct us to this theme. The text tells us that Jesus was listening to the teachers in the temple courts, thoughtfully "asking them questions" and impressing everyone around him with his "understanding and his answers" (Luke 2:46–47). When Mary and Joseph left for home, Jesus stayed. At first his parents didn't realize he wasn't with them, but when they couldn't find him, they returned to Jerusalem. On the third day when his parents finally found their son, Mary told Jesus that she and Joseph had been "anxiously searching for you" (verse 48), to which Jesus replied, "Why were you searching for me?" (verse 49). He asked them if they didn't know that the temple was where he had to be. Luke informs us that his parents "did not understand what he was saying to

⌄ *Bar mitzvah in Jerusalem*

them" (verse 50). At the conclusion of the narrative, Luke notes that Jesus "grew in wisdom and stature, and in favor with God and man" (verse 52), echoing the language used earlier in Luke 2:40: "He was filled with wisdom." Luke is emphasizing the importance of Jesus gaining knowledge and understanding.

What is most striking is who is doing the learning—it is Jesus. The gospel writers give us only this one story from the early life of Jesus in Nazareth, so we trust that it has something important to tell us. It does; it is challenging us to understand. During these early years of Jesus' life, he came to learn who he was and what he had to accomplish in life. To which we might respond, Didn't he already know? As true God, Jesus knew absolutely everything there was to know, including who he was and

∧ *Southern steps of the temple complex where Jesus may have sat with his teachers*

what he needed to do. But in a way that no mortal can fully understand, Jesus, who was also 100 percent mortal, did not allow himself full access to his divine knowledge. He put this self-imposed restriction on his divine knowledge because he had come to be our substitute. To be a substitute, Jesus could not just simulate the human experience, merely pretending to be human. He had to be human in every respect. He had to learn who he was and what he was to do in the same way every other human does—by studying God's Word. Only then would he be able to say to those who challenged his identity as the Messiah, "You study the Scriptures diligently because you think that in them you have eternal life. These are the very Scriptures that testify about me" (John 5:39). That is why he could say in his home synagogue in Nazareth after reading words from Isaiah that spoke about the coming Messiah, "Today this scripture is fulfilled in your hearing" (Luke 4:21). He could say that because he had done the hard work of studying the Scriptures, learning what the law required, and learning what he needed to do to secure salvation for a fallen world. Jesus had to learn from God's Word just as we do, so Luke tells us that he listened carefully to his teachers

and asked questions. "Jesus grew in wisdom and stature, and in favor with God and man" (Luke 2:52).

And it is for this reason that Jesus had to be in the temple complex in Jerusalem. Jesus had grown up in a Jewish family and lived in an orthodox Jewish village. There is no doubt that Jesus' parents and his local rabbi would have introduced him to the commands and promises of the Old Testament.[23] There is also no doubt that this ambitious and talented student would have exhausted the resources of Nazareth by the time he reached age twelve, extracting every morsel of theological knowledge that he could. The one place where he could turn next was the center of Jewish worship and learning, the place where the best of the Jewish teachers were—the temple in Jerusalem. Jesus had to be in that place because it was the one place where his quest for self-understanding could continue. He relentlessly pursued the scholars there with his questions. And when it was time to leave, he simply could not go despite the worry it would cause his parents. The most important thing Jesus was doing during his early years was growing in wisdom, and his Father's house became the best place for him to take his learning to a higher level.

Jesus Baptized near Bethany Beyond the Jordan

The baptism of Jesus is such an important event that all four gospel writers record it (Matthew 3:13–17; Mark 1:9–11; Luke 3:21–22; John 1:28–34).

To determine why Jesus was baptized by John, we begin by asking the significance or purpose of the baptism John was doing. John's baptism was different from all other water rites, or ceremonies, in the Old and New Testaments.[24] It is different from the water of cleansing used to mark the transition of the Levites into holy service (Numbers 8:5–11), and it is different from the baptism Jesus directed the disciples to do at the time of their commissioning (Matthew 28:19). Unfortunately, John's baptism is not discussed in the kind of detail that can fully satisfy all of our questions, but this much seems certain. People were baptized by John when they accepted, or acknowledged, their sinfulness, repented of those sins, and looked in faith to the Lord for forgiveness. It formally associated them with the teachings of John. This is the reason John tried to dissuade Jesus when he asked to be baptized by John. John replied, "I need to be baptized by you, and do you come to me?" (Matthew 3:14). Nevertheless Jesus insisted and John performed the baptism (see map 9.5).

John's baptism of Jesus was unique. Jesus' baptism demonstrates that he had fully accepted the teachings of his Father in heaven. Through it his Father in heaven says to the world that Jesus is his Son. John had baptized many who had come to him, but never before had the baptism concluded with the heavens opening, the Holy Spirit of God descending like a dove, and the voice of the heavenly Father pouring forth to announce, "This is my Son, whom I love; with him I am well pleased" (Matthew 3:17).[25] While Matthew, Mark, and Luke all give attention to these details as they relate the event, the gospel of John focuses on what the event means. Although John the Baptist and Jesus were cousins who had known each other, Jesus' baptism becomes the moment when John, after baptizing Jesus, finally got it and knew that Jesus was the Messiah. "Then John gave this testimony: 'I saw the Spirit come down from heaven as a dove and remain on him. And I myself did not know him, but the one who sent me to baptize with water told me, "The man on whom you see the Spirit come down and remain is the one who will baptize with the Holy Spirit." I have seen and I testify that this is God's Chosen One'" (John 1:32–34).

The baptism of Jesus marks him as the Chosen One, and where it happened provides a striking con-

*Left: Qasr el-Yahud on the Jordan River, the traditional site of Jesus' baptism; **Right:** Byzantine baptismal font in Church of the Nativity*

Map 9.5—Jesus' Baptism and Temptation

text for the event. John was baptizing up and down the lower Jordan River (Luke 3:3), but on the day of Jesus' baptism, he appears to have been near Bethany Beyond the Jordan (John 1:28–29). The exact location of this Bethany is not certain.[26] We favor the traditional location just a few miles or kilometers north of the Dead Sea opposite the city of Jericho, where baptism sites exist both east and west of the Jordan River at Qasr el-Yahud and Tel el-Kharrar. This location provides a striking setting for the moment the heavenly Father reveals that Jesus is his Son.

It is important to realize how connected the description of Jesus' baptism is to images and themes of the Old Testament. For example, the descent of the Holy Spirit calls to mind the Spirit of God hovering over the waters in the creation account (Genesis 1:2). Next note the Spirit of God's descent on Jesus recalls the language of Isaiah 11:2: "The Spirit of the LORD will rest on him." The heavenly Father's declaration of Jesus' identity recalls Psalm 2 that records this heavenly exchange between the Father and the preincarnate Jesus. "He said to me, 'You are my son; today I have become your father'" (verse 7). We hear echoes of Isaiah again when the Father speaks of Jesus as the one in whom he delights: "Here is my servant, whom I uphold, my chosen one in whom I delight; I will put my Spirit on him, and he will bring justice to the nations" (Isaiah 42:1).[27]

Knowing the connections to the Old Testament so evident in Jesus' baptism and the most likely location of Jesus' baptism near Bethany Beyond the Jordan, there is one more powerful Old Testament text we need to read. During the final days of Moses, the Israelites were camped east of Jericho on the Plains of Moab. This left the Moabites feeling unsettled, so they hired a man named Balaam to put a curse on the Israelites. Balaam was a professional who made his living manipulating deities, but he met his match when it came to the Lord. Every time he tried to curse the Israelites, he ended up blessing them instead (Numbers 22–24). In the end, Balaam even spoke of the coming Messiah. "I see him, but not now; I behold him, but not near. A star will come out of Jacob; a scepter will rise out of Israel" (Numbers 24:17). Balaam spoke those words on a mountain

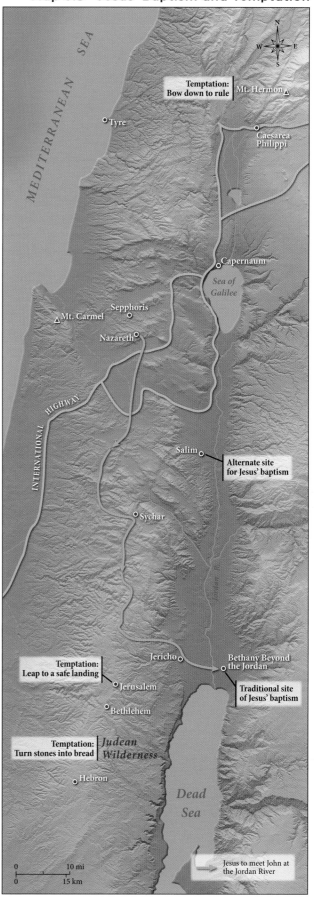

ridge just above the spot where Jesus would be baptized. You can see a long way from that ridge, but not into the future. God allowed Balaam to pick out the fuzzy images of this future event in the valley below on the day of Jesus' baptism. As the Father's voice booms in the Jordan Valley, we hear the faint echo of Balaam's prophecy that speaks of a time when a star and a scepter would arrive. Balaam said, "I see him, but not now; I behold him, but not near" (Numbers 24:17). This expectation expressed on the ridge above became real on the day Jesus was baptized in the river in the valley below.

Jesus Tempted in the Wilderness

Satan knew that he was in for a battle. Having been told by God that a descendant of Eve would engage him in an epic battle to determine the eternal destiny of mortals (Genesis 3:15), Satan had had lots of time to plot his strategy. But who would this challenger be? Promising candidates were picked off by Satan one after another. Then came Jesus' baptism, and Jesus' identity as the Son of God, the Messiah, is confirmed by God. Satan went to work tempting Jesus in the wilderness (Matthew 4:1–4; Mark 1:12–13; Luke 4:1–4).

The "wilderness" has many unnamed and non-descript places, so there is little chance that we can identify the precise location of this temptation (see map 9.5). Since John had been preaching in the Judean Wilderness (Matthew 3:1) and Jesus was baptized opposite Jericho near Bethany Beyond the Jordan just before going into this wilderness (John 1:28), it seems likely that Jesus faced this challenge on the dry ridges west of Jericho.[28] This wilderness is a rugged and menacing place with steep mountainsides that plunge into narrow, tortured canyons. It rains occasionally, but the 8 inches (20 cm) of annual precipitation won't change much, particularly since the rain that falls quickly runs off the steep, impenetrable ridges before the meager layer of soil can soak up much moisture. The lack of natural resources makes it difficult to survive there. Grain cannot be grown and there is little water to drink. The wilderness is a hauntingly beautiful landscape, a great place to find isolation and to fast, but one that defies human settlement.

The location of Jesus' temptation is important. Three gospel writers want to be sure we make that connection. But it is Matthew who lays bare the three parallels between the experience of Jesus and that of the Israelites who also spent time in the wilderness, although at different locations. First we note that both the Israelites and Jesus did not happen to go into the wilderness, they were led by God into the hostile terrain (Exodus 13:17–18, 21–22; Isaiah 63:14; Matthew 4:1).[29] The Israelites spent time in a variety of named wilderness areas, including the Deserts of Shur, Sinai, Sin, Paran, and Zin, all of which are far south of the location for Jesus' temptation. This may be why Matthew chooses to become more imprecise in identifying the location of Jesus' temptation. We know that Matthew had the language in his repertoire to speak of the Judean Wilderness because he did so at the start of the previous chapter (Matthew 3:1). The parallel between Jesus and the Israelites is not that they were in the same wilderness, but that they were in wilderness, hence the more vague language.

The second parallel has to do with the number 40. The Israelites spent 40 years in the wilderness (Deuteronomy 8:2); Jesus spent 40 days in the wilderness.

The third parallel has to do with the purpose behind the wilderness experience. Both the Israel-

∨ *The Desert of Zin was the setting for Israel's testing*

△ The Judean Wilderness was the setting for Jesus' testing

ites and Jesus faced the same question that is implied in Moses' description of the Israelites' experience: "Remember how the LORD your God led you all the way in the wilderness these forty years, to humble and test you in order to know what was in your heart, whether or not you would keep his commands. He humbled you, causing you to hunger and then feeding you with manna, which neither you nor your ancestors had known, to teach you that man does not live on bread alone but on every word that comes from the mouth of the LORD" (Deuteronomy 8:2–3). The question is, Will you trust me to provide even when you are in a place where the fundamentals for survival are missing? The Israelites faced that question, and Jesus faced the same question.

The need for Jesus to face this question in the wilderness just like the Israelites is because of his role as Savior-Substitute. Jesus had come to succeed in all the circumstances and situations where the Israelites and all other mortals had failed. He was "tempted in every way, just as we are—yet he did not sin" (Hebrews 4:15). The Spirit led Jesus into the wilderness, into terrain and circumstances that were like those of the Israelites, so that he could face that question in the same type of setting as the Israelites.

Jesus fasted for 40 days and nights. He "ate nothing" (Luke 4:2). Physically weakened by hunger, he probably appeared vulnerable. Satan made his play, urging Jesus to abandon his trust in the Lord. He urged him instead to tap into his power, taunting him with "if you are the Son of God" (verse 3). Satan was specific. He told Jesus to "tell this stone to become bread" (verse 3). There would be nothing morally wrong in the act itself; after all, the Lord had repeatedly provided manna in the wilderness for the Israelites. But this was different. Instead of helping others, as Jesus did later when he miraculously multiplied loaves and fish in his ministry, Jesus would be doing this miracle for himself and cut short the test of faith the wilderness imposed.

In response to this temptation, Jesus quotes the words of the Old Testament that addressed this situation at the time of Moses. "It is written: 'Man shall not live on bread alone, but on every word that comes from the mouth of God'" (Matthew 4:4). The Israelites repeatedly failed this test of faith during their wilderness experience by complaining, threatening, and lamenting their miserable circumstances. After being without food for 40 days in exactly the same kind of place, Jesus succeeds. He did not give in to temptation.

BIRTH AND EARLY YEARS OF JESUS · Jesus Tempted in the Wilderness | 243

∧ *Boat on the Sea of Galilee near Capernaum*

Chapter 10

JESUS IN GALILEE, SAMARIA, JUDEA, AND AMONG THE GENTILES

Jesus in Capernaum

The Gospels do not record every change in location Jesus made, but of those they mention, the most significant may have been his move from Nazareth, his hometown, to Capernaum (Matthew 4:13) (see map 10.1). By travel standards in Bible times, this was not a long journey, consisting of some 30 miles (48 km). What stands out is its permanence. Jesus left his hometown to establish a new residence in Capernaum, which becomes "his own town" (Matthew 9:1) and his "home" (Mark 2:1).

When Matthew reports on this move, he points out that it fulfills Old Testament prophecy. "Leaving Nazareth, [Jesus] went and lived in Capernaum . . . to fulfill what was said through the prophet Isaiah: 'Land of Zebulun and land of Naphtali, the Way of the Sea, beyond the Jordan, Galilee of the Gentiles—the people living in darkness have seen a great light; on those living in the land of the shadow of death a light has dawned'" (Matthew 4:13–16). This prophecy said the Messiah would have a significant and sustained impact in two geographic areas defined by Old Testament tribal land labels. Following the conquest of the Promised Land, Zebulun and Naphtali were two of the Israelite tribes assigned land parcels by Joshua (see map 10.1). Zebulun generally received the higher terrain north of the Jezreel Valley, including the Nazareth Ridge, while Naphtali received land northeast of Zebulun that included the area along the western shore of the Sea of Galilee (Joshua 19:10–16, 32–39).[1] These two tribal territories are mentioned twice by Matthew (4:13, 15) because they lie at the core of Isaiah's prophecy.[2] In terms of fulfillment of the prophecy, Jesus had already had a considerable influence on Zebulun because he had lived most of his life there in Nazareth. When he established his new residence in Capernaum, he placed himself in the heart of Naphtali, fulfilling the other dimension of Isaiah's prophecy.

The second portion of Isaiah's prophecy deals with the rehabilitation of this region's reputation following the Assyrian invasion at the time of Isaiah (2 Kings 15:29). Matthew repeats the unhappy description of this land used by Isaiah; Zebulun and Naphtali are called the "Galilee of the Gentiles" where people are "living in darkness" in the "land of the shadow of death" (Matthew 4:15–16). From an orthodox Jewish perspective, none of this language makes Galilee sound appealing. But the language captures the way of life that the Assyrians brought to the northern portion of the Promised Land. Following the fall of the Northern Kingdom, the Assyrians deported its Jewish residents and imported Gentiles to live in what had been Jewish homes. When problems developed, the

Map 10.1—Jesus Moves to Capernaum

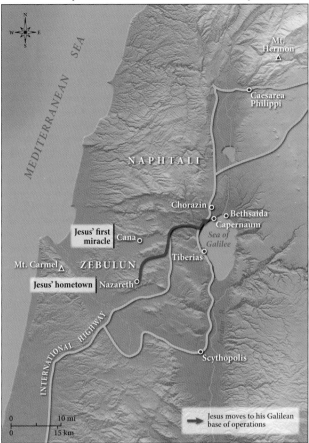

⌄ *Assyrian relief depicting the Israelites' exile*

Assyrians brought back some of the Jews, who then comingled their bloodlines and theology with the Gentiles there (2 Kings 17:24–41). Because so many Gentiles were living in Zebulun and Naphtali, those regions were identified by their dominant ethnic character, hence "Galilee of the Gentiles." And the theology was so confused that spiritual "darkness" aptly characterized the circumstances surrounding the people living there. Isaiah offers hope to his readers, writing of a day when all that will change. He declares that when the Messiah comes, he will bring light to this dark place. Considering that Shamash, one of the major Assyrian deities, was a solar deity who was regarded as the source of light,[3] the dawning of a new light is more than a metaphor for a new era. It is a new era marked by the arrival of God, namely the Messiah. Jesus' presence in Zebulun and Naphtali fulfilled this Old Testament prophecy and rehabilitated the reputation of this troubled area.

Jesus' move from Nazareth to Capernaum also changed the reach of Jesus' influence. This becomes apparent when we compare the geography and

∧ *Third/fourth-century synagogue at Capernaum*

character of Nazareth and Capernaum. Nazareth is a small village on the Nazareth Ridge. Tucked nicely into a valley near the top of the ridge, it is out of sight of the world, and the larger world is out of sight from Nazareth. The village was isolated both geographically and culturally. Nazareth was an orthodox Jewish village largely untarnished by the Hellenization of nearby cities. But this also means the views expressed in Nazareth, no matter how important, would remain in the village, disconnected from the rest of the world.

Capernaum is just the opposite. It is a medium-size town inhabited by a blend of Jews and Gentiles. Rather than being hidden, it sits in the open on the northwest shore of the Sea of Galilee. By contrast to Nazareth, it is an outward-looking place, easily seen and easily reached because it is near the International Highway.[4] This trade route was regularly traveled by merchants moving their wares between Asia, Africa, and Europe. Along with the olive oil, aromatics, and fibers they carried, the merchants also delivered the news of the day. Consequently, when Jesus moved from the isolated Nazareth to the exposed and outward-looking Capernaum, he completely changed the reach of his message. He could be certain that the important things he did and said would be carried to the far-flung corners of the world as the merchants moved their commodities. Long before Pentecost, people far from the Promised Land had a chance to learn of Jesus simply because he left Nazareth and moved to Capernaum.

The Mountain Setting for the Sermon on the Mount

The Sermon on the Mount (Matthew 5–7; Luke 6:12–49) is widely regarded as a theological treasure. But not everyone agrees on the setting. Even Matthew and Luke appear to be in conflict over the location. The Byzantine Christians in the fourth century AD resolved the dispute by locating the Sermon on the

Mount near the spot where they went to remember two "food" miracles, the Feeding of the 5,000 and the meal served by Jesus when he recalled the disciples to service after his resurrection (Mark 6:30–44; John 21). Near that spot on Mount Eremos, on a small rise west of the Sea of Galilee, is the Church of the Beatitudes, built in 1938.[5] While this is a wonderful spot for devotional reflection, our preference for the location of the sermon is the southern cliff of Mount Arbel, about 5 miles (8 km) southwest of Mount Eremos (see map 10.2).

Mount Arbel solves the apparent conflict between Matthew and Luke. When Matthew describes Jesus' discourse, he locates it on a mountain (Matthew 5:1). Luke locates it on a level place (Luke 6:17).[6] Mount Arbel's topography allows for the validity of both descriptions. When viewed from the Sea of Galilee, Mount Arbel offers a striking silhouette, a portion of which is nearly vertical, rising some 1,300 feet (396 m) above the Sea of Galilee. Once on top of this mountain, we discover that it flattens out and slopes gently westward, taking on the appearance of a level place. Thus Mount Arbel explains the different descriptions of Matthew and Luke. On one side it is a mountain and on the other, a level place.

Mount Arbel offered the isolation the Sermon on the Mount demanded. This discourse clearly is more sophisticated than other lessons Jesus presented in the Gospels. The character of the lesson itself suggests it was intended for a more advanced student, like the disciples who needed a higher level of training as the educators of God's people. The sophisticated content of the lesson and Matthew's statement that the disciples came to Jesus so he could teach them (Matthew 5:1–2) suggest that the Sermon on the Mount was not designed for wide public consumption, but was meant to be a private lesson for the disciples. This called for a quiet place, but a quiet place was difficult to find. Large and persistent crowds followed Jesus wherever he went (Matthew 4:25).[7] While Jesus taught in many places that made it easy for crowds to reach him, the strenuous climb up Mount Arbel was more likely to create the isolation that would have given Jesus quiet time in prayer as well as private time for teaching the disciples.

Mount Arbel also has the view and the full scope of imagery that Jesus uses in the Sermon on the Mount. This starts with the Beatitudes (Matthew 5:2–12). The language of the Beatitudes offers a remarkable survey of the seasons of life as well as the great reversals that are part of the life of the Christian. The poor are really rich, those who mourn will be comforted, the meek

∨ *Chapel of the Beatitudes, traditional location of the Sermon on the Mount*

∧ *Mount Arbel, a likely location for Jesus' Sermon on the Mount*

will inherit the earth, and the persecuted are blessed. The quiet isolation of high mountains provides a fitting place to reflect on such things. The view from the top of Mount Arbel calls to mind all the seasons of life. The view to the north looks directly into the Sea of Galilee basin and into the lives of those described in the Beatitudes. It is intriguing to consider that the specific circumstances in life mentioned by Jesus in the Beatitudes may have been prompted by the sight of real people having those experiences in the basin below.

In connection with this view from Mount Arbel, we also have within view all the imagery Jesus employs in the rest of the Sermon on the Mount. For example, Jesus challenges the disciples to see themselves as "the salt of the earth" (Matthew 5:13). At the foot of Mount Arbel was a place called Magdala (Taricheae) where fish were preserved in a process that used salt to dry them out.[8] As the salt of the earth, the disciples had a chance to bring about this kind of preservation in the lives of people. Next Jesus tells the disciples they are to be the light of the world, adding that a town built on

a hill cannot be hidden (Matthew 5:14). This language also comes to life when our eyes travel due east from Mount Arbel to the city of Hippos on the eastern shore of the Sea of Galilee. Hippos was a Decapolis city, extravagantly constructed and well lighted at night.[9] By design, such Greco-Roman cities located along important transportation routes were built to have a cultural influence on the local villages, showing them how grand and successful were those who espoused the ideology and religion of the Roman world. The disciples now had a different and more valuable kind of illumination to offer, and Jesus encouraged them to be that light for the world.

Beyond salt and light, we find an array of visual aids at Jesus' disposal that support the theology he taught. As he urges the disciples to put worry in its place, he invites them to consider the birds of the air who do not busy themselves in agricultural pursuits like those on the fertile Plain of Gennesaret below them. "Are you not much more valuable than they?" (Matthew 6:26). And he invites them to consider the flower-filled fields like those that occupy the top of Mount Arbel to this day. "If that is how God clothes the grass of the field, which is here today and tomorrow is thrown into the fire, will he not much more clothe you?" (Matthew 6:30). Although neither Matthew nor Luke gives us the name of the rising terrain that provided the setting for the Sermon on the Mount, when we consider the character, isolation, visual aids, and views available to Jesus from the top of Mount Arbel, it is hard to dismiss it as a viable candidate.

The Evangelical Triangle—Opportunity Squandered and Seized

The Evangelical ("Good News") Triangle is a relatively small parcel of land defined by the cities of Chorazin, Bethsaida, and Capernaum (see map 10.2). This triangle is less than 3 miles (5 km) per side, yet received more of the Savior's time and attention than any other place in the Promised Land. It was the place where "most of his miracles had been performed" (Matthew 11:20). The harsh words Jesus had for these towns were in direct proportion to the opportunities for repentance they squandered: "Woe to you, Chorazin! Woe to you, Bethsaida! For if the miracles that were performed in you had been performed in Tyre and Sidon, they would have repented long ago in sackcloth and ashes. But I tell you, it will be more bearable for Tyre and Sidon on the day of judgment than for you. And you, Capernaum, will you be lifted to the heavens? No, you will go down to Hades. For if the miracles that were performed in you had been performed in Sodom, it would have remained to this day" (Matthew 11:21–23; see also Luke 10:13–15).

Matthew tells us that Jesus spoke in towns throughout Galilee (Matthew 11:1), but he also tells us that three of those Galilean towns saw the most of Jesus. Capernaum is the most famous and becomes the second most

Map 10.2—Around the Sea of Galilee

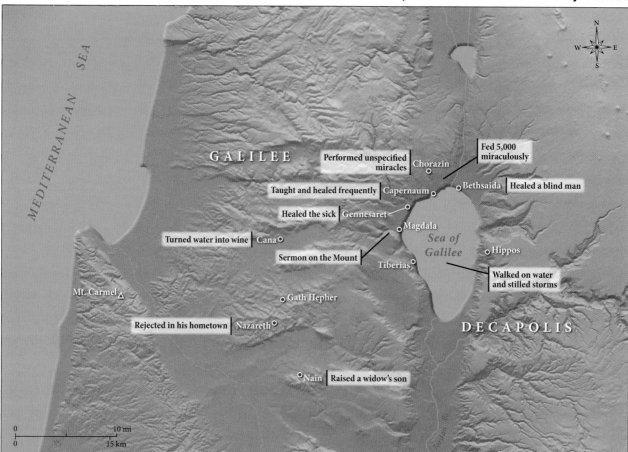

△ **Left:** *Third- to fifth-century ruins from Chorazin;* **Right:** *Foundations of first-century Capernaum homes*

mentioned place in the Gospels after Jerusalem. Its location on the northwest side of the Sea of Galilee has been confirmed by memories of the place passed down from one generation to the next and by archaeology.[10] Bethsaida is the third most frequently mentioned place in the Gospels, but its exact location is the subject of ongoing debate.[11] Without becoming unduly distracted by the debate, we can safely place the Bethsaida of Jesus' day on the north side of the Sea of Galilee near the inlet of the Upper Jordan River. That brings us to Chorazin, which we locate 2.5 miles (4 km) north of Capernaum. The first-century town has not been excavated, but we do have a striking third- and fourth-century AD village of Chorazin in the same area. Given this evidence, we place all three towns on the map on the north and northwest sides of the Sea of Galilee where an orthodox Jewish culture and mind-set dominated.

Of the three communities, the biblical authors were inspired by the Holy Spirit to tell us most about the experience Capernaum had with Jesus. We know that he moved into this location from Nazareth, establishing it as his "own town" (Matthew 9:1). We have examples of what the residents of Capernaum experienced as the Gospels tell us of profound teaching and astounding miracles Jesus performed there (Mat-

thew 8:5–17; 9:1–8; Mark 2:1–3:6; 4:1–34; Luke 7:1–10; 8:40–56). The Gospels are much stingier when reporting on events in Bethsaida and Chorazin. We know that Bethsaida was the home of Philip, Peter, and Andrew (John 1:44; 12:21). This certainly gave those living in this village an entry into the life of Jesus. And we know that in Bethsaida, Jesus healed a man who was blind (Mark 8:22–26). With Chorazin, we have little. The only time this village is mentioned in the Gospels is in the judgment directed against the three villages of the Evangelical Triangle. However, we can assume that both Bethsaida and Chorazin enjoyed an experience similar to that of Capernaum and one like that described in Matthew 4:23: "Jesus went throughout Galilee, teaching in their synagogues, proclaiming the good news of the kingdom, and healing every disease and sickness among the people."

What is so sad is that this opportunity Jesus provided was squandered. While a few accepted Jesus as their Savior, most did not. It is not that the residents of these villages attacked Jesus; they didn't. They dismissed or ignored him. And it is their disinterest that led them to squander the amazing opportunity they had. No wonder Jesus delivered such harsh language against these villages.

^ *The northwest shore of the Sea of Galilee, the site of much of Jesus' earthly ministry*

The other side of the geographic story in Jesus' harsh judgment speech has to do with the three cities mentioned as the foils to Chorazin, Bethsaida, and Capernaum. They are Tyre, Sidon, and Sodom (see map 10.3). We read about these cities in the Old Testament and find the crushing weight of Old Testament prophecy falling squarely on their shoulders. Tyre and Sidon were Phoenician cities that had grown wealthy through their skills with shipbuilding, shipping, and trade. But their pride, dishonest dealing, and violent behavior put them in the sights of Old Testament prophets (Ezekiel 28:11, 16–18). "Wail, you ships of Tarshish! For Tyre is destroyed and left without house or harbor" (Isaiah 23:1; see also Isaiah 23; Jeremiah 25:22; Ezekiel 28:11–23; Zechariah 9:3–4). Sodom has a similar pedigree whose character is best known from the time of Abraham in connection with her sister city of Gomorrah (Genesis 19). These cities had multiple strikes against them. They were outside the Promised Land. They were inhabited by Gentiles. And they had sinned so horribly that the Lord visited stern judgment on them. And yet in the language of Jesus' speech against Chorazin, Bethsaida, and Capernaum, these Gentile cities, bad as they were, stood a better chance on the day of judgment than the three in the Evangelical Triangle.

How did they get the chance to seize the opportunity for salvation that others squandered? People just like those in the cities of Tyre and Sidon, far removed from the ministry of Jesus, came to know Jesus as their Savior because the International Highway passed just to the west of the Evangelical Triangle. Because Jesus did so many miracles and taught so frequently on this small parcel of land, the merchants of the world who were passing through heard the stories. When they traveled to the farthest reaches of the world, they took the gospel message with them, giving those who would never know Jesus personally a chance to receive him as their personal Savior, including people from Tyre and Sidon (Mark 3:8). So while the Jewish villages in the Evangelical Triangle squandered the chance geography gave them, the Gentiles living far away from them seized the opportunity the geography gave them.

Jesus, Jonah, and the Nazareth Ridge

The book of Jonah does not contain a single direct prophecy about Jesus. But there is a geographic connection between Jesus and Jonah that joins with other parallels to link the messages of these two men. Their hometowns—Nazareth and Gath Hepher—are both located on the Nazareth Ridge, less than an hour's walk apart. All of those parallels come to the surface when some Pharisees ask Jesus for a sign they could see.

Ironically, their demand for such a sign comes right after a man possessed by a demon is brought to Jesus, who does a miracle they could have seen. The demon had deprived the poor man of both his sight and hearing. Jesus heals him. Those who witnessed the miracle wondered aloud if this might be the Messiah they had been waiting for. "Could this be the Son of David?" (Matthew 12:23). But when the Pharisees heard about it, they tried to discredit the miracle by claiming Jesus was manipulating spirits by Beelzebul, the prince of demons. Jesus, knowing what these guardians of orthodoxy were thinking, embarked on a strongly worded criticism designed to get them to think and change.

Jesus was teaching in Lower Galilee at the time,[12] the area that both Jesus and Jonah had lived in. In this location and in what Jesus says, three parallels between Jesus and Jonah emerge. First, Jesus and Jonah were both prophets. Jonah's story is told in the book that carries his name. The Lord summoned him from his home in Lower Galilee to travel to Nineveh at the top of the Fertile Crescent to convince Gentiles living there to repent of their sins. Once he got around to doing what he was told to do, his success is among the most dramatic recorded in the Bible. In answering the Pharisees who had asked for a sign, Jesus told them, "Now something greater than Jonah is here" (Matthew 12:41). The Pharisees did not understand the opportunity they were missing. They didn't understand the lesson Jesus was teaching them.

The second similarity between Jesus and Jonah is

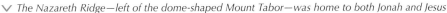

⌄ *The Nazareth Ridge—left of the dome-shaped Mount Tabor—was home to both Jonah and Jesus*

the authenticating sign that accompanied their ministries. Instead of going directly to Nineveh to preach against the sins committed there, Jonah decided to commit a few of his own. He disobeyed the Lord's command and boarded a boat, hoping to sail as far away from Nineveh as he could get. The Lord put a stop to this by stirring up a terrible storm on the Mediterranean Sea that threatened to end the lives of everyone aboard the vessel. When the casting of lots pointed to Jonah as the cause of the storm, he directed his fellow travelers to throw him into the raging water. We might have expected his life and mission to end there. But the Lord sent a large fish to swallow but not digest Jonah. He was kept alive in the fish for three days and nights before it vomited him out on shore. This is the sign Jesus said his detractors will be given. "For as Jonah was three days and three nights in the belly of a huge fish, so the Son of Man will be three days and three nights in the heart of the earth" (Matthew 12:40). Jonah's story of survival became an authenticating sign, marking him as a true prophet of God. In the same way, Jesus, who died on the cross, would spend three days and three nights in the tomb before his resurrection. This becomes the authenticating sign that Jesus is who he claimed to be and that the work of salvation he pursued has been accomplished (Acts 2:24, 32, 36; 3:15; 13:37; 17:31).

The third point of comparison between Jesus and Jonah is geographic. Jonah's hometown was in Gath Hepher (2 Kings 14:25), a small village on the Nazareth Ridge. Jesus' hometown of Nazareth was just 3 miles (4.8 km) to the southwest. In the minds of the Jewish leaders, Jesus' connection to Galilee worked against his credibility as the Messiah. When Nicodemus urged the other members of the Sanhedrin to give Jesus a fair hearing, his fellow Sanhedrin members turned on him.

∧ *Tomb with a rolling stone*

Nicodemus received this sharply worded reply: "Are you from Galilee, too? Look into it, and you will find that a prophet does not come out of Galilee" (John 7:52). They were wrong.

The ancestors of the Pharisees had Jonah as near as the Nazareth Ridge. Now the Pharisees had Jesus in the same location. But Jesus told them that those who lived far from the Nazareth Ridge in places like Nineveh and southern Saudi Arabia will rise up on the day of judgment to condemn this generation that asks for a sign. The people of Nineveh nearly missed the message because they were so far away. The Queen of the South traveled across the Arabian Desert to see for herself if the stories about Solomon were true. The Jewish leaders would be condemned at the judgment because they had someone greater than Jonah or Solomon who was speaking to them, and they failed to accept his message (Matthew 12:41–42).

Jesus Raises the Widow's Son at Nain

Unknown to either one, two crowds were heading toward each other, and their meeting would produce the experience of a lifetime. One crowd had walked from Capernaum to Nain; the other was leaving the town gates of Nain (see map 10.2). One was brimming with excitement, talking loudly about all that Jesus had done; the other was somber, carrying a dead man on a bier to the town cemetery. The dead man's mother, a widow, was going to bury her only son. All who saw her felt her pain and emptiness. She not only faced the grief of a bereaved mother but also a bleak economic future without the support of a husband or son. Jesus' heart went out to her. But Luke records this particular event not only because it demonstrates the compassion of Jesus, but also because it is an event that clearly identifies Jesus as the Messiah (Luke 7:11–17). Note that the story does not end with the happy reunion of mother and son but with the reaction of the crowd. They exclaimed, "A great prophet has appeared among us" (Luke 7:16). We will see how this extreme act of compassion combines with the geography to lead them to that conclusion.[13]

Ordinary people in the Promised Land were looking for someone special. When we finish reading the words of God recorded in the Old Testament, we know that the story is incomplete. The Old Testament ends with many threads still unwoven into the garment of history, a garment that will remain unfinished until someone special, the Messiah, arrives. So the people of Nain were looking for someone to complete the story of the Old Testament. God's people of the past expected a more important prophet than the many prophets whom they had already met. Moses said to expect "a prophet like me from among you" (Deuteronomy 18:15). In time, God's people came to think of the coming Messiah as the ultimate prophet. As Jesus moved among the people of Israel, some thought of him as "one of the prophets" (Matthew 16:14), but others saw him as "the Prophet" (John 7:40).

The Messiah would not only be a prophet, but also a man who was associated with the resurrection of the dead. The Old Testament says that the Messiah would rise from the dead (Psalm 16:10) and bring the world to a close with a great resurrection (Daniel 12:2). This resurrection connection to the Messiah explains why Martha speaks to Jesus as she does during their conversation following the death of Lazarus. Jesus tells Martha that her "brother will rise again" (John 11:23), and he asks her directly if she believes this. She does not answer by saying yes but by declaring, "I believe that you are the Messiah, the Son of God, who is come into the world" (John 11:27). In doing so, she offers the

∨ *Chapel in the village of Nain*

perspective of the ordinary man or woman, like those in Nain. These folks were looking for the Messiah, the Prophet, and they understood that resurrection would be associated with this Prophet.

These are the expectations that feed the passion Luke had for telling this story. There was nothing in the general appearance of Jesus to distinguish him as someone special. He could easily have gotten lost in the crowd had he chosen to do so. But he identifies himself as the Messiah by what he did. When John the Baptist sent some of his students to Jesus to confirm that Jesus was the one who was expected, Jesus told them to return to John and tell him what Jesus had done, particularly the fact that the "dead are raised" (Luke 7:18–23). No doubt the raising of the widow's son at Nain would be at the top of the list (verse 18).

However, it is not just that Jesus raised the dead but that he did so in Nain that is an important part of this story. Both the miracle and the location of the miracle tie Jesus with the prophet Elisha, who had an important connection to the general area of Nain. He often traveled between Mount Carmel and his hometown of Abel Meholah; the village of Shunem was located about halfway between the two and made for a convenient overnight stopping place.[14] A couple living there made a small room for Elisha so that he could use it whenever he passed through. This couple enjoyed financial security but had been unable to have children. That changed when Elisha prayed and the Lord provided them with a son. One day while this young man was helping his father in the grain fields, he collapsed and died. His father and mother placed him on Elisha's bed in their home and sent for the prophet. When Elisha reached the house, the Lord empowered him to perform a miracle to restore life to the boy (2 Kings 4:8–37).

∨ *The village of Nain resides on the side of Mount Moreh*

This is the kind of story that sticks in a place like Shunem. It's remembered for years. That is why Luke was so insistent that we know Jesus raised the widow's son at Nain. We can easily miss the geographic connection between the two places unless we note that Shunem (Elisha's miracle) and Nain (Jesus' miracle) are both on the same small mountain, Mount Moreh, only a few minutes' walk apart. Clearly Jesus' actions in Nain were driven by compassion he felt for the grief-stricken mother, a widow. But by doing a miracle like Elisha had done in almost the same location, he was identifying himself as the Messiah. The people of Nain remembered what Elisha had done on the other side of their mountain, and they got it. Their excited response shows that they were bringing together the miracle, the place, and its history. "They were all filled with awe and praised God. 'A great prophet has appeared among us'" (Luke 7:16).

The Geography of Forgiveness

When Jesus and his disciples traveled, it was necessary for them to bring along their own food. One day on a trip across the Sea of Galilee to its eastern shore, the disciples realized they had forgotten to bring bread. This prompted Jesus to start a conversation about yeast. "'Be careful,' Jesus said to them. 'Be on your guard against the yeast of the Pharisees and Sadducees'" (Matthew 16:6). The disciples mistakenly thought that Jesus was criticizing them for forgetting to bring bread, but instead Jesus was using the disciples' experiences of the feeding of the thousands to help them see the expansiveness and inclusiveness of the geography of forgiveness.

There are many similarities between the Feeding of the 5,000 and the Feeding of the 4,000, but a key difference is the geographical setting. John places the Feeding of the 5,000 on the "far shore of the Sea of Galilee" (John 6:1), and Luke puts it near Bethsaida on the north side of the lake (Luke 9:10) (see map 10.2). Jesus had gone to this area seeking some quiet time away from the crowds after receiving word of the execution of John the Baptist. Eventually a crowd finds

∨ *The Feeding of the 5,000 took place on the north side of the Sea of Galilee near Bethsaida*

Map 10.3—Jesus Beyond the Sea of Galilee

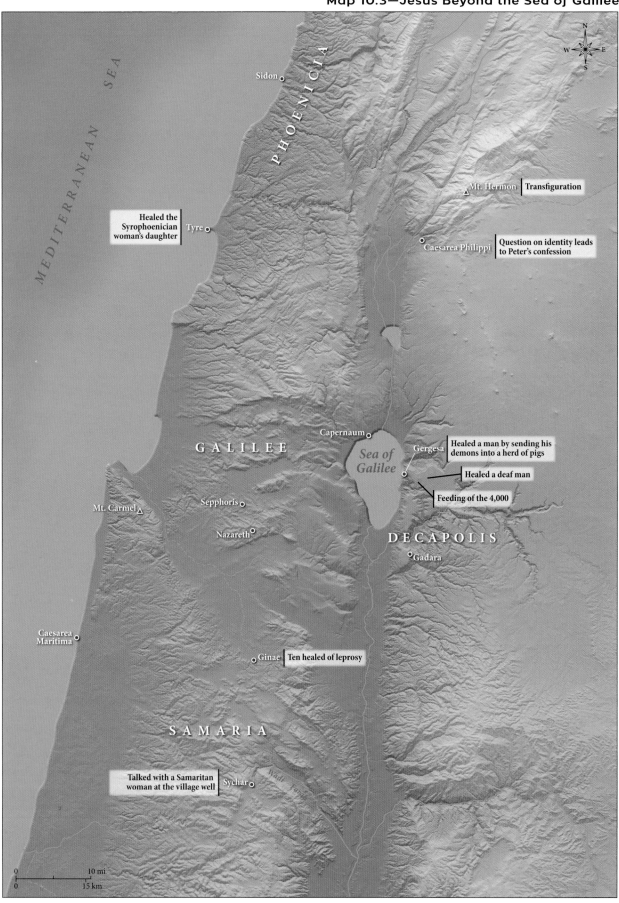

∧ *A Byzantine mosaic at Tabgha recalls the Feeding of the 5,000 miracle*

Jesus and stays so long that a miracle is needed to provide a meal for them. Because this segment of the lakeshore was predominantly settled by Jews in the first century, those who received the benefits of this blessing would have most likely been Jewish. This is supported not just by the geography but also by mention of Passover (John 6:4) and the collection of twelve baskets of leftovers, a number that recalls the twelve tribes of Israel (Matthew 14:20).[15]

This contrasts with the location for the Feeding of the 4,000 and its beneficiaries, which the Gospels place on the east side of the Sea of Galilee (see map 10.3). Just before reporting on this miracle, Mark places Jesus in the Decapolis (Mark 7:31) on the east side of the Sea of Galilee and has him returning to the west side of the lake after the miracle (Mark 8:10).[16] The Decapolis—the east side of the Sea of Galilee in the first century—was the "other side" of the lake in so many ways. Decapolis cities were Gentile in orientation, designed to project the authority of Rome and the culture of the Greco-Roman world into their geographic setting. By contrast to the northwest side of the Sea of Galilee, the Decapolis was home to pigs and pagan excesses that were shunned by orthodox Jews (Mark 5:1–20).[17] This means that the participants in the Feeding of the 4,000 were predominately Gentiles. This is suggested not only by the geography but by the number of baskets of leftovers gathered at the close of the miracle, seven. "Seven" is clearly meant to contrast with the "twelve" of the other miracle and so is best

interpreted as an ethnic marker. When we consider the use of numbers in the Old Testament, seven is a number associated with the Gentile population living in the Promised Land prior to the arrival of the Israelites (Deuteronomy 7:1; Acts 13:19).

While the ethnic difference in diners might seem to contribute little to our understanding of these two miracles, it lies at the heart of the miracles' interpretation. Jesus makes sure we notice by returning to the topic as he discusses the "yeast of the Pharisees and Sadducees" (Matthew 16:5–12). The yeast used to make first-century bread was a small amount of fermented bread dough that was mixed into a new batch of dough.[18] The small amount of "yeast" permeated the whole mixture as it was kneaded in the kneading trough. Jesus likens the errant theology of the Pharisees and Sadducees to yeast, mentioning it three times in the eight verses of this account. Their view was that the favor and forgiveness of God extended only to Jews, like those living on the northwest shore of the Sea of Galilee. Just as a small amount of yeast influences a large amount of bread dough, so the Jewish leaders' mistaken view had the ability to harm the growth of his kingdom.

Jesus responds to the notion by recalling the two feeding miracles. "Do you still not understand? Don't you remember the five loaves for the five thousand, and how many basketfuls you gathered? Or the seven loaves for the four thousand, and how many basketfuls

∨ *Modern boat on the Sea of Galilee*

you gathered?" (Matthew 16:9–10). His point? Jesus had done two parallel miracles in two different locations, one for Jews and one for Gentiles. In doing so, he was countering the "yeast" of those religious leaders that wished to narrow the geography of forgiveness to only Jews while leaving Gentiles out. The geogra-phy of forgiveness was much larger than they allowed. The Gospels speak of the worldwide nature of God's forgiveness (John 3:16). Jesus illustrated it in a memo-rable way by performing parallel miracles for Jews and Gentiles that countered the "yeast of the Pharisees and Sadducees."

Identity and Capability at Caesarea Philippi

Jesus moved from place to place, meeting hurting people where they lived. But there are also times when Jesus visited a location because it provided the right setting for a particular lesson he wanted to teach. That is the case when Jesus took the disciples to the region of Caesarea Philippi (Matthew 16:13–18) (see map 10.3).

On a quick read, this conversation in Matthew appears to be staged as a lesson on identity. It begins when Jesus asks the disciples to give him the word on the street. "Who do people say the Son of Man is?" (Matthew 16:13). Jesus listens to their answers and then turns the same question back on them. Peter is quick to speak for the group and gives the memorable answer: "You are the Messiah, the Son of the living God" (Matthew 16:16). His answer is so good that it merits a name change. Peter's given name was Simon;

Jesus says his new name is "Peter," or the "rock," a name that recalls his rock-like confession of his faith. "And I tell you that you are Peter, and on this rock I will build my church, and the gates of Hades will not overcome it" (Matthew 16:18). So far, the lesson seems to be focused on identity.

But the lesson is really about much more than that. It is about capability. Read the first question Jesus asked on who the "Son of Man" is. In that question, he is using a label linked to the Messiah in the Old Testament (Daniel 7:13–14). So when Jesus asks the disciples the follow-up question, he has already given the answer away. However, if we think of the mind-set of the ancient Near Eastern world, we see that this conversation goes beyond identity. In the mythology of the ancient world, a deity was considered a real being when it received a name and a function.[19] The

Left: Sanctuary for Greek god Pan at Caesarea Philippi; **Right:** Corinthian column from a temple at Caesarea Philippi

identity of a deity or a person is linked to their capability. Who you are is an indicator of what you can do. If we carry that mind-set into Matthew 16, we begin to hear the exchanges between Jesus and Peter in a different way. When Jesus asks the disciples who he is, Jesus is introducing a conversation not just about his identity, but about his capability. And when Jesus speaks about the identity of Peter, identity includes the notion of capability.

This conversation about capability will make even more sense when we see how vital it is in light of the changes that are about to occur. Immediately after this conversation, Jesus speaks about going to Jerusalem, surrendering his life, and rising from the dead (Matthew 16:21). It was important for the disciples to know who Jesus was so they could know everything he was capable of doing in Jerusalem. And the disciples had to know what they were capable of doing because

they were about to be left to advance the kingdom of God without him.

Jesus' selection of the location for this conversation on identity and capability made it clear and memorable. It takes place in the region of Caesarea Philippi, the largest city of the far north, tucked into the southern base of Mount Hermon just north of the swampy Huleh Basin.[20] Travelers on the International Highway were squeezed between the two natural obstacles—swamp and mountain—an ideal place to control movement and trade. That is why Herod Philip, a son of Herod the Great, established his capital city here. The administrative center doubled as a worship center for the pagan world. The natural setting and appearance certainly favored that. The worship center is located at the base of a 100-foot (30.5 m) cliff whose brilliant colors and eerie appearance make it seem otherworldly. At the base of this cliff, a large yawning cave spouted spring

∨ Illustration of the pagan worship complex at Caesarea Philippi

∧ *Cave at Caesarea Philippi that was regarded as the entrance to Hades*

water in such volume that its water collected into the Hermon River, one of the three major headwaters for the Jordan River. Here in this otherworldly place, so rich in water, the ancients established a worship site for Pan, the god of shepherds and nature. And here Herod the Great built an imposing marble temple right in front of the cave for his patron Augustus Caesar, who had given him the site in 20 BC.[21]

This place also had imagery Jesus used to illustrate and make memorable important things he had to say.

When he referred to Peter (who declared that Jesus is the Messiah) as a rock in this geographic setting, our eyes move to the one rock that dominates the horizon in this region, Mount Hermon. It stands out at an elevation of 9,232 feet (2,814 m), gleaming white a good share of the year because of the snow that crowns its long ridge. This rock beautifully illustrates the power of Peter's confession of faith. How could Christ's little church hope to survive when opposed by the power of Rome built on the foundation of its pagan theology? The answer is Peter's confession. Just as no army dared cross Mount Hermon's high tundra but was deflected at its base, so the church built on Peter's confession of faith would deflect all nations who opposed it. In fact, not even the gates of Hades would prevail against this church.

The disciples must have been concerned about the apparent power of false gods whose cultural presence is so aptly illustrated in the worship center at Caesarea Philippi. In fact, the Romans regarded the cave there as the gate to their gods' domain, Hades.[22] The pagan worship center at Caesarea Philippi was impressive, but it was no match for Christ's church. Caesarea Philippi was a place that made the discussion of Jesus' identity and capability both clearer and more memorable for the disciples.

Jesus Transfigured on a High Mountain

By our standards, the typical day spent with Jesus was anything but typical, given the insightful teaching he offered and the miracles he performed. But even among the atypical days of Jesus' life, the day of his transfiguration on the high mountain stands out (see map 10.3).

The transfiguration of Jesus has three interrelated parts. Peter, James, and John, who accompanied Jesus for this experience, were familiar with his appearance. But what they saw on the high mountain was awe inspiring. "His face shone like the sun, and his clothes became as white as the light" (Matthew 17:2). Jesus was joined by two others. The high mountain hike gave this small group some isolation but did not keep heavenly figures away. As Jesus glowed, Moses and Elijah appeared and talked with Jesus (Matthew 17:3). Just when the disciples thought this day could not be

any more surreal, a bright cloud enveloped them and a booming voice proclaimed, "This is my Son, whom I love; with him I am well pleased. Listen to him!" (Matthew 17:5).

The transfiguration marks a change in Jesus' direction and a change in his mode of speaking with the disciples. Before this, the majority of Jesus' time had been spent in the northern portion of the Promised Land, particularly in Galilee, with a few side trips into Gentile country. Now Jesus' face is firmly fixed on his final walk to Jerusalem. And as he makes this final turn toward the holy city, he speaks directly and clearly about what awaits him there. Jesus told his disciples that he would suffer and die (Matthew 16:21). This disturbing news created an opportunity for the disciples, particularly those closest to him, Peter, James, and

John, to rally behind their teacher and support him during these most difficult days. The transfiguration was meant to win their confidence and support for the challenges ahead.

This was accomplished in three ways. First, the message that Jesus was going to Jerusalem was accompanied by a change in Jesus' appearance. These men had spent many months with Jesus but never had seen him shine with the brightness of the sun. Second, the appearance of Moses and Elijah, whom Luke tells us were talking about Jesus' experiences ahead in Jerusalem (Luke 9:31), affirmed that this plan was an extension of prophecy. And finally, this unthinkable plan had the heavenly Father's support. He identified Jesus as his beloved Son and told the disciples, "Listen to him!" (Matthew 17:5). This directive with the change in Jesus' appearance and the presence of Moses and Elijah secured the support of Peter, James, and John for Jesus' plan to suffer and die in Jerusalem.

The location of the transfiguration helps shape our perception of the event. Both Matthew and Mark place Jesus' transfiguration on a "high mountain" (Matthew 17:1; Mark 9:2). We feel some frustration over the lack of precision in this description. But it is the nature of this description that allows us to identify the location of the mountain and the literary power it has. The description of this place as a "high mountain" starts our identification process. There are other mountains that stand out on the landscape of the Promised Land, like Mount Tabor that has been associated with the transfiguration.[23] But Mount Tabor, at 1,929 feet (588 m) simply is no match for Mount Hermon that towers above all other mountains in the region at 9,232 feet (2,814 m). Matthew employs the phrase "high mountain" only twice in his gospel, the other time in connection with the third temptation of Jesus (Matthew 4:8). This temptation involved the devil taking Jesus to a location from which he could see all the kingdoms of the world. Unless the Lord granted the devil powers he did not naturally possess, we must look for a physical location from which one could see at least representatives of all kingdoms of the earth. Because international travelers wanted nothing to do with navigating the tundra of Mount Hermon's high passes, they shuttled around its base on the International Highway. That makes Mount Hermon a high

⌄ *Mount Tabor, the traditional location of Jesus' transfiguration*

∧ *Mount Hermon, the most likely location for Jesus' transfiguration*

mountain from which one can view those who are from the kingdoms of the world.[24] Because Matthew uses the phrase "high mountain" in referring both to the mountain of temptation and the mountain of transfiguration, we may presume that he is referring to the same place, Mount Hermon (see map 10.3). This mountain also is in exactly the right region, based on the geographic indicator we have in the story immediately preceding the transfiguration. Matthew 16:13 has us in the region of Caesarea Philippi. The enigmatic "high mountain" is most likely Mount Hermon.

By using this same reference—"high mountain"—Matthew is providing a link between two temptations. The devil tempted Jesus to bow down to him and offered Jesus a pathway to kingdom without the cross (Matthew 4:9). Jesus commands, "Away from me, Satan!" (Matthew 4:10). In the same location, and immediately following the transfiguration designed to win Peter's support, this disciple ironically presses Jesus to abandon his plan to go to Jerusalem, where suffering and death await him (Matthew 16:22). Jesus sharply criticizes Peter: "Get behind me, Satan," revealing the true source behind Peter's language (Matthew 16:23). This "high mountain" in Matthew is where three events come together. It is where Jesus was tempted to abandon the necessary path to the cross on two occasions, once by Satan directly and once by Satan working though Peter, and where the absolute necessity of going to the cross is presented in his transfiguration.

The Stakes Are Raised in Bethany

The raising of Lazarus from the dead is a story that deserves telling and the gospel of John does not disappoint. Realizing the gravity of this event, John honors it by relating this story more slowly, providing a wealth of details. Thousands of Christians who have lost family members and friends have benefited from it, drying their tears with the powerful words of Jesus that speak about resurrection and reunion beyond the grave. But John also gives detailed attention to this event in Jesus' life because of how it raises the stakes (John 11:1–44).

To see that, we first must note how this action by Jesus identified him as the Messiah to ordinary people. Note the exchange that took place between Martha and Jesus following the death of Lazarus. Clearly a warm friendship existed between Jesus and this family, one that had developed over many evenings spent together in Bethany (Matthew 21:17; Mark 11:11; Luke 10:38–42). This closeness made the news of Lazarus's serious illness all the more difficult for Jesus to hear. Yet when that news reached him, he stayed put in another area for two days, allowing the illness to run its course and take the life of his friend Lazarus. Only then did Jesus travel up the road from Jericho toward Bethany to visit the bereaved sisters (see map 10.4). Martha could not wait for him to reach her home but ran out to meet Jesus, leading to the important exchange between the two. Jesus offers comfort by reminding Martha that her brother would "rise again" (John 11:23). Martha responds by acknowledging the resurrection that would come at the end of time. Jesus presses the matter, suggesting that a more imminent resurrection was possible. "I am the resurrection and the life. The one who believes in me will live, even though they die; and whoever lives by believing in me will never die. Do you believe this?" (John 11:25–26). It is Martha's answer that provides a powerful insight. We might expect her to respond by saying "Yes!" or "Yes, I believe you are capable of doing a resurrection miracle." But instead she responds by saying, "Yes, Lord, I believe that you are the Messiah, the Son of God, who is to come into the world" (John 11:27). Martha was not a theologian. But her simple statement of faith reveals a perspective held by her and other ordinary people of the land. By raising Lazarus, Jesus identified himself as the Messiah.

To further appreciate how the raising of Lazarus raised the stakes, we need to see it in contrast to the two other resurrection miracles of Jesus presented in the Gospels. He raised the widow's son at Nain (Luke 7:11–17) and he raised Jairus's daughter in Capernaum (Luke 8:40–56). There are two striking differences between these miracles and the one celebrated by Mary and Martha. One has to do with timing and the other with location. The miracles performed for the widow's son and Jairus's daughter were performed on the same day they died. In the case of the widow's son, his mother was en route to the cemetery, the body of her son being carried on a bier. Within the Jewish culture of the first century, the day of one's death was the day of burial.[25] In the case of Jairus's daughter, she died while this synagogue ruler was with Jesus pleading for his help. Because there had been instances where a person was presumed to be dead but was not, a person was not certified as having died until the fourth day after death.[26] Thus, while there is no doubt for us that these two died and were brought back to life by Jesus, there was room in the Jewish mind for another explanation. This explanation in the case of Lazarus was ruled out. He had been dead for four days when Jesus arrived (John 11:17, 39).

The second way the raising of Lazarus was distinct has to do with the proximity of this miracle to Jerusalem. The other two miracles occurred in Galilee, far from the holy city of Jerusalem. The raising of Lazarus occurred in Bethany. This detail is so important to the story that John mentions it twice (John 11:1, 18). Bethany was less than 2 miles (3 km) from Jerusalem (John 11:18). And because this miracle was so memorable,

∨ *Traditional tomb of Lazarus*

Map 10.4—Jesus' Journey to Jerusalem

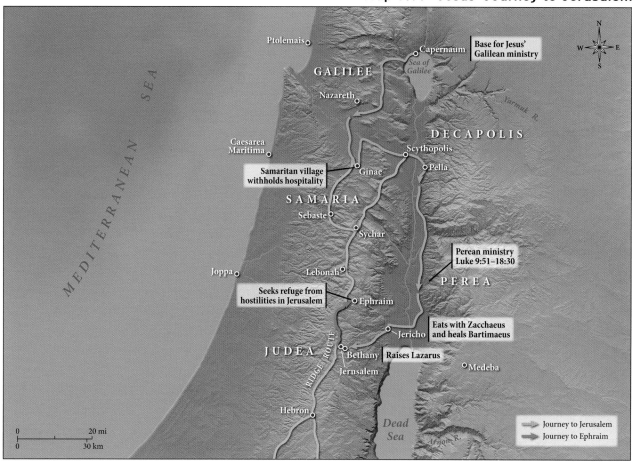

early Christian visitors to the land visited this village. In the fourth century, church historian Eusebius recorded that people were regularly shown the tomb of Lazarus located just outside Jerusalem. Within about a century of that, the historian Jerome added that there was a church built on the site.[27] This evidence allows us to locate Bethany in the modern Arab village of El-Azariya, a village whose name reflects the connection to Lazarus.

A resurrection miracle so close to Jerusalem and just before the Passover celebration that would bring thousands to Jerusalem meant that what happened in Bethany would be the big news, the talk of the festival. The eyewitnesses of Lazarus's resurrection and Lazarus himself were only a short distance from the temple, just over the Mount of Olives in Bethany. As a result, many came to think of Jesus as the Messiah, and it seemed that everyone might quickly follow suit (John 11:45, 48). But for the Jewish leaders in Jerusalem, the raising of Lazarus in Bethany was bad news. They plotted to end Jesus' life (John 11:49–53).

Jesus Enters Jerusalem via Bethphage

The small village of Bethphage is mentioned only three times in the Bible and only in connection with one event—Jesus' triumphal entry into Jerusalem on Palm Sunday (see map 10.5).[28] For the Jewish festivalgoers camped on the Mount of Olives, the geography of that day ignited a frenzied welcome the likes of which Jesus had not experienced any of the other times he had entered the holy city.

The gospel writers and early Christian pilgrims help us to locate Bethphage on the map of the greater Jerusalem area. The Gospels place Bethphage on the Mount of Olives, between downtown Jerusalem and the village of Bethany (Matthew 21:1; Mark 11:1; Luke 19:29).[29] Just east of the watershed of the Mount of Olives is a chapel built in 1883 intended to identify the location where Jesus got on the donkey he rode into Jerusalem. It was built over the top of a Crusader church that had been constructed around a 3-foot-tall (.9 m) mounting stone that tradition said Jesus used to get on the donkey (an animal much smaller than the Crusader stallions whose riders benefited from such a mounting stone). The mounting stone was covered with Crusader paintings depicting the raising of Lazarus, Jesus on a donkey, and the triumphal entry into Jerusalem.[30] This locates Bethphage in the modern village of et-Tur.

∧ *Bethpage is located near the Ascension Tower on the Mount of Olives*

On Palm Sunday, Jesus left Bethany and followed the well-worn path that led through Bethphage and the dip, or pass, in the extended ridge of the Mount of Olives, then down the slope into Jerusalem. Before he reaches Bethphage, Jesus issues his unusual request. He sends two of the disciples "ahead" to Bethphage to acquire the donkey they are to "bring to" Jesus before he enters the village because he "needs" it. Three gospels are clear on these instructions (Matthew 21:2; Mark 11:2; Luke 19:30). The unique request for a

Map 10.5—Events on the Mount of Olives

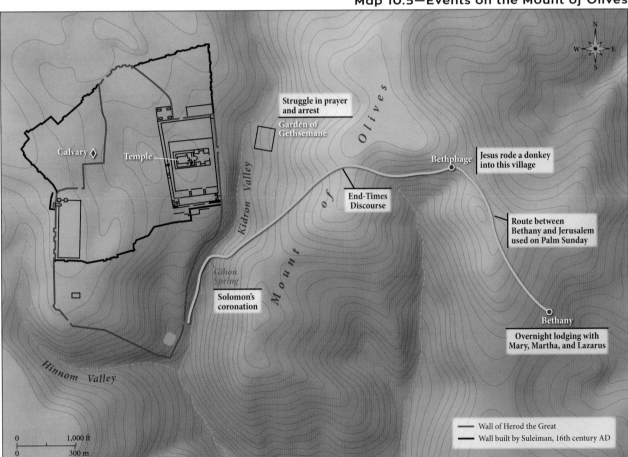

∧ *This dip on the Mount of Olives provided the easiest route to Bethany*

donkey and Jesus' insistence that he "needs" it signals the fulfillment of the Old Testament prophecy quoted by Matthew that "your king comes to you . . . riding on a donkey" (Matthew 21:5). The large crowd that had gathered on the Mount of Olives cheers when it sees Jesus coming. The people place their cloaks on the road, wave palm branches, and excitedly shout about the coming of the Son of David.

They respond as they do because Jesus' actions combine with geography to identify him as the Messiah who was to come. Jesus is coming from the correct direction as he enters Jerusalem. The Messiah was to enter Jerusalem from the east. This expectation comes from a number of prophetic texts. Isaiah said the highway via which the Messiah will come runs through the desert (Judean Wilderness) east of Jerusalem (Isaiah 40:3). Ezekiel, in his vision, saw the Lord returning to the new temple from the east to occupy the space he had abandoned during the time of judgment (Ezekiel 43:1–3). Zechariah saw the nations gathering in Jerusalem for the Messiah's final judgment that will occur east of Jerusalem on the Mount of Olives (Zechariah 14:4). And Malachi turns the eyes of his readers with these words: "But for you who revere my name, the sun of

righteousness will rise with healing in its rays" (Malachi 4:2). All of this eastward-looking language gave rise to the expectation that the Messiah would enter Jerusalem from the east. And the gospel writers want us to pay attention to the geography of this important day. Jesus' route from Bethany, to Bethphage, and down the Mount of Olives into Jerusalem was a route that brought Jesus into the holy city from the east.

The second important dimension of the geography in this narrative is linked to Bethphage being in the city limits of Jerusalem. When we think about ancient cities, we are tempted to think of their city limits in connection with the city's defensive wall. But the reality was that the effective reach of a city's economy and residential area extended well beyond those walls. If we were to mark Jerusalem's city limits with its defensive walls, we would never think of Bethphage as being in the city limits of Jerusalem because at no time in the history of Jerusalem did its defensive walls extend as far as the Mount of Olives. However, in the Jewish Mishnah, which preserves rabbinic points of view on a variety of topics, we get information about the perceived Jewish city limits of Jerusalem from a discussion centering on the baking of ritual bread for use in the temple. Though there was agreement on the fact that this bread needed to be baked in Jerusalem, there was a question on where the city limits were.[31] One view noted that bread baked in Bethphage was suitable for use in the temple, thus marking Bethphage as within the effective city limits of Jerusalem.[32] It is no wonder then that the Gospels are so insistent about this geography. By getting on a donkey outside of Bethphage and riding it into the village, Jesus was riding across the city limits of Jerusalem and into the city itself. This fulfills the prophecy found in Zechariah 9:9 quoted by Matthew: "See, your king comes to you, gentle and riding on a donkey, on a colt, the foal of a donkey" (Matthew 21:5). Jesus needed the donkey to fulfill this prophecy, but he also needed the geography to mark this entry into Jerusalem. By traveling through Bethany and then Bethphage, he arrived from the east, riding the donkey into Jerusalem.

Jesus, the Son of David, and Gihon Spring

The Christian celebration of Palm Sunday (the Sunday of Triumphal Entry) is a day filled with classic sights and sounds. Jesus rides on a donkey surrounded by adoring crowds who wave palm branches as they shout their hosannas. Those wonderful images and sounds of Palm Sunday are best explained by something that is not a familiar part of our celebration, the Gihon Spring (see map 10.5). An event associated with this spring is the most likely explanation not only for the actions of the crowd, but also for their use of the title "Son of David" as they welcome Jesus to Jerusalem.

An important Old Testament event happened at the Gihon Spring that helps to explain the actions and language of the crowd on Palm Sunday (1 Kings 1). As age robbed King David of his vigor and compromised his ability to lead, his son Adonijah began to promote himself as David's successor. Some of David's advisers were so worried about David's mental state that they fell in behind Adonijah and made plans to have him anointed as king without telling David. When Nathan, the prophet, and Bathsheba, the mother of Solomon, heard that Adonijah's coronation was under way at En Rogel, a spring located at the confluence of the Kidron and Hinnom Valleys, they went to speak with David. David immediately called for the coronation of Solomon, his intended successor. "Take your lord's servants with you and have Solomon my son mount my own mule and take him down to the Gihon. There have Zadok the priest and Nathan the prophet anoint him king over Israel. Blow the trumpet and shout, 'Long live King Solomon!'" (1 Kings 1:33–34).

The area of this spring remains in view from the Mount of Olives along the route Jesus followed. When Jesus left Bethphage on Palm Sunday, he traveled over the Mount of Olives in the direction of Jerusalem (Matthew 21:1). Given the topography of the Mount of Olives, those making this crossing typically saved some energy by using the lower pass in the middle of the ridge. We presume Jesus did the same. Then, as he descended, we assume he would have stayed

∧ The donkey played an important role in Jesus' Palm Sunday entry to Jerusalem

well north of the cemetery that stretched from the current location of the Dominus Flavit church toward the southern end of the Mount of Olives. By avoiding the cemetery, Jesus avoided the ritual contamination he otherwise would have experienced. Because we know the route of Jesus, we also know where the excited crowd was and what they were able to see as they watched Jesus descend the Mount of Olives. They saw

⌃ **Left:** *The Gihon Spring lies under the red-roofed building at the bottom of the Kidron Valley;* **Right:** *Gihon Spring, site of Solomon's coronation*

Jesus riding a donkey down the west side of the Mount of Olives, descending into the Kidron Valley, a route that would take him right past Gihon Spring.

The symmetry between Solomon's coronation day and Jesus' triumphal entry are striking. Although arriving from opposite directions, both Solomon and Jesus rode a beast of burden (Jesus a donkey, Solomon a mule) into the Kidron Valley, heading in the direction of Gihon Spring. This symmetry made the ride of Jesus look like a coronation, and that is how the crowd responded. They treated Jesus like royalty and filled the air with coronation language. "Hosanna to the Son of David!" (Matthew 21:9). "Blessed is the coming kingdom of our father David!" (Mark 11:10). "Blessed is the king who comes in the name of the Lord!" (Luke 19:38). God had promised David that one of his descendants would be the royal Messiah (2 Samuel 7:11–14). That day had come. And we will see it as clearly as the crowd did when we add the Gihon Spring to our Palm Sunday images.

End Times Discourse on the Mount of Olives

When illness or injury signal the final days of our life on earth, the things that had commanded our attention and controlled the content of our weeks change. The to-do list that stretches into the next half of the year becomes meaningless when we expect to die within weeks or days. Our attention turns to the things we would have done well to pay attention to all along. As Jesus faced the end of his life, his thoughts also turned to the last things. Three days prior to his death, Jesus had a long conversation on the end times with his disciples on the Mount of Olives (Matthew 24–25) (see map 10.5). Both Matthew and Mark see significance in the location and name it (Matthew 24:3; Mark 13:3).

The Mount of Olives is as easy to identify today as it was in the first century. It was well known to Jesus and his disciples. It is an extended ridge some 2 miles

(3.2 km) long that rises 300 feet (91.4 m) higher than Jerusalem and lies immediately to the east of the city. Between the Mount of Olives and Jerusalem runs the Kidron Valley. While dry most of the year, the valley hosts a flowing stream during the rainy season, carrying water from the mountains around Jerusalem all the way to the Dead Sea. During the last week of Jesus' life, Jesus and his disciples had been staying in the small village of Bethany on the east side of the Mount of Olives. That means every day, twice a day, Jesus would climb and descend the well-worn path over the Mount of Olives and across the Kidron.

Two days before Passover, while finishing the day in Jerusalem, the disciples were marveling at the temple complex that had been remodeled by Herod the Great. Sounding every bit the rural folk they were, one of the disciples said, "Look, Teacher! What massive stones! What magnificent buildings!" (Mark 13:1). That prompted Jesus to speak of their ruin. "Do you see all these great buildings? . . . Not one stone here will be left on another; every one will be thrown down" (Mark 13:2). Jesus had provided an example of just one of the things the disciples could expect to see in the years ahead. This destruction would be realized when Titus and the Romans destroyed Jerusalem at the close of the first Jewish revolt in 70 AD. The prophecy whet

their appetite for more. "As Jesus was sitting on the Mount of Olives opposite the temple, Peter, James, John and Andrew asked him privately, 'Tell us, when will these things happen? And what will be the sign that they are all about to be fulfilled?'" (Mark 13:3–4). This prompts Jesus to launch into a discourse that

∨ *Evidence of the 70 AD Roman destruction of the temple*

∨ *Model of the temple complex as it would be seen from the Mount of Olives*

Map 10.6—New Testament Jerusalem

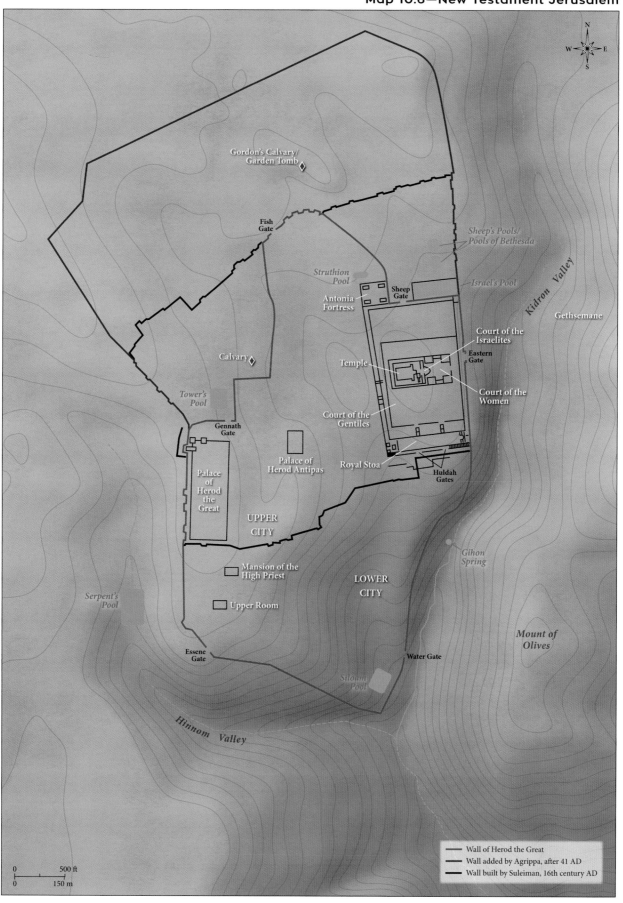

Gordon's Calvary/
Garden Tomb ◇

Fish
Gate

Sheep's Pools/
Pools of Bethesda

Struthion
Pool

Sheep
Gate

Antonia
Fortress

Israel's Pool

Kidron Valley

Gethsemane

Court of the
Israelites

Temple

Eastern
Gate

Calvary ◇

Court of the
Women

Tower's
Pool

Court of the
Gentiles

Gennath
Gate

Palace of
Herod Antipas

Royal Stoa

Huldah
Gates

Palace
of
Herod
the
Great

UPPER
CITY

Mansion of the
High Priest

LOWER
CITY

Gihon
Spring

Serpent's
Pool

Upper Room

Mount of
Olives

Essene
Gate

Water Gate

Hinnom Valley

Siloam
Pool

——	Wall of Herod the Great
——	Wall added by Agrippa, after 41 AD
——	Wall built by Suleiman, 16th century AD

0   500 ft

0   150 m

fills two chapters in Matthew (Matthew 24–25). Jesus speaks of the troubling news they will hear about wars, famines, and earthquakes. He speaks about the coming persecution of Christians. And he speaks of how Christians might best use their time. During those last days, Jesus urges his followers to show kindness to others and to steep themselves in thoughtful preparation, being intentional about where they place their attention. "Therefore keep watch, because you do not know the day or the hour" (Matthew 25:13).

Their location on the Mount of Olives above the Kidron Valley was ideal for this kind of reflection. It is a place that people associated with the end of time. Today that connection is apparent in the cemeteries that dot the landscape. Jews, Christians, and Muslims who have associated this place with the grand resurrection and final judgment have filled the place with tombs. There are Jewish graves on the Mount of Olives, Muslim graves just west of the Kidron Valley, and Christian graves on the floor of Kidron Valley.

Two Old Testament texts suggest this location will be the place of final judgment. The first is Joel 3:2, 14. Joel spoke to the people of God during a terrible locust plague that was devastating the landscape and the economy (Joel 1:16–20). Natural disasters like that can prompt deep reflection, and Joel urged his readers to use it as a time to reflect and repent. "Rend your heart and not your garments. Return to the LORD your God" (Joel 2:13). He urged these actions because

the Lord is coming to judge the nations and close this chapter of the world's history. Joel placed this event in the "Valley of Jehoshaphat" (Hebrew for "The Lord will judge"). While some have associated this valley with one east of Tekoa where King Jehoshaphat won victory over the eastern people during his reign (2 Chronicles 20:20–26), the early Christian community associated it with the Kidron Valley.[33]

This connection is likely influenced by Zechariah 14:4 that also speaks of the end times. In the final chapter of Zechariah, the prophet addressed the era of the Messiah. The nations that have spent their energy opposing the advance of God's kingdom will meet this Messiah in one last battle that will culminate in the final judgment. "On that day his feet will stand on the Mount of Olives, east of Jerusalem." If Joel and Zechariah are discussing the same event, we identify the Valley of Jehoshaphat with a valley near the Mount of Olives. The Kidron Valley is a good bet.

For some Christians today, the scene of the final battle at the close of time and the judgment to follow is connected to Megiddo and the Jezreel Valley (Revelation 16:16). But in the first century when people talked about these last days, they associated them with the Mount of Olives and the Kidron Valley. As Jesus sits on the Mount of Olives with the temple complex in view, he conducts his discourse on the end times in the area where the people of his age thought it would occur.

∨ **Left:** *Traditional tomb of Absalom;* **Right:** *Traditional tomb of Zechariah*

Jesus Struggles at Gethsemane

Gethsemane was located along the road Jesus traveled between Jerusalem and Bethany (see map 10.5), a quiet spot where he had stopped to have private conversations with the disciples (Luke 22:39; John 18:2). In the final week of Jesus' life before his crucifixion, Gethsemane becomes the place of Jesus' struggle in prayer.

The gospel writers identify the location of this struggle both with general and specific language. Following the celebration of Passover, the meal that turned into the Last Supper, Jesus and the disciples walked to the Mount of Olives (Matthew 26:30; Mark 14:26; Luke 22:39). The Mount of Olives is the extended ridge that lies just east of Jerusalem, stretching sharply skyward out of the Kidron Valley and rising 300 feet (91.4 m) above the city. On the side of this ridge was a healthy grove of olive trees and the installation for processing the harvested olives. This processing station was

called Gethsemane. This is the second and more precise way the writers identify the spot of Jesus' struggle in prayer (Matthew 26:36; Mark 14:32).

With the precision of this language, it would appear to be easy to pinpoint the location of this event in Jesus' life. Today the Mount of Olives is filled with churches, and no less than three of those church compounds claim to be the historic site of Jesus' struggle.[34] But the evidence allows us to point in only a general way toward the north side of the ridge of the Mount of Olives, affirming that the Gethsemane of the Gospels is located somewhere in this area.

We can be more certain about why the writers of the Gospels urge us to note the location of Jesus' struggle. The location of Gethsemane on the Mount of Olives highlights the intensity of Jesus' struggle in prayer and explains why this poignant moment of struggle occurs when it does. First, the name Gethsemane

∨ *Church of All Nations, traditional location of the Garden of Gethsemane*

highlights the intensity of Jesus' struggle. The word *Gethsemane* brings to mind the substantial mechanisms used to process olives to make olive oil. This valuable commodity was extracted from the harvested olives only when a mighty weight was brought to bear on them with a press.[35] Gethsemane is the place of the "oil press." It is the image of the olive press that highlights the devastating pressure this moment imposed on Jesus. We see it presented in the Gospels in both the physical and emotional descriptions of Jesus. Luke tells us that Jesus knelt to pray (Luke 22:41). Matthew depicts a more extreme posture. Jesus "fell with his face to the ground" (Matthew 26:39). Jesus was under so much duress that he not only began to sweat profusely, but blood became comingled with that sweat due to bursting of his capillaries.[36]

Jesus' emotional state is also described, with each of the writers selecting a unique combination to describe the intense emotions Jesus was experiencing. They employ language like "sorrowful," "troubled," "overwhelmed with sorrow to the point of death," "deeply distressed," and "in anguish" (Matthew 26:37–38; Mark 14:33–34; Luke 22:44). The diversity of their language highlights just how inadequate words are to describe the full reality of Jesus' suffering.[37] The brutal mental strain and hollow feelings of grief that come only when we know the circumstances are dire and irreversible cannot be expressed with words. Perhaps the intensity is best captured with the image of the olive press—Gethsemane.

Firmly bonded to the human race, the Son of God struggles with what lies ahead and seeks an alternative. "My Father, if it is possible, may this cup be taken from me. Yet not as I will, but as you will" (Matthew 26:39). This struggle may be better understood by considering the options the geographic location offered. If Jesus turned east, he would quickly find himself surrounded by the quiet isolation of the Judean Wilderness. This

∨ *Olive crushing press*

rugged and dry place was no friend to the farmer or city builder. But its austerity provided isolation and escape, a place to get away from the ravages of life. If there were only another way to redeem the world, Jesus could take this turn to the east and in short order be far away from the trumped-up charges, the mockery, the merciless beatings, and death on the cross. Feeling the full weight of the world's future, Jesus considers and even pursues the question of escape offered by the wilderness. But in the end, our salvation is not about an escape into the wilderness but a walk toward the cross that will be raised to the west of the Mount of Olives in the city of Jerusalem. Only there could Jesus fulfill his role as our Savior, our substitute, and offer the forgiveness we so desperately need. Jesus struggled in Gethsemane because it imposed a choice on him, a decision he made not in his own best interests but in ours.

"Rise! Let us go! Here comes my betrayer!" (Matthew 26:46).

∧ *Jesus' struggle in prayer depicted in a mosaic within the Church of All Nations*

Galilean Denial in a Judean Courtyard

There is much to love about Peter. He spoke out in support of Jesus when others were silent. He even struck out with his sword when others menaced Jesus at the time of his arrest. But when Peter promised more than he could deliver, insisting he would lay down his life for Jesus, the Savior turned to him and offered these words of rebuke and warning: "Will you really lay down your life for me? Very truly I tell you, before the rooster crows, you will disown me three times!" (John 13:38). After Peter received such a warning, how is it possible that he let his guard down and three times denied knowing Jesus? The writers of the Gospels include two details that do not excuse his denials but help to explain what distracted Peter so severely that he failed to heed Jesus' words of warning. They emphasize that Peter was a Galilean among Judeans and that he denied Jesus while in a courtyard.

Right after Jesus' struggle in prayer in Gethsemane, Judas arrived with those sent to arrest Jesus. The disciples with Jesus soon panicked and fled. However, as the armed men were taking Jesus from the Mount of Olives to the home of Caiaphas, the high priest, Peter

and John followed. Because John was known by the high priest, he was permitted to enter the courtyard, then came back out to obtain access for Peter (John 18:15–16) (see map 10.7).

Almost immediately Peter is identified as a Galilean, a fact revealed by his accent (Matthew 26:73; Mark 14:70; Luke 22:59). It was a short step from identifying Peter as a Galilean to identifying him with the Galilean prisoner, Jesus (Matthew 26:69, 71; Mark 14:67; John 18:17). To appreciate how this proved to be a distraction for Peter, we have to put ourselves in his Galilean sandals for a moment. Galilee lies in the northern portion of the Promised Land just west of the Sea of Galilee, and Judea lies in the southern portion that includes Jerusalem. The geography of the two places is quite different, and the Judean perspective on those living in Galilee was generally not favorable. Galileans were despised for their perceived rural simplicity and lack of sophistication. They were regarded as lax in practicing their Jewish faith and sloppy in vocalizing the consonants of the language they shared with the Judeans.[38] When one was called a Galilean by a Judean, it was

⌄ Extravagant mosaics on the floor of homes that likely belonged to Jerusalem's priestly aristocracy

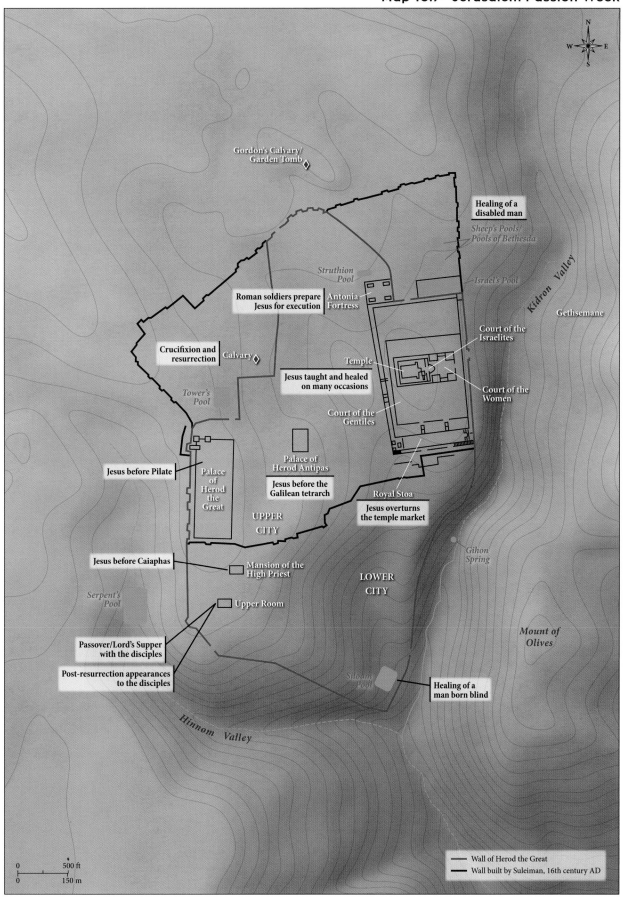

Map 10.7—Jerusalem Passion Week

∧ **Left:** *Church of St. Peter Gallicantu, traditional location of Peter's denial;* **Right:** *Mount Zion, another possible location for the home of Caiaphas*

meant as a criticism. Peter is not one to take that lightly. He could have been thrown by this insult, quickly and without thinking denying his Galilean roots and with them his association with the man being interrogated inside. That might explain why Peter, feeling the sting of this Judean criticism of his Galilean roots, allowed a denial of Jesus to fall from his lips. But why didn't he just leave rather than stay around and allow himself to be baited into two more denials of Jesus?

The answer to that may be found in the second element included in the description of the setting. Peter was in the courtyard of Caiaphas's home. All four gospel writers mention this detail, with Matthew and Mark each noting it twice in their short narratives (Matthew 26:58, 69; Mark 14:54, 66; Luke 22:55; John 18:15–16).

It would be helpful if we had archaeological evidence for the home mentioned in these texts so we could know its floor plan, but we do not. In fact, we have only early evidence with regards to the general area in which this home is found in Jerusalem. The first-century historian Josephus notes that the high priest of his day was living in the Upper City of Jerusalem.[39] Two early Christian pilgrims from the fourth and sixth centuries AD wrote that they had visited the home of Caiaphas, noting that it was located on what

they had come to call Mount Zion.[40] These Byzantine-era statements point to two locations now associated with the home of Caiaphas. The first is Saint Peter Gallicantu, a modern church on the lower slopes of Mount Zion constructed over a fifth-century church. Stronger Byzantine evidence takes us farther north. Here on the grounds of the Armenian Church of Saint Saviour, some 50 yards (46 m) north of the Dormition Abby, archaeologists have discovered a housing complex dating from the first century AD that has all the trappings of a wealthy Jewish neighborhood that would suit the likes of Caiaphas. Furthermore, this is about where the sixth-century report puts the home of Caiaphas. Beyond that, nothing more certain can be said about the specific location of this home.

But evidence from the Upper City of Jerusalem where first-century palatial homes have been found helps us understand the nature of the courtyard where Peter waited.[41] This courtyard is not a porch, deck, or patio that generally grants easy access to outsiders. This courtyard was centrally located within the building, surrounded on all sides by a maze of rooms and passages. Assuming Peter was in such a courtyard, it would explain why he didn't just leave. Peter was in a building he did not know. Given the stress of the moment, it is unlikely he paid attention to the way in when John came to get him. Peter clearly would have felt trapped in this strange building. Consequently, when the second and third verbal challenges came, Peter felt threatened not only by his Galilean connection but also by the Judean courtyard. The Judean bias against Galileans and the courtyard do not excuse what Peter did, but they help us to understand how the setting influenced his denial.

The Location of Jesus' Crucifixion and Resurrection

Of all the wonderful events preserved for us in the Bible, no set of events is more important to our eternal well-being than the death and resurrection of our Savior. For thousands of years, Christians have traveled to the Holy Land with their hearts set on seeing this place that changed their place in eternity. Usually, their quest has taken them to the Church of the Holy Sepulcher.

As the gospel authors provide us with the details surrounding the crucifixion and resurrection of Jesus, they include ones that narrow our search to this location. For example, we are given the name of the place. Mark tells us that "they brought Jesus to the place called Golgotha (which means 'the place of the skull')" (Mark 15:22). This rather unattractive name links the location with death, making it a grisly but fitting name for a cemetery or place of execution. In 1883 General Charles Gordon assumed it described the shape of a hill and so searched for a hill that looked like a skull. His eyes found a place that became known as Gordon's Calvary, or the Garden Tomb (see map 10.7). While this somewhat peaceful location offers a compelling setting for reflecting on the events of Good Friday and Easter Sunday, it is unlikely to be the authentic site we are seeking.[42]

If we link the name Golgotha with "cemetery," we find support in the gospel of John that the location of Jesus' crucifixion was a cemetery in which he would be buried. "At the place where Jesus was crucified, there was a garden, and in the garden a new tomb, in which no one had ever been laid" (John 19:41). Ideally the site we are seeking will have evidence of a first-century tomb and will be located outside the city wall of first-century Jerusalem. The ritual purity laws found in the Old Testament indicate that contact with the remains of the deceased makes a person ritually impure (Leviticus 15:31; Numbers 9:6–7; 19:13). As a result, Jewish communities did not bury their loved ones within the cities or villages, but in discrete locations outside the city or village to minimize the risk of ritual contamination.

There is one more clue in the Gospels that directs our search for the place of Jesus' crucifixion and resurrection. It must be in an accessible public location. Jesus did not endure the suffering imposed by the cross in isolation. He is not dying on a high hill far away from Jerusalem. John tells us that the crucifixion site was "near the city" (John 19:20). And Matthew speaks of the stream of people who walk past Jesus, hurling their venom-filled insults at him (Matthew 27:39–40). All of that is consistent with what we know about how the Romans used crucifixion. It was meant to be a deterrent for the most serious of crimes, so they would

∨ *Church of Holy Sepulcher, likely location of Jesus' crucifixion and resurrection*

∧ **Left:** *Byzantine and Crusader columns in the Church of the Holy Sepulcher;* **Right:** *A tomb whose door is a rolling stone*

crucify criminals in locations within easy view of the masses. Thus it is best for us to search for Golgotha where we have evidence of a first-century Jewish cemetery outside the city walls of Jerusalem and with easy access to those going about their daily routines.

The one place in Jerusalem that satisfies all these requirements is the Church of the Holy Sepulcher, also known as the Holy Resurrection Church (see Calvary on map 10.7).[43] Although the building itself is located inside the modern Old City Wall of Jerusalem, it clearly was outside the city walls of first-century Jerusalem. There is evidence in the church of tombs from the first century. And it is located near the bustling city center and a gate that would have given access to the execution site.

This is the one place in Jerusalem that has a strong chain of memory and archaeological evidence to mark this as the location of Jesus' crucifixion and resurrection. In the later portion of the Old Testament, the area of the Church of the Holy Sepulcher was a rock quarry from which limestone was cut for construction purposes. When this quarry went out of operation, soil blew in to form a garden that eventually was conscripted for use as a cemetery. The events of Good Friday and Easter Sunday most likely transpired here. This became a place that Christians visited regularly in the years that followed. The site was so popular

that it was targeted by the Roman emperor Hadrian. Responding to the Jewish revolt of 135 AD, he set about turning Jerusalem into a pagan city. Because he did not differentiate between Jews and Christians, seeing both as springing from the same soil, he began destroying all the Christian sites, including the place people had identified with Golgotha. Hadrian began by filling in the quarry and then built a pagan temple on a platform there.[44] The rich irony of Hadrian's efforts becomes clear in the fourth century. In that century, the Roman emperor Constantine came to know Jesus as his Savior as did his mother, Helena. Together they set about identifying important Christian sites in the Promised Land and building churches on them. Unwittingly Hadrian had marked this most critical of Christian holy spots with a pagan monument that Helena removed before constructing the first church in this location, dedicated in 335 AD.[45] Many early Christian pilgrims visited and wrote about this church.[46] Although the first church building was damaged many times, its reconstruction on the same location has left a continuous mark on the land, and elements of its early Byzantine architecture remain. While a visit to this location is not necessary to know the fullness of our forgiveness, it remains a powerful place to visit for those who trace their redemption to the events that transpired there.

The Great Commission on a Grand Mountain in Galilee

Of the 13 occasions when Jesus appeared to his followers after his resurrection,[47] Matthew saves the most powerful moment and language for last. "All authority in heaven and on earth has been given to me. Therefore go and make disciples of all nations, baptizing them in the name of the Father and of the Son and of the Holy Spirit, and teaching them to obey everything I have commanded you. And surely I am with you always, to the very end of the age" (Matthew 28:18–20). What a compelling way to end a book! It turns our eyes from the pages before us to the next step each Christian must take to advance the kingdom of God. This Great Commission has appropriately become the topic of many sermons and books.

Matthew mentions the geography of the Great Commission four times, three in his final chapter. Just before leaving the upper room for Gethsemane, Jesus tells the disciples that they are to meet him in Galilee after his resurrection (Matthew 26:32). At the tomb, the angel who appeared to the women explained why the tomb was empty. "He has risen, just as he said" (Matthew 28:6). But the topic soon turns to what is next. The women are to return to the disciples and tell them the news of Jesus' resurrection and that he is "going ahead of you into Galilee" (Matthew 28:7). As the women began to run to tell the disciples, Jesus appeared to them and reinforced the message: "Go and tell my brothers to go to Galilee; there they will see me" (Matthew 28:10). When Matthew reports that the disciples do what they have been directed to do, a new detail shows up. "Then the eleven disciples went to Galilee, to the mountain where Jesus had told them to go" (Matthew 28:16). We learn that Jesus directed them to a specific mountain for their meeting. It was on this mountain that the Great Commission was given.

The other gospel writers make no mention of the mountain. And we must confess that identification of this mountain in Galilee remains elusive. But a compelling case can be made for Mount Arbel, a mountain whose former history and view make it a winsome candidate for what Jesus has to say. Mount Arbel is on the west side of the Sea of Galilee, cutting a sharp and distinctive profile when viewed from the north or east. It rises abruptly from the lake, climbing to 600 feet (183 m) above its waters and offers one of the most awe-inspiring views in Galilee (see map 10.8).

Matthew may have had several reasons for providing

∨ *Mount Arbel on the Sea of Galilee*

Map 10.8—Post-Resurrection Appearances

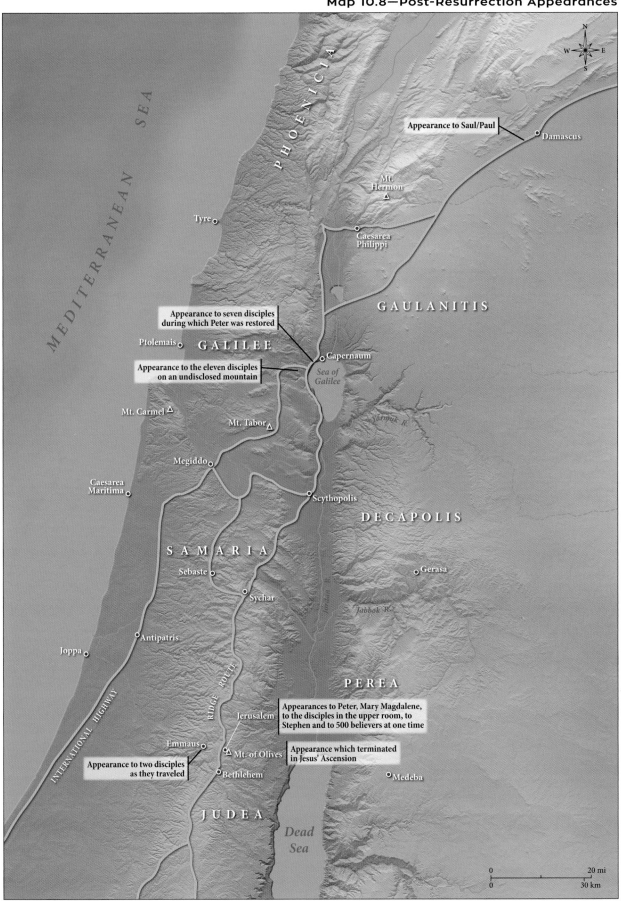

MEDITERRANEAN SEA

PHOENICIA

Appearance to Saul/Paul

Damascus

Mt. Hermon △

Tyre ○

Caesarea Philippi ○

GAULANITIS

Appearance to seven disciples during which Peter was restored

Ptolemais ○   GALILEE

Capernaum ○

Appearance to the eleven disciples on an undisclosed mountain

Sea of Galilee

Mt. Carmel △

Mt. Tabor △

Yarmuk R.

Megiddo ○

Caesarea Maritima ○

Scythopolis ○

DECAPOLIS

SAMARIA

Gerasa ○

Sebaste ○

Sychar ○

Jabbok R.

Antipatris ○

Joppa ○

PEREA

RIDGE ROUTE

Appearances to Peter, Mary Magdalene, to the disciples in the upper room, to Stephen and to 500 believers at one time

Jerusalem

Emmaus ○

△ Mt. of Olives

Appearance which terminated in Jesus' Ascension

Appearance to two disciples as they traveled

Bethlehem ○

Medeba ○

INTERNATIONAL HIGHWAY

JUDEA

Dead Sea

0 — 20 mi
0 — 30 km

∧ *The view north from Mount Arbel may be linked to the Great Commission*

the geographic details surrounding this meeting up north. We can appreciate how helpful an escape from Jerusalem may have been for the disciples, given all they experienced during the final week of Jesus' time on earth. They had a great deal to think about. And they needed to think about those things without feeling the constant threat of the Jewish and Roman leaders who would be scrambling to respond to the resurrection of the man they had presumed was dead and silenced. Galilee was home to the disciples. And a return to this familiar area promised a measure of security and an opportunity to reflect on what Jesus had told them about what would happen.

Mount Arbel itself has something to contribute to the disciples' experience. Earlier we had made the case that Mount Arbel was the location for the Sermon on the Mount (Matthew 5–7). If we place not only that event but also the Great Commission on this mountain, then there is a striking geographic link to consider. The Sermon on the Mount was the first intensive theological instruction that Matthew reports Jesus having with the disciples. This must have been an unforgettable time as they sat with him and learned that there was so much more to the teachings of Scripture than they had dared to imagine. How fitting it was that the final and critical words of instruction they

needed to take Jesus' teaching out into the world were said to them at the same place.

The view from Mount Arbel would have prompted a reminder of the Sermon on the Mount and other experiences they had with Jesus. Matthew quotes Jesus' criticism of three communities that had the best opportunities to hear him speak and to watch him at work. They were Chorazin, Bethsaida, and Capernaum (Matthew 11:21–24). All three as well as the rest of the Sea of Galilee are plainly in view. Mount Arbel was not just a place to recall what Jesus had said while sitting with them on this mountain, but a place to think about all they had seen him do and say within view of their high perch on Mount Arbel.

And finally it is the horizon-to-horizon view from the top of this mountain that creates the visual that supports the scope of the Great Commission. Earlier Jesus had lowered the vision of the disciples, instructing them to proclaim the kingdom only among the lost sheep of the house of Israel rather than to Gentiles or Samaritans (Matthew 10:5–6). But now that the disciples understand the message they have to deliver, the view from the top of Mount Arbel with the international travelers moving along its base on the International Highway erased the old limitations. Lifting their eyes to the horizon, Jesus called for them to disciple all nations.

⌃ *The island of Patmos where John received the content of Revelation*

Chapter 11

FROM JERUSALEM TO THE ENDS OF THE EARTH

Jesus Ascends from the Mount of Olives

Luke pays more attention to the ascension of Jesus than the other gospel writers, using it as a literary hinge between the two substantial works attributed to him. It is the last event in his gospel and the first mentioned in the book of Acts. The attention it gets is fitting because the ascension of Jesus marks a new stage in life both for Jesus and for the disciples. Jesus' mission on earth was drawing quickly to its close. He had died for the sins of all and had risen from the dead. For the next 40 days, he had shown himself to hundreds of people, giving convincing proof that he was alive, that he had risen from the dead (Acts 1:3). Now it was time for him to return to heaven where he would take his rightful seat at the right hand of his Father (Romans 8:34), "far above all rule and authority, power and dominion, and every name that is invoked, not only in the present age but also in the one to come" (Ephesians 1:21). The time of Jesus' humiliation had given way to his full exaltation. "Therefore God exalted him to the highest place and gave him the name that is above every name, that at the name of Jesus every knee should bow, in heaven and on earth and under the earth, and every tongue acknowledge that Jesus Christ is Lord, to the glory of God the Father" (Philippians 2:9–11).

The disciples had spent years as students and now were about to become the church's teachers. When Jesus sent the Holy Spirit to them, their memories were sharpened and their understanding of all they had learned was honed so that they might accurately and effectively present the teachings of Jesus to others (John 16:13; Acts 1:4–5). Their mission is defined geographically. It starts in Jerusalem, expands to Judea and Samaria, and reaches to the ends of earth (Acts 1:8). So the ascension marked a time of transition. Jesus gathered the disciples around him, lifted his hands to bless them, and then lifted from the earth, rising heavenward until he was hidden from their view by a cloud (Luke 24:50–51; Acts 1:9).

Luke includes the location of the ascension in his gospel account and in Acts (Luke 24:50; Acts 1:12). Jesus was on the Mount of Olives, about three-quarters of a mile (1.2 km) east of Jerusalem, with the village of Bethany in view (see map 11.1). Attempting to be even more precise, Helena, the mother of the Roman emperor Constantine, built a church near the top of the Mount of Olives that was to have marked the spot where Jesus' feet left the earth.[1] Many early Christian visitors speak of visiting this church, starting in the fourth century. Over time, church replaced church on the site until the building was taken by Saladin in 1187 AD. From then on, the site has been known as the Mosque of the Ascension.[2]

In his gospel, Luke reports the location of Jesus' ascension as being in "the vicinity of Bethany" (Luke 24:50). But in Acts he refers to "the hill called the Mount of Olives" (Acts 1:12). Jesus' ascension from the Mount of Olives had important ramifications both for the disciples and for Jesus. It put the disciples back in the location where they needed to be to take the next steps in fulfilling Jesus' Great Commission to "go into all the world and preach the gospel to all creation" (Mark 16:15). After the resurrection of Jesus, these men left Jerusalem and traveled to Galilee where Jesus had promised to meet with them (Matthew 28:7–10, 16). This put

Map 11.1—Location of Jesus' Ascension

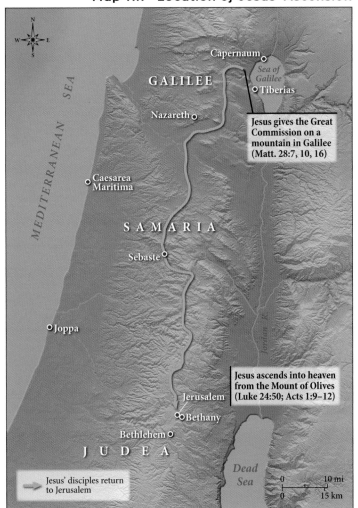

Jesus gives the Great Commission on a mountain in Galilee (Matt. 28:7, 10, 16)

Jesus ascends into heaven from the Mount of Olives (Luke 24:50; Acts 1:9–12)

Jesus' disciples return to Jerusalem

∨ *Mosque of the Ascension on the Mount of Olives*

^ *The Tower of the Ascension rises distinctively above the Mount of Olives*

some distance between the disciples and Jerusalem, where those who had relentlessly pursued the execution of Jesus now presented a threat to his disciples. But within less than a month and a half, the disciples had to be back in Jerusalem and had to stay put. Jesus gave them stern instructions in this regard: "Do not leave Jerusalem, but wait for the gift my Father promised, which you have heard me speak about" (Acts 1:4). The location of Jesus' ascension in Luke illustrates that the disciples are right where they need to be, in Jerusalem. In fact as soon as Jesus left their view, both Luke's gospel account and Acts report that the disciples left the Mount of Olives and returned to Jerusalem (Luke 24:52; Acts 1:12).

The ascension from the Mount of Olives creates a wonderful symmetry when we link it to the past and future celebration of Jesus as eternal King of the world. It was on this ridge, not far from the area of Jesus'

ascension, that the crowds celebrated the entry of Jesus into Jerusalem on Palm Sunday. "When he came near the place where the road goes down the Mount of Olives, the whole crowd of disciples began joyfully to praise God in loud voices for all the miracles they had seen. 'Blessed is the king who comes in the name of the Lord!'" (Luke 19:37–38). The ascension from the same ridge takes Palm Sunday one step further. The prophet Zechariah, in speaking about the return of the King of Kings on the last day, says that the Messiah will return to judge the nations with his feet firmly planted on the Mount of Olives (Zechariah 14:4). Thus, whether we read of events of the past or the future, the Mount of Olives is associated with the exaltation of Jesus as King. We see it on Palm Sunday, we see it on the day of his ascension, and we see it on the day of his second coming. He "will come back in the same way you have seen him go into heaven" (Acts 1:11).

The Day of Pentecost

Readers of the Old Testament knew the day was coming. The prophet Joel had announced it. "And afterward, I will pour out my Spirit on all people. Your sons and daughters will prophesy, your old men will

dream dreams, your young men will see visions. Even on my servants, both men and women, I will pour out my Spirit in those days" (Joel 2:28–29). Readers of John's gospel had heard Jesus speak about the day.

"Unless I go away, the Advocate will not come to you; but if I go, I will send him to you" (John 16:7). Nevertheless, when the day of Pentecost dawns, the profound changes it brings catch us by surprise as the disciples speak boldly and miraculously to thousands who come to know Jesus as their Savior from sin.

The day of Pentecost for the disciples begins at one location and ends at another. The day begins in a "house" where the disciples are staying (Acts 2:2). There is no reason to think that this is a different building than the one in Acts 1:13 that describes them staying in the upper room of a house. And there is no good reason to assume this is not the upper room that hosted the events of the Passover meal, turned into Last Supper, on the night of Jesus' arrest (Mark 14:15).[3] This familiar place changed character the morning of Pentecost. The sound of a violent wind filled the house, and what appeared to be "tongues of fire that separated and came to rest on each of them" (Acts 2:2–3). The Holy Spirit had come, just as Joel and Jesus

had said it would, and lest there be any doubt, these physical changes marked the moment. The extraordinary sights and sounds of the morning began to draw a crowd. At first they must have pushed and jostled to get a closer look and to listen at the door of the house. But as the crowd grew in size, it became clear that a new venue was needed.

The book of Acts does not tell us where the disciples went, but given the details we have in Acts 2, a likely spot is the southern steps of the temple complex, the main entrance for those going to worship there. This location seems best for four reasons.

First, Pentecost required a place that could accommodate hundreds of people and provide them with the acoustics to hear Peter. A high festival like Pentecost brought thousands of people to Jerusalem; estimates range from 125,000 to 500,000.[4] Even if only a few thousand gathered in one place, a significant space was required. One of the few places in Jerusalem large enough for such a gathering is on

Map 11.2—Homes of the Visitors to Jerusalem on Pentecost

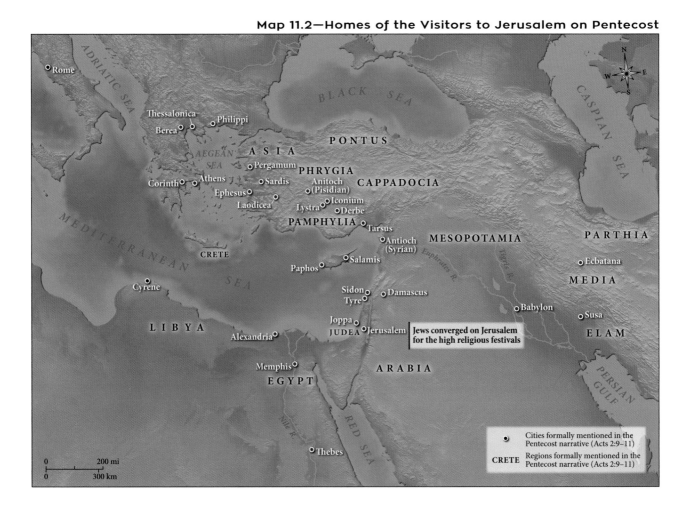

∧ *The southern steps provide a likely setting for Peter's Pentecost sermon*

the broad staircase that provided access to the temple from the south.[5] Immediately above these steps rose the solid façade of a retaining wall, part of the infrastructure that held up the temple platform. Sound rebounds from this wall in a way that allows a voice to be amplified. Thus the southern steps provide not only the physical space, but also the acoustics needed to accommodate those who had gathered and who heard Peter speak.

Second, Pentecost required a place where the kind of audience Peter addressed would gather naturally. Acts 2:36 refers to them as "Israel," a label that identifies them as Jewish people who had come to Jerusalem for the festival of Pentecost (also called the Feast of Weeks; Exodus 34:22; Numbers 28:26–31; Deuteronomy 16:10, 16). Their passion for the Jewish faith is evidenced by the wide array of places from which they have come (see map 11.2). Starting in the east and moving counterclockwise, we read of visitors who have come to Jerusalem from all corners of the known world (Acts 2:6–12). The challenge of finding

accommodations in Jerusalem during the high festival likely would have spread the visitors throughout the greater Jerusalem area. But the one place they would all gather is the temple, the geographic focal point of the festival. Because the southern steps of the temple are the main entry, placing Peter's Pentecost address on these steps would provide him with just the kind of audience Acts describes.

The third detail that supports this location for Peter's speech is related to a visual aid that Peter uses in his address. He quotes Psalm 16 that speaks of dying but not remaining in the grave to decay (Acts 2:25–28). Although this psalm was written by David, it describes the experience of the Messiah, Jesus, who had risen from the dead. Lest there be a question about the fact that David was not the one spoken of, a short walk from the southern steps to the City of David ridge would bring them to David's tomb. Peter told the crowd, "Fellow Israelites, I can tell you confidently that the patriarch David died and was buried, and his tomb is here to this day" (Acts 2:29).

Finally, this day witnessed the baptism of some three thousand (Acts 2:41). This would require a rather substantial facility with plenty of water. The temple was a large consumer of water and so had a water delivery system designed to collect water in the north and deliver it downhill through the complex. On the south, we find a ritual bathing facility adjacent to the southern steps with enough stations to accommodate the crowds coming to the temple and the crowds needing baptism on Pentecost.[6] The day of Pentecost signaled the beginning of a new era in the history of God's kingdom. The best place in Jerusalem to understand how the activities of that day looked are the southern steps of the temple complex.

^ *Mikvah, a ritual bathing station, adjacent to the southern steps of the temple complex*

Philip in Samaria

The glorious day of Pentecost gives way all too quickly to the challenging days of persecution felt by the Christians in Jerusalem. Following the stoning of Stephen (Acts 7), the safest future for many believers was outside Jerusalem. Among those taking flight was a man named Philip. This is not the Philip who had been the disciple

Map 11.3—Events in the Lives of Peter and Philip

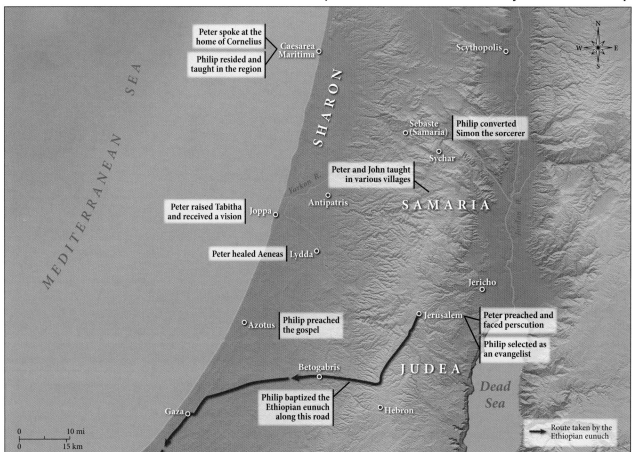

Peter spoke at the home of Cornelius
Philip resided and taught in the region
Caesarea Maritima
Scythopolis

SHARON

Sebaste (Samaria)
Philip converted Simon the sorcerer
Sychar

Peter and John taught in various villages

Yarkon R.

Antipatris
SAMARIA

Peter raised Tabitha and received a vision
Joppa

Peter healed Aeneas
Lydda

Jericho

Azotus
Philip preached the gospel

Jerusalem
Peter preached and faced perscution
Philip selected as an evangelist

Betogabris
JUDEA
Dead Sea

Philip baptized the Ethiopian eunuch along this road

Gaza
Hebron

MEDITERRANEAN SEA

0   10 mi
0   15 km

→ Route taken by the Ethiopian eunuch

of Jesus, but Philip the Evangelist, who was selected with others, like the martyred Stephen, to assist the apostles in their work (Acts 6:5). Philip traveled north to the region of Samaria (see map 11.3), performed stunning miracles, and preached the good news about Jesus to those who gathered to listen. Because of his work, many living in Samaria came to know Jesus as their Savior and were baptized (Acts 8:6–12).

The specific location of Philip's work is not known because of the vague language used for the location. "Philip went down to a city in Samaria" (Acts 8:5).[7] Some regard this as the Old Testament city of Samaria that Herod the Great had rebuilt and renamed; Samaria became the Hellenistic city of Sebaste.[8] Or the "city in Samaria" could be the ancient Shechem, based on the fact that Philip was dealing with those who had a worldview unlike what we might expect to find in Sebaste.[9] Perhaps the author of Acts left ambiguity here because the importance is not in the name of the city but in the region. The gospel was expanding in Samaria. The regional name is repeated four times in this chapter, twice in one verse (Acts 8:5, 9, 14), focusing our attention on the region rather than on a city within the region.

Why is that regional identification so important? The book of Acts is organized geographically, and the region of Samaria is the next step as the gospel expands outward from Jerusalem. Jesus had told his disciples that they would become his witnesses "in Jerusalem, and in all Judea and Samaria, and to the ends of the earth" (Acts 1:8). Because the third step of this process moved the gospel from its home turf of Jerusalem and Judea, it merits special attention.

But there is more. The author of Acts is speaking about the advance of the gospel into a region that had acquired a negative reputation. Here Luke's detail on place works to change our perspective on Samaria. During the Old Testament, this region was the same as the tribal territories of Manasseh and Ephraim. The author of 2 Kings presents these tribal territories at the heart of the Northern Kingdom of Israel in an unflattering way. Because the people of Manasseh and Ephraim had incessantly combined the worship of idols with the worship of the true God, the Lord had allowed Assyria to invade and deport these Jews from their land. The policy of Assyria was to remove conquered people from their homeland and resettle them in new places. When the Jews were removed from Samaria, people from other conquered lands were brought in. When these new residents failed to worship the Lord as he intended in the Promised Land, he sent lions among them. This propelled the Assyrians to

∨ *Left:* Region of Samaria; *Right:* Staircase to the Augustan temple built at Samaria (Sebaste)

⌃ **Left:** The Byzantine church on Mount Gerizim used materials from the destroyed Samaritan temple; **Right:** The region of Samaria was tainted with pagan practices from the time of Jeroboam I into the New Testament era

return some of the corrupted Jewish religious leaders of the Northern Kingdom to teach the new locals how to worship (2 Kings 17:24–28). The outcome is summarized in 2 Kings 17:40–41: "They would not listen, however, but persisted in their former practices. Even while these people were worshiping the LORD, they were serving idols. To this day their children and grandchildren continue to do as their ancestors did."

The 400 years between the Old and New Testaments saw additional developments that further compromised the reputation of this region, now occupied by people known as Samaritans. Samaria's residents built a temple for themselves on Mount Gerizim in 388 BC. When a Jewish king, John Hyrcanus, came to the throne in Jerusalem, he expanded the influence of his government north into Samaria and, in the process, destroyed the Samaritan temple in 128 BC. This appears to have pushed the relationship between the two groups in the direction of racial hatred.[10] This dislike between Jews and Samaritans is mentioned in the Gospels. In a parenthetical note, John says, "For Jews do not associate with Samaritans" (John 4:9). An unnamed Samaritan village showed hostility toward Jesus and the disciples, forcing them to take a different route to Jerusalem (Luke 9:53). This imposed detour caused Peter and John to ask in the next verse, "Lord, do you want us to call fire down from heaven to destroy them?"

The negativity and hostility associated with Samaria and the Samaritans begin to change in the time of the Gospels and Acts. Jesus tells the story of a man traveling between Jerusalem and Jericho who is harmed by thieves. The kindly actions of a Samaritan man illustrate what it means to show love to one's neighbor (Luke 10:30–37). When Jesus heals ten men afflicted by leprosy, the one Samaritan among them is the only one who returns to give thanks (Luke 17:11–19). And while so many of Jesus' fellow Jews did not accept him as the Messiah, it was the people in the Samaritan village of Sychar who could not get enough of his time (John 4:39–42). The remaking of Samaria continues in Acts when persecution in Jerusalem sends Philip to the region. When word got back to the Christians in Jerusalem about the growing community of believers in Samaria, they dispatched Peter and John—not to rebuke Philip for taking the gospel there, but to confirm and expand the kingdom of God in this region (Acts 8:14–25). This story, which gets attention in Acts, is a story of the gospel spreading into a region whose reputation is changing.

Peter Gains a New Perspective at Caesarea Maritima

A change in scenery can do us a world of good. Day-to-day living in the same location can wear deep ruts that wear us out and trap us in patterns of thinking that can become unhealthy. Peter was in that kind of rut, but a trip to Caesarea Maritima would help him and the Christian movement. A substantial amount of space is set aside in the book of Acts to explain how this city participated in changing the perspective of Peter (Acts 10:1–11:18).

Caesarea on the sea was founded by one of the most famous builders of the ancient world, Herod the Great (see map 11.3). He built this expansive 165-acre (67-hectare) harbor city because he wanted an outlet that could connect him to Europe and an inlet through which he could bring all the best of Europe to the land he ruled. After the days of Herod the Great, this Caesarea became the favorite haunt of the Roman procurators who were in charge of the Roman province of Judea, including the infamous Pontius Pilate, who used it as his base of operations, traveling to Jerusalem only when necessary.[11] The public buildings and facilities of Caesarea Maritima made it one of the most impressive cities in Israel. The city was built around a harbor that required the first extensive use of hydraulic cement to establish the foundations for the breakwater. It boasted a large temple dedicated to Augustus Caesar as well as a luxurious seaside palace. Entertainment venues included a 4,000-seat theater as well as a hippodrome designed for chariot racing, though it was used for other sporting events as well. Thousands came to live here. But the place lacked a decent local source for water, so Herod designed a water-delivery system that brought this precious resource into the city from 13 miles (21 km) away. The delivery system was half in a rock-cut channel and half on a raised aqueduct. To this day, a walk among Caesarea's ruins reveals the imposing grandeur and sophistication of the Roman world.[12]

The response to all this grandeur was mixed. For those who felt at home in Europe and loved the culture of the Greco-Roman world, this city was ideal. In the middle of the Middle East, this city was Rome away from Rome. But for the Jews living in the land, Caesarea represented a blight on the landscape. They saw it as contributing to the cultural pollution that had infiltrated their homeland.[13] Peter was in this camp.

∨ The sprawling city of Caesarea Maritima

∧ **Left:** *An aqueduct carried water to Caesarea Maritima from the base of Mount Carmel;* **Right:** *Stone boat anchors from the harbor at Caesarea Maritima*

He had grown up with orthodox Jewish laws and passions. He ate kosher and observed the Sabbath. He regarded all expressions of the Greco-Roman world's ideology with a great deal of suspicion. For him, this was the broad road that Jesus had warned about, a road that led to destruction. Peter's preference was for Jewish communities like Lydda and Joppa. For Peter, Caesarea Maritima was a foreign place, and as a result, it was a place that had much to teach him.

That lesson begins with a vision. Peter was in Joppa praying as the noontime hour approached. He was hungry. While his meal was being prepared, Peter fell into a trance. As he looked heavenward, he saw a large sheet or sail descending toward him, carrying a wide array of animals. Some of these animals were approved for Jews to eat and others were not (Leviticus 11). When a voice urged Peter to eat indiscriminately, he thought it was a test and vehemently objected to eating nonkosher food. But the

∧ *The sign in the temple courtyard warning Gentiles to advance no closer to the sanctuary*

Lord responded to Peter's objection with the same language three times: "Do not call anything impure that God has made clean" (Acts 10:15). This vision was not so much about food as it was about people. While Peter was experiencing the vision, Gentiles were approaching the door of the home with an invitation for Peter from a Roman officer, Cornelius, asking Peter to come to Caesarea Maritima to speak with him and his family. The vision overcame the initial objection Peter would have felt about traveling to this Hellenistic city to meet with non-Jewish people.

Peter's language demonstrates his changing perspective. When he arrives at the home of Cornelius, Peter sounds anything but convinced that this was a good idea. "He said to them: 'You are well aware that it is against our law for a Jew to associate with or visit a Gentile.'" But then he tells them about his vision from God to "not call anyone impure or unclean" (Acts 10:28). Once Cornelius speaks of his faith and acts of kindness to the poor, Peter understands that this Gentile is truly seeking a relationship with Jesus. Peter's response shows that the Lord is working a change in Peter's perspective. "I now realize how true it is that God does not show favoritism but accepts from every nation the one who fears him and does what is right" (Acts 10:34–35).

Gentiles were never out of the picture. God had told Abraham that one of his descendants would work a change in the world so dramatic that all nations of the earth would be blessed through him (Genesis 12:3). Jesus had cautioned the Jews in the synagogue at Nazareth that they dare not exclude Gentiles from the spiritual revolution that was under way (Luke 4:23–27).

But this division remained an important issue even after the death and resurrection of Jesus. The early church was a Jewish church. Suspicion of Gentiles and of cities like Caesarea Maritima was tightly woven into the fabric of first-century Judaism. Even leaders like Peter were infected with hesitation, and so the Lord used a Roman soldier from Caesarea Maritima to change Peter's perspective. Peter got it. And when he spoke to others in Jerusalem about his experience in Caesarea Maritima, they got it too. "When they heard this, they had no further objections and praised God, saying, 'So then, even to Gentiles God has granted repentance that leads to life'" (Acts 11:18).

Damascus and the Book of Acts

The gospel was meant to reach all locations; and some locations were better than others at facilitating that outcome. Damascus is one of those places. It may not be among the top five places that come to mind in terms of gospel outreach. But it is among the most frequently mentioned cities in Acts, apart from Jerusalem. In Acts, Damascus is mentioned twelve times, Antioch twenty times, Ephesus nine times, and Rome

Map 11.4—Saul's Conversion and Early Years

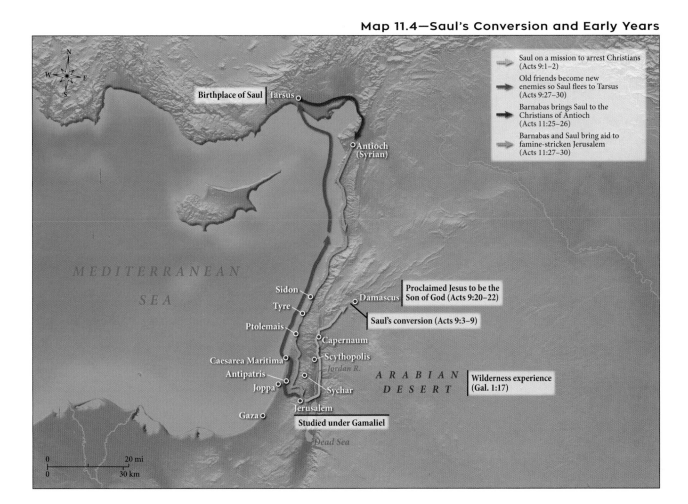

Saul on a mission to arrest Christians (Acts 9:1–2)

Old friends become new enemies so Saul flees to Tarsus (Acts 9:27–30)

Barnabas brings Saul to the Christians of Antioch (Acts 11:25–26)

Barnabas and Saul bring aid to famine-stricken Jerusalem (Acts 11:27–30)

Birthplace of Saul | Tarsus

Antioch (Syrian)

MEDITERRANEAN SEA

Sidon

Tyre

Ptolemais

Damascus | Proclaimed Jesus to be the Son of God (Acts 9:20–22)

Saul's conversion (Acts 9:3–9)

Capernaum

Scythopolis

Caesarea Maritima

Antipatris

Joppa

Jordan R.

Sychar

ARABIAN DESERT | Wilderness experience (Gal. 1:17)

Jerusalem

Gaza

Studied under Gamaliel

Dead Sea

0   20 mi
0   30 km

∧ *Saul was converted as he traveled near Mount Hermon on the road to Damascus*

eight times. Here we focus on Luke's persistent mention of Damascus in the narrative that describes Saul's conversion.

Damascus is approximately 130 miles (209 km) north of Jerusalem on a plain between the Syrian Desert to its east and Mount Hermon to the west (see map 11.4). Good soils and access to rivers result in an irrigated oasis to house a large city. Because of these resources and the natural obstacles to travel met by taking routes around Damascus, this city became a wealthy transportation hub. Routes went out from Damascus to the populated regions of the known world (Ezekiel 27:18).[14] These transportation links guaranteed that Damascus would have a strong multicultural flavor. Included was a sizable Jewish population served by multiple synagogues.

The Old Testament mentions the city as early as the time of Abraham (Genesis 14:15), but refers to it most frequently during the time when Israel was ruled by the kings. During this time, Damascus and the Arameans fought with Israel to control the route for trade goods flowing from Arabia and Moab. Both were vitally interested in playing the roles of middleman and tax collector (1 Kings 20:1–34; 22:1–40). It was also during this time that the strong anti-Assyrian

posture of the city caused a rift between Israel and Judah (2 Kings 16:5–9).[15] The gospel writers do not mention Damascus, but this quickly changes in the book of Acts.

Luke pays particular attention to Damascus in relating the story of Saul's conversion. Saul (renamed Paul) describes himself in these early years of his life as being one of the most staunch and passionate men among the Hebrews, "a Hebrew of Hebrews" (Philippians 3:5–6). He perceived the movement that claimed Jesus as the Jewish Messiah to be a terrible perversion of Judaism and dedicated himself to punishing its followers. "Still breathing out murderous threats against the Lord's disciples" (Acts 9:1), Saul headed for Damascus with letters of support from the Jewish leaders of Jerusalem in hand. These letters enlisted the aid of the synagogues in Damascus during Saul's quest to take followers of the "Way" into custody so they could be tried and punished in Jerusalem (Acts 9:1–2). Geography helps explain his destination. Damascus not only housed a large Jewish population, which in his mind had become vulnerable to the heretical message of the Way, but there were also Jewish pilgrims traveling through Damascus on the way to Jerusalem who were being infected by this Jesus message. Because

Damascus could facilitate the spread of the Christian movement, that Christian movement, he decided, had to be stopped in Damascus.

The Lord had quite a different perspective. First he planned to turn the zeal of Saul around. "This man is my chosen instrument to proclaim my name to the Gentiles and their king and to the people of Israel" (Acts 9:15). He would use Damascus in exactly the way that Saul feared it might be used, to spread the gospel. Before Saul reaches the city and can do any harm there, the risen Lord Jesus appears to him on the road to Damascus, takes away his sight, and starts the process that will completely revolutionize the way Saul thinks about Christians. Afterward, his conversion complete and his sight restored, Saul goes to the synagogues of Damascus whose aid he had planned to solicit in arresting followers of Jesus. "Saul spent several days with the disciples in Damascus. At once he began to preach in the synagogues that Jesus is the Son of God" (Acts 9:19–20; see also verse 22). His passion and skill in presenting the gospel baffled the opposition. He later returned to Damascus and continued to advocate for Jesus in this city (Galatians 1:15–17).

As Luke tells this story, Damascus does not lie at the periphery but at the heart of Saul's conversion. Luke mentions the city seven times in Acts 9 alone. This detail is important. We might expect someone like Saul—who perceives the followers of Jesus as heretics harming the cause of the Jewish faith—to be actively persecuting that faith in Jerusalem. So why would Saul travel for days to pursue his mission in Damascus, so far from Jerusalem? The answer lies in the geography. Damascus was a particularly effective tool in getting the gospel circulating widely in the inhabited world. But Saul's plan to stop the gospel spread from Damascus ran headlong into the Lord's agenda. The Lord wanted Damascus to function as a dissemination point for the gospel, and Saul would be among those who would make the city's geography work toward that goal. That lays bare the second reason for Luke's emphasis on Damascus in Acts. While many verses speak about Saul's life, the real subject of Acts is the spread of the gospel to the world. In reality, and in Luke's reporting of that reality, it is the geography of Damascus—its location—that played a vital role in accomplishing the goals for the church that Acts lays before its readers.

∧ *Damascus street*

The Celebrated City of Antioch

The three most important cities in the Roman world were Rome, Alexandria, and Antioch of Syria (see map 11.4). Of these, the last is the least familiar to most Bible readers. Luke seems intent on changing that. He mentions this Antioch (Syrian, not Pisidian Antioch) in Acts no less than 17 times. He repeatedly commends the city of Antioch for its Christian character and example, while acknowledging the important ways geography helped it become an important city to the spread of Christianity.[16]

The modern city of Antakya, Turkey, sits on the footprint once occupied by the city of Antioch, nestled in the Orontes River valley with mountains rising to the north and south. As the Orontes River coursed through this valley westward to the Mediterranean Sea, it provided an abundance of water for the farmers tilling the fertile farmland of the valley. With plenty of food and water, this becomes the ideal location for a major city to grow, and Antioch does not disappoint. The so-called "Queen of the East" boasted a population of 500,000 people.[17] Politics and geography joined with agriculture to make the city a prominent political and commercial center. Under Rome's Augustus Caesar, Antioch was elevated to the status of capital city of the imperial province of Syria. This change in rank was quickly followed by a string of architectural improvements that made the place stand out from the local landscape and stand above its neighbors.[18]

The Orontes River valley provided a conduit to the Mediterranean coast and the seaport city of Seleucia Pieria, granting trade access to every shore that the Mediterranean Sea touched. The same valley traveled east from Antioch to Aleppo (see map 11.5), where it joined roads that led deep into Mesopotamia as well as into Egypt. Antioch became a hub in the ancient transportation system and the envy of those who lived in the ancient world. Many people of diverse backgrounds passed through the city.

Antioch of Syria served as a model for Jewish-Christian relationships. A sizable segment of Antioch's population was Jewish with synagogues established to meet their worship needs.[19] This community of

Jews came to know about Jesus in part because Jewish believers who had been driven from Jerusalem by persecution came to Antioch and spread the gospel message (Acts 11:19). But there was an even larger seg-

∨ *Orontes River in Antioch*

Map 11.5—First Missionary Journey

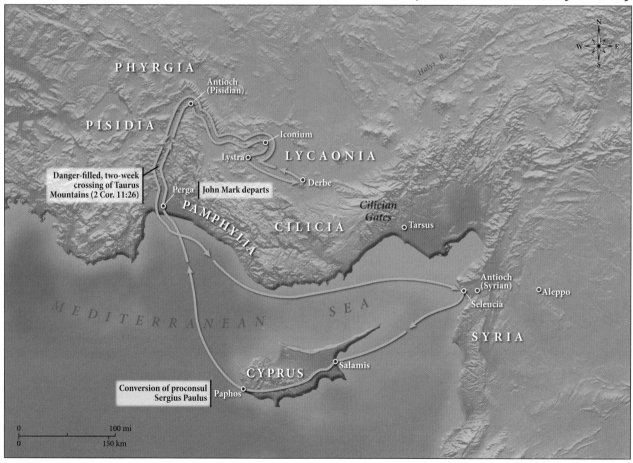

ment of Antioch's population that was Gentile. These Gentiles came to know Jesus because Christians from Cyprus and Cyrene traveled to Antioch and spoke about Jesus, and "a great number of people believed and turned to the Lord" (Acts 11:21). Problems could easily have developed in this mixed community, but the city itself played a role in diminishing any frictions between Jew and Gentile. With the wide array of people who passed through Antioch, the city was accustomed to hearing new ideas. It was a place where cultural barriers were more easily negotiated and new ideas were discussed.[20] The differences between the Jewish and Christian perspectives were debated honestly. In fact the Christian message was so clear in Antioch that its followers received a label that set them apart from Judaism. "The disciples were called Christians first at Antioch" (Acts 11:26).

When trouble did come to the Christian church in Antioch, it typically came from the outside, as it did when men from Judea went to Antioch insisting that Gentile Christians had to submit to circumcision (Acts 15:1). This disturbance led to a meeting of the Council at Jerusalem to deal with the issue. The Council immediately dispatched a letter to Antioch to quell the concern (Acts 15:22–29). Peter also caused a problem in Antioch. He initially socialized freely with Gentiles but suddenly pulled back, fearing the reaction of other Jews. Paul confronted him and fixed the problem before it bloomed into something more problematic for the church (Galatians 2:11–21). Luke includes this Christian church in Antioch because it sets an example of a culturally mixed church whose members get along with each other.

Antioch is also deserving of the attention it gets in the book of Acts because it is a church that demonstrates how to use the resources God gave them. The Lord clearly blessed many within the Christian community of Antioch through the various financial opportunities the city offered. Rather than turning their attention inward, using the gifts themselves, they looked outward from the city to see how they might benefit others. Acts mentions a severe famine that gripped the entire Roman world. Concern for their extended spiritual family living in Judea led the

∨ *Modern Antakya in Turkey is the Bible's Antioch of Syria*

Christians in Antioch to collect aid that was taken as a gift to the region by Barnabas and Saul (Acts 11:27–30). But the Christians in Antioch had an even greater opportunity along the roads that led from their city to the world. Antioch gave the apostle Paul a base from which to begin his three missionary journeys (Acts 13:1–4; 15:35–36; 18:23). The Christians in Antioch had been blessed by the geography of their city and they, in turn, saw an opportunity because of their location to be a blessing to others.

The Macedonian Call

The book of Acts pays so much attention to the memorable people and places we meet on its pages that we can lose sight of the Lord's vital involvement in managing the expansion of his church. Even prominent missionaries like Paul were simply enacting a divine agenda. This becomes clear as Acts narrates the events of the second missionary journey of Paul that included a vision and a call to Macedonia.

Paul's second missionary journey, like the first, begins in Antioch and retraces familiar pathways, revisiting the young Christian churches in places like Derbe, Lystra, Iconium, and Antioch (Pisidian) (see map 11.6). The purpose of these visits was to strengthen the faith of God's people and deliver the decision of the Council at Jerusalem (Acts 16:1–5). When it was time to break new ground, Paul planned to make his way to the important city of Ephesus. But his visit would have to wait because the Holy Spirit kept him from preaching the Word there (Acts 16:6). A turn to the northeast into the region of Bithynia was also precluded by intervention of the Spirit of Jesus (Acts 16:7). This left a corridor that landed Paul and his companions in Troas on the Aegean Sea, across from Macedonia. Once they arrived in that city, the Holy Spirit's plan

Map 11.6—Second Missionary Journey

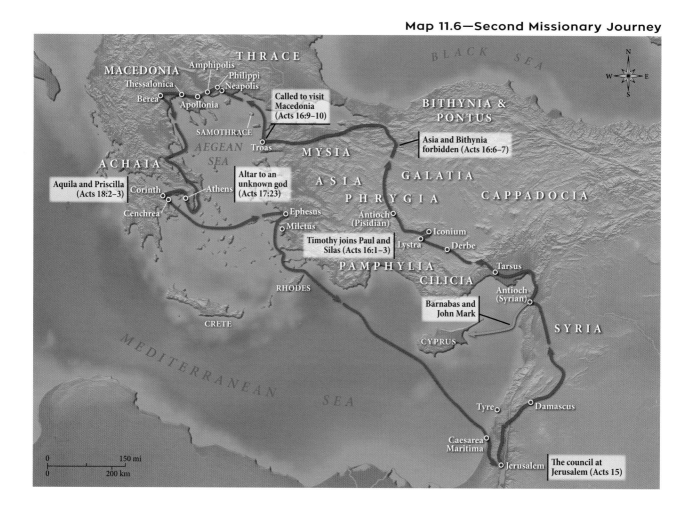

˄ *Remains of the ancient harbor at Troas*

became clear. "During the night Paul had a vision of a man of Macedonia standing and begging him, 'Come over to Macedonia and help us.' After Paul had seen the vision, we got ready at once to leave for Macedonia, concluding that God had called us to preach the gospel to them" (Acts 16:9–10). Note that Luke makes sure we see the direction their mission efforts take, repeating mention of Macedonia three times.

The logic of this move is evident when we consider both the geographic and spiritual dimensions of opening a mission field in Macedonia. Paul made extended stops at two important Greek cities in Macedonia, Philippi and Thessalonica. Philippi was "a Roman colony and the leading city of that district of Macedonia" (Acts 16:12). This was primarily a Gentile place occupied by Roman war veterans who enjoyed the privileges typical of a city in Italy.[21] Thessalonica was the capital of the province of Macedonia and the seat of its governor. These two important cities were bound to one another and the world via an important road called the Egnatian Way. Thessalonica was about at the midpoint on this road, and Philippi had the Egnatian Way as one of its main streets. It is the Egnatian Way that made Macedonia so important to Rome because it connected to shipping lanes that linked Rome with its eastern provinces. Macedonia was an international crossroads with Philippi and

Thessalonica at the heart of the action.[22] If the gospel was preached here, it had the potential of traveling thousands of miles or kilometers both east and west from Macedonia. Leaping ahead, we can see that this is exactly what happened. In Paul's first letter to the Thessalonians, he observed, "Your faith in God has become known everywhere" (1 Thessalonians 1:8).

The spiritual need is clearly evident in this region. The passionate begging of the Macedonian man in Paul's vision made that clear. The urgency is in part due to the geographic gap we find in Acts 2. Here

˅ *The odeum at Thessalonica*

⌃ *The Roman forum at Philippi*

Luke lists the places the people who heard Peter speak at Pentecost had come from, returning to those regions as changed people who carried the gospel with them. Notable by its absence is any mention of visitors from Macedonia. This quietly but powerfully speaks of a gap that needed to be filled. The people Paul met in Macedonia confirm the need for mission work there. When Paul and Silas were imprisoned in Philippi by the local authorities, they met a man, their jailer, who was searching for hope. His simple question suggests that he was the one who was imprisoned. "Sirs, what

⌄ *The traditional site of Paul's imprisonment in Philippi*

must I do to be saved?" (Acts 16:30). When Paul and his companions went to Thessalonica, a large number of Jews and God-fearing Greeks who came to know Jesus as their Savior provide evidence of the need for the gospel in the region (Acts 17:4). And Paul's preaching in Berea prompted a search of the Old Testament among the Jews living there that is celebrated in these words: "Now the Berean Jews were of more noble character than those in Thessalonica, for they received the message with great eagerness and examined the Scriptures every day to see if what Paul said was true" (Acts 17:11). Thus the geography and stories in Acts tell of the great opportunity to spread the good news that was just across the Aegean Sea from Troas in Macedonia.

The Spirit-filled success of the second missionary journey continues on Paul's third missionary journey. He returned to Macedonia, visiting the communities there not just once but twice (Acts 20:1–3) (see map 11.7). These visits were reinforced by correspondence that left an enduring voice of encouragement and direction. Of the letters of Paul preserved for us in the New Testament, we find three addressed to people in Macedonia: Philippians and 1 and 2 Thessalonians. Directed by the Holy Spirit, Paul's work was meant to encourage and sustain the churches he founded in this geographically influential location.

Paul's Extended Stay in Ephesus

The maps of Paul's missionary journeys can give the impression that he was a man constantly on the move, interrupting the rhythm of his itinerary only to make brief stops before he was on his way again. In reality Paul did make extended stays, the longest in Ephesus. Ephesus is located on the west side of the Roman province of Asia just 3 miles (4.8 km) from the Aegean Sea, connected to the maritime trade of the Aegean via the Cayster River (see map 11.7). This city was the most important urban center in the province, reaching its zenith during the Roman era. During that time, it functioned as the seat of the governor of Asia and became a center of banking, commerce, and worship. An array of beautiful public buildings signaled to every visitor that they were in a special place. City planners included a harbor, theater, agora (a meeting place), temples, and even a street paved with marble.[23] Upwards of 400,000 people called Ephesus home.

Paul had wanted to make an extended visit to Ephesus, but it took three attempts before he got to stay. At the start of his second missionary journey, Paul seems to have targeted Ephesus, but the Holy Spirit prevented him from entering the province of Asia (Acts 16:6). At the close of the second missionary journey, Paul was able to stop briefly. The Jews asked him to extend his stay, but Paul declined, saying he would come back if God created the opportunity (Acts 18:19–21). The Lord was willing and so, during Paul's third missionary journey, he spent more than two years at work in Ephesus (Acts 19:8–10).

Luke reports on this stay in Acts 19. When we combine what we know of the location and culture of Ephesus with what Luke says in Acts about this visit, we get a pretty good idea of why Paul selected Ephesus for this extended visit. We note the large Jewish population that was given special privileges by

Map 11.7—Third Missionary Journey

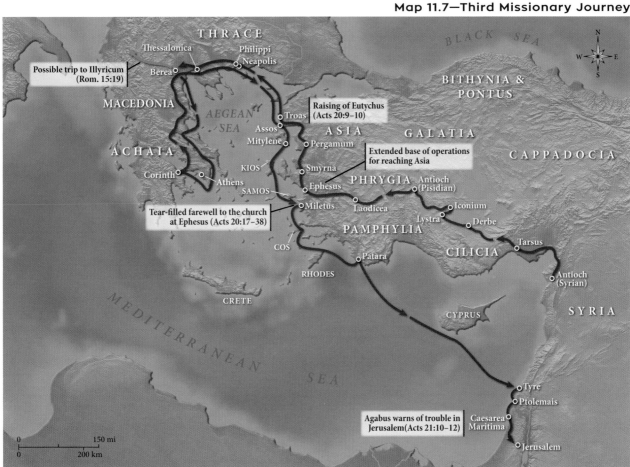

Rome, including exemption from military service and the right to observe their religious laws.[24] Paul had a heart for his own people and invested three months among them "arguing persuasively about the kingdom of God" (Acts 19:8). When he was no longer welcome in the synagogue, Paul moved into a public lecture hall that provided space for an even larger audience (Acts 19:9–10).

There also were a number of elements of the Christian faith that had either not been taught to this community or had been taught incorrectly. Luke highlights two of them. When Paul arrived in Ephesus, he met disciples and asked them if they had received the Holy Spirit at the time they came to know Jesus as their Savior. Stunningly, they had never heard mention of the Holy Spirit. This led Paul to ask about their baptism, to which they replied that the only baptism they knew was the baptism of John. Paul immediately set about filling these gaps in understanding (Acts 19:1–7).

Paul not only had to teach new information, he also had to correct mistaken information. Ephesus was a city given over to the worship of false gods, including the worship of the emperor of Rome and the goddess Artemis. One way the Roman emperors tried to strengthen the loyalty of their citizens was through the imperial cult. It was assumed that identifying the emperor as divine and establishing temples in his honor would assist the collection of taxes and the keeping of the peace. Asia was home to some of the most ardent supporters of this imperial cult. Ephesus itself had two temples dedicated to Augustus Caesar, making it the chief city for the emperor cult in the province.[25]

But long before this emperor worship was initiated in Ephesus, the city was known for its dedication to the goddess Artemis (Roman, Diana). During the time of Paul, the city had built a lavish palace for her on a platform that was 420 feet by 240 feet (128 m by 73 m). It had more than a hundred 60-foot (18.3 m) columns and was the first monument building constructed completely of marble.[26] Architecturally, it

∨ *Street leading from Ephesus to its harbor*

△ The theater at Ephesus

merited being counted as one of the Seven Wonders of the World. Luke pays particular attention to the cult of Artemis in describing Paul's visit to Ephesus. Paul did not shy away from a fight. Rather than presenting the Christian faith as an equal alternative to others, he adamantly argued for monotheism in this polytheistic setting. When he did, the gospel simply overpowered the opposition. Luke humorously illustrates this by telling the story of a disturbance that occurred in Ephesus (Acts 19:23–41). The guild members who made trinkets associated with the worship of Artemis were going through hard financial times because people stopped buying their stuff. The account drips with irony as the local craftsmen riot and attempt to prop up the reputation of Artemis that had been severely damaged by Paul's teaching. A crowd gathered in the theater but "the assembly was in confusion: Some were shouting one thing, some another. Most of the people did not even know why they were there"

△ Statue of Artemis

(Acts 19:32). Finally the city clerk calmed the people, urged use of the court system for disputes, and dismissed the crowd.

Ephesus was connected to the world through its harbor and the valleys that stretched east into Asia, providing access to important cities in the interior. It was at the geographic center of all the places Paul had visited, making it an excellent administrative hub.[27] The success of the gospel there had an impact beyond Ephesus. "In this way the word of the Lord spread widely and grew in power" (Acts 19:20). Clearly Paul was a man who lived his life on the move. New Testament reports suggest he traveled some 13,450 miles (21,646 km)![28] But when he stopped, he stopped for a good reason. As a base of operations, Ephesus benefited from the correction Paul offered and became a conduit through which the gospel moved east to those living throughout Asia Minor and west via shipping lanes into Europe.

Paul, Rome, and Caesarea Maritima

As the gospel of Jesus Christ moves ever outward from Jerusalem, following the plan outlined in Acts 1:8, we read many place names. None may be more familiar to us than Rome. As we read the book of Acts, we are aware of the possibility of Paul's visit to Rome long before we get to his actual departure for Italian shores.

The first mention of the church in Rome comes with the day of Pentecost. Among the Jews who heard Peter speak were Jews from Rome (Acts 2:10). The news about Jesus they carried home brought new life to a community of believers that continued to grow as Christian travelers from Asia went to Rome on business or as immigrants or as slaves.[29] During Paul's third missionary journey, he expressed his desire to get to Rome as soon as he could (Acts 19:21). When Paul was arrested in Jerusalem, the Lord himself stood near him and said, "Take courage! As you have testified about me in Jerusalem, so you must also testify in Rome" (Acts 23:11). All of this creates an expectation that we will soon read of Paul walking the streets of Rome just as he walked the streets of Antioch, Ephesus, Corinth, and Athens.

There was good reason for Paul to get to Rome, both because of a need to advocate for the Christian community there and to interact with them about the basics of the faith. The need for advocacy involved the Roman requirement for public meetings. Because of a concern that groups might meet to plan for revolution, Roman law permitted groups to meet only if they had become approved associations. Judaism was one of the approved religious associations in Rome. And it appears that the Christians in Rome could meet because they were not distinguished from Judaism and so met under the auspices of the Jewish license.[30] This worked well for the newly formed Christian community until an edict was issued by Emperor Claudius in 49 AD.[31] This edict expelled Jews from Rome because of continuing disturbances associated with the instigation of a man named Chrestus. Christians were swept up in the purge, including Aquila and Priscilla, two Jewish Christians from Rome whom Paul met in Corinth (Acts 18:2). Christians were in need of an advocate to speak for them at the highest levels of government, providing one powerful reason for the articulate Paul to travel to Rome.

The other reason for Paul to be in Rome is quietly

Left: Reconstructed columns of Herod's seaside palace at Caesarea Maritima; *Right:* Bust of Emperor Claudius

Map 11.8—Paul Travels to Rome

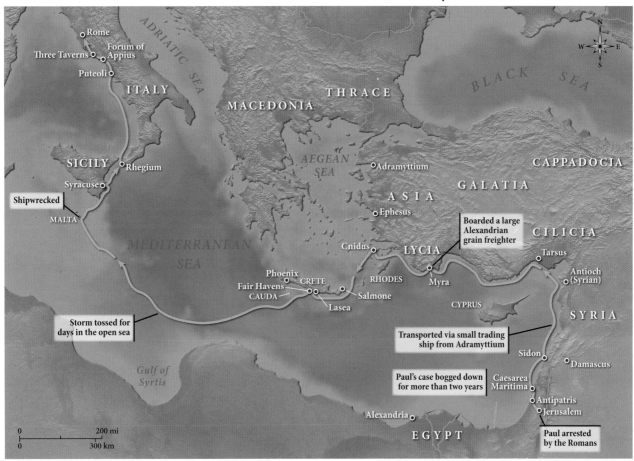

Map 11.8—Paul Travels to Rome

but firmly suggested in Paul's letter to the church at Rome written during his third missionary journey prior to his visit (Romans 1:10–15; 15:22–29). Perhaps the signature element of Paul's letter to the Romans is its simple presentation of the basics of the Christian faith. The content of the book of Romans indicates that the church in Rome was in need of this kind of fundamental instruction. While we cherish having it in writing, this letter to the church in Rome did not give the community there an opportunity to ask the questions they needed to ask Paul to clarify what he had written. They needed Paul to visit with them.

We might expect that this trip to Rome will be undertaken as expeditiously as possible. So it is a bit surprising to find Paul idled for more than two years in Caesarea Maritima, held in the custody of the Roman governor (see map 11.8). The problems began not in Caesarea, but in Jerusalem. A statement about the Gentiles got Paul into trouble there. When he spoke of his need to get the news of Jesus as Messiah to

Gentiles (Acts 22:21), he caused such a strong disturbance that Paul was taken into protective custody by Roman soldiers. The Jewish leaders wanted to press charges against Paul as they had against Jesus, hoping to assassinate Paul long before he ever came to trial. But the Lord had other plans. Roman soldiers spirited Paul away to Caesarea Maritima, the seat of the Roman governor, so that his trial might be held in a more secure location. The hearing before Felix, the governor, began in less than a week. We expect Paul will be on his way to Rome in short order. Ever the cautious politician, Felix tried to resolve the disagreement between Paul and his angry Jewish detractors by tabling the whole matter until a later date. Paul waited for more than two years. When Festus succeeded Felix as governor, he too coddled the favor of the Jewish leaders by leaving Paul in custody (Acts 21:27–24:27).

We do wonder what the Lord's plan was in all of this, given the urgent need for Paul to get to Rome.

∧ *Paul was detained in Herod's palace for two years*

The answer may be in the character of Caesarea Maritima, the place Paul was being detained. Paul was well schooled in the Jewish world, but if he was going to Rome to advocate for the Christian church there, he would need to learn how Romans thought and how business got done. Caesarea was founded by Herod the Great to be his Rome away from Rome. His goal was to re-create a European port in the Middle East with the architecture, entertainment, and worldview of Rome. That is why the Roman governors established their base of administration there. It also proved to be an ideal place for Paul to immerse himself in the pragmatics of Rome before he traveled to Rome. More than two years later, during Paul's trial before Festus, Paul made his plea for a hearing before the highest court in the Roman Empire. "After Festus had conferred with his council, he declared: 'You have appealed to Caesar. To Caesar you will go!'" (Acts 25:12).

The Seven Cities of Revelation

If we randomly open the book of Revelation to almost any of its pages, we read some of the most vivid language and see some of the most surreal imagery found in Holy Scripture. But this book, so full of otherworldly imagery, gets under way with some real-world geography. The author introduces us to seven cities that host seven Christian communities. They are to be the first beneficiaries of what this book has to offer.

In its format, the book of Revelation is a circulating letter that begins by introducing the writer, John, and the recipients, "seven churches in the province of Asia" (Revelation 1:4). In short order, we learn the names of the cities where those seven churches are located. Jesus directs John to "write on a scroll what you see and send it to the seven churches: to Ephesus, Smyrna, Pergamum, Thyatira, Sardis, Philadelphia and Laodicea" (Revelation 1:11) (see map 11.9). After John briefly describes the appearance of Jesus in the vision he had on the island of Patmos and how he received the information contained in the letter (Revelation 1:12–19), he dedicates a block of text to each of the seven churches (Revelation 2–3). The churches are addressed in an order that reflects real-world geography. The city closest to the place of John's exile on Patmos is Ephesus. That is the first city mentioned in chapter 2. All the cities that follow are along the imperial road that connects the seven cities with a circuit that required traveling about 350 miles (563 km). In fact, the order of the cities likely reflects the itinerary for the delivery and reading of Revelation to the churches, starting in Ephesus, proceeding clockwise, and listing the cities in the order they would be visited when traveling on the imperial road system.[32]

From a literary perspective, this repeated mention of the seven cities located in the western quarter of the province of Asia establishes a real-world setting and tone for the reading that follows. It creates the expectation that everything we read in the book of Revelation will have value for those facing real-world challenges in the first century. In other words, the exotic language of Revelation should not be read as the musings of a man gone mad. As elegant and beautiful as the book is, it is not presented to its readers as art for the sake of art. And it is not a road map designed to precisely confirm the date of Jesus' expected return to this earth.

It is a letter written to assist the people living in seven cities who are facing serious challenges.

The big problem for the Christian church in that area was the imperial cult of the Roman Empire. Emperor worship had deep roots in the Roman province of Asia and even among the cities listed in Revelation. The citizens of Pergamum started it by asking to honor Augustus Caesar with a temple. Augustus welcomed the offer, and in 29 BC the first temple to the emperor was built in Pergamum. In the words that John addresses to Pergamum, he speaks of this city as the place "where Satan has his throne" (Revelation 2:13), a likely reference to the temple associated with the imperial cult. When Augustus died, the Roman Senate posthumously recognized the deity of Augustus. That opened the door for his son and successor, Tiberius (14–37 AD), to declare himself "the son of god." But it was the emperor Domitian who made worship of the emperor a litmus test of loyalty. He insisted that every citizen under his rule refer to him as *dominus et deus*

Map 11.9—Churches of the Revelation

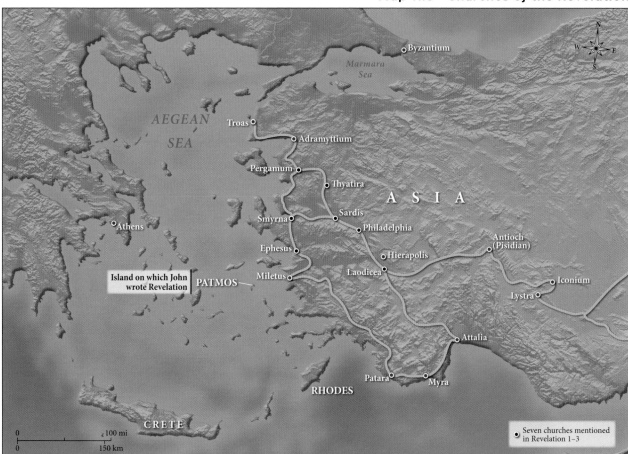

noster ("our lord and god").[33] Domitian is the one who appears to have exiled John to the island of Patmos. And he is the one who is on the stage of history as John writes this letter to the churches in the seven cities of the province of Asia. The Christian church is now recognized as something quite distinct from Judaism and is threatened by the state's insistence on worshiping the emperor.[34]

In response to this challenge and other spiritual failures, Revelation was composed as a circulating letter. Each of the Christian communities who heard it

∧ *Bust of Domitian*

in each of the seven cities had its own history, its own geography, its own experiences as a growing Christian community, and its own potential failure points.[35] We might have expected John to write seven individual letters, one for each of the churches. But instead Jesus directed John to combine them in the one circulating letter preserved for us in the book of Revelation.

The combining of these letters into one emphasizes the shared need for correction and support that would make it possible for these Christians to get through the perilous days ahead. It was with the Lord's help and the mutual support of one another that they would succeed.

The threats from outside were real and were faced not just by the churches in one city but by all the churches. Other communities needed to hear what John was directed to say to the church in Smyrna. "Do not be afraid of what you are about to suffer. I tell you, the devil will put some of you in prison to test you, and you will suffer persecution for ten days" (Revelation 2:10). All faced the fate of Antipas of Pergamum who refused to renounce his faith in Jesus and so died as a martyr and faithful witness (Revelation 2:13). The letter needed to circulate because the threat was real and would invade the life of each community.

∨ *Emperor Trajan's temple at Pergamum*

∧ **Left:** *Remains of the aqueduct at Laodicea;* **Right:** *The main street of Laodicea*

In similar fashion, Christians in each of the cities faced the same temptation from within the church. This is the part of the circulating letter that the Christians of the cities probably were not happy about having it read to others; it is the part where John identifies their failures. These were risks each Christian community faced and so needed to be on guard against them. Ephesus had misplaced love issues. "Yet I hold this against you: You have forsaken the love you had at first" (Revelation 2:4). Pergamum and Thyatira had an issue with hosting false teaching. "Nevertheless, I have a few things against you: There are some among you who hold to the teaching of Balaam. . . . Likewise you also have those who hold to the teaching of the Nicolaitans" (Revelation 2:14–15). "Nevertheless, I have this against you: You tolerate that woman Jezebel, who calls herself a prophet. By her teaching she misleads my servants into sexual immorality and the eating of food sacrificed to idols" (Revelation 2:20). Sardis and Laodicea had issues with apathy. "I know your deeds; you have a reputation of being alive, but you are dead" (Revelation 3:2). "I know your deeds, that you are neither cold nor hot. I wish you were either one or the other! So, because you are lukewarm—neither hot nor cold—I am about to spit you out of my mouth" (Revelation 3:15–16). These stinging criticisms needed to be heeded by the church to which they were addressed, but the warning needed the attention of all the churches.

The encouragement that John offered each church was also meant for all. To Ephesus, he wrote, "You have persevered and have endured hardship for my name, and have not grown weary" (Revelation 2:3). To the church in Smyrna, he wrote, "Be faithful, even to the point of death, and I will give you life as your victor's crown" (Revelation 2:10). And to the church in Philadelphia, John wrote these encouraging words, "I am coming soon. Hold on to what you have, so that no one will take your crown. The one who is victorious I will make a pillar in the temple of my God. Never again will they leave it. I will write on them the name of my God and the name of the city of my God, the new Jerusalem, which is coming down out of heaven from my God; and I will also write on them my new name" (Revelation 3:11–12).

All the churches faced the same threats from the outside, the same temptations from within, and needed the same words of encouragement. This binds the Christians of this entire region into one social unit and tacitly encourages the churches in each of the cities to form a support network through which they might encourage one another. This could have been communicated in individual letters, but a circulating letter had the added benefit of inviting the churches in

Map 11.10—Growth of the Christian Church

Cities hosting Christian communities at the close of the first century

these seven cities to see themselves as linked to all the others—a community of faith (see map 11.10).

The first chapters of Revelation are firmly anchored in the geography of western Asia Minor, in the ancient cities named. This builds real-world connections to what is being said and urges us to look for the value for us today. As the final word of revelation from Jesus, the book of Revelation becomes an extended commentary on how to live in this world while we wait for him to return. We will face troubles of many kinds. He told us that. "I have told you these things, so that in me you may have peace. In this world you will have trouble. But take heart! I have overcome the world" (John 16:33). But we can be assured that Jesus is aware of the troubles we face and offers his support.

We can be assured that our "names are written in the Lamb's book of life" (Revelation 21:27). And we can find hope and encouragement in every season of life within the book of Revelation. Its real-world language and otherworldly images combine to sound the note that Christians need to hear. The book of Revelation sings the distant song of triumph.

John lived in the real world. And the first three chapters of Revelation offer the real-world direction and encouragement we need to live as children of God. We can live in hope and confidence through all the mayhem, assured that Jesus is coming back to this earth to bring us to a place of eternal rest. "He who testifies to these things says, 'Yes, I am coming soon.'"

"Amen. Come, Lord Jesus" (Revelation 22:20).

Appendix:
IMPORTANT DATES

KEY:
Bold type: key individuals named in the Bible
Regular type: events recorded in the Bible
Italic type: individuals and world events not recorded in the Bible

BIBLE BOOK	DATE/ERA	EVENT DATE	PERSONS AND EVENTS
Genesis	*Origin–1805 BC*	*2700*	*Egypt's Old Kingdom period begins*
		2589–2504	*Pyramid building at Giza*
		2334	*Akkadian Empire begins under Sargon*
		2166–1991	**Abraham**
		2091	Covenant with Abraham
		2070	*Xia dynasty begins in China*
		2066–1886	**Isaac**
		2006–1859	**Jacob (Israel)**
		2000	*Stonehenge in England*
		2000	*Rise of the Old Assyrian kingdom*
Job	*1900 BC*	**1915–1805**	**Joseph**
		1885	Joseph to power in Egypt
		1876	Jacob's family to Egypt
		1775	*Law code of Hammurabi*
		1750	*Old Assyrian demise*
		1700	*Chariots in Middle East*
		1600	*Shang dynasty begins in China*
Exodus	*1570–1446 BC*	1570	Oppression in Egypt begins
Leviticus	*1446–1445 BC*	**1526–1406**	**Moses**
Numbers	*1445–1406 BC*	*1526–1512*	*Thutmose I*
Deuteronomy	*1406 BC*	*1512–1504*	*Thutmose II*
		1504–1450	*Thutmose III*
		1466–1356	**Joshua**
		1450–1425	*Amenhotep II*
		1446	Exodus from Egypt
		1446–1406	Years in the wilderness
Joshua	*1406–1380 BC*	1406–1399	Conquest of Canaan
Judges	*1356–1050 BC*	*1361–1352*	*Tutankhamen (King Tut)*
Ruth	*1370 BC*	**1356–1050**	**Judges rule Israel**
		1320–1318	*Ramses I*
		1318–1304	*Seti I*
		1304–1236	*Ramses II*

BIBLE BOOK	DATE/ERA	EVENT DATE	PERSONS AND EVENTS
		1210	*Merneptah Stele*
		1200	*Philistines arrive in SW Canaan*
		1115–1076	*Tiglath-Pileser I and resurging Assyria*
		1085–1051	**Samuel as judge**
		1070	*Decline in Egyptian power*
		1046	*Zhou dynasty in China*
1–2 Samuel	*1100–971 BC*	1050–931	United Kingdom
		1050–1011	**Saul**
Psalms	*1020–500 BC*	**1011–971**	**David**
1–2 Chronicles	*971–586 BC*	977	Ark of the covenant to Jerusalem
1–2 Kings	*971–560 BC*	**971–931**	**Solomon**
Proverbs	*971–931 BC*	966	Construction of temple begins
Ecclesiastes	*971–931 BC*	945–924	Shishak (Shoshenq) in Egypt
Song	*971–931 BC*	931	Kingdom divides
		931–913	**Rehoboam (Judah)**
		931–910	**Jeroboam I (Israel)**
		930	Golden calves at Bethel/Dan
		885–874	**Omri (Israel)**
		880	Omri founds Samaria
		874–853	**Ahab and Jezebel (Israel)**
Joel	*830 BC*	**841–814**	**Jehu (Israel)**
		835–796	**Joash (Judah)**
		835	*Mesha Stele*
		827	*Black Obelisk*
Jonah	*770 BC*	**793–753**	**Jeroboam II (Israel)**
Amos	*760–750 BC*		
Hosea	*760–722 BC*	745	*Rise of Neo-Assyrian Empire*
Micah	*750–705 BC*	**735–716**	**Ahaz (Judah)**
Isaiah	*740–701 BC*	733–732	Tiglath-Pileser III campaigns in Israel
		732–722	**Hoshea (Israel)**
		722	Samaria falls to Assyria
		716–687	**Hezekiah (Judah)**
		705	Hezekiah's reforms
		704–681	Sennacherib
		701	Assyria attacks Jerusalem
Nahum	*663–612 BC*	**641–609**	**Josiah (Judah)**
Zephaniah	*630 BC*		
Jeremiah	*628–580 BC*	625	*Rise of Neo-Babylonian Empire*
Habakkuk	*615 BC*		
		612	*Nineveh falls to Babylonians and Medes*
Daniel	*605–536 BC*	605	First deportation to Babylon
		597–586	**Zedekiah (Judah)**
		597	Second deportation to Babylon

BIBLE BOOK	DATE/ERA	EVENT DATE	PERSONS AND EVENTS
Ezekiel	*593–573 BC*		
Obadiah	*586–550 BC*	586	Third deportation to Babylon
Lamentations	*586 BC*	586	Jerusalem and temple destroyed
		559–530	Cyrus the Great
		535	*Cyrus Cylinder*
Ezra	*538–440 BC*	538	Exiles return under Sheshbazzar
		536	Temple reconstruction begins
		530–520	Temple reconstruction halted
Haggai	*520–516 BC*	**522–486**	**Darius I**
Zechariah	*520–516 BC*		
		515	Temple dedication
		509	*Roman republic established*
Obadiah	*500 BC*		
		490	*Battle of Marathon*
Esther	*483–474 BC*	**486–465**	**Xerxes I (Ahasuerus)**
		485–425	*Herodotus*
		478	**Esther, queen in Persia**
		464–424	**Artaxerxes I**
		458	Return led by Ezra
Nehemiah	*445–410 BC*	445	Return led by Nehemiah
		445	Jerusalem's walls rebuilt
Malachi	*433 BC*		
		390	*Gauls attack Rome*
		175–164	*Antiochus IV Epiphanes*
		167–164	*Maccabean revolt, temple purification*
		164	*First celebration of Hanukkah*
		164–63	*Hasmoneans*
		142	*Jewish independence from Syria*
		109/108	*John Hyrcanus destroys Samaritan Temple on Mt. Gerizim*
		63	*Pompey defeats Jerusalem*
		47	*Antipater, governor of Judea*
		47	*Herod, governor of Galilee*
		44	*Julius Caesar assassinated*
		42	*Battle of Philippi, Octavian and Mark Antony defeat Brutus and Cassius*
		40	*Rome senate proclaims Herod king of Judea*
		40–37	*Herod battles Parthians*
		37–4	Herod the Great rules
		31	*Battle of Actium, Octavian defeats Antony and Cleopatra*
		27 BC–AD 14	Octavian becomes Caesar Augustus (first Roman emperor)
		20	*Temple restoration begins*

BIBLE BOOK	DATE/ERA	EVENT DATE	PERSONS AND EVENTS
		4 BC–AD 6	Archelaus rules Judea
		4 BC–AD 39	Herod Antipas rules Galilee and Perea
		4 BC–AD 34	Herod Philip rules Iturea, Trachonitus, and Gaulanitis
Mathew, Mark,	*4 BC–AD 30*	**6/4 BC**	**Jesus' birth**
Luke, John		**4 BC**	**Herod the Great dies**
		AD 7	*Judea made a Roman imperial province*
		14–37	**Tiberius Caesar, Roman emperor**
		15–30	Paul studies with Gamaliel in Jerusalem
		18–36	**Caiaphas, High Priest in Jerusalem**
		26	Jesus' baptism by John
		26	Pilate begins to rule in Judea
		29	Lazarus is raised
		30	Jesus' death and resurrection
Acts	*AD 30–62*	30	Pentecost
		31–33	Saul persecutes the church
		32/33	Stephen martyred
		34	**Conversion of Saul (Paul)**
		34–37	Paul in Arabia and Damascus
James	*AD 40–60*	*37–41*	*Caligula, Roman emperor*
		37–95	*Josephus*
		41–44	Herod Agrippa I, King of Israel
		41–54	Claudius, Roman emperor
		42	James the apostle executed
		47	Barnabas brings Saul to Antioch
		47/48	Paul's first missionary journey
Galatians	*AD 49*	49	Jews expelled from Rome by Claudius
		49/50	Council at Jerusalem
		49–51	Paul's second missionary journey
1-2 Thessalonians	*AD 51*	50–93	Herod Agrippa II
1-2 Corinthians	*AD 55*	52–57	Paul's third missionary journey
Romans	*AD 57*	52–60	Felix, governor of Judea
		53–56	Paul in Ephesus
		54–68	*Nero, Roman emperor*
		57–59	Paul awaits trial in Caesarea Maritima
1 Peter	*Early 60s*	59–60	Paul travels to Rome
Ephesians	*AD 60*	60–61	Paul in Rome
Philippians	*AD 60–62*	60–62	Festus, governor of Judea
Colossians	*AD 60–62*	62	*James, the Lord's brother executed*
Philemon	*AD 60–62*	62	*Paul released and travels to Spain*
1 Timothy	*AD 63–65*	63	*Temple restoration completed*
Titus	*AD 63–65*	63–67	Paul again imprisoned in Rome
Jude	*AD 65*	64–65	*Rome burns, Christians blamed*

BIBLE BOOK	DATE/ERA	EVENT DATE	PERSONS AND EVENTS
Hebrews	*AD 60s*	*64–68*	*Paul and Peter executed by Nero*
2 Timothy	*AD 66–67*	*66–70*	*First Jewish revolt*
2 Peter	*Late 60s*	*66*	*Jerusalem Christians flee to Pella*
		69–79	*Vespasian, Roman emperor*
		70	*Titus destroys Jerusalem*
		73	*Fall of Masada*
		79–81	*Titus, Roman emperor*
		79	*Eruption of Mt. Vesuvius, destruction of Pompeii and Herculaneum*
1, 2, 3 John	*AD 85–95*	*81–96*	*Domitian, Roman emperor*
Revelation	*AD 95*	*94–96*	John exiled to Patmos
		98–117	*Trajan, Roman emperor*
		100	*John's death*

NOTES

Introduction

1. This revealing of divine characteristics is called "general revelation," which is designed to work in concert with "special revelation." Special revelation is the more complete unveiling of God found in our Bibles.
2. John Muir, *Our National Parks* (Boston: Houghton Mifflin, 1901), 56.
3. John Muir, *The Yosemite* (New York: Century Company, 1912), 256.
4. Andson F. Rainey and R. Steven Notley, *The Sacred Bridge* (Jerusalem: Carta, 2006), 9.
5. Jerome, *Commentary on Chronicles* as quoted in Yohanan Aharoni, *The Land of the Bible: A Historical Geography*, 2nd ed. (Philadelphia: Westminster Press, 1979), x.

Chapter 1

1. The approximate area of the Promised Land is 10,700 square miles (2,771,287 hectares). Barry J. Beitzel, *The New Moody Atlas of the Bible* (Chicago: Moody, 2009), 40.
2. For a more complete introduction of each zone and accompanying subregions, see John A. Beck, *The Land of Milk and Honey: An Introduction to the Geography of Israel* (St. Louis, MO: Concordia, 2006), 29–146.
3. Efraim Orni and Elisha Efrat, *Geography of Israel*, 3rd ed. (Jerusalem: Jewish Publication Society of America, 1971), 57.
4. Beitzel, *Moody Atlas of the Bible*, 48.
5. For a discussion, see David A. Dorsey, *The Roads and Highways of Ancient Israel*, ASOR Library of Biblical and Near Eastern Archaeology (Baltimore: Johns Hopkins University Press, 1991), 147–50.
6. W. F. Lynch, *Narrative of the United States' Expedition to the Jordan River and the Dead Sea* (Philadelphia: Lea and Blanchard, 1849), 264–65.
7. The most comprehensive and focused treatment of this topic in a single publication can be found in Arie S. Issar, *Water Shall Flow from the Rock: Hydrogeology and Climate in the Lands of the Bible* (Berlin: Springer-Verlag, 1990).
8. For a discussion of the theological implications of this reality, see Beitzel, *Moody Atlas of the Bible*, 58–64.
9. A more detailed summary of this issue can be found in Orni and Efrat, *Geography of Israel*, 142–46.
10. "Renewable Internal Freshwater Resources per Capita," The World Bank, http://data.worldbank.org/indicator/ER.H2O.INTR.PC.
11. For a discussion of the use of wells and cisterns as tools in the hands of the Bible's authors, see John A. Beck, ed., *Zondervan Dictionary of Biblical Imagery* (Grand Rapids: Zondervan, 2011), 48–50, 268–71.
12. Orni and Efrat, *Geography of Israel*, 147.
13. For a more detailed summary of the science and realities of the summer and winter seasons, see Orni and Efrat, *Geography of Israel*, 135–63.
14. The biblical authors were familiar with the awful consequences of rain that falls short of expectation as well as a rainy season that begins late or ends too early. For a discussion of drought and its consequences, see Beck, *Land of Milk and Honey*, 160.
15. For a more detailed discussion of these winds and their use by the biblical authors, see Beck, *Zondervan Dictionary of Biblical Imagery*, 271–72.
16. Given the complexity of moving an army, military movements are more modest and limited to 14 to 15 miles (22.5 to 24 km) per day. The army of Alexander the Great was considered fast moving due to its ability to move 18 to 20 miles (29 to 32 km) per day. Dorsey, *Roads and Highways of Ancient Israel*, 12–13.
17. Yohanan Aharoni, *The Land of the Bible: A Historical Geography*, 2nd ed. (Philadelphia: Westminster Press, 1979), 43.
18. Dorsey, *Roads and Highways of Ancient Israel*, 26–27. What was true in the Iron Age persisted well into the Roman period; see Michael Avi-Yonah, *The Holy Land: A Historical Geography from the Persian to the Arab Conquest 536 BC to AD 640* (Grand Rapids: Baker, 1966), 181–87.
19. Orni and Efrat, *Geography of Israel*, 350.
20. An alternative route east of the Jordan avoided the deep river canyons but put travelers on the fringe of the Syrian Desert. This is referenced as the Desert Road of Moab (Deuteronomy 2:8). The King's Highway and the Desert Road meet at Rabbath-Ammon after taking different routes north from the Gulf of Eilat. At Rabbath-Ammon, the Desert Road ends and the King's Highway continues north to Damascus.
21. Aharoni, *Land of the Bible*, 54.

Chapter 2

1. For an overview of all the options, see Eric H. Cline, *From Eden to Exile Unraveling Mysteries of the Bible* (Washington, DC: National Geographic Society, 2007), 1–15.

2. Barry J. Beitzel, *The New Moody Atlas of the Bible* (Chicago: Moody, 2009), 88. The same term has also been linked to the Aramaic notion of "delight." See John H. Walton, ed., *Bible Backgrounds Commentary* (Grand Rapids: Zondervan, 2009), 1:27.

3. For a more detailed discussion, see Beitzel, *Moody Atlas of the Bible*, 89–90.

4. Victor P. Hamilton, *The Book of Genesis: Chapters 1–17*, NICOT (Grand Rapids: Eerdmans, 1990), 346.

5. For a thorough treatment of each location discernible in this list, see Beitzel, *Moody Atlas of the Bible*, 91–97.

6. John H. Sailhamer, *The Pentateuch as Narrative: A Biblical-Theological Commentary*, Library of Biblical Interpretation (Grand Rapids: Zondervan, 1992), 130.

7. Carl G. Rasmussen, *Zondervan Atlas of the Bible* (Grand Rapids: Zondervan, 2010), 90.

8. See the discussion in Beitzel, *Moody Atlas of the Bible*, 98–100. J. Wilkinson, *Egeria's Travels to the Holy Land* (Jerusalem: Ariel, 1981), 120.

9. Walter C. Kaiser Jr., *The Promise-Plan of God: A Biblical Theology of the Old and New Testaments* (Grand Rapids: Zondervan, 2008), 35.

10. This is the *hithpael* form of *hlk*. For a discussion see, Willem A. VanGemeren, ed., *New International Dictionary of Old Testament Theology and Exegesis* (Grand Rapids: Zondervan, 1997), 1:1034.

11. The exchange of sandals worn during the process provided the culminating moment of the property transfer. Philip J. King and Lawrence E. Stager, *Life in Biblical Israel*, Library of Ancient Israel (Louisville, KY: Westminster John Knox Press, 2001), 273.

12. James K. Hoffmeier, *Israel in Egypt: The Evidence for the Authenticity of the Exodus Tradition* (Oxford: Oxford University Press, 1996), 68.

13. John A. Beck, "Faith in the Face of Famine: The Narrative-Geographical Function of Famine in Genesis," *The Journal of Biblical Storytelling* 11 (2001): 58–66.

14. The difficulty in understanding "Moriah" led those translating the Old Testament into the Samaritan Aramaic, Greek, and Latin languages to alter the spelling of this word to better identify the location. The more difficult spelling is likely the most authentic. (The versions noted here handle this lexeme in more than one way. In all cases, they translate using a term with which they are more familiar.)

15. David A. Dorsey, *The Roads and Highways of Ancient Israel*, ASOR Library of Biblical and Near Eastern Archaeology (Baltimore: Johns Hopkins University Press, 1991), 12–13.

16. For more on graves of the biblical period, see John A. Beck, ed., *Zondervan Dictionary of Biblical Imagery* (Grand Rapids: Zondervan, 2011), 116–18.

17. For a sustained discussion, see Augustine Pagolu, *The Religion of the Patriarchs* (Sheffield: Sheffield Academic Press, 1998), 145–70.

18. Anson F. Rainey and R. Steven Notely, *The Sacred Bridge* (Jerusalem: Carta, 2006), 60.

19. Since the fourth century AD, the location of the tomb of Rachel has been stated to be on the outskirts of Bethlehem. But the text indicates Jacob and his family were traveling toward Bethlehem, yet were some distance away when Rachel died (Genesis 35:16–20). First Samuel 10:2 places the tomb near Zelzah (location unknown) on the border of Benjamin. With Saul's likely line of movement that day, we place the tomb between Ramah and Gibeah.

20. Dorsey, *Roads and Highways of Ancient Israel*, 120.

21. For a more detailed comparison of the incidents related to the use of famine in Genesis as a way of revealing faith, see Beck, "Faith in the Face of Famine," 11:58–66.

22. For more discussion of the Amorites and Canaanites, see Keith N. Schoville, "Canaanites and Amorites," in *People of the Old Testament World*, eds. Alfred J. Hoerth, Gerald L. Mattingly, and Edwin M. Yamauchi (Grand Rapids: Baker, 1994), 157–82.

23. Walton, *Bible Backgrounds Commentary*, 1:126.

Chapter 3

1. James K. Hoffmeier, *Israel in Egypt: The Evidence for the Authenticity of the Exodus Tradition* (Oxford: Oxford University Press, 1996), 121–22.

2. Carl G. Rasmussen, *Zondervan Atlas of the Bible* (Grand Rapids: Zondervan, 2010), 67–68.

3. James K. Hoffmeier, "Egyptians," in *Peoples of the Old Testament World*, ed. Alfred J. Hoerth, Gerald L. Mattingly, and Edwin M. Yamauchi (Grand Rapids: Baker Books, 1994), 270–71.

4. Thutmose III alone conducted 17 campaigns into the Levant. Anson F. Rainey and R. Steven Notley, *The Sacred Bridge* (Jerusalem: Carta, 2006), 65–69.

5. Paul H. Wright, *Greatness, Grace, and Glory: Carta's Atlas of Biblical Biography* (Jerusalem: Carta, 2008), 17.

6. Hoffmeier, *Israel in Egypt*, 177.

7. For a detailed discussion of the options for locating Mount Sinai and the strengths and weaknesses of the proposals, see Barry J. Beitzel, *The New Moody Atlas of the Bible* (Chicago: Moody, 2009), 109–13.

8. Rainey and Notley, *The Sacred Bridge*, 119.

9. Succoth has been linked to Tell el-Maskhutah on the east side of the Wadi Tumilat. Although a camp near an Egyptian fortress would seem out of the question. Perhaps it would be better for us to understand that they camped along the main route in the region of Succoth. See Hoffmeier, *Israel in Egypt*, 181.

10. The translation Red Sea comes from the Greek edition of the Old Testament called the Septuagint. In translating the Hebrew with "Red Sea," they have employed a classical reference which encompasses a wide range of water bodies. See Beitzel, *Moody Atlas of the Bible*, 108–9.

11. K. A. Kitchen, *On the Reliability of the Old Testament* (Grand Rapids: Eerdmans, 2003), 260.

12. The pros and cons of various identifications for Mount Sinai are carefully listed here. Beitzel, *Moody Atlas of the Bible*, 109–13.

13. Efraim Orni and Elisha Efrat, *Geography of Israel,* 3rd ed. (Jerusalem: The Jewish Publication Society of America, 1971), 359.

14. The word for spy which is used in Genesis 42:9 and Joshua 2:1 is absent from this narrative; consequently it is better to construe this delegation as a scouting team rather than as a group of military spies.

15. Here we understand the more generic language of "good" and "bad" according to the Rabbinic interpretation which sees this as a reference to hydrology. Rabbi A. M. Silbermann, ed., *Chumas with Targum Onkelos, Haphtaroth and Rashi's Commentary, Bamidbar* (Jerusalem: Silbermann Family, 1934), 62.

16. These observations are based on the evidence provided in the el-Amarna correspondence from the mid-fourteenth century BC and upon archaeological surveys of the Central Mountain Range during this period. See Rainey and Notley, *The Sacred Bridge,* 79. Yohanan Aharoni, *The Land of the Bible: A Historical Geography,* 2nd ed. (Philadelphia: Westminster Press, 1979), 174–75. Amihai Mazar, *Archaeology of the Land of the Bible, 10,000–586 BCE,* The Anchor Bible Reference Library (New York: Doubleday, 1992), 243.

17. Up to ten different explanations have been offered for Moses' disqualification. We find the explanation we offer the one which most closely follows the trajectory of text and geography. For alternate explanations see, Jacob Milgrom, *Numbers,* JPS Torah Commentary (Philadelphia: The Jewish Publication Society, 1990), 448.

18. The Hebrew term used here is not the typical Hebrew term for rock. Five of its seven occurrences in the Pentateuch are within this chapter. And it is a different Hebrew term for rock than the one used in Exodus 17 to present an earlier miracle of providing water from stone. For a discussion see, John A. Beck, "Why Did Moses Strike Out? The Narrative-Geographical Shaping of Moses' Disqualification in Numbers 20:1–13," *Westminster Theological Journal* 65 (2003): 139.

19. Orni and Efrat, *Geography of Israel,* 24.

20. Arie S. Issar, *Water Shall Flow from the Rock: Hydrogeology and Climate in the Lands of the Bible* (Berlin: Springer-Verlag, 1990), 117–18, 121.

21. For a discussion on the realized northern border of Moab, see Rainey and Notley, *The Sacred Bridge,* 124.

22. See also Judges 3:12–30; 1 Samuel 14:47; 2 Samuel 8:2, 13–14; 10; 11:1, 12:26–31; 2 Kings 3; 16:6; 1 Chronicles 19:1—20:3; 2 Chronicles 20 and all the many judgment speeches against Ammon, Moab, and Edom found within the prophetic books of the Old Testament.

23. The question regarding the eastern border of the Promised Land is unresolved. Some suggest that it extends only to the Jordan River and that the area east of the Jordan is more of a land grant like that made to Ammon, Moab, and Edom. Others contend that the Promised Land includes all the land assigned to Reuben, Gad, and the half tribe of Manasseh east of the Jordan River. For a discussion, see Beitzel, *Moody Atlas of the Bible,* 26–29.

Chapter 4

1. For a more sustained discussion of this important event, see John A. Beck, "Why Do Joshua's Readers Keep Crossing the River?" *JETS* 48 (December 2005): 689–99.

2. Carl Ritter, *The Comparative Geography of Palestine and the Sinaitic Peninsula* (New York: Greenwood, 1968), 4:51–53.

3. For a discussion on the use of salt in the culture of Bible times, see, John A. Beck, *Zondervan Dictionary of Biblical Imagery* (Grand Rapids: Zondervan, 2011), 217–19.

4. Zertal discovered an Iron Age altar on the northeast side of Mount Ebal made of uncut stones, 6.5 feet (2 m) in diameter. The bones associated with this apparent altar were all from animals defined in the Israelite law as clean animals. Adam Zertal, "Has Joshua's Altar Been Found?" *Biblical Archaeology Review* 11 (January–February 1985), 26–43.

5. For a discussion of this road system, see David A. Dorsey, *The Roads and Highways of Ancient Israel* (Baltimore: Johns Hopkins University Press, 1991), 140–46.

6. For a discussion of this miracle and its geographical connections, See Barry J. Beitzel, *The New Moody Atlas of the Bible* (Chicago: Moody, 2009), 118–19.

7. For a detailed discussion of this city, see LaMoine F. DeVries, *Cities of the Biblical World* (Peabody, MA: Hendrickson, 1997), 182–88.

8. The reader looking for a detailed discussion of the individual tribal boundary lines will find it in Carl G. Rasmussen, *Zondervan Atlas of the Bible* (Grand Rapids: Zondervan, 2010), 113–19.

9. Because the lists of cities at times reflect a later reality in Israel's history, some have suggested that the origin of these lists ought to be tied to Israel's monarchy. It is more

likely that these lists are authentic to the time of Joshua, that they continued in use as administrative lists into the time of the monarchy, and that late features evident in the lists are a product of their being updated during time of the monarchy. See Iain Provan, V. Philips Long, and Tremper Longman III, *A Biblical History of Israel* (Louisville: Westminster John Knox Press, 2003), 156.

10. There remains a question as to whether or not the Levites actually owned these villages or merely had use of these towns which remained under the ownership of the other Israelite tribes. On the one hand, the Lord told Aaron that he would not have an inheritance in the land but that the Lord himself was their inheritance (Numbers 18:20); while on the other hand, the villages are "given" to the Levites (Numbers 35:1–5).

11. While the Hebrew text of Judges 18 indicates that Judah was successful against the Philistine cities of Gaza, Ashkelon, and Ekron, the Septuagint (early Greek translation of the Old Testament) inserts a negative particle here indicating they were not successful against these cities.

12. Rainey suggests the Canaanite industrialists welcomed the agricultural contribution of the Asherites. Anson F. Rainey and R. Steven Notley, *The Sacred Bridge* (Jerusalem: Carta, 2006), 135.

Chapter 5

1. Barry J. Beitzel, *The New Moody Atlas of the Bible* (Chicago: Moody, 2009), 143.

2. Kenneth A. Kitchen, *On the Reliability of the Old Testament* (Grand Rapids: Eerdmans, 2003), 96–97.

3. The heads and hands of defeated soldiers were collected by the victorious army to tabulate enemy casualties and demonstrate the total defeat of the opposing army on the battlefield. John H. Walton, ed., *Zondervan Illustrated Bible Backgrounds Commentary* (Grand Rapids: Zondervan, 2009), 2:293.

4. Alfred J. Hoerth, *Archaeology and the Old Testament* (Grand Rapids: Baker, 1998), 243.

5. Josephus, *Antiquities of the Jews* 6.5.1.

6. For a discussion of maiming in battle contexts, see Walton, *Zondervan Illustrated Bible Backgrounds Commentary*, 2:322–23.

7. For a discussion of Geba's location see, Anson F. Rainey and R. Steven Notely, *The Sacred Bridge* (Jerusalem: Carta, 2006), 145–46.

8. This outpost may have been established on higher ground which afforded the lookouts a better view both south and east from Mikmash to warn of an approaching attack.

9. Paul H. Wright, *Greatness, Grace, and Glory: Carta's Atlas of Biblical Biography* (Jerusalem: Carta, 2008), 41.

10. The Hebrew word "stronghold" used to describe this location is likely the prominent butte of Masada which later would become a fortress-palace of Herod the

13. The narrative and poetic version of this event in Judges 4 and 5 differ in the way they describe participation of the northern tribes. For a discussion see, Rainey and Notley, *The Sacred Bridge*, 138–39.

14. Mount Tabor occupies a unique position in that it is the geographical meeting point of the parcels of land given to Zebulun, Issachar, and Naphtali (Joshua 19:10–23, 32–39).

15. Unfortunately many English translations blur this symmetry by translating the verbs in these two verses with different English equivalents. The NIV translates in Exodus with "threw . . . into confusion" and in Judges with "routed."

16. For a discussion of Philistine origins and culture, see David M. Howard Jr., "Philistines," in *People of the Old Testament World,* ed. Alfred J. Hoerth, Gerald L. Mattingly, and Edwin M. Yamauchi (Grand Rapids: Baker Books, 1994), 231–50.

17. Philip J. King and Lawrence E. Stager, *Life in Biblical Israel,* Library of Ancient Israel (Louisville: Westminster John Knox Press, 2001), 61–63.

18. Bethlehem is formally mentioned in 1:1–2, 19, 22; 2:4; 4:11.

19. Moab is mentioned in 1:1–2, 4, 6, 22; 2:2, 6, 21; 4:3, 5, 10.

Great. See Yohanan Aharoni, *The Land of the Bible: A Historical Geography,* 2nd ed. (Philadelphia: Westminster Press, 1979), 290.

11. Rainey and Notely, *The Sacred Bridge*, 148.

12. The parallel grows even stronger if the "spring of Jezreel" (1 Samuel 29:1) is the same as the "spring of Harod" (Judges 7:1). See Rainey and Notely, *The Sacred Bridge*, 150.

13. This association with the Philistines allowed David to escape from Saul, to obtain wealth which he could use to foster the well-being of those in Judah, and to learn about the military technology and strategies of the Philistines. See John H. Walton, Victor H. Matthews, and Mark W. Chavalas, *The IVP Bible Background Commentary: Old Testament* (Downers Grove, IL: InterVarsity Press, 2000), 317.

14. In Chronicles, Ish-Bosheth is identified by the name Eshbaal (1 Chronicles 8:33; 9:39). It is hard to imagine that parents would name their son Ish-Bosheth, which is the Hebrew for "man of shame." This likely is an attempt by the author of 2 Samuel to diminish our confidence in and respect for this man.

15. It seems unlikely that the troublesome "Ashuri" is a reference to the tribal unit of Asher.

16. This Jezreel is not the well-known Jezreel on the east side of the Jezreel Valley but the city located in Judah (Joshua 15:56).

17. The combination of family ties and security guaran-

teed David a loyal following in Judah and Simeon. See Aharoni, *Land of the Bible*, 292.

18. Carl G. Rasmussen, *Zondervan Atlas of the Bible* (Grand Rapids: Zondervan, 2010), 47–48.

19. Kings naming cities after themselves was not new in the ancient Near East. See Walton, *Zondervan Illustrated Bible Backgrounds Commentary*, 2:435. But here the renaming clearly has a rhetorical role to play in defeating old civil war affinities.

20. For a discussion of the relationship between the Abrahamic and Davidic covenants, see Walter C. Kaiser Jr., *The Promise-Plan of God: A Biblical Theology of the Old and New Testament* (Grand Rapids: Zondervan, 2008), 118–24.

21. For an attempt at reorganizing the information in chronological order, see Rainey and Notely, *The Sacred Bridge*, 160–61.

22. Not all translations reflect the change in Hebrew vocabulary which distinguishes what happened to the Philistines from the report given about other people groups in 2 Samuel 8.

23. For a detailed discussion of the geography within this list, see Rainey and Notely, *The Sacred Bridge*, 174–78.

24. See Beitzel, *Moody Atlas of the Bible*, 166.

25. Rainey and Notely, *The Sacred Bridge*, 177.

26. Walton, *Zondervan Illustrated Bible Backgrounds Commentary*, 3:23.

27. In contrast to a solid wall, the casemate wall is composed of two parallel wall lines that encircle the city being defended. The intervening space between the walls can serve as storage space during peace time; but when the city is put under siege, this open area can be filled to substantially widen the defensive wall of the city. John A. Beck, *Zondervan Dictionary of Biblical Imagery* (Grand Rapids: Zondervan, 2011), 265–66.

28. The Jewish traditional writings narrow the application of these psalms even further, indicating that these 15 psalms were to be recited while climbing the 15 steps between the court of the women and the court of the Israelites. See *Middoth* 2.5.

29. For a more detailed introduction to these psalms, see C. Hassel Bullock, *Encountering the Book of Psalms: A Literary and Theological Introduction* (Grand Rapids: Baker Academic, 2001), 79–82.

30. For more on this visit and its purpose, see Kitchen, *On the Reliability of the Old Testament*, 116–19.

31. For an introduction to the broad maritime trading network of the Phoenicians, see Beitzel, *Moody Atlas of the Bible*, 164–65).

Chapter 6

1. For a discussion of the roads which converge on Shechem, see David A. Dorsey, *Roads and Highways of Ancient Israel*, The ASOR Library of Biblical and Near Eastern Archaeology (Baltimore: Johns Hopkins University Press, 1991), 140–45, 165–67, and 174–78.

2. Israelites were not pressed into the same required government services as non-Israelites. See Anson F. Rainey and R. Steven Notley, *The Sacred Bridge* (Jerusalem: Carta, 2006), 168.

3. There is some debate on exactly what Jeroboam's intentions were. It seems that he may have been attempting to create a state religion which would please both his Baal worshiping Canaanite subjects and Israelites who still held a nominal affiliation with worship of the Lord. See James C. Martin, John A. Beck, and David G. Hansen, *A Visual Guide to Bible Events* (Grand Rapids: Baker, 2009), 106.

4. For a summary of the archaeology associated with the worship facility at Dan, see Richard S. Hess, *Israelite Religions: An Archaeological and Biblical Survey* (Grand Rapids: Baker Academic, 2007), 301–3.

5. Yohanan Aharoni, *The Land of the Bible: A Historical Geography* (Philadelphia: Westminster Press, 1979), 323.

6. Ibid., 334.

7. For a discussion of this dye industry, see John A. Beck, *Zondervan Dictionary of Biblical Imagery* (Grand Rapids: Zondervan, 2011), 73–75.

8. Paul H. Wright, *Greatness, Grace, and Glory: Carta's Atlas of Biblical Biography* (Jerusalem: Carta, 2008), 61.

9. For a more detailed treatment of the geography associated with this narrative, see John A. Beck, "Geography as Irony, The Narrative-Geographical Shaping of Elijah's Duel with the Prophets of Baal (1 Kings 18)" *Scandinavian Journal of the Old Testament* 17 (2003): 291–302.

10. Carl G. Rasmussen, *Zondervan Atlas of the Bible* (Grand Rapids: Zondervan, 2010), 40.

11. Rainer Albertz, *A History of Israelite Religion in the Old Testament Period, Vol. 1: From the Beginnings to the End of the Monarchy* (London: Vandenhoeck and Ruprecht, 1994), 319.

12. The biblical authors know of more than one village named Gilgal. While it is tempting to see it as the same Gilgal along the Jordan River mentioned in Joshua 4:20, it is more likely to be a Gilgal located in Ephraim, north of and at a higher elevation than Bethel.

13. The empire of Assyria had been in the region subjugating both Aram and Israel at the start of Jehu's reign. However from 838–806 BC, Assyria was occupied with difficulties at home that opened the door for Aram to expand its landholdings. Rainey and Notley, *The Sacred Bridge*, 210.

14. John H. Walton, Victor H. Matthews, and Mark W. Chavalas, *The IVP Bible Background Commentary: Old Testament* (Downers Grove, IL: InterVarsity Press, 2000), 397.

15. For a more detailed discussion of this Assyrian campaign, see Rainey and Notley, *The Sacred Bridge*, 208.

16. This period of Assyrian inactivity in the west lasted from 782–745 BC. The latter date marks the beginning of aggressive campaigning in the west by Tiglath-Pileser III, who imposes dark days on the Northern Kingdom (Isaiah 9:1–2).

17. For a discussion see, John A. Beck, *Translators as Storytellers: A Study in Septuagint Translation Technique*, Studies in Biblical Literature 25 (New York: Peter Lang, 2000), 117.

18. Tarshish has been variously identified as Tartessus on the southwest coast of Spain, Carthage in North Africa and points beyond. Barry J. Beitzel, *The New Moody Atlas of the Bible* (Chicago: Moody, 2009), 159–62.

19. Eusebius had identified the Valley of Jehoshaphat with both the Hinnom Valley and the Kidron Valley. G. S. P. Freeman-Glenville, Rupert L. Chapman III, and Joan E. Taylor, eds., *The Onomasticon by Eusebius of Caesarea* (Jerusalem: Carta, 2003), 141.

20. Wright, *Greatness, Grace, and Glory*, 192.

21. Evidence for this system of provisions has survived in four-handled jars which have a special stamp indicating their contents belonged to the king. For more information, see Rainey and Notley, *The Sacred Bridge*, 251–53.

22. Fortunately a segment of this wall has been discovered and can be seen in Jerusalem today. This segment of the wall, known as the Broad Wall, is 23 feet (7 m) thick. Its width appears to be related to topography. This segment of Hezekiah's wall was transiting a saddle which means that it would have naturally dipped lower than the wall on either side of it if constructed to the same height. The wall builders had to increase its height as it transited the saddle; and to increase its stability, they increased its width as well.

23. Philip J. King and Lawrence E. Stager, *Life in Biblical Israel*, Library of Ancient Israel (Louisville: Westminster John Knox Press, 2001), 219–23.

24. Aharoni, *The Land of the Bible*, 405.

25. It is striking to note the similarities between the biblical author's description of Josiah's death and that of Ahab and Saul. Although the biblical author does not formally censure Josiah's choice, these parallels added to what is said and shows us the dim view which the Lord took of Josiah's fatal decision. Sara Japhet, *1–2 Chronicles: A Commentary*, The Old Testament Library (Louisville: Westminster John Knox Press, 1993), 1043.

26. K. A. Kitchen, *On the Reliability of the Old Testament* (Grand Rapids: Eerdmans, 2003), 67.

27. Wright, *Greatness, Grace, and Glory*, 107.

Chapter 7

1. Egypt was standing firm against the Babylonian war machine and was currently ruled by Pharaoh Hophra who had brought a time of prosperity and progress to Egypt. See Anson F. Rainey and R. Steven Notley, *The Sacred Bridge* (Jerusalem: Carta, 2006), 270.

2. This has been identified with Tell Defenneh. Carl G. Rasmussen, *Zondervan Atlas of the Bible* (Grand Rapids: Zondervan, 2010), 300.

3. For a broader introduction to the Edomites, see Kenneth G. Hoglund, "Edomites," in *Peoples of the Old Testament World*, eds. Alfred J. Hoerth, Gerald L. Mattingly, Edwin M. Yamauchi (Grand Rapids: Baker, 1994), 335–47.

4. Yohanan Aharoni, *The Land of the Bible: A Historical Geography*, 2nd ed. (Philadelphia: Westminster Press, 1979), 40.

5. The family relationship between Israel and Edom is highlighted by Obadiah. See verses 6, 9–10, 12, 18–19, 21.

6. A series of archaeological finds and texts builds a continuous link indicating the Edomites settled into the southern portions of the Promised Land from the fourth century BC into the second century BC. The Persian Darius apparently demanded that the Edomites return southern villages to the Jews (1 Esdras 4:50). For the archaeological picture, see Rainey and Notley, *The Sacred Bridge*, 285.

7. For examples of other nations who enjoyed this policy change and for a discussion of the way in which this benefited the national interests of Persia, see K. A. Kitchen, *On the Reliability of the Old Testament* (Grand Rapids: Eerdmans, 2003), 76–77.

8. Storage jar seal impressions which date to this period and which mention either the province of Yehud or Jerusalem generally confirm the boundaries of Yehud we have. See Rainey and Notley, *The Sacred Bridge*, 295.

9. While this list generally defines a northern border for Yehud, we must turn to other sources to discover the southern boundary which runs south of Beth Zur and north of Hebron. Southern Judah had been invaded by Edomites and turned into the separate province of Idumea. Aharoni, *The Land of the Bible*, 416.

10. An archive discovered near Nippur, 60 miles (96.6 km) southeast of Babylon, suggests that Jews who lived in this area had become successful in a variety of business exploits. See Alfred J. Hoerth, *Archaeology and the Old Testament* (Grand Rapids: Baker, 1998), 387.

11. A large Jewish colony complete with its own temple was established at Elephantine (Yeb). See Joseph Modrzejewski, *The Jews of Egypt: From Rameses II to Emperor Hadrian* (Princeton: Princeton University Press, 1995), 21–46.

12. Paul H. Wright, *Greatness, Grace, and Glory: Carta's Atlas of Biblical Biography* (Jerusalem: Carta, 2008), 111.

13. At this time, rebellions had begun to spring up in the western holdings of Persia, so it makes sense that

Artaxerxes would want to have what he perceived to be a trusted friend in Nehemiah at the helm. See Walter C. Kaiser Jr., *A History of Israel from the Bronze Age Through the Jewish Wars* (Nashville: Broadman and Holman, 1998), 441–42.

14. Many of the more significant are briefly discussed in Edwin Yamauchi's discussion of Nehemiah within John H. Walton, ed., *Zondervan Illustrated Bible Backgrounds Commentary* (Grand Rapids: Zondervan, 2009), 3:429–31.

15. Ephraim Stern, *Archaeology of the Land of the Bible: The Assyrian, Babylonian, and Persian Periods,* The Anchor Bible Reference Library (New York: Doubleday, 2001), 343–46.

Chapter 8

1. For a more detailed summary of this period, see Barry J. Beitzel, *The New Moody Atlas of the Bible* (Chicago: Moody, 2009), 207–11.

2. There is debate on the authenticity of this ancient story. For a discussion, see Anson F. Rainey and R. Steven Notely, *The Sacred Bridge* (Jerusalem: Carta, 2006), 298–99.

3. The four books of Maccabees together with the other Apocryphal books are not accepted as part of the biblical canon by most Protestants. Nevertheless, they offer helpful historical and cultural insights into the time between the Old and New Testaments.

4. Assyrians in the eighth century BC started referring to the region as "Philistia," which morphed into "Palestine," a term used by Herodotus in late fifth century BC.

5. The Ptolemies also used Palestine as a source for olive oil, wine, and slaves. Carl G. Rasmussen, *Zondervan Atlas of the Bible* (Grand Rapids: Zondervan, 2010), 185.

6. Donald E. Gowan, *Bridge Between the Testaments,* Pittsburg Theological Monograph Series (Allison Park, PA: Pickwick, 1986), 63.

7. Josephus, *Antiquities of the Jews* 12.3.3–4.

8. For a detailed account of this period of history including its intimate relationship to the geography of the Promised Land, see Rainey and Notely, *The Sacred Bridge,* 308–33.

9. The leaders of the new Jewish state were called Hasmoneans because of their family connection with Mattathias who was a descendant of a priest whose name was Hasmonias.

10. The complete story is best read in Josephus, *Antiquities of the Jews* 14.1–9.

11. Josephus, *Antiquities of the Jews* 14.1.3.

12. For the details of this land editing, see Rainey and Notely, *The Sacred Bridge,* 336.

13. Josephus, *Antiquities of the Jews* 14.4.5.

Chapter 9

1. For a more detailed introduction to the time of Herod the Great, see Paul H. Wright, *Greatness, Grace and Glory: Carta's Atlas of Biblical Biography* (Jerusalem: Carta, 2008), 127–46.

2. Josephus, *Antiquities of the Jews* 14.15.2.

3. For a summary see, John McRay, *Archaeology of the New Testament* (Grand Rapids: Baker Academic, 1991), 91–149. For a comprehensive treatment of Herod's building program, see Ehud Netzer, *The Architecture of Herod the Great Builder* (Grand Rapids: Baker Academic, 2006).

4. Read the speech he gave in advance of the temple rebuilding project and you will see his powers of persuasion at work. Josephus, *Antiquities of the Jews* 15.11.1.

5. Noting Herod's practice of avoiding pork to maintain a semblance of eating kosher, Augustus observed, "I'd rather be Herod's pig than Herod's son." Macrobius, *Saturnalia* 2.4.11.

6. Josephus, *Antiquities of the Jews* 17.8.1.

7. The word "desert" rather than "wilderness" used in a variety of English translations when speaking of this region can leave a mistaken impression. The Greek word employed here indicates a place where people are unlikely to establish permanent residence.

8. A discussion that appears to have started at the time of Origen is reflected in the *Onomasticon* which changes *Bethania* to *Bethabara*. This would move John to the west side of the river but near the same ford. The earliest Greek manuscripts do not support this change. See Joan E. Taylor, ed., *The Onomasticon by Eusebius of Caesarea* (Carta: Jerusalem, 2003), 38.

9. For a discussion on changing the location of Bethany to Batanea thus moving these events north into Bashan, see Anson F. Rainey and R. Steven Notley, *The Sacred Bridge* (Jerusalem: Carta, 2006), 351.

10. For an overview of the archaeology of Bethlehem, see Jack Finegan, *The Archeology of the New Testament: The Life of Jesus and the Beginning of the Early Church* (Princeton: Princeton University Press, 1992), 29–43.

11. Note that in John 7:42 some were having difficulty accepting Jesus' claim to be the Messiah because they presumed he was born in Galilee rather than in Bethlehem.

12. As heinous as this crime is, we need to be careful about inflating the number of infants who died here. Given the size of Bethlehem at this time, it is likely that less than two dozen children perished in this ruthless attack. Paul L. Maier, *In the Fullness of Time: A Historian Looks at Christmas, Easter, and the Early Church* (San Francisco: Harper Collins, 1991), 64.

13. For a list of these Coptic Christian traditions, see Wright, *Greatness, Grace and Glory*, 167.

14. We know for example that Alexandria, Egypt, had a large Jewish quarter.

15. For the details on Archelaus's rule and his banishment to Gaul in 6 AD, see Josephus, *Antiquities of the Jews* 17.10.1–10; 17.13.2.

16. James Strange, "Nazareth," in David N. Freeman, *Anchor Bible Dictionary* (New Haven, CT: Yale University Press, 1992), 4:1050–51.

17. G. K. Beale and D. A. Carson, ed., *Commentary on the New Testament Use of the Old Testament* (Grand Rapids: Baker Academic, 2007), 11.

18. Taylor, *The Onomasticon by Eusebius of Caesarea*, 65.

19. George A. Turner, *Historical Geography of the Holy Land* (Grand Rapids: Baker, 1973), 88–89.

20. David A. Dorsey, *The Roads and Highways of Ancient Israel*, The ASOR Library of Biblical and Near Eastern Archaeology (Baltimore: Johns Hopkins University Press, 1991), 161.

21. The Greek text of this story appears to be intentionally ambiguous here. Jesus may be making reference to his "Father's house" (as the NIV) or "my Father's business," which occurs at the temple. In either case, the location of Jesus is confirmed as the temple complex. See Beale and Carson, *Commentary on the New Testament Use of the Old Testament*, 274.

22. See the Jewish Midrash, *Yoma* 8:4; *Niddah* 5:6.

23. Ben Witherington III, *New Testament History: A Narrative Account* (Grand Rapids: Baker Academic, 2001), 90–91.

24. For other examples, see F. F. Bruce, *New Testament History* (New York: Doubleday, 1969), 155–56.

25. This language can further be understood as the moment when Jesus became a Rabbi according to Jewish custom. See James C. Martin, John A. Beck, and David G. Hansen, *A Visual Guide to Gospel Events* (Grand Rapids: Baker, 2010), 40–41.

26. For a discussion on changing the location of Bethany to Batanea thus moving these events northeast of the Sea of Galilee, see Rainey and Notley, *The Sacred Bridge*, 351. For a parallel discussion which moves the baptism site to the confluence of the Yarmuk and Jordan Rivers, see Barry J. Beitzel, *The New Moody Atlas of the Bible* (Chicago: Moody, 2009), 240.

27. For additional Old Testament allusions, see the presentation in Beale and Carson, *Commentary on the New Testament Use of the Old Testament*, 14 and 279–81.

28. Early church tradition becomes more precise identifying the mountain just west of Jericho as the site. It is called Jebel Quarantal, "Mount of the Forty" to recall the 40 days Jesus spent in the wilderness. For more in the Christian tradition, see Finegan, *The Archeology of the New Testament*, 146–47.

29. Mark's language here is even stronger than that of Matthew suggesting that the Holy Spirit "sent him" into this region (Mark 1:12).

Chapter 10

1. For a detailed discussion of the boundary, see Carl G. Rasmussen, *Zondervan Atlas of the Bible* (Grand Rapids: Zondervan, 2010), 116–17.

2. The NIV can add to our confusion here by translating with the singular "area" rather than plural "areas." This makes it sound as if Capernaum is in both which it is not. A more accurate rendering of the geography would be "in Nazareth and Capernaum by the lake, in the areas of Zebulun and Naphtali."

3. John H. Walton, *Zondervan Illustrated Bible Backgrounds Commentary* (Grand Rapids: Zondervan, 2009), 4:50.

4. Barry J. Beitzel, *The New Moody Atlas of the Bible* (Chicago: Moody, 2009), 241–43.

5. The Church of the Beatitudes resides on a small hill just above the two chapels which recall the food miracles, Tabgha and the Primacy of Peter. For more on these Byzantine sites, see George A. Turner, *Historical Geography of the Holy Land* (Grand Rapids: Baker, 1973), 104–6.

6. But if we begin reading this account at Luke 6:12, it would seem that Luke also set this event on a mountain before Jesus moves to the level place.

7. In support of this notion, we note Jesus was looking for an isolated place to pray. See Luke 6:12.

8. Anson F. Rainey and R. Steven Notley, *The Sacred Bridge* (Jerusalem: Carta, 2006), 355.

9. John J. Rousseau and Rami Arav, *Jesus and His World: An Archaeological and Cultural Dictionary* (Minneapolis: Fortress Press, 1995), 128.

10. John McRay, *Archaeology and the New Testament* (Grand Rapids: Baker Academic, 1991), 162–66.

11. For more on the debate surrounding Bethsaida Julius and el-Araj, see Rousseau and Arav, *Jesus and His World*, 19–24, and Rainey and Notley, *The Sacred Bridge*, 356–59.

12. There is no specific geographical reference in this narrative. However when we examine the geographical indicators in the verses which surround this narrative, they suggest that Jesus is at work in the greater Galilee area (Matthew 11:1, 20–24; 12:9; 13:53).

13. See also, James C. Martin, John A. Beck, and David G. Hansen, *A Visual Guide to Bible Events* (Grand Rapids: Baker, 2009), 174–75.

14. Paul H. Wright, *Greatness, Grace, and Glory: Carta's Atlas of Biblical Biography* (Jerusalem: Carta, 2008), 183.

15. For more on this miracle and its location see, Martin, Beck, and Hansen, *A Visual Guide to Bible Events*, 176–77.

16. Dalmanutha is likely the harbor for Magdala located on the south side of the Plain of Gennesaret. Rasmussen, *Zondervan Atlas of the Bible*, 208.

17. For more on this miracle and its location see, Martin, Beck, and Hansen, *A Visual Guide to Bible Events*, 180–81.

18. Philip J. King and Lawrence E. Stager, *Life in Biblical Israel,* Library of Ancient Israel (Louisville: Westminster John Knox Press, 2001), 65.

19. John H. Walton, *Ancient Near Eastern Thought and the Old Testament* (Grand Rapids: Baker Academic, 2006), 91–92.

20. Josephus notes the distinction between Caesarea on the sea, Caesarea Maritima, and this Caesarea associated with Philip, Caesarea Philippi. *War* 3.9.7 and 7.2.1.

21. Josephus, *Antiquities of the Jews* 15.10.3.

22. Eusebius, *History* 7.17.

23. The Byzantine Christians identified Mount Tabor as the site of the transfiguration of Jesus. Ton Hilhorst, "The Mountain of the Transfiguration in the New Testament and Later Traditions," in *The Land of Israel in Bible, History, and Theology: Studies in Honour of Ed Noort,* eds. Jacques Van Ruiten and J. Cornelis De Vos (Leiden: Brill, 2009), 317–38.

24. Martin, Beck, and Hansen, *A Visual Guide to Bible Events*, 157.

25. Mishnah, *Sanhedrin* 6:5.

26. Alfred Edersheim, *The Life and Times of Jesus the Messiah* (Grand Rapids: Eerdmans, 1971), 2:324–25.

27. Joan E. Taylor, ed., *The Onomasticon by Eusebius of Caesarea* (Jerusalem: Carta, 2003), 38. For a record of early Christian visits and churches on the site, see Jack Finegan, *The Archeology of the New Testament: The Life of Jesus and the Beginning of the Early Church* (Princeton: Princeton University Press, 1992), 155–62.

28. Bethphage is also spelled Bethpage and Bethfage in various Bible translations.

29. Responding to their readers' need to locate the less well-known village of Bethphage, both Mark and Luke add mention of Bethany in a parenthetical way. Our English translations can be a bit confusing here, making it sound as though Bethphage lay east of Bethany.

30. Finegan, *Archeology of the New Testament*, 164.

31. Mishnah, *Menahot* 11:2.

32. Rainey and Notley, *The Sacred Bridge*, 363.

33. In the *Onomasticon* Eusebius says the Valley of Jehoshaphat is the Kidron Valley, although he also seems to have connected it to the valley which ran around the west side of New Testament Jerusalem, the Hinnom Valley. See Taylor, *The Onomasticon by Eusebius*, 67, 171–72.

34. Turner, *Historical Geography of the Holy Land*, 262–63.

35. For a description of the presses and process used, see John A. Beck, *Zondervan Dictionary of Biblical Imagery* (Grand Rapids: Zondervan, 2011), 185–87.

36. For a discussion of this phenomenon, see William D. Edwards, Wesley J. Gabel, and Floyd E. Hosmer, "On the Physical Death of Jesus Christ," *Journal of the American Medical Association* 255 (March 1986): 1456.

37. Matthew knew what it felt like because he uses the same language to describe the way he felt when Jesus told him that he was on the way to Jerusalem to die (Matthew 17:23).

38. R. T. France, *The Gospel of Matthew* (New International Commentary on the New Testament; Grand Rapids: Eerdmans, 2007), 6.

39. Josephus, *Wars of the Jews* 2.17.5.

40. In 333 AD the Bordeaux Pilgrim places it on "Mount Zion" and in 530 AD Theodosius places it some 140 feet (42.7 m) from the Holy Zion Church. Rousseau and Arav, *Jesus and His World*, 136.

41. McRay, *Archaeology and the New Testament*, 78–79.

42. The archaeological evidence simply does not support the identification of the tomb on this property with the first-century tomb of Jesus. Gabriel Barkay, "The Garden Tomb: Was Jesus Buried Here?" *Biblical Archaeology Review* 12 (March–April 1986): 49. McRay, *Archaeology and the New Testament*, 207–210.

43. Dan Bahat, "Does the Holy Sepulcher Church Mark the Burial of Jesus?" *Biblical Archaeology Review* 12 (May–June 1986): 26–45.

44. Eusebius, *The Lie of Constantine* 3.26.

45. Ibid., 3.27–33.

46. See Finegan, *The Archeology of the New Testament*, 262–63.

47. See Beitzel, *Moody Atlas of the Bible*, 248.

Chapter 11

1. Eusebius, *Life of Constantine* 3.43.

2. For an overview of this history, see Jack Finegan, *The Archeology of the New Testament: The Life of Jesus and the Beginning of the Early Church* (Princeton: Princeton University Press, 1992), 167–70.

3. Early Christian tradition from the fourth century assumes that it is the same room. Paul H. Wright, *Greatness, Grace, and Glory: Carta's Atlas of Biblical Biography* (Jerusalem: Carta, 2008), 217.

4. Ben Witherington III, *New Testament History: A Narrative Account* (Grand Rapids: Baker Academic, 2001), 180.

5. Anson F. Rainey and R. Steven Notley, *The Sacred Bridge* (Jerusalem: Carta, 2006), 370.

6. John McRay, *Archaeology and the New Testament* (Grand Rapids: Baker Academic, 1991), 106–7.

7. Certain Greek manuscripts indicate that we ought to translate Acts 8:5 as "the city of Samaria."

8. Rainey and Notley, *The Sacred Bridge,* 370 and Barry J. Beitzel, *The New Moody Atlas of the Bible* (Chicago: Moody, 2009), 251.

9. F. F. Bruce, *The Acts of the Apostles: Greek Text with Introduction and Commentary* (Grand Rapids: Eerdmans, 1990), 216.

10. Witherington, *New Testament History,* 191.

11. LaMoine F. DeVries, *Cities of the Biblical World* (Peabody, MA: Hendrickson, 1997), 255–57.

12. Ehud Netzer, *The Architecture of Herod the Great Builder* (Grand Rapids: Baker Academic, 2006), 94–118.

13. Wright, *Greatness, Grace, and Glory,* 220.

14. McRay, *Archaeology and the New Testament,* 233.

15. For a broader discussion of the history of Damascus, see DeVries, *Cities of the Biblical World,* 60–66.

16. Luke mentions two different cities by the name of Antioch. Pisidian Antioch is noted just twice (Acts 13:14; 14:19), while the remainder of the references are to Syrian Antioch.

17. James S. Jeffers, *The Greco-Roman World of the New Testament Era* (Downers Grove, IL: InterVarsity Press Academic, 1999), 287.

18. For an overview of the archaeology, see Charles F. Pfeiffer and Howard F. Vos, *The Wycliffe Historical Geography of Bible Lands* (Chicago: Moody, 1967), 249–52.

19. Some of the earliest Jewish families to settle here may have been mercenaries who had fought for Alexander the Great. Jeffers, *The Greco-Roman World of the New Testament Era,* 288.

20. McRay, *Archaeology and the New Testament,* 232.

21. F. F. Bruce, *New Testament History* (New York: Doubleday, 1969), 307.

22. Jeffers, *The Greco-Roman World of the New Testament Era,* 281–83.

23. DeVries, *Cities of the Biblical World,* 376–77.

24. Josephus, *Antiquities of the Jews* 14.11–12, 25.

25. Jeffers, *The Greco-Roman World of the New Testament Era,* 265.

26. McRay, *Archaeology and the New Testament,* 256.

27. Beitzel, *Moody Atlas of the Bible,* 262.

28. For a discussion on the extent of Paul's travels, see Beitzel, *Moody Atlas of the Bible,* 253.

29. J. C. Walters, "Romans, Jews, and Christians: The Impact of the Romans on Jewish/Christian Relations in First-Century Rome," in *Judaism and Christianity in First-Century Rome,* eds. K. Donfried and P. Richardson (Grand Rapids: Eerdmans, 1998), 176–77.

30. Jeffers, *The Greco-Roman World of the New Testament Era,* 75.

31. Suetonius, *The Life of Claudius* 25:4.

32. Beitzel, *Moody Atlas of the Bible,* 266–67.

33. D. A. Carson, Douglas J. Moo, and Leon Morris, *An Introduction to the New Testament* (Grand Rapids: Zondervan, 1992), 475.

34. Witherington, *New Testament History,* 405.

35. For a discussion of each individual city, see Carl G. Rasmussen, *Zondervan Atlas of the Bible* (Grand Rapids: Zondervan, 2010), 235–39.

PHOTOGRAPHY CREDITS

Cover photographs © Mordechai Meiri/Shutterstock. com, Vladislav Gurfinkel/Thinkstock, Steven Frame/ Thinkstock, and Our Daily Bread Ministries.

Unless otherwise indicated, photographs © John A. Beck.

Photographs on pages 4, 6, 7, 11, 20, 22, 27, 28, 31, 34, 41, 42, 45 (right), 47, 52, 54, 62, 63, 75, 86, 88, 101, 102, 103, 113, 114–15, 128, 139, 140, 144, 146, 149, 152, 153, 161, 165, 167, 168, 176, 177, 179, 183, 205, 210 (2x), 224, 232, 235, 244, 246, 247, 248, 249, 251, 253, 259 (2x), 260 (2x), 265, 269, 271, 273 (2x), 276, 280, 281, 283, 289, 294 (2x), 305, 306 taken by Terry Bidgood or Alex Soh © Our Daily Bread Ministries.

Photographs on pages 47, 62, 66, 88, 91, 101, 107, 113, 126, 140, 161, 165, 172, 174, 177, 184, 187 (top), 199, 210, 219, 237, 246, 271, 292, 294, and 305 used by permission of the Israel Museum in Jerusalem.

Photographs on pages 67, 69, 70, 124 (2x), 128, 164, 189, 195, 211, 218, 236, 284, 299, 301 (2x), 302 (2x), 305, 310 (bottom), 311 (2x) © Todd Bolen /BiblePlaces.com. Used by permission.

Photograph on page 66 © A. D. Riddle/BiblePlaces. com. Used by permission.

Photographs on page 110 courtesy of Jerusalem University College.

Photograph on page 146 courtesy of the museum at Megiddo National Park.

Photograph on page 169 courtesy of the Church of St. George Madaba, Jordan.

Photograph on page 174 taken by Steven G. Johnson, Wikimedia Commons, http://wikimediafoundation. org/wiki/File:Jehu-Obelisk-cropped.jpg.

Photograph on page 187 (top) © A. D. Riddle /BiblePlaces.com. Used by permission.

Photograph on page 187 (bottom) © A. D. Riddle /BiblePlaces.com. Used by permission. Courtesy of the Walters Art Museum, Baltimore, Maryland.

Photograph on page 189 courtesy of the British Museum.

Photograph on page 197 (left) © A. D. Riddle /BiblePlaces.com. Used by permission. Courtesy of the Pergamon Museum (Museum of the Ancient Near East) in Berlin.

Photographs on pages 197 (right), 200, and 203 courtesy of the Oriental Institute, University of Chicago.

Photograph on page 214 (top) taken from Wikimedia Commons, http://commons.wikimedia.org/wiki /File:POxy_v0075_n5021_a_01_hires.jpg.

Photograph on page 214 (bottom) © Todd Bolen /BiblePlaces.com. Used by permission. Courtesy of the Eretz Israel Museum, Tel Aviv, Israel.

Photograph on page 216 courtesy of the Tower of David Museum, Jerusalem.

Photograph on page 220 © plrang/iStock. Taken at Warsaw's Royal Baths Park, Poland.

Photograph on page 221 © Todd Bolen/BiblePlaces. com. Used by permission. Courtesy of Athens Archaeological Museum, Greece.

Photograph on page 224 courtesy of Masada National Park.

Photograph on page 255 © Stephen Bramer /BiblePlaces.com. Used by permission.

Photograph on page 261 courtesy of the Hermon Stream (Banias) Nature Reserve.

Photographs on page 276 courtesy of the Wohl Archaeological Museum.

Photograph on page 286 © Alexander Gatsenko /iStock.

Photograph on page 297 © Ugurhan Betin/iStock.

Photograph on page 298 © A. D. Riddle/BiblePlaces. com. Used by permission.

Photographs on pages 299 and 311 © Mark Wilson. Used by permission.

Photograph on page 304 © Barry Beitzel/BiblePlaces .com. Used by permission.

Photograph on page 306 (right) © Todd Bolen/ BiblePlaces.com. Used by permission. Courtesy of the Naples Archaeological Museum, Italy.

Photograph on page 310 (top) © Todd Bolen /BiblePlaces.com. Used by permission. Courtesy of Athens Archaeological Museum, Greece.

SCRIPTURE INDEX

SUBJECT INDEX

Note: *f* denotes a figure; *m*, a map; *p*, a photograph.

Deborah and Barak, 105–107, 106*m*
    Hazor, 106, 107*p*
    pagan practices, 105–106
    rainfall, role of, 106
    repentance of Israelites, 106
    victories, 107
Deserts, 72*m*
Divided kingdom, 160*m*
Division at Shechem, 157–159, 158*m*
Domitian portrait, 310*p*

E

East and hope, 177
Edom, 83*p*
Edomite highlands, 197*p*
Edomite highlands across Dead Sea, 192–193*p*
Edom's incursions, 198*m*
Egypt, Alexander's conquest of, 210–211
Egypt, exodus, and wilderness, 64–85
    Canaan exploration, 73–76, 74*m*
    Exodus route, 67–70
    Israel in Egypt, 65–67
    Moses barred from Promised Land, 76–78
    Moses' death on Mount Nebo, 83–85
    mountains and wilderness, 71–73
    other promised lands, 78–80
    Transjordan conquest and distribution, 81–84, 82*m*
Egypt, extended stay, 62–64
    fertility figurine, 62*p*
    immorality, 62–63
    necessity of, 63
    pagan worship of Amorites, 62
    sheep and shepherd, 63
Egyptian Pharaoh Necho II, 187*p*
Egypt, Jesus' flight to, 230–233
    Herod, 232
    Herodium, 232*p*
    Magi, 232
    theological significance, 232–233
Elah Valley, 11*p*, 131*p*
Elephantine Island from east bank of Nile, 195*p*
Elijah, 165*p*, 167–168
Elijah and Elisha, 166*m*, 168–170
    transition to leadership, 168–169
    translation to glory, 169–170
Emperor Claudius, 306*p*
End times discourse, 270–273
    Jerusalem model, from Mount of Olives, 271*p*
    Mount of Olives, 271
    New Testament in Jerusalem, 272*m*
    place of final judgment, 273
    70 AD Roman destruction of the temple, 271*p*
En Gedi, 118–119*p*
Ephesus, 303–305
    Artemis statue, 305*p*
    connection to the world, 305
    Great Theater, 305*p*
    Harbor Street, 304*p*
    paganism, 304–305
    statue of Artemis, 305
    third missionary journey, 303*m*

Esther, 203–204
Evangelical Triangle, 250–252
    Capernaum general, 251*p*
    Korazin, 251*p*
    Sea of Galilee, 250*m*, 252*p*
Events in lives of Peter and Philip, 290*m*
Exile and return, 192–207
    flight to Egypt, 193–197
    Jewish diaspora, 202–204
    Nehemiah's Jerusalem, 204–207
    Obadiah and Edomites, 197–199
    return from exile, 199–201, 200*m*
Exile image, 199*p*
Exodus route, 67–70, 68*m*
    beginning, 67, 69
    Lake Timsah, 70*p*
    to Mount Sinai, 70
    purposes, 70
    starting point, 69
    trust, 70
Ezra, 199–201

F

Famine, 165, 167, 299–300
Feeding of the 5,000, 257, 257*p*, 259
Feeding of the 4,000, 259
Fertility figurine, 62*p*
First missionary journey, 298*m*
Flight to Egypt, 193–197
    Babylonian Empire, 196*m*
    Elephantine Island from east bank of Nile, 195*p*
    Jeremiah to Egypt, 194*m*
    Jerusalem defensive wall in ruin, 194*p*
Foods and impurity, 294
Four geographic zones, 21*m*

G

Garden of Eden, 43–46
    as eternal home, 46
    location, 43–45, 44*m*
    Upper Jordan River, 45*p*
Gentile relations, 295
Geography of forgiveness, 257–260
    boat on Sea of Galilee, 259*p*
    Feeding of the 5,000, 257, 257*p*, 259
    Feeding of the 4,000, 259
    interpretation of miracles, 259–260
    Tabgha mosaic, fish and loaves, 259*p*
Gethsemane, 274–75
    Church of All Nations, Mount of Olives, 274*p*, 275*p*
    olive crushing press, 275*p*
Geographical cross section of Afro-Arabian rift valley, 25*f*
Gezer coastal plain, 22
Gibeon, pact with, 93–95, 95*p*
    appeal of land, 93
    deception of Gibeonites, 93–94
    solution, 94–95
Gideon, 109, 109*m*
Gihon Spring, 270*pp*
Golgotha, 279

NOTE TO THE READER

The publisher invites you to share your response to the message of this book by writing Discovery House Publishers, P.O. Box 3566, Grand Rapids, MI 49501, U.S.A. For information about other Discovery House books, music, or DVDs, contact us at the same address or call 1-800-653-8333. Find us on the Internet at dhp.org or send e-mail to books@dhp.org.

ABOUT THE AUTHOR

John Beck earned his PhD in theology (Hebrew and Old Testament) from Trinity International University in 1997. For 16 years, he taught courses in Hebrew and Old Testament at various colleges and universities. Currently he is a writer and permanent adjunct faculty at Jerusalem University College, Israel, where he teaches field study courses about the physical geography of the biblical world, its natural history, and culture.

Beck has long studied the relationship between the land of the Bible, Bible history, and Bible communication. He has published articles in *JETS, SJOT, WTJ*, and *BibSac*. He also authored the article on geography for Baker's *Dictionary for Theological Interpretation of the Bible*. Among his most recent books are *The Land of Milk and Honey: An Introduction to the Geography of Israel; God as Storyteller: Seeking Meaning in Biblical Narrative; A Visual Guide to Bible Events; A Visual Guide to Gospel Events; Zondervan Dictionary of Biblical Imagery; Understand Your Bible*; and *The Baker Illustrated Guide to Daily Life in Bible Times*. His forthcoming books include the *Baker Book of Maps Charts and Timelines* and *A Christian Guide to the Holy Land*.